ANSI C

PROBLEM-SOLVING AND PROGRAMMING

Kenneth A. Barclay

Napier Polytechnic, Edinburgh, Scotland

PRENTICE HALL

New York   London   Toronto   Sydney   Tokyo   Singapore

First published 1990 by
Prentice Hall International (UK) Ltd

66 Wood Lane End, Hemel Hempstead
Hertfordshire HP2 4RG
A division of
Simon & Schuster International Group

Disc conversion in 10/12pt Plantin
by Columns Typesetters of Reading

Printed and bound in Great Britain
at the University Press, Cambridge

Library of Congress Cataloging-in-Publication Data

Barclay, Kenneth A., 1947–
 ANSI C: problem solving and programming/
 Kenneth A. Barclay.
  p. cm.
 Includes bibliographical references and index.
 ISBN 0–13–037326–5 (paperback)
  1. C (Computer program language) I. Title.
QA76.73.C15B3648 1990
005.26′2—dc20   90–42373
                                 CIP

British Library Cataloguing in Publication Data

Barclay, Kenneth A. Sept. 27, 1947–
 ANSI C: problem solving and programming.
  1. Computer systems. Programming languages:
  C language
 I. Title
 005.133

  ISBN 0–13–037326–5

4 5 94 93 92

Contents

v

Case studies

Preface

THIS BOOK provides a comprehensive introduction to the C programming language and is suitable for use both by novice programmers and by those with a knowledge of other programming languages. The complete language is described and fully illustrated. More general programming principles, consistent with current methods of abstraction, structured programming and stepwise refinement, are also featured.

In addition to a full study of the C programming language, the important principle of 'Programming into a programming language, not in it', is emphasized. In general, this principle deals with data and its representation, as well as commands. There is, therefore, a strong emphasis on structured problem solving. 'Program refinement' is now well-established and is present in many modern programming texts. 'Data refinement' has, however, not received the same attention. This concept is concerned with data structures which match the problem space. Once a correct program design has been developed, the data structures are refined to make them more efficient and more easy to implement in the chosen programming language. In both cases the relevant C language features in support of this principle are described.

Considerable effort has been taken to present the topics in a clear and concise manner. Chapter 2 introduces a small number of the features of C, and provides an introduction to the detailed studies of the later chapters.

Chapter 3–6 present four fundamental aspects of programming: data types, operators, program flow control, and program design. In particular, Chapter 5 provides a full exposition of the C function. The function is one of the pivotal concepts in structuring large software systems. For this reason, it is introduced early in the text and is reinforced through continual use.

Chapter 7 addresses the problem of 'programming in the large', using the concept of a program unit to maintain a clear separation of the definition and use of a resource from its implementation. These divisions are supported by the storage classes of C. The scope rules and the proper use of each class is discussed.

Within this general model, subsequent chapters participate in the evolution of the concept of the abstract data type. For a number of standard types specifications are developed, external representations are defined, implementations are programmed, and practical applications are illustrated.

A particular feature of the book is the inclusion of a number of major case-studies. They are used to illustrate various aspects of the C language, fundamental computing algorithms and systematic program design, in a relevant context, something not otherwise achievable with small programs. Where appropriate, each chapter includes many complete programs. All program listings are reproduced directly from the computer and should execute correctly on any machine supported by a standard C compiler.

A short list of the major issues raised in each chapter are repeated as a summary at the end. Most chapters include a set of exercises. The exercises include the construction of new programs as well as modifications and extensions to the given examples.

ANSI standard C

The original definition of the C programming language is *The C Programming Language* by Brian W Kernighan and Dennis M Ritchie (Prentice Hall, 1978). For many years this book was the definitive reference for the language. With a growing number of C language implementations came variants of C based on different interpretations of the definition as well as language extensions. Despite the diversity of implementations, the C used by its practitioners has remained consistent. This, in part, is attributable to the unifying influence of the UNIX community.

By 1983, however, the maturity of the C language and its adoption by a community of users beyond its original environment, dictated the need for a standard. In 1983 the American National Standards Institute (ANSI) formed the X3J11 committee to provide a new definition for the C language independent of any particular implementation.

The X3J11 committee has aimed to retain the original spirit of the C language, codifying common existing practices. Thus, much consideration was given to what existing programs do. An important consideration has been to ensure, where practicable, that existing C source code should continue to function normally.

The Standard ratifies constructs alluded to in the original definition. In particular, enumerated types, structures as function arguments and structure assignment are defined.

Perhaps the most significant change to the language is the new form of function declaration and definition. The Standard borrows from C++ the notion of a function prototype declaration incorporating parameter types. Further, functions with variable number of arguments have been formalized, improving associated portability issues. For the present, the original style of function declaration/definition is supported to retain compatibility. In the text, however, I have presented solutions exclusively in the new form, to benefit from the improved compiler diagnostics.

The Standard has also defined more carefully the preprocessor, which has, in the past, not had any formal specification and has been subject to numerous interpretations. The preprocessor has also been extended with new operations and control lines. The preprocessor is the subject of Chapter 8.

A large part of the Standard defines the library functions for performing input/output, string manipulation, memory management, date and time routines, etc. The lack of a well defined library has previously caused portability problems for application programmers. Appendix F summarizes the facilities of the new Standard library.

Acknowledgements

My special thanks go to Dr John Savage, Napier Polytechnic of Edinburgh, who read the first drafts of all chapters and gave technical and stylistic suggestions on virtually every paragraph. He also provided many useful insights on programming practice and methodology.

My gratitude goes also to the Napier Polytechnic Computer Studies Department. The students of this Department have been compelled to be the subjects of many experiments in my teaching of the C programming language. The thoughtful criticisms, suggestions and encouragement of colleagues is much appreciated.

Finally, I thank my wife, Irene, and children Dawn, Ria and Kim, for their love and patience while this book was in preparation.

1

Introduction: the C programming language

C is a general purpose programming language. It was designed by Dennis Ritchie of Bell Laboratories and implemented there in 1972 on a PDP-11. It was designed as the systems programming language for the UNIX† operating system. It is not, however, tied to any one operating system, and has proved very adaptable. In addition to being used to implement operating systems, language compilers and software tools, it has been used to write major numerical, text processing and data base management systems.

C evolved from the programming languages B and BCPL. BCPL is a typeless systems programming language developed by Martin Richards at Cambridge in 1967. B was written by Ken Thompson in 1970 for the first UNIX system on a PDP-7 and borrowed many features from BCPL. B is also a typeless programming language. The only data type supported by these languages is the machine word. In C, a richer set of data objects are supported, including characters, integers of several sizes, and two precisions of floating point numbers. Additionally, a hierarchy of derived data types may be created using arrays, structures, unions and pointers.

C is a 'middle-level' language, occupying a position between the low-level or machine-oriented languages and the high-level or problem-oriented languages. C is sufficiently close to the underlying hardware to allow detailed program control, yet supports advanced program and data structuring capabilities. It removes the need to program in CPU-specific assembly languages, removing retraining costs, reducing programming time, increasing reliability and improving portability.

C is also a small, lean language. Its modest size means that it is relatively easy to learn. Further, C compilers are simple, compact and straightforward to implement. This is evident by the availability of compilers for a wide range of hardware.

C provides the fundamental flow control primitives: statement grouping, selection (if and switch), and iteration (while, for and do). Subroutines are provided by recursive external functions with parameters. Modular programming is supported by the use of storage classes within program files. C has a rich and powerful set of operators giving considerable expressive powers to the programmer. By providing the correct control structures and data types, and allowing almost unrestricted meaningful usage, C offers an uncommonly productive programming environment.

---

† UNIX is a registered trademark of Bell Laboratories.

1

2

The essentials of a C program

THIS CHAPTER provides an introduction to the elements of a C program. The aim is achieved by exploring the features of a number of 'actual' programs. In no sense are the programs of any real value or use. They are technically complete, however, and will compile and execute on a computer supporting a standard C compiler.

The features of C introduced are covered in greater depth later in this book. Details, formal specifications, exceptions and so on, are deliberately avoided. This way we concentrate on the structure of a C program without being overwhelmed by the volume of technical detail. Armed with these essentials, we may progress to later chapters and explore the fine detail.

2.1 A first program

We start by considering a very modest program to display the message "My first program." on the computer terminal. In C, the program to print this message is:

PROGRAM 2.1(a)

```
#include <stdio.h>

main()
{
  printf("My first program.");
}
```

In the C programming language, use is made of both upper case and lower case letters to name program objects which are considered distinct. In many other programming languages, notably FORTRAN and COBOL, upper case letters are used exclusively. The names 'main' and 'printf' in the above program must appear as shown. The names 'MAIN' and 'Printf', for example, would be interpreted as different from their lower case forms.

C programs are described as free-format. This means that there are few restrictions on the appearance of the program, and that it is the programmer's responsibility to choose the layout of the program. Languages such as FORTRAN dictate the program form. This programmer freedom may be used or abused. The following two versions of the original program are equally acceptable to the C compiler. They all achieve the same result. They are, however, very difficult to read and are of doubtful quality. Certain stylistic conventions have been adopted by the C programming community and these are noted below and in subsequent programming examples.

PROGRAM 2.1(b)

```
#include <stdio.h>

main() { printf("My first program."); }
```

PROGRAM 2.1(c)

```
#include <stdio.h>

main
(
)
{
printf
(
"My first program."
)
;
}
```

A C program, no matter what its size and complexity, is composed of one or more *functions*. Each function specifies the actual computation to be performed by that piece of code. In this respect C functions are similar to FORTRAN subroutines or Pascal procedures/functions. Each function in C is identified by its name. The name of the function is chosen by the programmer. The exception to this rule is that there must exist one, and only one, function called main in any given program. A program starts executing from the first instruction in the function main.

The function main usually executes instructions and invokes other functions to perform their operations. The instructions are given as program *statements*. These other functions may be part of the same program or be members of *libraries* of previously developed functions. Function printf is an example of the latter, being a member of the *standard library*. The standard library is a collection of C functions designed to provide, among other things, standard input/output facilities. The functions are meant to exist in compatible form on any computer system which supports the C language (see Appendix F), and programs which confine themselves to the facilities of the standard library will be portable and can be moved among computer systems with minimum change.

Function `printf` delivers output to the user's terminal. The program line:

```
printf("My first program.");
```

is known as a *function call* statement. It calls or invokes the library function `printf`. The actual objects to be printed by `printf` are supplied as *arguments* to the function. One or more arguments are given as a comma separated list enclosed in parentheses (and). The single argument in the above example is the *character string* that is to be displayed. The sequence of characters enclosed between the double quotes is produced as the program output.

Finally, the braces { and } enclose the statements that constitute the function. The braces are analogous to the begin–end pair of Algol and Pascal. The statement or statements enclosed within the braces is the *function body*. In C, the semicolon is the statement terminator, rather like the full stop in natural language. Every C statement must have a terminating semicolon. Program 2.2 extends our first program by including two `printf` function call statements, both with associated semicolons.

PROGRAM 2.2(a)

```
#include <stdio.h>

main( )
{
  printf("My first program.\n");
  printf("It is wonderful.\n");
}
```

In this program two stylistic guidelines are being followed. First, each statement appears on separate lines. This is not essential but it does improve program readability. Second, the two statements are indented a number of character places from the left margin using blank or space characters. This helps to identify the program structure under consideration, particularly when dealing with large multi-function programs.

The sequence \n in the two character strings is the C notation for a newline symbol. When a newline is printed, all subsequent output starts from the left margin of the next line. Thus the output from the last program is:

```
My first program.
It is wonderful.
```

Note that two `printf` function calls does not imply two separate lines of output. Consider a second version of this program:

PROGRAM 2.2(b)

```
#include <stdio.h>

main( )
{
  printf("My first program.");
  printf("It is wonderful.\n");
}
```

Without the explicit newline symbol appearing in the first character string, the output from this program is:

```
My first program.It is wonderful.
```

In these first examples, the printf function was used to display a character string. The printf function is also capable of displaying the value of *expressions* and *variables*. Consider the following program employing these two new concepts.

PROGRAM 2.3

```
#include <stdio.h>

main( )
{
  int sum;

  sum = 10 + 20;
  printf("The sum of 10 and 20 is %d\n", sum);
}
```

The first line of the function body is known as a *declaration*. In common with many other programming languages, C requires that all variables be declared before they are used. A variable is a name for a region of memory in which values may be stored. The variable sum is declared to be of type int (integer), that is, a variable which represents numbers without fractional parts.

The second line causes the integer constants 10 and 20 to be added and the resulting value placed in the memory location known as sum. This is an example of the C *assignment*. The expression 10 + 20 to the right of the equal symbol (=) is evaluated and the result assigned to the variable on the left. The integer constants are separated by a plus symbol (+). This is an example of a C *operator* which informs the computer that the two values are to be added together.

Finally, the printf function call has two arguments: a character string and the variable sum. The second argument is an example of an expression, the value of which is to be printed. In this case, the expression value is that of the variable sum, namely 30, which is printed together with the character string. The percent character within the string is a special character recognized by the `printf` function. It and the immediately following single character d determines that the value 30 is to be displayed at that point in the string as a decimal integer number. The program output is thus:

```
The sum of 10 and 20 is 30
```

Punctuation is used in C to define program and part program structures, and to separate constituent parts. In Program 2.3 a number of common punctuation symbols are present. We have already noted that blank space is used to form indentation. To heighten readability a blank line has been placed between the declarations and the statements of function `main`. Blank spaces, line separators and tab characters are classes of *whitespace* characters used extensively in C programs to improve their readability.

Besides whitespace characters, Program 2.3 uses a variety of punctuation symbols. Braces { and } have been noted as function body delimiters. Parentheses (and) are used to group related items, for example the arguments of the function `printf`. Character strings are delimited by double quote (") characters. The semicolon is the statement terminator. The comma separates related items, such as the arguments of `printf`.

The final program we look at introduces the *comment*. A comment is used by the programmer to annotate the program code. Comments enhance a program's readability and provide a useful documentation tool. Proper documentation is an essential programming habit. Comments serve to inform the reader of the program – the original program author or the programmer responsible for its maintainance – of the intended logic. Comments can be applied to the overall program, to individual functions, or to a particular sequence of statements.

A comment is any sequence of characters enclosed between /* and */. In both cases, there should be no embedded spaces in /* and */. A comment may appear anywhere that whitespace is permitted in a program. A comment is ignored by the C compiler. An example of a comment is:

```
/* This is a comment */
```

A comment can extend over several program lines. Such a block of commenting is frequently used to describe the behaviour of a piece of code. An example is:

```
/*
**      This comment extends over seven lines in total.
**      The first and last lines are simply the opening
**      and closing comment symbols. All other lines
**      are marked with a leading pair of asterisks. They
**      are used to emphasize a unit of commenting.
*/
```

The one restriction which applies to comments is that they may not be nested.

Thus it is impossible to, say, take the comment:

```
/* Program 1 version 3 */
```

and comment it out with:

```
/* /* Program 1 version 3 */ developed 28 October */
```

Program 2.4 repeats the last problem but includes imbedded comments. The two programs are otherwise identical. The comments clarify the program's operation and improve its readability.

PROGRAM 2.4

```
/*
**      This program assigns the sum of two integer
**      constants to an integer variable, then displays
**      the result along with some annotation.
*/

#include <stdio.h>

main ()
{
   int sum;          /* declare variable, ... */

   sum = 10 + 20;
                     /* ... then assign value, and ... */
                     /* ... display the result. */
   printf("The sum of 10 and 20 is %d\n", sum);
}
```

It is a good habit to insert comments into a program as it is being prepared. There are a number of reasons for this. First, it is easier to document the program when the logic is established. This saves having to return to the coding to insert appropriate commenting. Second, it is frequently the case that comments are not included once the program is operational. Given that a program is written once but read many times, comments can aid the programmer in reading the text, and facilitates debugging erroneous programs.

2.2 Compiling and running

Before a program can be compiled and run, the source text must first be placed in a file. Generally, this is achieved with a text editor. The file containing the program text is identified by its *filename*. Most C compilers require that a source filename has a suffix or extension '.c', as in the filename 'example.c'.

The source program may then be *compiled* to create an *executable* image of the program. Compilation procedures differ considerably between compilers. Under UNIX, the C compiler is called `cc`. To compile the program in the file `'example.c'`, the command is:

```
cc example.c
```

If there are no program errors in the source code, the executable program file `'a.out'` is automatically created, and the program is ready for execution.

The compilation process consists of translating a program in the high-level language C into the equivalent sequence of machine code instructions. During the translation process, the compiler may detect errors in the programming language usage, for example a missing comma or semicolon. The compiler reports these errors in a printout identifying the source and nature of the error. These are known as *compile time* errors.

If the program compiles correctly, it can be executed by entering the command:

```
a.out
```

When running this executable program produced by the compiler, further situations, known as *run time* errors may occur. These cause programs to terminate abnormally during execution, and arise from executing perfectly plausible instructions but with erroneous data. For example, division of one number by another is perfectly acceptable provided the second number is not zero, otherwise the answer is infinity. Protection against run time errors to improve program robustness is discussed in later chapters.

A program that is free of both compile time and run time errors may still not produce the correct results. These errors, known as *logical errors*, arise from an incorrect specification of the program solution. A methodical approach to programming, as emphasized in the text, can significantly reduce this type of problem.

Appendix G gives a full exposition of the compilation process and the command `cc` under UNIX. In other systems the commands will be different and the reader is referred to the appropriate documentation and/or a local expert.

2.3 Summary

1. A simple program consists of the function `main`. The body of the function consists of declarations and statements enclosed within the braces { and }.

2. Every C statement and declaration concludes with a terminating semicolon.

3. C programs are free-format. Certain stylistic guidelines have, however, been adopted. Generally, programs do not have more than one program statement per line. Indent to highlight the program structure and use whitespace characters to separate the program tokens.

4.   Comments are written between /* and */. They are vital to good program documentation. Comments should assist the reader to understand the program logic.

5.   The compiler translates a C program into its equivalent machine instructions. The input to the compiler is the source C program and the output is the executable program image.

6.   Programs can exhibit compile time, run time and logic errors, all of which must be corrected to produce an operational program.

2.4 Exercises

1.   Explain the meaning of the following terms:

    (a) function   (b) standard library
    (c) argument   (d) declaration
    (e) statement   (f) variable
    (g) expression   (h) constant
    (i) assignment   (j) compile time error
    (k) run time error   (l) logic error

2.   Carefully enter Program 2.1(a) into a file with an editor or word processor then compile it and run it to ensure it produces the required output.

3.   What output would you expect from the following program?

```
#include <stdio.h>

main()
{
  printf("One.....");
  printf("Two.....");
  printf("Three\n");
}
```

4.   Write a program which divides the value 47 by the value 12 and displays the result with an appropriate message. The division operator is denoted by the slash symbol (/).

5.   The following program contains a run time error. Carefully enter it into a file, and check that it compiles without any errors. What happens when you run the program? What messages, if any, are produced.

Consult a local expert or compiler documentation to obtain an explanation:

```
#include <stdio.h>

main()
{
  int first, second;

  first = 0;
  second = 27 / first;
  printf("second is %d\n", second);
}
```

3

Types, operators and expressions

A C PROGRAM describes the computational processes to be carried out on items of data. It is necessary in a C program to classify each and every item of data according to its type. In C, an infinite number of distinct types is possible. They are, however, all derived from four basic types: *integer*, *character*, *float* and *double*. For these simple types there are *denotations* or *constants*, i.e. a sequence of symbols possessing a specific value of a particular type. Constants are the subject of Sections 3.1–3.4 of this chapter.

The data items manipulated by a program may be divided into two classes – those whose values remain fixed during execution of a program, and those whose values change. The former are the constants in a program. The latter are known as *variables*, since the values possessed by such objects are allowed to vary during the program run. Items of both classes share the properties of the type as described above. Variables are considered in Sections 3.5–3.7.

An *expression* is a rule by which a value may be computed. It consists of one or more *operands* (or values) combined by *operators*. C has an unusually rich set of operators which provide access to most of the operations implemented by the underlying computer hardware. The full complement of available operators naturally divide into a number of groups. The arithmetic operators, such as addition, are discussed fully in this chapter. The other operators are introduced in the chapters in which they are applied.

3.1 Integer constants

An integer constant is a whole number which may be positive, zero or negative (strictly, a negative integer is obtained by applying the unary negative operator to a positive integer; see section 3.8). Integer constants may be specified in either the decimal, octal or hexadecimal notation.

A decimal integer constant is written as a sequence of decimal digits (0 through 9), the first of which is not 0 (zero). The values:

```
1234     255     10     9999
```

are all valid examples of decimal integer constants. No embedded spaces or commas are permitted between the digits. The value 10,000, for example, is not a decimal integer constant because of the comma; it must be expressed as 10000.

A computer can only represent a finite subset of all possible integers. The precision of an integer depends on the particular hardware. For instance, on the IBM PC[†] an integer is held using a 16-bit 2's complement notation. An integer can therefore assume values from − 32767 through 32767 inclusive.

An octal integer constant is written as a sequence of octal digits (0 through 7) starting with a zero (0). The values:

        0377   0177   00000   01

are all valid examples of octal integer constants.

A hexadecimal integer constant is a sequence of hexadecimal digits starting with 0x or 0X. The hexadecimal digits include 0 through 9, and the letters A through F (or a through f). The letters represent the values 10 through 15 repectively. Examples of valid hexadecimal integer constants include:

        0XFF   0x4B   0x1f   0XfF

Octal and hexadecimal constants frequently find their way into system programming applications. Examples of their use will appear later in this book.

The precision of an integer constant can also be *qualified*. A decimal, octal or hexadecimal integer constant immediately followed by the letter L (or letter l) is an explicit *long* integer constant. On the DEC VAX[‡], long integers employ 32 bits, and can thus express values in the range − 2147483647 to 2147483647 inclusive. Valid explicit long integer constants are:

        123L   04774771   0XFFL

Integer constants which exceed the single precision range are also implicitly long integers (examples are for a 16-bit integer):

        32768   0100000   0X4FFF

Table 3.1

C constant	True value	C type	C value
0	0	int	0
32767	$2^{15}-1$	int	32767
077777	$2^{15}-1$	int	32767
32768	2^{15}	long	32768
0x10000	2^{16}	long	65536
2147483647	$2^{31}-1$	long	2147483647
2147483648	2^{32}	undefined	

[†] IBM is a registered trademark of International Business Machines Corporation.
[‡] DEC is a registered trademark of Digital Equipment Corporation.

If the value of an integer constant exceeds the largest representable value, the result
is unpredictable. Most C compilers generally warn the programmer of the problem.

To illustrate some C integer constants, consider the IBM PC implementation. In
Table 3.1 some integer constants, their true mathematical value, and their type and
values are presented.

3.2 Floating point constants

Numbers with fractional parts may be represented as floating point constants. If
there is a preceding minus sign attached to the number, it is taken to be the unary
negation operator applied to the constant, and not part of the constant itself (see
Section 3.8). Floating point constants may be written in two different forms. The
first, and simplest, is a sequence of decimal digits including the decimal point. Valid
examples include:

```
3.1415926    12.0    0.1    0.00001
```

Note that the decimal point need not necessarily be embedded, allowing both
leading and trailing decimal point forms. The second and third examples above
might also be shown as:

```
12.    .1
```

It is recommended, however, that the readability is improved if the former notation
is used.

In the second form, a floating point constant is expressed as an integer or as a
floating point constant as defined above, multiplied by some integer power of ten.
This power is shown as the letter E (or letter e) followed by an optionally signed
integer constant. Examples of this form include:

```
1.0E2  (=100.0)      12.34e-3 (=0.01234)
1E-2   (=0.01)       1E+3     (=1000.0)
```

This latter representation is frequently referred to as scientific notation.

The range of floating point constants permitted by implementations is restricted
like integers. Further, whereas integers are held exactly, floating point constants are
held as an (close) approximation. The type of a floating point constant is always
double. On the DEC VAX a double precision floating point constant has a 64-bit
representation, with a magnitude between about 10E−38 and 10E+38, and an
accuracy of approximately seventeen decimal digits. A single precision representation
for floating point values is also available with the same range as doubles but with
only some seven significant decimal digits. These values are of type float. These
are distinguished by the qualifying suffix f or F as in:

```
1.234F    98.76f
```

Finally, we may qualify a floating point constant with the suffix l or L to denote a long double.

If the magnitude of a floating point constant is too great to be represented, the result is unpredictable. Most compilers generate an appropriate error message in this case. If the magnitude of a floating point constant is below 10E−38, zero is substituted.

The standard header files <limits.h> and <float.h> contain symbolic constants for the sizes of the data types (respectively the integers and the floats). For example, on an IBM PC the maximum value for an int and the maximum value for a long might be given as:

```
INT_MAX      32767
LONG_MAX     0x7FFFFFFFL
```

in the file <limits.h>.

For some further details on number representation for a range of computer hardware and sample values for <limits.h> and <float.h> see Appendix A.

3.3 Character constants

A character constant is a single character written within single quotes (apostrophe) as in 'X'. The value of a character constant is the integer numeric value of the character in the machine's character set. Character constants have type int. C programmers must be aware of the character set of the target computer. The two most commonly used character sets are EBCDIC (Extended Binary Coded Decimal Interchange Code) and ASCII (American Standard Code for Information Interchange). The two sets are not the same. In the ASCII character set, the character 'X' has decimal encoding 88, while the EBCDIC encoding is 231. The full ASCII character set is given in Appendix B.

Escape sequences can be used to represent characters that would be awkward or impossible to enter in a source program directly. An escape sequence consists of the backslash symbol (\) followed by a single character. The two symbols taken together represent the single required character. The characters which may follow the backslash, and their meanings, are listed below:

alarm bell	\a
newline	\n
horizontal tab	\t
vertical tab	\v
backspace	\b
carriage return	\r
formfeed	\f

single quote	\'
double quote	\"
backslash	\\
question mark	\?

Thus the character constant to represent the formfeed symbol in a program is '\f', and the character constant for a backslash is '\\'.

The escape sequence may appear as a backslash symbol followed by one, two or three octal digits, or as a backslash symbol followed by the letter x and one or more hexadecimal digits. The resulting octal (hexadecimal) value is taken as the octal (hexadecimal) number of the character from the machine's character set. The character constant 'X' (with ASCII encoding octal 130 and hexadecimal 58) may be represented as '\130' ('\x58'). More generally, this representation is used for non-printing characters. The ASCII character ACK (acknowledge) would be represented by '\006' ('\x6'). The first of the ASCII collating sequence is the character NUL and is shown as '\0'. This symbol is reserved for a particular role in C and is discussed fully later.

If the character following the backslash is neither an octal digit nor one of the character escape codes listed above, the result is considered unpredictable. Commonly, the effect is simply to ignore the backslash.

3.4 String **constants**

A string constant is a possibly empty sequence of characters enclosed in double quotes. The same escape mechanism provided for character constants can also be used in string constants. Examples of string constants include:

```
"Hello world"
"The C Programming Language"
""
"She said \"Good morning\""
"This string terminates with a newline\n"
```

A string is allowed to extend over one or more lines provided each line terminates with a backslash character followed immediately by a newline symbol. In this case, the backslash and the newline symbols are ignored:

```
"This string extends \
over two lines."
```

and is textually equivalent to:

```
"This string extends over two lines."
```

Two adjacent string constants are concatenated at compile time into a single string. For example:

```
"This " "string"
```

is converted into:

```
"This string"
```

This concatenation is convenient for splitting long strings across several source lines.

For each string constant of N characters, there is a block of N + 1 consecutive characters whose first N are initialized with the characters from the string, and whose last character is the ASCII NUL character '\0'. Thus the string:

```
"hello"
```

is stored as shown in Figure 3.1.

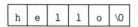

Figure 3.1

As we shall discover later, the NUL character is used to delimit the end of all strings.

Care must be taken to recognize that the character 'X' and the string "X" are not the same. On the majority of computers the character 'X' is a single character 8-bit byte (see Figure 3.2), while the string "X" is two character bytes (see Figure 3.3).

```
x
```

Figure 3.2

```
x | \0
```

Figure 3.3

Strings and characters are thus distinct, and must on no account be operated upon as if they were the same.

3.5 Identifiers

The C programming language requires that various quantities used in a program be given names by which they can then be referenced. These names are known as *identifiers* and are created by the programmer.

An identifier is created according to the following rule:

An identifier is a combination of letters and digits the first of which must be a letter. The underscore symbol (_) is permitted in an identifier and is considered to be a letter.

From this, the following are valid examples of identifiers:

```
time       day_of_the_week      BUFFER
x          unit_cost            program_name
_MAX       h2o                  AVeryLongIdentifier
```

Two identifiers are the same when they have the same spelling, including the case of all letters. The identifiers abcd and abcD are thus considered distinct.

Strictly, an identifier may be any length. However, the Standard dictates that compilers consider at least the first thirty-one characters as significant. Subsequent characters in identifiers are ignored by Standard conforming compilers.

A C program may reference objects defined elsewhere. These are known as *external* objects. For example, the function printf is a member of the standard C library and is defined external to the program containing its use. Identifiers in a C program which refer to external objects are often subject to additional restrictions. These identifiers have to be processed by software other than compilers. Linkers and librarian managers may have their own limitations on the length of identifiers. Further, these software tools may not distinguish between the case of letters. Frequently, external identifiers are restricted to six characters and are not case sensitive. This is the guarantee provided by the Standard.

Notwithstanding all these restrictions, the programmer is encouraged to use meaningful identifiers. The name of the identifier should reflect the purpose of the object in a C program. If a program operates on, say, a time of day, then the identifiers hours, minutes and seconds are superior to the shorter, but less obvious h, m and s.

Certain identifiers are reserved for use as *keywords* in a C program. A complete list of the C keywords is given below (and repeated in Appendix C). They may not be used as programmer-defined identifiers:

```
auto       double     int        struct
break      else       long       switch
case       enum       register   typedef
char       extern     return     union
const      float      short      unsigned
continue   for        signed     void
default    goto       sizeof     volatile
do         if         static     while
```

3.6 Variable declarations

Variables are data items whose values vary during execution of a program. Variables in a C program are made to possess one of the four fundamental types – integers, characters, single precision floating point and double precision floating point. Variables must have their type indicated so that the compiler can record all the necessary information about them, and generate the appropriate code during translation. This is done by means of a *variable declaration*. A variable declaration has the form:

type-specifier list-of-variables

The list-of-variables is a comma separated list of identifiers representing the program variables. Each named variable posseses a fundamental type as given by the type-specifier. The type-specifiers for the four fundamental types are introduced by the reserved keywords:

```
int      (integer)
char     (character)
float    (single precision floating point)
double   (double precision floating point)
```

A complete variable declaration is then:

```
int hours, minutes, seconds
```

Thereafter, the variables `hours`, `minutes` and `seconds` may assume any legal integer value. Integer values may be assigned to these variables, and the integer value associated with a variable may be called upon in a program statement.

A sequence of variable declarations may appear using the semicolon symbol as the terminator. For improved readability, each declaration appears on separate lines:

```
int    day, month, year;
float  centigrade, fahrenheit;
char   initial;
double epsilon;
```

Separate variable declarations may employ the same type-specifier as in:

```
int day, month, year;
int hours, minutes, seconds;
```

This facility is often employed to bracket together related variables. In the first declaration, the variables are concerned with a calendar date. In the second, the variables are used to represent a time. Because C is free-format, we are, of course, free to extend a declaration over one or more lines. It is perfectly acceptable to write:

```
int day, month, year,
    hours, minutes, seconds;
```

where the six variables are declared in the single declaration.

A variable may not be redeclared in a second declaration. Such declarations would cause the C compiler to issue an appropriate error message:

```
int  time, interval, period;
float time;
```

The compiler would be unable to determine the correct type for the variable `time`. The compiler message would report that in the second declaration, variable `time` has been redeclared.

The declaration of variables can also be accomplished by initialization. A variable is initialized to some value by appending an equal symbol (=), the assignment operator (see Section 3.10), and an expression (see Section 3.8). For example:

```
int sum = 0;
float fahrenheit = 32.0;
```

3.7 Qualifiers

In the same way that the accuracy of a variable containing a floating point number may be extended by declaring it to be of type double, so it is possible to control the range of an integer variable.

If the qualifier long is placed before the type-specifier int in a declaration, then the declared integer variables will have extended range. Long integer variables provide the largest range of signed integer values. An example of a long declaration is:

```
long int memory_address, factorial;
```

On the IBM PC the range of values that may be stored in a long integer variable is that for long integer constants (see Section 3.1 and Appendix A). Operations on objects of type long are sometimes slower than the same operations on objects of type int, depending upon the implementation.

The qualifier short placed ahead of the type-specifier int in a variable declaration specifies that the named variables are used to represent a limited range of signed integer values. The motivation for using short integer variables is primarily one of conservation of memory space. An appropriate declaration is:

```
short int day_of_week, week_of_year;
```

In both the examples above, the specifier int is optional, and the declarations may be alternatively presented as:

```
long  memory_address, factorial;
short day_of_week, week_of_year;
```

Strictly, C does not specify the exact number of bits used to represent int, long and short variables. These quantities are implementation-dependent, usually determined by the underlying hardware. The only relation guaranteed by C is that a short is shorter than a long. It is permissible for an int to be the same size as either a short or a long. On the DEC VAX both int and long are 32-bit quantities, while short is 16 bits.

Finally, the qualifier unsigned may also precede int in a variable declaration. This restricts the integer variables to positive values. On the IBM PC an unsigned integer variable is represented in 16 bits and can assume values from 0 through 65535 inclusive. Examples of these declarations are:

```
unsigned int  natural;
unsigned      record_number;
```

In the last example, the optional int is omitted.

All arithmetic operations on unsigned integers behave according to the values of modulo arithmetic. If the number of bits in an unsigned integer is N, the arithmetic is modulo 2^N. This amounts to computing the N low-order bits of the true 2's complement result.

Suppose unsigned int's are represented using 16 bits. The range of possible values is 0 to 65535 inclusive. The arithmetic is then modulo 65536 (2^{16}). Adding 1 to the largest unsigned value is guaranteed to produce 0. Subtracting the unsigned value 9 from the unsigned value 6 produces the unsigned value 65533, that is 65536 − 3 since this is modulus 65536 to the true arithmetical value − 3.

The type long double specifies extended precision floating point variables. Along with integers, the sizes of floating point objects are implementation-defined. The types float, double and long double could represent up to three distinct sizes.

The qualifier signed may be applied to char or to any size of int. This specifier is permissible but redundant when used with integral types. The signed specifier is useful for forcing char objects to have a sign. So, for example, if characters are 8-bit bytes, then unsigned char variables have values 0 to 255 inclusive, while signed char's have values between − 127 and 127 in a 2's complement machine. Whether plain char variables (without any qualifier) are signed or unsigned is machine-dependent. Printable characters are, however, guaranteed to be positive.

The qualifier const can be applied to the declaration of any variable to specify that its value will not be changed. Such an object may not be used on the left side of an assignment (see Section 3.10), or have its value modified in any manner whatsoever. An implementation is then free to place const objects in read-only memory, and perform additional optimizations. When introducing const objects we must also initialize them to the required value:

```
const double pi = 3.1415926;
const int dozen = 12;
```

3.8 Arithmetic expressions

The C programming language supports the normal *arithmetic operators*: addition (+), subtraction (−), multiplication (*) and division (/). Also provided is the modulus operator, denoted by the percent symbol (%), used to compute the remainder on dividing two integer values. These are the *binary arithmetic operators* which apply to two operands. The *unary negation* operator, − (and *unary plus* operator, +) is also available and is applied to a single operand to produce the arithmetic negative (arithmetic value) of its operand.

Examples of expressions involving such operators are:

```
12 * feet
- 1023
3.1415926 * radius * radius
60 * hours + minutes
distance / time
cents % 100
```

In the first example, the integer constant 12 is multiplied by the current value of the variable feet. In the second example, the integer constant 1023 is made negative using the unary negation operator.

As with normal arithmetic expressions, a C expression is evaluated according to the precedence of its operators. The precedence or priority of an operator dictates the order of evaluation in an arithmetic expression. An extract of the full table of precedences for all C operators is given in Table 3.2 below. The full table is given in Appendix E.

Table 3.2 Precedence and associativity of the arithmetic operators

Operator	Description	Associativity
+	Unary plus	Right to left
−	Unary minus	
*	Multiplication	Left to right
/	Division	
%	Modulus	
+	Addition	Left to right
−	Subtraction	

From Table 3.2, unary minus and unary plus are shown to have the highest precedence, while addition and subtraction have the lowest equal precedence. The multiplication, division and modulus operators have intermediate precedence. From this, an expression involving a mixture of these operators will first perform all unary minus and plus operations, then any multiplication, division and modulus operations, and then, finally, addition and subtraction. Thus:

```
2 + 3 * 4
```

yields 14, since 3 is first multiplied by 4 giving 12, and then 2 is added producing 14.

An expression involving operators of equal precedence is resolved by reference to the column labelled *associativity* in Table 3.2. Associativity refers to the order (or direction) in which operators possessing the same precedences are executed. The expression 2 + 3 * 4 + 5 is evaluated in the following way. Multiplication has the highest precedence of the three operators and is evaluated first. The expression now reduces to 2 + 12 + 5. The two addition operators have equal precedence, and associate left to right. Thus, the 2 and 12 are first added to give 14, before finally the 14 and 5 are summed producing 19 as the final result.

If, in the expression 2 + 3 * 4 + 5, it is required to perform both the additions before executing the multiplication, then this is indicated by employing the parentheses (and) around the subexpressions. The expression would then be written as (2 + 3) * (4 + 5), and evaluate to 5 * 9, or 45.

The division operator functions normally, except in situations where both operands are of type integer. For two integer operands, the division operator determines the quotient with any fractional remainder truncated. Thus:

13.0 / 5	evaluates to 2.6
13 / 5.0	evaluates to 2.6
13 / 5	evaluates to 2

When two positive integers are divided, truncation is always towards zero. If either operand is negative, however, the truncation is machine-dependent. Usually, the quotient is positive if the signs of both operands are the same, negative otherwise. Thus:

− 13 / 5	evaluates to − 2
13 / − 5	evaluates to − 2
− 13 / − 5	evaluates to 2

The modulus operator (%) yields the integer remainder from the division of two integer operands. Therefore:

13 % 5	evaluates to 3
15 % 5	evaluates to 0

Again, if either operand is negative, the remainder usually has the same sign as the dividend. Thus:

− 13 % 5	evaluates to − 3
13 % − 5	evaluates to 3

Irrespective of the particular implementation, it is always true that:

a % b	evaluates to a − (a/b) * b

where a and b are integer values and b is not zero. This is shown in Table 3.3:

Table 3.3

a	b	a/b	(a/b) * b	a % b	(a/b) * b+a % b
13	5	2	10	3	13
− 13	5	− 2	− 10	− 3	− 13
13	− 5	− 2	10	3	13
− 13	− 5	2	− 10	− 3	− 13

3.9 Type conversions

All integer arithmetic is performed with at least the range of an int. As a consequence, a character or short integer appearing in an expression is first converted to int. This process is called *integral promotion*. The promotion results in an int if an int can hold all of the values of the original type; otherwise the conversion will be to unsigned int.

We know that whether plain characters are signed or unsigned is implementation-dependent. As a result, on some machines a char will be converted to a negative integer by a process of *sign extension* where the leftmost bit of that char is a 1. On other machines, a char is promoted to a positive int by prepending zeros to the left of the character bit pattern.

The promotion of a short is to either an int or an unsigned int. If, for example, a short has the same number of bits as an int, then the value is converted to an int; an unsigned short would be converted to an unsigned int. However, if a short used fewer bits than an int, then both a short and an unsigned short are converted to an int.

With the following declarations:

```
char            pc; /* plain char */
short           ps; /* assume shorts have same .. */
unsigned short  us; /* .. size as int */
int             pi; /* plain int */
```

we can list some expressions and show how the operands are first promoted (see Table 3.4):

Table 3.4

C expression	Original types	Promoted types
pc − pi * ps	char − int * short	int − int * int
3 * us − pi	int * unsigned short − int	int * unsigned int − int

The promotion of operands of type char to type int means that it is sensible to perform arithmetic operations on data objects of type char. From the ASCII character set 'D' is represented by decimal 68; 'A' by 65; 'z' by 122 and 'a' by 97. Thus:

```
'D' − 'A'         evaluates to: 68 − 65 = 3
'z' − 'a' + 1 evaluates to: 122 − 97 + 1 = 26
```

If ch is a variable of type char and currently represents any upper case letter in the ASCII character set, then the expression:

```
ch − 'A' + 'a'
```

evaluates to the integer value with the ASCII code that represents the equivalent lower case letter. For example, if variable ch represents the character 'D', then using decimal representation of the ASCII encodings of the characters, the expression evaluates to:

```
68 - 65 + 97 = 100
```

and the corresponding ASCII character is 'd'.

An arithmetic expression such as a + b computes a value of some type. For example, if both a and b are of type int, then the value of a + b is also of type int. However, if a and b are of different types, then a + b is a mixed expression, and we require rules to establish the type of the result itself.

In a mixed expression *arithmetic conversions* determine whether and how operands are converted before a binary operation is performed. When two values are to be operated upon in combination, they are first converted to a single common type. The result after applying the operation is also of that same common type.

The conversion is performed according to a hierarchy of types. Operands of the lower type are converted to that of the higher type before executing the operator. The implicit arithmetic conversions operate much as expected. In the absence of unsigned quantities the following informal rules apply:

If either operand is long double, convert the other to long double.

If either operand is double, convert the other to double.

If either operand is float, convert the other to float.

Perform the integral promotions.

If either operand is long, convert the other to long.

Otherwise, both operands are of type int.

In the context of the following declarations:

```
int   i;
short s;
```

consider the evaluation of the mixed expression:

```
3.0 * i + s
```

Assume that the current values for the variables i and s are, respectively, 32 and 10. First, the integral promotions cause the short to be promoted to type int. The resulting *representation change* will leave the value unaltered as 10. The expression is then viewed as:

```
double * int + int
```

operating on the values:

```
3.0 * 32 + 10
```

Since multiplication has higher precedence than addition, it is evaluated first. The left operand to the multiplier operation is a double. Therefore, the right operand is also promoted to type `double` if it is not already one. The expression is now:

    double * double + int

The integer value 32 undergoes a representation change to the equivalent double precision floating point value:

    3.0 * 32.0 + 10

Following execution of the multiplying operator, we have:

    96.0 + 10

and the types involved in the expression are now:

    double + int

Following the same argument, the `int` (`10`) is promoted to type `double` (`10.0`) before performing the addition. The final result is of type `double` and has the value:

    106.0

These implicit arithmetic conversions operate much as expected. The programmer is cautioned, however, to be fully aware of the conversions. Without a full understanding, some unexpected results are possible.

Some pitfalls surround the use of unsigned integral quantities in expressions. The full set of rules for arithmetic conversions is:

If either operand is `long double`, convert the other to `long double`.

If either operand is `double`, convert the other to `double`.

If either operand is `float`, convert the other to `float`.

Perform the integral promotions on both operands and:

if either operand is `unsigned long int`, convert the other to `unsigned long int`. Otherwise, if one operand is `long int` and the other is `unsigned int`, then if a `long int` can represent all values of an `unsigned int` then the latter is converted to a `long int`; if not, both are converted to an `unsigned long int`.

If either operand is `long int`, convert the other to `long int`.

If either operand is `unsigned int`, convert the other to `unsigned int`.

Otherwise, both operands are of type `int`.

The conversion rules are complicated by the introduction of unsigned operands. For example, consider the declarations:

    unsigned int ui = 10U;   /* note the suffix */
            int pi = -7;

and the expression:

```
ui + pi
```

Here we are mixing signed and unsigned quantities. By the rules of arithmetic we must convert `pi` to `unsigned int`. Unsigned integers obey the laws of arithmetic modulo 2^N where N is the number of bits in the representation. Arithmetic on unsigned quantities can never produce overflow. For N = 16, an `unsigned int` has a range of 0–65535 inclusive. Converting the signed value -7 to `unsigned int` involves adding 65536 producing the result 65529. The final expression value is `10 + 65529`, the `unsigned int` value 3.

Similarly, given the declarations:

```
long int     li = -1L;
unsigned int ui = 1U;
```

then the expression:

```
li + ui
```

involves mixing a `signed long int with an unsigned int`. Suppose that a standard sized `int` is 16 bits and a `long` is 32 bits. Then since a `long int` can represent all the values of an `unsigned int`, `ui` is converted to `long int` and this is the type of the expression. If, however, both `int` and `long` are 32 bits, then a `long int` cannot represent all the values of an `unsigned int` and both operands are converted to `unsigned long int` (the result type).

The moral is to avoid unsigned quantities in programs. Where they are present, one must be especially careful when they are mixed with signed quantities.

For certain operations in C, it may be that the true mathematical result of the operation cannot be represented as a value of the expected result type (as determined by the usual conversion rules). This condition is referred to as overflow. For example, multiplication of two `int`'s result in an `int`. But if, as on the IBM PC `int`'s are held as 2's complement 16-bit values, with largest integer representation of 32767, then multiplying 700 by 800 produces the true mathematical value 560000 which is not representable as an `int`. Another example is attempted division by zero, where the result is infinity.

Generally, C does not specify the consequences of overflow. A number of possibilities may arise. One is that an incorrect value of the correct type is generated. Another possibility is that the program is prematurely terminated with or without some appropriate error message. A third possibility is to trap the exception within the program and take the appropriate action. In all cases, the programmer must guard against these occurrences and, where possible, handle them within the program. A program that terminates prematurely is not a good program.

3.10 The assignment operator

The *assignment* operator allows the assignment of some new value to a program variable. The simplest form of the assignment operator is:

```
variable = expression
```

The effect of the operator is to evaluate the expression to the right of the assignment operator (=), and the resulting value is then assigned to the variable on the left. If both operands to the assignment operator are arithmetic, the type of the expression is converted to the type of the variable on the left before executing the assignment. Examples of assignments are:

```
(a)   interest  = principal * rate * time / 100
(b)   speed     = distance / time
(c)   total_min = 60 * hours + minutes
(d)   count     = count + 1
```

Since the assignment mechanism in C is implemented as an (binary) operator, like all other operators it has a precedence, an associativity, and indulges in automatic type conversions. The precedence and associativity are given in Appendix E. The low priority of the assignment operator guarantees that the right-hand expression is first evaluated before the assignment is performed.

In the same way that `operand1 + operand2` evaluates to the arithmetic addition of the two operands, the assignment:

```
variable = expression
```

also evaluates to a value. That is, after evaluation of the expression and assigning it to the variable on the left, a value is delivered. The type and value is that of the variable, and may be discarded or used in multiple assignment expressions:

```
variable1 = variable2 = .... variablek = expression
```

The right to left associativity of the assignment operator means that the expression is evaluated, assigned to variable k; the value of this variable is then the delivered value, which in turn is assigned to variable k − 1, and so on. Thus the expression:

```
x = y = z = p + q
```

is interpreted as:

```
x = (y = (z = p + q))
```

Implicit type conversions also occur across the assignment operator. For example, in an expression in which the left operand is a `double` and the right operand is an `int` as in:

```
double = int
```

the value of the integer expression will be converted to a `double` before performing the assignment. The integer is automatically promoted to type `double`. A promotion or *widening* is normally well behaved, but *narrowing* or *demotion* such as in:

```
int = double
```

can result in the loss of information. Precisely what happens in each case is implementation-dependent. In this example if the double were to evaluate to, say, 12.345 then we should reasonably expect the integer value 12 to be assigned after discarding the fractional part. The behaviour of the conversion is undefined if the double value cannot be represented as an integer. For example, the magnitude of the double may be too large to be represented as an integer, or if a negative double is assigned to an unsigned integer. Questions of rounding versus truncation are also left to the discretion of the implementor. Again, the reader is advised to seek out the appropriate local documentation.

Some possible assignments and the likely effects are as follows:

Assignment	Effect
int = int	no conversion
float = double	truncate (possibly round) the double
int = long	implemented by truncation
char = int	implemented by truncation

Care must be taken when employing the multiple assignment. If iii is a variable of type integer, then in the assignment:

```
iii = 12.34
```

the floating point constant 12.34 will normally be truncated to integer 12 before assigning to the integer variable. The value of this integer variable is then the value delivered by this operation. Then in the multiple assignment:

```
fff = iii = 12.34
```

with variable fff of type float, the expression to the right of:

```
fff = ....
```

is of type integer, with value 12. The integer is converted back to a floating point representation (12.0) before assignment. One must not therefore read the value 12.34 as assigned to both iii (after truncation) and to fff.

3.11 The compound assignment operators

Assignments of the form:

```
count = count + 2
```

occur repeatedly in programming problems. The effect is to take the current value of the variable count and to it add the literal value 2. The resulting value is then assigned back to the variable count. Overall, the value of the variable count is increased by 2. Such an assignment may also be represented in C by:

```
count += 2
```

In fact, this *compound assignment* operator is applicable to all five binary arithmetic operators. Thus we may have:

```
count += 2
stock -= 1
power *= 2.71828
divisor /= 10.0
remainder %= 10
```

In all cases, except the modulus operator assignment (%=), the two operands may be of any arithmetic type. For the operator %= the two operands must be integral types.

All these new operators have the same precedence level as the simple assignment and associate right to left (see Appendix E).

If op= is a generalized denotation for the compound assignment operators, then the semantics of the expression:

```
variable op= expression
```

is specified by:

```
variable = variable op (expression)
```

Note the parenthesized subexpression is evaluated before applying the operator op. Thus the expression:

```
sum /= 3 + 7
```
is equivalent to:

```
sum = sum / (3 + 7)
```

Multiple assignments employing both the simple assignment and the compound assignment are possible. Again, some care is required in their interpretation. If variable iii is of type integer and value 12, and variable fff is of type float and value 1.234, then the assignment:

```
fff = iii *= fff
```

operates as:

```
fff = ( iii = iii * fff)
```

with iii assigned the value 14 (12 * 1.234 = 14.808, truncated) and fff is assigned the value 14.0.

3.12 The increment and decrement operators

In the preceding section, the compound assignment operators were introduced. With these operators, simple assignments of the form:

```
x = x + 1
```

may be represented by:

```
x += 1
```

In fact, incrementing by one is such a commonly occurring operation in a program, that C supports two forms of unary increment operator. They are known as the *preincrement* operator and the *postincrement* operator. The preincrement expression has the form:

```
++ variable
```

while the postincrement expression appears as:

```
variable ++
```

In both cases the constant 1 is added to the arithmetic operand. The usual arithmetic conversions are performed on the operand and the constant 1 before addition is performed, and the usual assignment conversions are performed when storing the arithmetic sum back into the variable.

Both increment operators produce a side effect. In addition to incrementing the value of the variable operand, a value is delivered. In the case of the preincrement operator, the delivered value is the new (incremented) value of the variable. The type of value delivered is the same as the type of the operand. Given two integer variables called sum and count, then the effect of the assignment:

```
sum += ++count
```

is twofold. First, the value of the variable count is increased by 1. Second, this new value of count is added to the current value of the variable sum.

The postincrement operator also delivers a value, but this time it is the old value of the variable before it was incremented. The assignment:

```
sum += count++
```

again increments the value of the variable count by 1, and then adds the original value of count (before the incrementing took place) to the variable sum. Thus if the initial values of sum and count are 10 and 20 respectively, then evaluation of the expression is twofold:

1.   Variable count is postincremented to produce 21.
2.   Variable sum is incremented by the original value of variable count and evaluates to 30.

Instead of incrementing a variable value by 1 we can also decrement its value by

1. This is achieved by the *predecrement* and *postdecrement* operators. The former has the form:

```
-- variable
```

while the latter appears as:

```
variable --
```

In both cases the constant 1 is subtracted from the operand. Again, the usual arithmetic conversions apply. The same side effects also apply with a value delivered after decrementing. The value delivered by the predecrement operator is the new variable value after decrementing. The value delivered by the postdecrement operator is the original value of the variable before decrementing.

The precedence and associativity of the increment and decrement operators are shown in the table in Appendix E.

In certain constructions the side effects caused by these operators can produce unintended results. Consider the expression:

```
a = ++c + c
```

Here ++ is prefixed to variable c, meaning that c is to be incremented before it is used. But variable c occurs twice in the expression, and when c is incremented it changes both the values of c. The computation is unclear about whether the original or the new value of c is used in the part . . . + c. Such expressions are considered bad programming practice and should be avoided by writing code that isolates the effect of the ++ operator, as in:

```
++c;
a = c + c;
```

or by:

```
a = 2 * (++c);
```

3.13 The type cast operator

In addition to implicit type conversions which can occur across the assignment operator and in mixed expressions, there is an explicit type conversion called a *cast*. If variable date is an int, then:

```
(double) date
```

will cast or coerce the value of date so that the expression has type double.

A cast expression consists of a left parenthesis, a type-specifier, a right parenthesis and an operand expression:

```
(type-specifier) expression
```

A cast is implemented as an operator. It possesses both a precedence and an associativity. Its relation to other operators is shown in Appendix E.

Some examples of the use of the cast operator are:

```
(char) x
(int) dl + d2
```

Note how in the last example, the type cast `int` applies only to the operand `dl`. This is because the type cast operator has higher precedence than binary addition. To apply the cast to the result obtained by adding `dl` and `d2`, parentheses are required:

```
(int) (dl + d2)
```

The cast operator is a specialized explicit type conversion operator. We shall discuss its use and application in later chapters.

3.14 The comma operator

The *comma* operator finds applications in a number of specialized areas. For completeness, we discuss it here, since it is an operator. Use of this operator will appear in later chapters.

The comma operator consists of two expressions separated by a comma symbol:

```
expression , expression
```

Of all the C operators, the comma operator has lowest precedence, and associates left to right (see Appendix E).

In the comma expression:

```
expression1 , expression2
```

`expression1` is fully evaluated first. It need not produce a value but if it does that value is discarded. The second expression is then evaluated. The type and value of the comma operator is that of the final expression.

An example of the comma operator is:

```
sum = 0, k = 1
```

If variable `k` has been declared an `int`, then this comma expression has value 1 and type `int`. In the comma expression:

```
s = (t = 2, t + 3)
```

variable `t` is assigned the value 1, and the value of the comma expression is 5 (the result of `t + 3`). The value 5 is then assigned to the variable `s`. This effect is achieved only through use of the parentheses, since the comma operator has lower precedence than the assignment operator. Without the parentheses:

```
s = t = 2, t + 3
```

then both s and t would be assigned the value 2 and the result of the expression is 5. Depending upon the context of this comma expression, the result value may or not be discarded.

3.15 Summary

1. The four fundamental types are char, int, float and double. Float and double provide two precisions for decimal numbers. The qualifiers short, long and unsigned offer several sizes for integral types. Long doubles also feature.

2. Denotations or constants represent specific instances of a particular type. Integer constants preceded with 0 and 0X (or 0x) designate octal and hexadecimal integer constants respectively. Integer constants of type long are prepended with an L (or l). Unsigned integer constants are prepended U or u. A constant with a decimal fraction is implicitly of type double. A floating point constant may be prepended with either F or f for constants of type float, or with L or l for constants of type long double.

3. A character value is delimited by single quotes ('). A string value is delimited by double quotes ("). Both may involve escape sequences.

4. Identifiers are used to name objects in a program. An identifier is a letter/digit sequence starting with a letter. The underscore symbol (_) is considered to be a letter. Good mnemonic names should always be chosen to improve program clarity.

5. The three types of identifiers are reserved words, standard identifiers and user-defined identifiers. Reserved identifiers (keywords) have a special predefined meaning to the C compiler and cannot be redefined by the programmer. Standard identifiers (e.g. printf) may be redefined but it is not recommended.

6. A declaration contains the names and types of the variables used in a program.

7. An expression is a combination of operators and operands. The operators determine the computation to be performed. The precedence and associativity of operators determines the order of evaluation in an expression. Assignment is an operator and can occur as part of an expression.

8.   When evaluating mixed mode expressions, automatic type conversions apply. Integral conversions promote integer data values of a lower type to one of a higher type. Arithmetic conversions apply to operands before performing a binary operation.

9.   The comma operator is used for sequential evaluation of a sequence of expressions. The value of the final expression is the value of the entire expression.

3.16 Exercises

1.   Which of the following are valid C constants? For those which are valid, identify their type. If invalid, state why:

(a) − 123   (b) .123   (c) 10E−4
(d) '4'   (e) 'four'   (f) '\z'
(g) 106

2.   Which of the following are invalid identifiers in C, giving explanations.

(a) June   (b) int   (c) BBC_1
(d) b   (e) a$ (f) X_RAY
(g) _Z   (h) _12_

3.   Given the following declarations and initial assignments:

```
int  i, j, m, n;
float f, g;
char c;

i = j = 2;
m = n = 5;
f = 1.2;
g = 3.4;
c = 'X';
```

use the rules of precedence and associativity of the operators to evaluate the following expressions, showing any conversions which take place and the type of the result.

(a) 12 * m   (b) m / j
(c) n % j   (d) m / j * j
(e) (f + 10) * 20   (f) (i++) * n
(g) i++ * n   (h) −12L * (g − f)
(i) 2 + c   (j) (n++), (n++)
(k) m = n = --j   (l) (int) f

(m) `(double) m`   (n) `(double) m + 10`

(o) `(double)(m + 10)`

4.   Find the errors in the following series of declarations:

```
int     kilometres, metres;
float   metres;
integer weeks;
int     fm, medium, long;
short   char, tiny;
```

4

Input and output

STRICTLY, INPUT AND OUTPUT FACILITIES are not part of the C language, unlike FORTRAN, for example, where the READ and WRITE statements are defined as part of the language. None the less, real programs do communicate with their environment. In this chapter we will describe a subset of the standard I/O (input/output) library, consisting of a set of functions designed to provide a standard facility for performing input and output.

We will not attempt to describe the entire I/O library here. We restrict our discussion to four functions which communicate with the user's terminal. This will be sufficient to permit us to write complete operational programs. In Chapter 14 we will revisit input/output and consider programs which operate on data held in computer files. Appendix F4 provides a reference section for those I/O functions of the standard library.

4.1 Access to the standard library

Whenever a C program executes, three 'files' are automatically opened by the operating system environment for use by that program. These files are known as the *standard input*, the *standard output* and the *standard error*. It is intended that normal input by the program will be read from the standard input. In an interactive environment the standard input normally associates with the user's terminal (keyboard). Similarly, normal output is written to the standard output and, again, is the user terminal (screen). Finally, an additional output file is opened. It is intended that any error messages produced by the program be written to this standard error file. In an interactive environment, this is also the user's terminal.

In this chapter we are concerned only with programs that operate with the standard input and standard output. In Chapter 14 where input/output through files is discussed, we consider more fully the standard input, standard output and the standard error.

All source program files which refer to a standard I/O library function must contain the line:

```
#include <stdio.h>
```

near the beginning of the file. Strictly this is not entirely true, since only certain functions from this library need the information contained in the standard I/O header file, stdio.h. By always including it we then do not need to worry whether it is required or not. A detailed description of this #include statement is reserved until the next chapter. Suffice it to say that a file called stdio.h defines certain items required by the standard I/O library. For example, the standard input, standard output and standard error files are defined here. These details are incorporated or 'included' into the application program from this header file.

4.2 Formatted output

Formatted lines of output are achieved with the standard I/O library function printf. We used printf informally throughout Chapter 2. The complete and generalized description of printf is:

```
printf(format, argument1, argument2, .... )
```

The function printf formats and prints its arguments on the standard output. The arguments are any expressions delivering the values to be printed. The display of these arguments is under the control of the formatting string *format*. This string (see Section 3.4) contains two types of information: ordinary characters, which are simply copied to the output; and *conversion specifications* which cause conversion and printing of the arguments to printf.

The simplest example of printf is one with a format string containing no conversion specifications and with no arguments. In this case, the string is copied verbatim to the standard output:

```
printf("A simple message.\n")
```

The result of executing this statement is to produce on the standard output the content of the format string. As the string contains a newline symbol as the last printed character, any subsequent output appears at the left margin on the line immediately following this output. Equally, this output follows any previous output to the standard output.

For each argument to printf, a corresponding conversion specification should appear in the format string. There should be exactly the right number of arguments of the right type to satisfy the conversions; otherwise the result of executing printf is unpredictable. If any conversion specification appearing in the format string is malformed, then the effect is also unpredictable.

A conversion specification in the format string is introduced by the percent (%) character. There then follows a sequence of none or more options to the conversion. The specification terminates with a conversion operation expressed as a single character. A full definition for a conversion specification is then:

$$\text{percent symbol} \left\{ \begin{array}{l} \text{flag} \\ \text{character} \end{array} \right\}_{\text{opt}} \left\{ \begin{array}{l} \text{minimum} \\ \text{field} \\ \text{width} \end{array} \right\}_{\text{opt}} \left\{ \begin{array}{l} \text{precision} \\ \text{specification} \end{array} \right\}_{\text{opt}} \left\{ \begin{array}{l} \text{long} \\ \text{size} \\ \text{specification} \end{array} \right\}_{\text{opt}} \text{conversion operation}$$

Note that only the percent symbol and the single character conversion operation need be present. All the other fields are optional (opt). Further, not all combinations of the fields are meaningful. For example, the precision specification controls the number of decimal places printed in a decimal number. This is meaningless if an integer value is being formatted and printed.

Not all the possible combinations are explored in this section. There are simply too many. Here we provide an explanation of a range of examples of the fundamentals of formatted output. A full explanation of the functions in the standard I/O library and in particular the conversion specifications of `printf` are given in Appendix F4.

A minimum conversion specification is the percent symbol and a conversion operation. The latter is expressed as any one of the single characters:

```
c d E f g G i n o p s u x X or %
```

The last conversion character shown is used to represent the percent symbol itself, since otherwise it is reserved to introduce conversion specifications in format strings. The output from:

```
printf("Tax is 10%%\n")
```

is:

```
Tax is 10%
```

Detailed explanations of how each conversion operation performs is given in Appendix F4. A brief description of each operation is given in Table 4.1, and provides a convenient reference. Some common examples then follow.

Table 4.1 Conversion operations for use with `printf`

Conversion operation	Application
d, i	signed decimal conversion of int
u	unsigned decimal conversion of unsigned
o	unsigned octal conversion of unsigned
x, X	unsigned hexadecimal conversion of unsigned
c	single character conversion
s	string conversion
f	signed decimal floating point conversion
e, E	signed decimal floating point conversion
g, G	signed decimal floating point conversion
p	pointer conversion
n	number of characters written

An argument expression evaluating to an integer value is formatted with the d conversion operator. In the context of the declarations and assignations:

```
int a, b;
a = 10;
b = 15;
```

the function call:

```
printf("The sum of %d and %d is %d\n", a, b, a+b)
```

produces the following output:

```
The sum of 10 and 15 is 25
```

The conversion operation %d causes signed decimal conversion of the argument value to be performed. For each %d, one argument is consumed. The argument value should be of type int. The converted value consists of a sequence of decimal digits. The sequence is as short as possible, necessary to print the value. Thus the value of the variable a (10) requires two character positions in the output stream.

A minimum field width may also be present in the conversion specification. In its simplest form this consists of an unsigned decimal integer constant. If the argument value results in fewer characters than the specified field width, then the characters are right justified in the field and padded on the left with space characters. The function call:

```
printf("The sum of %d and %d is %4d\n", a, b, a+b)
```

produces the output:

```
The sum of 10 and 15 is   25
```

with the value of the expression a + b displayed in a field width of four characters. If, however, the converted argument value results in more characters than the specified field width, the field is expanded sufficiently to accommodate the printed value. The value is not truncated but the formatted output is now different from that expected. The example:

```
printf("The sum of %d and %ld is %3d\n", a, b, a+b)
```

produces the output:

```
The sum of 10 and 15 is   25
```

The conversion specification corresponding to the argument b is %ld. This directs the value to be printed in a field width of one, but since the converted argument value requires a field of two, the latter takes precedence.

Floating point values are displayed using the conversion specification %f. The converted value consists of a sequence of decimal digits with an embedded decimal point, but no more than is necessary to represent the value. When no precision is specified, a precision of six decimal places is assumed. In the context of the declarations and assignments:

```
float x, y;
x = 1.234;     y = 56.78;
```

then:

```
printf("%f from %f gives %f\n", y, x, x-y)
```

produces the output:

```
56.780000 from 1.234000 gives -55.546000
```

The minimum field width and the precision can be expressed as two unsigned integer constants separated by a period symbol. Both these elements are optional. If the precision is not present, then the period symbol is omitted and the default precision is 6. If necessary, rounding of the converted value may be performed. The example:

```
printf("%5.2f from %4.2f gives %7.2f\n", y, x, x-y)
```

produces:

```
56.78 from 1.23 gives -55.55
```

Finally, we demonstrate how to control the formatting of a string. The required conversion operation is %s. When no field width is given, the characters of the string are printed in the minimum field necessary:

```
printf("[%s]\n", "Hello there")
```

produces:

```
[Hello there]
```

A field width is represented as an unsigned decimal integer constant preceding the conversion operation. The string is right justified in the field and padded on the left with spaces:

```
printf("[%20s]\n", "Hello there")
```

produces:

```
[         Hello there]
```

None of the examples we have introduced used a *flag* character. Flag characters modify the meaning of the main conversion operation. In all the examples where the converted value requires fewer characters than the explicit field width, then the value is displayed right justified in the field and padded on the left with spaces. Left justification in the field and padding on the right with spaces is achieved by prefixing the conversion specification with a hyphen symbol flag character:

```
printf("[%-20s]\n", "Hello there")
```

produces:

```
[Hello there         ]
```

A number of other flag characters are available. They are fully detailed in

Appendix F4. We may choose to employ any of these other flags in the programs which follow. It is therefore assumed that the reader has reviewed Appendix F4.

4.3 Formatted input

The function `scanf` is the counterpart of `printf`. The stream of input characters from the standard input are parsed according to a control string and input values assigned to program variables. The form of the function call is:

```
scanf(format, argument1, argument2, .... )
```

Note:

> Each argument is the address of the memory location to receive the input value. Each argument must therefore be the address of the receiving variable. This is expressed in C by preceding the variable name with the address operator, denoted by the ampersand (&) symbol. Further details of this operator is given in Chapter 5.

To input two data values and to store them in locations referred to by the identifiers `month` and `year`, we use:

```
scanf(" .... ", &month, &year)
```

The *format* string is a *picture* of the expected form of the input. One may think of `scanf` as performing a simple parse of the stream of input characters according to the format string. The format string uses conversion specifications similar to those found with `printf`. There should be exactly the correct number of arguments of the correct type to satisfy the conversion specifications in the format string; otherwise the results are unpredictable. If any conversion specification is malformed the effect is also unpredictable.

In addition to conversion specifications, a format string may also include whitespace characters. A whitespace character in the format string causes one or more whitespace characters to be read from the standard input and discarded. The first non-whitespace character encountered in the input remains as the next character to be read.

Finally, a format string may include characters other than whitespace characters and the sequence of characters representing a conversion specification. These other characters must match exactly the next characters of the input stream. If there is no match, `scanf` terminates and the conflicting character remains in the input as the next available character.

A conversion specification commences with a percent (%) symbol. The form of a conversion specification for use with `scanf` is:

| percent symbol | $\left\{ \begin{array}{l} \text{assignment} \\ \text{suppression} \\ \text{flat} \end{array} \right\}_{opt}$ | $\left\{ \begin{array}{l} \text{maximum} \\ \text{field} \\ \text{width} \end{array} \right\}_{opt}$ | $\left\{ \begin{array}{l} \text{size} \\ \text{specification} \end{array} \right\}_{opt}$ | conversion operation |

The conversion operations supported by scanf are similar to those of printf and are summarized in Table 4.2. Full details are given in Appendix F4.

Table 4.2 Conversion operations for use with scanf

Conversion operation	Application
d, i	signed decimal conversion to int
u	unsigned decimal conversion to unsigned
o	unsigned octal conversion to unsigned
x	unsigned hexadecimal conversion to unsigned
c	single character conversion
s	string conversion
f	signed decimal floating point conversion
e	signed decimal floating point conversion
g	signed decimal floating point conversion
[	string conversion (special)
p	pointer input
n	number of characters read

The number of characters read from the input stream depends on the conversion operation. Generally, a conversion operation processes a sequence of one or more characters until either (a) a whitespace or other inappropriate character is read, or (b) the number of characters read equals the specified maximum field width.

Given the declarations:

```
int  day, month, year;
char ch1, ch2;
```

then the scanf invocation:

```
scanf("%d %d %d", &day, &month, &year)
```

expects three integer values to be supplied. The first integer value read is assigned to the variable day. Any amount of leading whitespace characters before the digits of the number are ignored. The second integer value is separated from the first by one or more whitespace characters and is assigned to the variable month. Similarly for the final variable year. The input:

```
31     12

1985
```

causes the value 31 to be assigned to the variable day, 12 to the variable month and 1985 to the variable year. The input values are separated by a series of whitespace characters. The values 31 and 12 are separated by spaces and/or tabs, while 12 and 1985 are separated by newline symbols. The value 1985 is also terminated by a newline character. This final character remains in the input buffer to be processed by any subsequent scanf call.

In the example:

```
scanf("%d/%d/%d", &day, &month, &year)
```

each integer value is expected to be separated by the slash (/) character. A valid input stream to the above is then:

```
12/4/1985
```

A conversion specification may also include a maximum field width. This is presented as an unsigned decimal integer constant not equal to zero. The conversion terminates when either the required number of characters are read or the input value terminates with whitespace or some invalid character. The last scanf example might also have been written as:

```
scanf("%2d/%2d/%4d", &day, &month, &year)
```

allowing for a two-digit day and month, and a four-digit year.

When maximum field widths are employed, it is no longer necessary to use whitespace characters. The input:

```
12051985
```

can be parsed so that the variable day is assigned the value 12, month the value 5, and year the value 1985. The scanf call to achieve this is:

```
scanf("%2d%2d%4d", &day, &month, &year)
```

Care is required when using the %c conversion specification. This operation does not skip over any initial whitespace characters. The example:

```
scanf("%d%c%d%c%d", &day, &ch1, &month, &ch2, &year)
```

with input:

```
5-9/1985
```

assigns the value 5 to the integer variable day, 9 to the integer variable month and 1985 to the integer variable year. The character variables ch1 and ch2 are assigned, respectively, the hyphen (–) symbol and the slash (/) symbol.

4.4 The functions getchar and putchar

From the preceding two sections we know how to perform single character transfers using formatted I/O routines. Given the declaration:

```
char ch;
```

we may read a single character from the standard input and print it to the standard output with:

```
scanf("%c", &ch);
printf("%c", ch);
```

An unnecessary overhead is incurred by doing it this way. This is attributable to both scanf and printf having to process their respective format strings.

Two simpler facilities are provided for single character input and output: getchar and putchar. Strictly, we should not refer to them as functions, for as we shall show later in the book they are not library functions at all. Precisely what they are is given in Chapter 14. For the present, however, they can be considered as functions.

The function putchar takes a single argument and prints the character which it represents on the standard output. To output the value of the character variable ch, we use:

```
putchar(ch)
```

To output a single newline character we could use:

```
putchar('\n')
```

The function getchar reads the next character from the standard input stream. No arguments are given to getchar, but the parentheses are obligatory. The value of the character read is returned as an int as the function value. This can be captured by a suitable assignment:

```
ch = getchar()
```

If variable ch is of type char then appropriate conversions take place across the assignment operator.

The original problem to input and then echo a single character can then be expressed by:

```
ch = getchar();
putchar(ch);
```

Mixing the input/output operations scanf, printf, getchar and putchar is freely supported. For example, the input date:

```
12-10/1985
```

could be read with the functions:

```
scanf("%d", &day);
ch1 = getchar();
scanf("%d", &month);
ch2 = getchar();
scanf("%d", &year);
```

with the character variables ch1 and ch2 holding the delimiters between the three numbers.

When using formatted input with scanf, we must be aware that the input of, say, a number continues until the first occurrence of whitespace or a character that is not part of a number. From our earlier discussions, the above input could have been read by:

```
scanf("%d%c%d%c%d", &day, &ch1, &month, &ch2, &year)
```

The value for variable day is read as the character sequence up to but not including the hyphen symbol. This remains in the input stream for the next assignation. The next conversion specification is %c and hence a single character is entered and assigned to variable ch1. This single character is the hyphen symbol.

When a number is read and is terminated by whitespace, then the whitespace character remains as the first character in any subsequent input operation. Consider, then, a program which prompts the user for a number, reads the newline terminated value, asks the user if the value is correct, and reads the reply expected as the single character Y or N (respectively, yes or no). A first attempt at this programming might suggest the solution:

```
printf("Please enter the number: ");
scanf("%d", &number);
printf("Correct? ");
reply = getchar();
```

After the number has been read, the terminating newline symbol remains in the input buffer. When the prompt "Correct?" is displayed, the program does not await user input, but takes the newline symbol in the buffer as the reply. Processing continues without any user input. Clearly, this is not the desired effect.

One simple solution to this problem is to discard the newline symbol before the reply is required. Provided that the number is terminated by an immediate newline character, we can insert an additional single character read. This can be done either in the first scanf itself, or as a separate getchar. We show the latter solution:

```
printf("Please enter the number: ");
scanf("%d", &number);
discard = getchar();      /* remove newline from input */
printf("Correct? ");
reply = getchar();
```

4.5 Summary

1. Input/output facilities in C are provided by a suite of functions from the standard library.

2. When using input/output constructs, the system header file stdio.h should be included in a program by means of the control line #include <stdio.h>.

3.   Formatted output is provided by the libraray function `printf`. Formatted input is provided by the library function `scanf`. Formatting is the process of controlling the layout of the printed output and the program input.

4.   Formatting strings include a mixture of whitespace characters, plain characters and conversion specifications.

5.   Single character transfers is accomplished with the library 'functions' `getchar` and `putchar`.

4.6 Exercises

1.   Produce the following two lines of output:

```
PROGRAMMING IN C
IS FUN
```

using

(a) two `printf` function calls
(b) one `printf` function call.

2.   Given the integer variable `staffno` and the floating variable `salary`, write output statement(s) to produce:

```
STAFF      PAY
ddd        ddd.dd
```

where each 'd' represents a decimal digit.

3.   Write program statement which reads a sum of money in the form `ddd.dd`, increases it by 10%, and prints out the increased sum. If the input was of the form `ddd:dd`, how would the program have to be modified?

4.   In the context of the variable declarations:

```
int   j, k;
float x, y, z;
char  c;
```

and the three lines of program input data:

```
12.34      56.7
      -89E10
0.012
```

What is the effect of executing each of the following sequence of input statements:

    (a) `scanf("%f %f %f", &x, &y, &z);`

    (b) `scanf("%f", &x);`
        `scanf("%f %f", &y, &z);`

    (c) `scanf("%f %f %f", &x, &y, &z);`
        `scanf("%d", &j);`

    (d) `scanf("%d%c%d %f", &j, &c, &k, &x).`

5

Program structure

IN CHAPTER 2 we explored the fundamental features of a C program. In particular, a number of complete programs were presented. No attempt was made to specify the exact construction of a program. We merely explored the essentials of a C program. In this chapter we will define the exact composition of a basic program. In later chapters, where we introduce additional language features, extensions to this basic form are given.

5.1 The structure of a function

A C program consists of one or more functions. Functions within C facilitate partitioning large programs into smaller, manageable units, thus simplifying the programming task. In addition, functions developed in one program may be incorporated into others, saving the need to reprogram them. The value of functions to the C programmer will be fully appreciated, when, in this and later chapters we construct major items of software.

A C function describes the computational processes to be carried out on its data. The function must thus describe both its data objects (declarations) and its processing actions (statements). The simplest form of function definition reflects this minimum requirement:

```
function-name()
{
  optional-declaration-list
  optional-statement-list
}
```

The *function-name* is the programmer-defined name (identifier) for that function. Function-names must be unique, otherwise the compiler is unable to distinguish between two distinct functions bearing the same name. A function-name is constructed according to the rule for identifiers. The unit of text surrounded by and including the braces { and }, is called a *compound statement* – also called a *block*. A block consists of a (possibly empty) sequence of declarations, followed by a (possibly empty) sequence of statements. Individual declarations and statements are terminated by semicolon (;) symbols. The declarations identify the data items and the statements specify the processing actions.

48

All the programs introduced in Chapter 2 conform to this structure. Program 2.1(a), repeated as Program 5.1(a), consists of the single function main. As noted in Chapter 2, all complete C programs must have a function called main. A program starts executing from the the first executable statement in function main.

PROGRAM 5.1(a)

```
/*
**      A program to display a simple message to
**      the operator's console.
*/

#include <stdio.h>

main()
{
  printf("My first program.\n");
}
```

The function main has no variable declarations but does have a single statement. The statement is a *function call* to the standard C library function printf. This single statement is terminated with a semicolon symbol.

When a function is called (such as printf, above), the actual objects to be manipulated by that function are supplied as *arguments*. In the case of printf, the item to be printed is the string:

```
"My first program.\n"
```

This single argument is enclosed in the parentheses (and). Equally, main is a function. It has, for the present, no arguments and its definition is shown by:

```
main() ....
```

It is not permissible to omit the parentheses in a function with no arguments. The parentheses are obligatory.

A program which uses input/output functions from the standard C library must also have a #include statement as shown. This statement supplies the C compiler with details relating to the standard input/output functions. Strictly, not all input/output functions from the library require the presence of this particular #include. Rather than try to remember which functions need the #include and which do not, it is easier to put it into all programs. This redundancy is harmless.

Program 5.1(a) might alternatively have been written as in Program 5.1(b).

PROGRAM 5.1(b)

```
/*
**      This program displays a simple message through
**      three separate calls to the printf function.
**      The output is the same as that of Program 5-1(a).
*/

#include <stdio.h>

main()
{
  printf("My ");
  printf("first ");
  printf("program.\n");
}
```

This time the function main employs three statements. Each is a separate invocation of the printf function. Again, no variable declarations are present. To assist with program readability, each function call appears on separate lines. This does not, however, imply that the outputs appear on separate lines. Output on to separate lines is governed by the arguments to printf and not by the program layout. Indentation and alignment are used to emphasize the structure of this program. The program output is:

```
My first program.
```

A function need not have any declarations, as in the examples above, or any statements. For example, Program 5.2 is a perfectly valid C program. The function main, and hence the program, does absolutely nothing, except, perhaps, consume some processor time. Such a program has no real practical value. A null function, other than main, can sometimes prove useful as a placeholder during program development.

PROGRAM 5.2

```
/*
**      A program to do nothing !
*/

#include <stdio.h>

main()
{
}
```

Consider now a program which includes variable declarations. The program is required to read two integer data values and to print them in reverse order. To achieve this the function `main` must include a declaration for two integer variables. These variables will be the repositories for the two data values.

PROGRAM 5.3

```
/*
**      This program accepts two integer data values
**      and displays them in reverse order.
*/

#include <stdio.h>

main()
{
  int first, second;      /* data stores */

  printf("Enter two integer values: ");
  scanf("%d %d", &first, &second);
  printf("Reversed data: %d and %d\n", second, first);
}
```

Program 5.4 is similar to the last example. It reads some data, processes it, then displays the result of its computations. The processing this time involves some arithmetic operations. The program reads three integer data values representing a time expressed as `hours`, `minutes` and `seconds`. The time is converted into a total number of `seconds`, then printed.

PROGRAM 5.4

```
/*
**      This program accepts as input a time measured
**      in hours, minutes and seconds. The time is then
**      converted to the equivalent number of seconds.
*/

#include <stdio.h>

main()
{
  int hours, minutes, seconds;    /* original data values */
  int time;                       /* converted value */

  printf("Enter the time to be converted: ");
  scanf("%d %d %d", &hours, &minutes, &seconds);
```

```
    time = (60 * hours + minutes) * 60 + seconds;
    printf("The original time of:\n");
    printf("%d hours, %d minutes and %d seconds\n",
        hours, minutes, seconds);
    printf("converts to %d seconds\n", time);
}
```

The last two programs incorporated a prompt to the user before reading the data values. For interactive programs this is good practice since the user then knows when data is required to be entered (on some systems the output for the prompt may have to be 'flushed', see Chapter 14). Without a prompt, the program hangs awaiting input from the user, which might be misconstrued as the program having, in some way, failed.

How did we arrive at the solution for Program 5.4? It is sufficiently complex to warrant applying some design process prior to its implementation. The technique of designing a system or program in steps that gradually define more and more detail is called *functional decomposition*.

Functional decomposition is a step-by-step process that begins with the most general functional view of what is to be done, breaks the view down into subfunctions, and then repeats the process until all subfunction units are simple enough to be easily understood and small enough to be easily coded. This method of systematically applying *stepwise refinements* is a powerful tool for dealing with the complexity of many related elements.

We express our functional decomposition through a *program design language* or PDL. The PDL is a design description language specifically intended for documenting software designs. It is not a compiled language in the sense of C. The language has no formal syntax, but is an extensible language which provides constructs to express the necessary program logic.

PDL descriptions may include informally stated actions, intended to be a self-explanatory description of the program. In our PDL we shall reserve upper case for formalizations in terms of the programmming language. We shall see examples of this in later chapters. Material in lower case is an informal description of some action to be performed. The context of this description should be sufficient to make the action clear.

A first level PDL description of Program 5.4 might then be:

```
    prompt the user for the data
    accept the data
    perform the calculations upon the data
    print the results
```

Each of these actions is at a level where no further decomposition is required. Each action is directly expressible as C code. The second action, for example, is encoded as:

```
scanf("%d %d %d", &hours, &minutes, &seconds)
```

Applying the same to all other actions we can synthesize a complete program including all the necessary declarations. The result is Program 5.4.

Had any actions required further analysis, then the process of functional decomposition would have been repeated on these. Each action would be further refined and again expressed in our PDL.

As we progress through the remainder of the book introducing new program features, we shall also introduce an appropriate statement in our PDL.

5.2 Multi-function programs

As noted in the preceding section, a C program may consist of one or more functions. One of the functions must, of course, be called `main`. Functions offer a means of controlling the complexity of large programs. A function provides a convenient way to encapsulate some discrete programming task. When the function is *called* or *invoked*, the task is executed. Consider a function as a named black box. The name given to the box is the means by which we select the box or function to execute. The box has one entry point and one exit point. During execution of the function some action is performed as described by the executable statements in the function body. Pictorially we represent this by Figure 5.1.

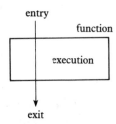

Figure 5.1

Where one function calls a second function, the effect is to temporarily suspend execution of the first function at the *point of call* of the second. The second function is entered (at its entry point), executed and then exited. Upon completion, control returns to the calling function and execution continues with the statement immediately following the point of call. We can express this diagramatically by showing function 1 calling function 2 in Figure 5.2.

Functions can call other functions, building a hierarchical layer of interconnected functions, reflecting the functional decomposition performed during program design. The design can then map directly on to the programming language. For example, a first-level PDL description of a program might give rise to three actions: input the data, process the data, and output the results. If all three actions require

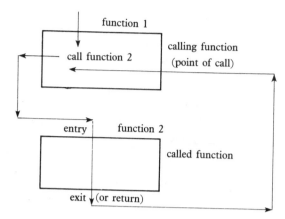

Figure 5.2

further refinement, the same PDL analysis may be applied. Since the first-level refinement is also a top-level description of the problem, it is implemented in function `main`. Each action in `main` then becomes a call to a subsidiary function containing the details of the corresponding second-level refinement.

So far, all our programs have consisted of the single function `main`. Each `main` function specified the totality of actual operations to be performed. In Program 5.4, for example, the six operations are:

```
printf( .... );
scanf( .... );
time = .... ;
printf( .... );
printf( .... );
printf( .... );
```

Consider now extending this program to operate upon, say, four sets of data. Each data set consists of a time measured in hours, minutes and seconds, and for each set the time is to be converted to its equivalent number of seconds. One possible solution would be to repeat the above six statements a total of four times. This leads to a much larger `main` function, but is, nevertheless, a viable solution.

Further analysis of this programming problem identifies that two subtasks are present. The first subtask is that there are four data sets to be operated upon and that the operations are identical. The second is that for a given data set a distinct series of operations is to be performed. These operations are captured by the six statements outlined above.

Expressed in our PDL, the subtask to control the processing of four data sets might appear as:

```
process the first data set
process the second data set
process the third data set
process the fourth data set
```

Informally, each statement is a description of the required action. The statements cannot, however, be directly expressed in our chosen programming language. We must further refine the actions. A second-level refinement of the operation 'process one data set' is the PDL description we arrived at for Program 5.4, namely:

```
prompt the user for the data
accept the data
perform the calculations upon the data
print the results
```

Given that the second-level refinements to process the second, third and fourth data sets are the same, the implementation is then realized by relegating the second subtask to a separate function. This function is fully responsible for the operations on a single data set. The function is subordinate to function main, which calls or invokes this subsidiary function four times, and, in so doing implements the first subtask.

PROGRAM 5.5

```
/*
**      This program operates on four data sets. Each set
**      consists of a time measured in hours, minutes and
**      seconds. For each set, the time is converted into
**      the equivalent number of seconds and printed.
*/

#include <stdio.h>

main()
{
   convert();      /* Four function .... */
   convert();      /* .... calls to .... */
   convert();      /* .... convert */
   convert();
}

/*
**      Function convert operates on a single data set,
**      reading, processing and printing.
*/

convert()
{
   int hours, minutes, seconds;      /* data values */
   int time;                         /* computed result */

   printf("Enter the time to be converted: ");
   scanf("%d %d %d", &hours, &minutes, &seconds);
   time = (60 * hours + minutes) * 60 + seconds;
   printf("The original time of:\n");
```

```
    printf("%d hours, %d minutes and %d seconds\n",
        hours, minutes, seconds);
    printf("converts to %d seconds\n\n", time);
    return;
}
```

The program shown above consists of two functions. The function `main` is, of course, always present. In addition, a function called `convert` is defined. This function contains all the variable declarations and statements required to operate on a single data set. Since it is this function which requires the variable space to hold the data and the computed values, then we declare the variables in this function. It would be illegal to, say, declare the variables in function `main` and then use them in function `convert`. We shall have more to say on this matter shortly.

Function `main` now no longer possesses any variable declarations. They are, in this example, unnecessary since no values are processed by this function. Were this the case, then appropriate variable declarations would also be present in the function body of `main`. The actual body of function `main` consists of the statements to control processing the four data sets. This is achieved with four *function calls* to `convert`:

```
    convert();
```

Each such statement causes the named function (`convert`) to be executed. Each invocation of this subsidiary function processes a single data set. When the function `convert` is complete, control reverts back to the calling function `main`. The called function (`convert`) is said to return control to the calling function (`main`). This return of control is explicitly specified by the `return` statement, the last executable statement in `convert`. Function `main` then arranges for three further calls to function `convert`.

The `return` statement is new and its effect is described above. The general form of this command is:

```
    return
```

or

```
    return expression
```

where `return` is a reserved keyword. We shall discuss the second form of the `return` statement in a later section of this chapter. If no `return` statement is present in a called function, then processing continues until the end of the function body, as indicated by the closing brace symbol, }. Upon encountering the function end, control returns to the calling function as if an explicit `return` had been present. The use of the implicit `return` is so common that we shall adopt it in all further examples.

The order in which the functions appear in a C program text file is unimportant.

We might equally well have placed the function `convert` first. Since, normally, function `main` will describe the overall processing, with detail reserved for the subordinate functions, reflecting our functional decomposition of the problem, we will always choose to place function `main` first.

The invocation of a programmer-defined function is no different to that of calling a function from the standard library. A call to `printf`, for example, has the form:

```
printf( .... )
```

Equally, a call to function `convert` from function `main` is:

```
convert( .... )
```

The items to be printed by function `printf` are supplied to it through function arguments. These appear as a comma separated list enclosed within parentheses. For example:

```
printf("converts to %d seconds\n\n", time)
```

No communication of data takes place between function `main` and function `convert`. Neither function sends or receives any information to/from the other function. The function declaration for `convert` indicates this by showing no arguments with the empty parentheses:

```
convert()
{
    ....
    ....
}
```

Similarly, when this function is called in `main`, the empty argument list is shown by the parentheses:

```
convert()
```

In both cases the parentheses are obligatory and may not be omitted.

A principle, present in Program 5.5, is that the program text is an expression of the idea of how the program operates (its *algorithm*). Functional decomposition facilitates expressing this algorithm. The question we must answer is where did this algorithm come from?

Programs are composed of two related elements: data items, and the process to which the data is subject. These elements are also present in a C function which includes both data declarations and executable statements. A program then specifies what to do and what to do it to. The program structure is thus derived from the structure of its data. The justification for this approach is that the program data is a model of the real world. During its lifetime, a program may undergo many functional changes. We might, as shown in Program 5.8, operate on the same data set as above, yet produce a total of the number of seconds for the four supplied times. The structure of the data has, however, remained the same. Only the processing is different.

If the structure of the problem data is:

```
data item 1
data item 2
data item 3
```

which means data items 1, 2 and 3 in that order, then the program will consist of a *sequence* of processing actions, such as:

```
process data item 1
process data item 2
process data item 3
```

Since Program 5.5 operates upon four data sets, four sequential processing actions appeared in the PDL:

```
process the first data set
process the second data set
process the third data set
process the fourth data set
```

Since the actions for each data set are identical, we relegate this task to a subsidiary function `convert`, and code function `main` as four sequential calls to `convert`. Had each data set been different and had each process also been different the same sequential structure would still have been appropriate. This is a consequence of the problem data.

Thus we shall deliberately set out our programs so that they reflect the structure of the problem data. Later problems introduce data structures other than sequential structures, and to maintain this one-to-one mapping new program control structures are presented.

5.3 Automatic variables

In the last section we developed a program with two functions – `main` and `convert`. It was noted that the variables in the program were declared in function `convert` since it is here that data space is required. Also, since no data items are required by function `main`, then no variable declarations are necessary.

It is known from Chapter 3 that the declaration:

```
int time;
```

appearing in function `convert`, introduces a data object called `time` and is of type `int`. Strictly, all variables have an attribute in addition to its type and name, which is referred to as its *storage class*. The term refers to the manner in which memory is allocated by the compiler for variables.

The term *scope* refers to the extent of the meaning of a particular variable in a program. Variables defined in a function are said to be *local* to that function and their scope is the block in which they are declared. This means that they have no meaning outside that function. The storage class for such variables is known as *automatic*. Variables declared within a function have storage class `auto`. This association is implicit. It is quite legal to state this explicitly by the declaration:

```
auto int time;
```

where `auto` is a reserved keyword. Since the storage class automatic is implicit because the declaration appears in the body of a function, most C programmers choose to omit this keyword.

To illustrate the concept of the scope of a variable, the program below is presented. The variable `two` declared in the function `func` is only referenced by this function. However, the variable `one` is defined in function `main`, but is illegally referenced by function `func`. The C compiler meeting such an illegal reference would generate a compilation error indicating that variable `one` is not declared in function `func`.

PROGRAM 5.6

```
/*
**      WRONG !
**      The automatic variable "one" is defined in function
**      main. Its scope is the body of function main. It is
**      illegal to reference it outside of main.
*/

#include <stdio.h>

main()
{
    int one;        /* scope = main */
    one = 1;        /* valid reference, within scope */
    func();         /* call subordinate function */
}

func()
{
    int two;        /* has scope of func */

    two = one;      /* variable one undefined here !! */
}
```

Automatic variables are only *visible* within the function in which they are declared. Each automatic variable is said to be *local* or *private* to its corresponding function. Because of this, variables with the same name appearing in declarations in separate functions are unrelated, except that they have been chosen with the same identifier. Operations performed on one automatic variable in one function have no

effect whatsoever on an automatic variable with the same name in another function.
This is illustrated by the following program. The variables local declared in both
program functions are quite distinct. This is shown by the program's output.

PROGRAM 5.7

```
/*
**        A program to illustrate local variables, with the
**        same identifier appearing in two subroutinetions.
*/

#include <stdio.h>

main()
{
    int local;          /* this "local" belongs to main */

    local = 1;          /* "local" in main set to 1 */
    printf("Function main: local = %d\n", local); /* confirm */
    subroutine();       /* call subordinate */
    printf("Function main check: local = %d\n", local); /* unchanged */
}

subroutine()
{
    int local;          /* this "local" belongs to subroutine */

    local = 2;          /* set subroutine's "local" */
    printf("Function subroutine: local = %d\n", local);
}
```

The output produced by this program is:

```
Function main: local = 1
Function subroutine: local = 2
Function main check: local = 1
```

The final line of output demonstrates that the two variables called local are
unrelated and are unaffected by the operations performed upon them in separate
functions.

This feature means that the C programmer is free to use the same variable name
in any number of functions without fear of confusion. It also implies that where
functions are written independently by a number of programmers, each has
unrestricted use of automatic variable names.

In addition to declaring an automatic variable in a function, it is also permissible
to assign an initial value. This process is called initialization. A variable is initialized
with a value by following its name in the declaration with an equals symbol (=) and
an expression. For example:

```
int time = 10;
int period = 20 + time;
```

Semantically, the declaration is equivalent to:

```
int time, period;

time = 10;
period = 20 + time;
```

Since semantically an initialized declaration is equivalent to a declaration and an assignment, then the usual conversions apply. Thus, for example:

```
float sum = 0;
```

converts the integer constant 0 to the floating point constant 0.0 before performing the assignment. In this situation, the programmer might avoid the unnecessary run time conversion with the declaration:

```
float sum = 0.0F;
```

5.4 Function values

Program 5.5 in Section 5.2 employed a subordinate function convert, responsible for processing a single data set. The main function called convert the correct number of times. No data was actually communicated between these functions. The C language provides a mechanism whereby the result of a calculation performed by a called function may be transmitted back to the calling function. This is achieved with the return statement. The syntax of this construct is:

```
return expression
```

To ensure that the returned expression is adequately highlighted from the surrounding program text, it is often presented as a bracketed subexpression. Thus, commonly, the statement form is:

```
return (expression)
```

The statement indicates that control is to return immediately from the called function, and that the value of the expression is to be made available to the calling function. The value returned may be 'captured' by the calling function with an appropriate assignment. For example, if convert is a function returning an integer value, and period is a variable of type int, then we may use:

```
period = convert();
```

to record the returned value.

Where a function returns a value, then the type of this returned value must precede the function name in the function declaration. Strictly, a function definition has the extended form:

```
type-specifier function-name()
{
  optional-declaration-list
  optional-statement-list
}
```

The type-specifier is any of the fundamental types supported by C. If, for example, function func delivers a floating point value through a return statement, then the definition should include:

```
float func()
{
      _____
      _____
  return (expression);
}
```

The type of the expression returned must match the the type of the function, or be capable of being converted to it as if by assignment. For example, the function func could contain:

```
return (1);
```

and the integral value will be converted to float.

The calling sequence for such a function is now different. Since the function makes available a returned value, a mechanism must allow the calling function to capture this value. The assignment operator, or one of its variants, is normally used. Assuming a floating point variable called result, then function func might be called by:

```
result = func();
```

The statement calls function func and picks up the returned value in the variable result.

In the preceding sections no functions have returned any values. If a function definition now includes a type-specifier, then what is the type for a function with no return value? A function definition with no type-specifier is implicitly of type int. Thus the function definition:

```
convert()
{
      _____
      _____
}
```

is interpreted by the compiler as:

```
int convert()
{
      _____
      _____
}
```

The call for such a function is also different. The function call is expected to return an integer value, yet no assignment is performed:

```
convert();
```

The compiler arranges that the expected value is simply discarded. Many of the standard I/O library functions, including `printf`, also return function values. For the present we choose to ignore the value by having the compiler dispose of it in the same way by:

```
printf( .... );
```

The Standard introduces a new type specifically for a function with no return value. This new type is called `void`. Function `convert` of Program 5.5 should then have had the definition:

```
void convert()
{
    .....
}
```

and similarly for function `subroutine` in Program 5.7. Henceforth, we shall adopt type `void` for functions with no associated value.

In C a data object is declared before it is used. This is necessary so that the C compiler can collect details of the attributes of the object, and then use this information when the object is referenced. A function, however, may be referenced (called) before it is defined. Unless otherwise told, the C compiler will assume that the return value of the function is of type `int`. Thus any function, such as `main` below, calling function `func` will erroneously interpret the returned value as an integer when the function is actually defined as one returning type `float`.

```
main()
{
    float result;
    _____

    _____
    result = func();     /* erroneously interpreted */
    _____

    _____
}

float func()
{
    _____

    _____
    return (expression);
}
```

In function `main` the compiler will generate code for an integer returning function `func`. When function `func` is ultimately compiled, code is generated to return a floating point value since the function type is now known to be `float`. Strictly, a compilation error is generated at the start of the definition of function func:

```
float func()
```

This is because the compiler has already assumed the existence of the integer function func:

```
int func()
```

The error would report that the function func has already been declared.

From Section 5.2 we know that function order is unimportant in a C program. If function main and function func are interchanged, then the compiler will meet the definition for func first, and will record the fact that the function returns a float. Then when function func is subsequently called in function main, the correct code will be generated.

This approach is very much dependent upon the textual ordering of the functions and is best not relied upon. When a function is called before it is declared, then the calling function must indicate to the compiler the type of value returned by a called function. A declaration, called a *function prototype* is present in the calling function, and indicates the value delivered by a called function. The simplest form for a prototype declaration is:

```
type-specifier function-name(), function-name(), ....

The program fragment above would now appear as:

main()
{
   float result;
   float func();          /* function prototype */
   -----------

   -----------
   result = func();    /* correctly interpreted */
   -----------

   -----------
}

float func()
{
   -----------

   -----------
   return (expression);
}
```

Similarly, Program 5.5 should contain a function prototype declaration indicating that the subordinate function convert is of type void:

```
main()
{
   void convert();     /* prototype declaration */
   .....
}
```

```
void convert()          /* function definition */
{
    .....
}
```

These ideas are encapsulated in Program 5.8, a variant of Program 5.5. Again we have two functions main and convert. This time convert does not print the result of its computations, but returns with the value computed from processing one data set. Function main calls function convert four times, and computes and prints a running total of the returned values.

PROGRAM 5.8

```
/*
**      A program to operate on four data sets each representing
**      a time measured in hours, minutes and seconds. Each set
**      is converted to its equivalent number of seconds.
**      Additionally, a running total of the number of seconds
**      is maintained.
*/

#include <stdio.h>

main()
{
    int total_time = 0;     /* accumulated total */
    int convert();          /* forward reference */

    total_time += convert();
    total_time += convert();
    total_time += convert();
    total_time += convert();

    printf("The total time is %d seconds\n\n", total_time);
}

int convert()
{
    int hours, minutes, seconds;    /* data values */
    int time;                       /* computed result */

    printf("Enter the time to be converted: ");
    scanf("%d %d %d", &hours, &minutes, &seconds);
    time = (60 * hours + minutes) * 60 + seconds;
    return (time);
}
```

5.5 Function arguments

The multi-function programs which we developed either had no data transferred between individual functions, or had a single value returned from the called function by the `return` statement. Many programming problems exist in which functions are required to return more than one item to the calling function. Further, the calling function may wish to transmit values to the called function. We introduce *function arguments* by which values may be conveyed between functions. In this section we restrict the discussion to arguments passed from the calling function to the called function. Passing arguments in the opposite direction is considered in a later section of this chapter.

The concept of a called function receiving arguments passed from the calling function has already been alluded to. Most of the programs which we have developed use the standard library function `printf`. When calling this function a number of arguments are supplied. The arguments are a comma separated list enclosed in parentheses. The call:

```
printf("My first program.")
```

invokes the function `printf` and passes it the single string argument `"My first program."`. This represents the actual string to be printed by `printf`. For this reason, the string is referred to as the first *actual argument*. In the call:

```
printf("The sum is %d\n", first + second)
```

two actual arguments are supplied. Once again the first actual argument is a string. It represents the string to be printed and includes a conversion specification for the second actual argument. The second argument is the expression:

```
first + second
```

The value of this expression is computed and is delivered to `printf` as the second actual argument.

The means by which a function is invoked is known as the *calling sequence*. The calling sequence in C consists of the function name followed by a comma separated list of actual arguments enclosed in parentheses. If any actual argument is an expression, that expression is first evaluated and the value is passed as the argument. For this reason, argument passing in C is implemented by the method known as *call by value*.

A function definition including arguments has the form:

```
type-specifier function-name(argument-type-list)
{
  optional-declaration-list
  optional-statement-list
}
```

The new feature is the *argument-type-list* appearing within the parentheses. The argument list in a function call is a list of actual arguments. The argument-type-list in a function definition is referred to as the list of *formal arguments*. The formal and actual arguments should agree in number and type. For every formal argument, there should be a corresponding actual argument of the same type in the function call. The type of each formal argument is given in the argument-type-list part of the function definition. These argument declarations have the same basic form as declarations for automatic (local) variables.

To illustrate, consider a function called sum which receives two floating point values as arguments and which delivers their sum through the return statement. One complete definition is:

```
float sum(float first, float second)
{
   float temp;

   temp = first + second;
   return (temp);
}
```

The formal argument list is a comma separated list of argument declarations giving the type and name of a formal argument identifier. These identifiers represent the arguments to be received when the function is called. The behaviour of the function is described fully in terms of these formal arguments and any local variables. The names of arguments and of any local variables must be distinct since they both have the same scope – namely, the function body.

The corresponding function prototype for function sum would appear as:

```
float sum(float first, float second);
```

and informs the compiler that the function expects two float arguments and returns a float. Parameter names in a prototype need not necessarily agree with the names in the function definition. Indeed, parameter names may be omitted. They do, however, act as a source of documentation. Hence, this example may also be presented as:

```
float sum(float arg1, float arg2);     /* other names */
```

or:

```
float sum(float, float);          /* no names */
```

To call function sum we use the assignment mechanism introduced earlier. In addition, we provide two actual arguments. They may be any expression delivering floating point values. Possible uses are:

```
main ()
{
   float result, total, second;  /* local data */
   float sum(float, float);      /* prototype */
   ----------
```

```
    ----------
    result = sum(12.3, 17.21);      /* = 29.51 */
    ----------

    ----------
    total = sum(result, second);
    ----------

    ----------
    result = sum(total * 3, result - 17.111);
    ----------

    ----------
}
```

Functions such as these have all been shown with the returned value captured by an assignment. The delivered values may equally appear in larger arithmetic expressions. To multiply the returned value from function sum before assigning we may write:

```
    result = 3 * sum(total, 10.0)
```

Additionally, we might call the function sum and use its return value as the actual argument to another call on sum:

```
    quadratic = sum(x*x, sum(x, 1.04))
```

The first or outer function call to sum has the square of the value for x as its first actual argument. Its second actual argument is the value delivered by the inner call to sum which has arguments x and 1.04. This inner call is executed first. The value delivered then becomes the second actual argument value to the outer call on sum.

Program 5.9 illustrates these features. The integer function hms_time translates its integer arguments representing a time measured in hours, minutes and seconds into a total number of seconds. The actual data values are collected by main and passed as actual arguments to this function. The returned value is then printed.

PROGRAM 5.9

```
/*
**      Read a time measured in hours, minutes and seconds
**      and convert it to the equivalent number of seconds.
*/

#include <stdio.h>

main ()
{
    int hours, minutes, seconds;    /* data values */
    int time;                       /* computed value */
    int hms_time(int, int, int);    /* referencing declaration */

    printf("Enter the time: ");
```

```
      scanf("%d %d %d", &hours, &minutes, &seconds);
      time = hms_time(hours, minutes, seconds);
      printf("Converted time is %d seconds\n", time);
}

int hms_time(int h,int m,int s)
{
      int t;                              /* computed time */

      t = (60 * h + m) * 60 + s;
      return (t);
}
```

Note how function `hms_time` is now responsible for a single task – namely, converting a time in hours, minutes and seconds to the equivalent number of seconds. In an earlier version of this function, it was responsible for three tasks – input, processing and output. In this new form we now have a primitive function that may find uses in other applications. We shall strive for this independence in other functions which we shall develop.

When a function with arguments is called, the value of each actual expression is calculated. The computed values are then matched with the corresponding formal argument. The formal argument within the function body behaves as an initialized local variable (initialized to the value of the actual argument). Thereafter, they may be treated as local variables and have their local copies modified. Only the local copy is changed. The changes do not alter the actual argument. This is demonstrated in Program 5.10.

PROGRAM 5.10

```
/*
**      A program to demonstrate that a function argument
**      behaves as an initialised (by the actual argument)
**      local variable, having no effect whatsoever on the
**      actual argument.
*/

#include <stdio.h>

main()
{
    int actualarg = 20;
    void subroutine(int);       /* referencing declaration */

    printf("Main: actual argument is %d\n", actualarg);
    subroutine(actualarg);
    printf("Main check: actual argument is %d\n", actualarg);
}
```

```
void subroutine(int formalarg)
{
   formalarg += 10;            /* change (local) value */
   printf("Subroutine: formal argument is %d\n", formalarg);
}
```

The output from this program is:

```
Main: actual argument is 20
Subroutine: formal argument is 30
Main check: actual argument is 20
```

The value of the actual argument (actualarg) is unchanged even when the local copy in function subroutine is modified.

Functions without arguments have been shown thus (see Program 5.5):

```
void convert();             /* prototype declaration */
void convert(){ ... }       /* function definition */
```

Presenting an empty argument list is supported by the new Standard to maintain backward compatibility with the original C definition. A prototype declaration such as the one above does not permit the compiler to check that the function is called with the correct number and type of arguments. To define and declare a function with no arguments (and hence supporting the necessary checking) we use:

```
void convert(void);         /* prototype */
void convert(void){ ... }   /* definition */
```

5.6 Function argument agreement and conversion

When employing a function with arguments we have stated that the actual and formal arguments must agree in number and type. The full set of rules on argument passing is especially complicated because of the need to support a mixture of new and old style function declarations. We can, however, simplify matters because of our insistence that a function prototype be present and in scope. In that case, the arguments are converted as if by assignment to the types specified in the prototype. Thus in the call to the function square in the following fragment, the actual parameter 2 is converted to type double:

```
main()
{
   double answer;
   double square(double);
   .....
   answer = square(2);
   .....
}
```

Because comma symbols are used to separate argument expressions, the comma operator may not be used in argument expressions unless enclosed by parentheses to prevent mistaking it for an argument separator. Conceivably, we might have the example:

```
main()
{
  int s, t, ...;
  void subroutine(int, int);     /* prototype */
  ..........
  ..........
  subroutine(s, (t = s+1, t));    /* legal!! */
  ..........
  ..........
}

void subroutine(int a, int b)
{
  ..........
  ..........
}
```

The actual arguments passed to function subroutine are the values of variables s and t (the latter from the second expression of the comma operator t = s + 1, t). The first expression of the comma operator caused the value of s + 1 to be assigned to variable t. More naturally we might expect to find the call to subroutine to consist of:

```
t = s + 1;
subroutine(s, t);
```

5.7 Pointers and function arguments

The parameter passing which we have developed is asymmetric in so far as the calling function can supply values to the called function, but there is no equivalent in the opposite direction. We know from Section 5.5 (Program 5.10) that changes to the values of formal arguments within a function do not alter the original actual argument values. This is attributable to the call by value method of parameter passing in C.

To allow a called function access to a value in the calling function, the latter must supply the *address* of one of its automatic (local) variables. If the called function then has the address of a variable in the calling function, it can arrange to assign a new value at that address. This is not a new concept, it has already been presented. Recall, that to use the function scanf, the addresses of variables are passed as arguments. The address of a variable is obtained by applying the unary *address operator* &:

```
scanf("%d %d", &first, &second)
```

To write functions that operate with addresses we must first introduce the idea of a *pointer*. Pointers are one of the most sophisticated features of the C programming language. They are also one of the most dangerous. The power and flexibility that C provides in dealing with pointers is one of the language's most distinguishing qualities. In this section we will introduce sufficient features to allow us to use pointers with function arguments. In later chapters we shall look at further applications of pointers.

Let us, for a moment, revisit declarations. Consider the declaration and initialization:

```
int x = 27;
```

Our understanding of such a declaration is that an area of memory sufficient to accommodate an integer value is set aside. This area of memory is referenced in the program by the identifier x. At the machine level, this memory area has an address (say 5678). The area of memory is initialized with the binary pattern representing decimal 27. Pictorially we have Figure 5.3. The result of the expression x is 27, since this is the value of the variable. The result of the expression &x is 5678, since the & operator delivers the address of its variable operand x.

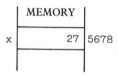

Figure 5.3

Our normal understanding of a variable (such as x) is that it represents a location in memory which has a unique address (5678 in the example), the content of which is a representation of some value currently assigned to the variable.

A pointer, however, is a variable which contains the address of some other object. If a pointer is a variable itself, then like all other variables it must occupy an area of memory which will have an address. The content of that area of memory is the address of some other variable. If `ptrx` is a variable capable of addressing the integer variable x, and if `ptrx` resides at memory location 1234, then the arrangement is shown in Figure 5.4.

The unary operator & gives the address of an object, so the statement:

```
ptrx = &x;
```

assigns the address of x to the variable `ptrx`; `ptrx` is said to point to the variable x. This is shown in Figure 5.4.

If variable x were to appear in an expression, we understand that the value of x would be required. For example, in the assignment:

```
y = x;
```

MEMORY

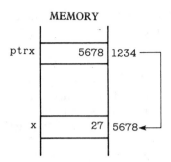

Figure 5.4

for some integer variable y. The value of the integer variable x, namely 27, is assigned to y. Equally, if the variable ptrx were to appear on the right of an assignment operator, the value of ptrx is required (5678 in this example):

```
.... = ptrx;
```

On the other hand, the unary *indirection operator* * treats its operand as the address of the ultimate target, and accesses that address to fetch its content. Thus:

```
y = *ptrx;
```

assigns to y the content of the memory location to which ptrx points. Now ptrx points to x and so y is assigned the value of x (that is, 27). The expression to the right of the assignment operator is evaluated in two stages. First, the value of ptrx is obtained (namely, 5678). This is interpreted as the address of an integer object. The unary indirection operator then delivers the value of the integer at this address (namely, 27). The sequence:

```
ptrx = &x;
    y = *ptrx;
```

assigns the same value to y as does:

```
y = x;
```

The value of x is, however, obtained indirectly through the variable ptrx. This concept is known as *indirect addressing*, or simply *indirection*, and is implemented with the *indirection operator* (*). The precedence and associativity of this operator and the address operator are shown in Appendix E.

To declare all the variables which participate we arrive at:

```
int x, y;
int *ptrx;
```

The declaration for x and y is normal. The declaration for the pointer variable ptrx is new. The declaration:

```
int *ptrx;
```

is intended as a mnemonic; it states that the combination `*ptrx` is an `int`. It is no different, then, from saying that:

```
int x;
```

declares x as an `int`. If `ptrx` occurs in the context `*ptrx` it is equivalent to a variable of type `int`. It indirectly references the actual variable.

Pointers can appear in generalized expressions. If `ptrx` points to the integer variable x, then `*ptrx` can occur in any context where an integer could be found:

```
y = *ptrx + 1;
```

sets y to be one more than x. Equally:

```
printf("The value of x is %d\n", *ptrx);
```

prints the current value of x. Since integer variables can occur on the left side of an assignment operator, then so too can `*ptrx`. Then:

```
*ptrx = 0;
```

initializes x to zero.

Care must be taken when using the indirection operator with the increment and decrement operators. To increment the value of the variable to which `ptrx` points, we use:

```
(*ptrx)++;
```

The parentheses are necessary as both operators are of equal precedence and associate right to left. Without the parentheses:

```
*ptrx++;
```

would increment `ptrx` then access the value indirectly referenced by the original value of `ptrx`. In Chapter 11 we will discover what an incremented pointer value actually means.

Lastly, since pointers are variables, they can be manipulated like other variables. Given:

```
int x;
int *ptrx, *ptry;

ptrx = &x;
```

then:

```
ptry = ptrx;
```

copies the content of `ptrx` into `ptry`, making both `ptrx` and `ptry` point to x.

Strictly, when we declare `ptrx` as, say, a pointer to an integer variable, as in:

```
int *ptrx;
```

then we are constraining that pointer to point to a particular kind of object (int in this case). Given the declaration:

```
double x;
```

it is illegal to execute the assignment:

```
ptrx = &x;
```

We are now in a position to proceed and to discuss how pointers are used in function arguments. Consider a main function wishing to convert a time measured in hours, minutes and seconds to a total number of seconds. The function main will employ a subsidiary function hms_time to perform this processing. The function has four arguments: the final three represent the original time, while the first argument is the converted time computed by the function. The first argument needs to be an address (or pointer) so that function hms_time can place the computed value at that location. The function main might then appear:

```
main( )
{
    int  hours, minutes, seconds;
    int  time;
    void hms_time(int *, int, int, int);

    scanf("%d %d %d", &hours, &minutes, &seconds);
    hms_time(&time, hours, minutes, seconds);
    printf("Converted time is %d\n", time);
}
```

Note how the address of the local variable time is given as the actual argument to function hms_time. Operationally this is the same as giving the address of variable hours to function scanf in the preceding statement.

In the definition for the function hms_time we must indicate that the first formal argument is the address of an integer. In the function body we need also to assign a value to the integer pointed to by the argument. The coding is:

```
void hms_time(int *t, int h, int m, int s)
{
    *t = (60 * h + m ) * 60 + s;
}
```

The formal argument t is a pointer to an integer. This is shown by:

```
int *t, ....
```

The integer to which t refers is assigned a value by:

```
*t = .... ;
```

As a complete example, a program is required to input a time measured as a number of seconds and to convert that value to its equivalent form expressed in hours, minutes and seconds. The program is organized so that function `main` performs all the input and output, and the subordinate function `time_hms` performs the necessary conversions.

PROGRAM 5.11

```
/*
**      The program inputs a time measured in seconds
**      and converts it to its equivalent in hours,
**      minutes and seconds.
*/

#include <stdio.h>

main ()
{
  int   time;                                /* original data value */
  int   hours, minutes, seconds;             /* computed values */
  void time_hms(int, int *, int *, int *);   /* forward ref. */

  printf("Enter the time in seconds: ");
  scanf("%d", &time);
  time_hms(time, &hours, &minutes, &seconds);
  printf("The time %d seconds\n", time);
  printf("converts to %d hours, %d minutes and %d seconds\n",
      hours, minutes, seconds);
}

void time_hms(int t, int *h, int *m, int *s)
{
  int temp = t / 60;    /* total minutes */

  *s = t % 60;          /* number of seconds */
  *m = temp % 60;       /* number of minutes */
  *h = temp / 60;       /* number of hours */
}
```

In any function, if a data value is to be read and recorded in a local variable, then the address of that variable is given to the `scanf` function:

```
void subroutine(int *arg, .... )
{
  int local;
  .....
  .....
  scanf("%d", &local);
  .....
}
```

If the formal argument `arg` is to be used in the call to `scanf` instead of `local`, then the call is:

```
scanf("%d", arg);
```

No address operator is applied to `arg` since in the formal argument declaration part, `arg` is already a pointer to an `int`.

Program 5.12 illustrates this feature in the function `input`. The program is a repeat of Program 5.11 and is structured into three subordinate functions: one to read the data, one to process it and one to display the results. The `main` function coordinates each, passing and receiving the necessary values.

PROGRAM 5.12

```
/*
**      Input a time expressed in seconds and convert to
**      the equivalent time in hours, minutes and seconds.
*/

#include <stdio.h>

main()
{
    int time;                        /* original data */
    int hours, minutes, seconds;     /* computed results */
    void input(int *);               /* forward decls. */
    void process(int, int *, int *, int *);
    void output(int, int, int, int);

    input(&time);
    process(time, &hours, &minutes, &seconds);
    output(time, hours, minutes, seconds);
}

void input(int *t)
{
    printf("Enter the time in seconds: ");
    scanf("%d", t);                  /* note: no address operator */
}

void process(int t, int *h, int *m, int *s)
{
    int mins = t / 60;

    *s = t % 60;
    *m = mins % 60;
    *h = mins / 60;
}
```

```
void output(int t, int h, int m, int s)
{
  printf("The time %d seconds\n", t);
  printf("converts to %d hours, %d minutes and %d seconds\n",
      h, m, s);
}
```

Decomposing the program in this manner allocates separate tasks to separate functions. The generalization of the functions permit their possible use in other programs. Further, the tasks are localized so that changes are readily implemented. If, for example, a new layout of the results is required, only function output need be modified, and this can be done without consideration for the other program elements. This is a consequence of the completeness of the function. The function is independent of its environment, described completely in terms of its arguments and any local variables.

This type of function exhibits *functional abstraction*. During program decomposition, we are concerned with what the function does, not *how* it does it. Abstractly we are only interested in the *what*. Pictorially, a function at this level of refinement is a black box. For example, function process might be shown as in Figure 5.5, receiving a time (t) in seconds as input and delivering the equivalent time expressed in hours (h), minutes (m) and seconds (s). Later during development, the how is established by further refinement.

Figure 5.5

5.8 Constant parameters

From Chapter 3 we know that the adjective const can be applied to a declaration to yield a type that is the same as the original except that the value of the object cannot be changed. As a consequence, we cannot take the address of a const object, because if that were permitted we could assign a value to the object indirectly via its pointer. Thus the following is illegal:

```
const int june = 6;
int *p = &june;         /* error */
```

To declare a pointer to be a constant rather than the object itself, the declarator *const is used in place of *. For example:

```
int june = 6, august = 8;   /* normal */
int *const p = &june;       /* constant pointer */
```

```
. . . . .
*p = 7;          /* ok, june is now the value 7 */
p = &august;     /* error, the pointer cannot change */
```

Variable p is a pointer to an `int`, which is what would be meant if the `const` were omitted. The presence of the `const` means that p cannot be modified. The object to which p points can, however, be changed.

To permit the pointer to be modifiable but the object to which it points be constant we write it as:

```
int june = 6, august = 8;
const int *p = &june;    /* modifiable constant */
. . . . .                /* but not pointed object */
p = &august;             /* ok, p may be changed */
*p = 10;                 /* error, object cannot be changed */
```

Finally, to make both the object and the pointer constant, both the declarators `const` and `*const` are employed:

```
int june = 6, august = 8;
const int *const p = &june;
. . . . .
*p = 7;          /* error, cannot change object */
p = &august;     /* error, cannot change pointer */
```

The qualifier `const` may also be applied to function arguments to indicate where values are unchanged. For example, the function `process` in Program 5.12 might have the prototype declaration:

```
void process(const int, int *const, int *const, int *const);
```

and function definition:

```
void process(const int t, int *const h, int *const m,
                  int *const s)
{
  const int mins = t / 60;

  *s = t % 60;
  *m = mins % 60;
  *h = mins / 60;
}
```

5.9 The C preprocessor

The power and notation of the C programming language is extended by the use of a *preprocessor*. This preprocessor is associated with the C compiler and is used to recognize preprocessor statements embedded in a C program. The features offered by the preprocessor are used to develop programs which are easier to read, easier to modify and easier to transfer to different computer systems.

As implied by the name, the preprocessor actually analyses the preprocessor statements before full compilation takes place. Preprocessor statements are identified by the character #, which must be the first character on the line. The syntax of these preprocessor statements is independent of the C language. We will begin by examining the two most widely used preprocessor statements, the #define and the #include statements. A detailed study of all the facilities of the preprocessor is delayed until Chapter 8.

A *macro* is an identifier which represents and is replaced by a string composed of one or more tokens. The preprocessor statement #define accomplishes this function. The simplest form of this statement is:

```
#define identifier     token-string
```

The end of the identifier is taken as the first whitespace character. The token-string (or replacement text, as it is sometimes known) is the remainder of the line. After a directive of this form is encountered in a program, all subsequent occurrences of the specified identifier are replaced with the specified token-string.

The following example illustrates the use of this directive:

```
#define PI     3.14159
```

Conventionally, the identifier is in upper-case. This is not, of course, obligatory. Reserving only upper-case letters in the identifier indicates to the reader that this is a #define'd item. From the point of definition, throughout the rest of the program text file, all occurrences of PI will be replaced by the preprocessor with the token-string 3.14159. This replacement is only valid outwith string constants. Any occurrence of PI inside a string is ignored. The statements:

```
circumference = PI * diameter;
printf("PI is %f\n", PI);
```

would be transformed by the preprocessor into:

```
circumference = 3.14159 * diameter;
printf("PI is %f\n", 3.14159);
```

There are many important uses for simple #define statements. If a large C program contains many literal occurrences of the value 3.14159, say, then the #define above would allow us to use PI in its place. The program is now more readable since the *symbolic constant* PI reflects the actual processing being performed. Further, if we wish to use 3.1415926 instead, for this geometric value, then we merely have to change the single #define rather than all the appearances of 3.14159:

```
#define PI     3.1415926
```

The preprocessor will now replace all occurrences of PI with the new token-string during the next program compilation.

The token-string can be any valid section of C code. The token-string is taken as the string immediately following the whitespace characters after the identifier. Normally this replacement text is the remainder of the line. Where a long replacement string is required, it may be extended over several lines, provided each line (except the last) terminates with a backslash symbol (\) followed immediately by a newline character. For example:

```
#define LONG_MESSAGE     "A very long message extending "\
        "over two lines"
```

The scope of a named identifier in a #define statement is from its point of definition to the end of the source program text file. It is perfectly valid to put the #define statements anywhere in a file provided they precede their use. It is common, however, to find all the #define statements grouped together at the head of the program file. Generally, we will adopt this convention in all our programs.

The #include preprocessor statement causes the entire content of a specified source text file to be processed as if those contents had appeared in place of the #include command. The name of the file to be included is given as the command argument. The two basic forms of this statement are:

```
#include "filename"
```

and:

```
#include <filename>
```

In the first example, the named file is searched for in the same directory in which the file containing the #include was found. In the second case, the named file is searched for in *standard places*. In UNIX and UNIX-like systems this is usually the directory /usr/include. We have already met and used this last form. We incorporate into all our programs details of the standard I/O library functions with the file stdio.h from this directory.

Generally, the #include mechanism is reserved to collect related groups of #define statements and other items. This way, if we are writing a series of programs, they can all share the same definitions. Consistency can then be better guaranteed by having all these definitions in one place. Such files are referred to as *header files*. Under UNIX the filenames normally have a .h suffix, for example stdio.h.

Consider, for example, a header file to package together a collection of symbolic constants defining characteristics of the Zilog Z80 microprocessor:

```
/*
**      File : z80.h
*/
#define WORD_SIZE     16
#define BYTE_SIZE     8
#define REGISTERS     6
#define ACCUMULATORS  1
```

```
#define LDAB              0x78      /* hex opcodes */
#define ADDB              0x80
#define JMP               0xC3
                   etc.
```

5.10 Mathematical functions

There are no mathematical functions as part of the C language. Functions such as:

```
sqrt()      square root
exp()       exponential
sin()       trigonometric
```

occur in a special library. If a programmer wishes to use these functions, the library must be available to the linker as shown in Appendix G. Many of these functions take an argument of type double and return a value of type double. Any program including any of these functions must, therefore, include appropriate prototype declarations, for example:

```
double exp(double);
```

The library header file <math.h> is provided and contains all the necessary declarations. They may be incorporated into a program with the statement:

```
#include <math.h>
```

Program 5.13 computes the area of a triangle given by the formula:

```
sqrt(s(s-x)(s-y)(s-z))
```

where:

```
s = (x + y + z)/2
```

and x, y, z are the lengths of the sides of the triangle.

PROGRAM 5.13

```
/*
**      Determine the area of a triangle given
**      the lengths of its sides.
*/
#include <stdio.h>
#include <math.h>

main()
{
   float a, b, c;
   float triangle(const float, const float, const float);
```

```
    printf("Enter lengths of sides: ");
    scanf("%f %f %f", &a, &b, &c);
    printf("Area of triangle is %6.2f\n", triangle(a, b, c));
}

float triangle(const float x, const float y, const float z)
{
    float s;      /* semi-perimeter */

    s = (x + y + z)/2.0;
    return (sqrt(s * (s-x) * (s-y) * (s-z)));
}
```

5.11 Summary

1. A C program consists of one or more *functions*. A complete C program has one function called `main`, and processing commences with the first statement in `main`. A function is a named *compound statement* or *block*.

2. A function block may include the declarations for *local* or *automatic* variables. Automatic variables are private to a function and only exist when the function is called, and are deallocated when the function terminates.

3. When a function is called in a *function statement*, program control is passed to the called function. When a *return statement* is executed explicitly, or implicitly at the function end, control is passed back to the calling function. If the return statement contains an expression, the value of the expression is made available to the calling function.

4. Functions implicitly return a value of type `int`. Where a function returns a value other than an integer, a *function prototype* declaration is required. A function with no associated value is of type `void`.

5. *Arguments* are used to communicate data between the calling and the called functions. When a function is called, the *actual* arguments listed replace the *formal* arguments. Argument passing in C is implemented as *call by value*. The values passed as arguments may be data items or variable addresses (pointers).

6. *Stepwise refinement* consists of repeatedly decomposing a problem into smaller subproblems. A large program should be written as a collection of functions, each responsible for some identifiable task from the overall problem.

7. The structure of the problem data should be reflected in the structure of the program. Sequential data items give rise to sequential program structures.

Do 1,2,6,7,8

5.12 Exercises

1. Write a program that will convert a length measured in centimetres to its equivalent number of inches. Modify the program to process five data sets.

2. Write a program that reads a data set containing an invoice number, quantity of an item ordered and the unit price of the item. The total price should then be calculated, and the output should appear as follows:

```
INVOICE      QUANTITY      UNIT PRICE      TOTAL
  xxx          xxxx         xxxx.xx       xxxxx.xx
```

3. Write a program to read four decimal values representing the coordinates of two points on a plane. Calculate the distance between the points and output the result. Use the formula:

$$\text{distance} = \sqrt{(x2 - x1)^2 + (y2 - y1)^2}$$

4. Write a program to determine the number of gallons of paint required to paint a rectangular room. The windows and doors are to be ignored in the calculation. The width and length of the room and the height of the walls will be entered in feet. A gallon of paint is assumed to cover about 250 square feet.

5. Write a program that will convert a given number of minutes and seconds to the correct fraction of an hour. For example, 37 minutes and 30 seconds is 0.625 of an hour.

6. Assuming that the population of a city is 650,000 and that its rate of growth is 4.5% a year, write a program to calculate the population each year over the next five years.

7. Write a program consisting of the single function `main` which reads two integer values representing the length and breadth of a rectangular figure, and which computes and prints the perimeter length.
   Repeat the same problem, but this time employ a second function called `perimeter` which performs the necessary calculation, given, as arguments, the dimensions of the rectangle. The function header is:

**x the thing at address x,
&x the address of x*

```
int perimeter(int length, int breadth)
```

8. Prepare a function called `denominations` which, when supplied with a positive integer argument representing a sum of money expressed in pence less than one pound in value, will print a list of each coin and the quantity required. The function header is to be:

```
void denominations(int money)
```

The sample call:

```
denominations(34);
```

would produce the output:

```
34 pence is:    0 fifty pence
                3 ten pence
                0 five pence
                2 two pence
                0 one pence
```

Test this function in a program.

9. ✓ Predict the output from the following five programs and explain your reasoning.

(a)
```
#include <stdio.h>
main()
{
    int x;
    void change(void);
    x = 0;
    change();
    printf("%d\n", x);
}
void change(void)
{
    int x;
    x = 1;
}
```
x = 0

(b)
```
#include <stdio.h>
main()
{
    int x;
    void change(int *);
    x = 0;
    change(&x);
    printf("%d\n", x);
}
void change(int *y)
{
    *y = 1;
}
```
x = 1

(c)
```
#include <stdio.h>
main()
{
    int x;
    void change(int);
    x = 0;
    change(x);
    printf("%d\n", x);
}
```

Wk 4

Do 9,10,12

```
        }
        void change(int y)
        {
          y = 1;              x =0
        }
(d)  #include <stdio.h>
     main()
     {
       int thing;
       void cheat(int *, int *)
       thing = 1;
       cheat(&thing, &thing);
       printf("%d\n", thing);
     }
     void cheat(int *hee, int *haw)
     {
       *hee = -1;
       *haw = -(*hee);
     }
(e)  #include <stdio.h>
     main()
     {
       int thing;
       void untrue(int *, int *);
       thing = 10;
       untrue(&thing, &thing);
       printf("%d\n", thing);
     }
     void untrue(int *hee, int *haw)
     {
       *hee = 20 + *haw;
     }
```

10. Prepare a function called `swap` which interchanges the values of its two integer arguments. The function header is:

```
void swap(int *x, int *y)
```

Test this function in a program.

11. The function `min`, defined below, determines the least of its two integer arguments.

```
int min(int a, int b)
{
  return (a < b ? a : b);
}
```

Design and write the corresponding function called `max` which finds the larger of its two integer arguments. Function `max` should make a call to function `min` in determining the correct value.

Similarly, write a function called `min3` which returns the least of its three integer arguments. Use function `min` to determine the result.

12. A time, expressed in terms of the twenty-four-hour clock, is provided by three integer values: hours (0 <= hours <= 23), minutes and seconds (0 <= minutes, seconds <= 59). Write a function called `hms_time` which converts such a time to a total number of seconds. The function header is:

```
long int hms_time(int hours, int minutes, int seconds)
```

Why is it reasonable to declare the function returning a `long int` rather than an `int`?

Write also the converse function `time_hms` which converts a time in seconds back into its equivalent twenty-four-hour-clock value. The function header is:

```
void time_hms(long int time,
        int * hours, int *minutes, int *seconds)
```

in which the `long int` argument, time, represents the number of seconds, and the three pointer arguments are the recipient addresses of the converted value.

Prepare a program that checks the execution of both these functions.

Write a function called `add_time_hms` which adds a time in seconds on to a twenty-four-hour-clock time. The final answer is also expressed as a twenty-four-hour-clock time, updates the original input values, and ignores any advance of one or more days. This function should be written in terms of the preceding two functions. The function header is:

```
void add_time_hms(long int time,
        int * hours, int *minutes, int *seconds)
```

Prepare a program to show that:

```
add_time_hms(0L, ...)
```

produces no change of values.

Write a further function called `difference` which finds the number of seconds between two twenty-four-hour-clock times. It can be assumed that the first time (hr1, min1, sec1) is later in the day than the second time (hr2, min2, sec2). The function header is:

```
long int difference(int hr1, int min1, int sec1,
        int hr2, int min2, int sec2)
```

Prepare a program to show that:

(a) `difference(hr, min, sec, hr, min, sec)`
    is OL for some twenty-four-hour-clock time (`hr`, `min`, `sec`).

(b) `add_time_hms(difference(h1,m1,s1,h2,m2,s2),`
    `&h2,&m2,&s2)`
    sets the twenty-four-hour-clock time (`h2`, `m2`, `s2`) to the value of (`h1`, `m1`
    `s1`).

6

Flow of control

THE EXECUTION OF C programming statements causes actions to be performed. The programs that we have developed execute one statement after another in a linear fashion. We can create abstract actions with function definitions and then treat these as if they likewise were primitive statements of the language. The simple statements which we have explored can be considered *sequential*, and include the assignment and the function call.

In addition, statements are available to alter the flow of control in a program. The full repertoire of C language statements then classified into one of three control structures:

(a)   sequence;
(b)   selection; and
(c)   iteration.

The new program control structures of *selection* and *iteration* permit us to process data with structures other than sequential. Repetitive data items are processed by iteration statements. Alternative data items are processed by selection statements. Through these statements we retain the correspondence between the structure of the problem's data and the program structure which we introduced in the preceding chapter.

We shall now examine further C statements as instances of the two control structures iteration and selection. A feature of these new statements is the *condition*. A condition determines the *truth* or *falsity* of some expression. We commence this chapter by considering expressions yielding values which are either true or false.

6.1 Relational operators and expressions

The relational operators are:

$$
\begin{array}{rl}
\text{less than:} & < \\
\text{greater than:} & > \\
\text{less than or equal:} & <= \\
\text{greater than or equal:} & >=
\end{array}
$$

All four operators are binary. They each take two expressions as operands and yield one of two possible values. Just as with arithmetic operators, the relational operators have rules of precedence and associativity that determine how expressions involving these operators are evaluated. All four operators have the same precedence levels and associate left to right. Their relationships with the other operators are shown in Appendix E.

Some examples of relational expressions include:

```
x < 0.0
ch2 >= 'A'
y * y <= 2 * y + 1
pointer > end_of_list
```

From Appendix E we observe that the relational operators have lower precedence than the arithmetic operators. Expressions like:

```
index <= limit - 1
```

are, therefore, interpreted as:

```
index <= (limit - 1)
```

The greater than or equal and less than or equal operators are described with two symbols. No embedded spaces are allowed, nor can the operators be expressed as equal or greater than, or equal or less than. The following are illegal expressions:

```
p < = q     /* imbedded space disallowed */
r => s      /* no such operator */
```

Consider the relational expression a < b. Intuitively, if the value of a is less than the value of b, then the expression is true. If the value of a is not less than the value of b, then the expression is false. In C, the logical value false is represented by the integer value zero (0), and the logical value true by any non-zero integer value. In particular, the relational operators generate either the integer value 0 (for false) or the integer value 1 (for true).

In the context of the following declarations:

```
char c = 'x';
int i = 1, j = 3, k = -4;
```

Table 6.1 gives a number of expressions involving the relational operators, together with the derived value. For each expression, the parenthesized equivalent is also shown. The logical value upon evaluation of the expression is indicated.

Table 6.1

Expression	Equivalent expression	Logical value	Derived value
'b' + 1 < c	('b' + 1) < c	true	1
5 * j >= 12 - k	(5 * j) >= (12 - k)	false	0
i + j <= -k	(i + j) <= (-k)	true	1

In C, the following relational expression may be derived:

```
2 < index < 6
```

For the reasons given below, it is inadvisable to use such a construct. The expression is frequently used in mathematics to indicate that the variable `index` has the property of being greater than 2 and less than 6. It can also be considered as a C expression which, depending on the value of `index`, may or not be true. For example, if `index` is 5, then the mathematical statement:

```
2 < index < 6
```

is true, but if `index` is 0, then the statement is false. Now consider:

```
2 < index < 6
```

as a C relational expression. Since the relational operators associate left to right, the expression is equivalent to:

```
(2 < index) < 6
```

For `index = 5`, the subexpression:

```
2 < index
```

evaluates to the logical value true, represented as the integer value 1. The expression then reduces to the subexpression:

```
1 < 6
```

and also evaluates to logical true or integer 1. In this case the C relational expression delivers the same as the mathematical statement.

However, when index = 0, the subexpression:

```
2 < index
```

evaluates to the logical value false, integer value 0, and:

```
0 < 6
```

evaluates to the logical value true, integer value 1. This time the C relational expression delivers a different interpretation from the mathematical statement. The correct way to express such a relationship of this form is described in Section 6.3.

6.2 Equality operators and expressions

The equality operators are:

> equal: ==
> not equal: !=

These binary operators act on two expressions and yield either of the two logical value true or false. Appendix E shows these two new operators alongside the other operators.

Some valid examples of expressions using these operators include:

```
ch == LTRZ
j + k != t
```

No embedded spaces are permitted between the two characters which represent these operators. Equally, the operator not equal may not be written =!.

The operator equal works perfectly correctly with integer operands. When used with operands of type floating point (float or double), some suprising results can arise. This is entirely attributable to the limited precision of the floating point representation. If we were to divide 1.0 by 3.0 and then multiply the result by 3.0, we might reasonably expect the answer to be 1.0. If the variable x is declared as:

```
float x = 1.0;
```

then we might assume the expression:

```
x == x / 3.0 * 3.0
```

to evaluate to the logical value true. The mathematical result of the division is 0.33333333 .... If on some hypothetical computer, floating point values are held with six decimal digits of accuracy, then the result is 0.333333. When we multiply by 3.0 the result is 0.999999. The expression now reduces to:

```
1.0 == 0.999999
```

which is clearly false.

The equality operator should be avoided when comparing two floating point expressions. The solution is normally not to ask if the two expressions are equal, but if the two expressions are approximately equal. This is expressed by asking if the difference between each expression is small enough to be considered negligible. We will show in a later section how to formulate this.

Care is required not to confuse the equality operator (==) and the assignment operator (=). This is a common programming mistake which can lead to unexpected results. For example, if we wish to determine if the integer variable a is equal to 2, the expression is:

```
a == 2
```

and yields either true or false according to the value of a. However, if the expression is mistakenly written as:

```
a = 2
```

then the expression is valid, has the effect of assigning the value 2 to the variable a, and delivers the value 2 interpreted as logical true. The expression is always true, irrespective of the original value of a.

6.3 Logical operators and expressions

The logical operators are:

> logical and: &&
> logical or: ||
> (unary) negation: !

The logical *and* and logical *or* operators are binary, both acting on two expressions and yielding either the logical value true or logical false. Both operators treat their operands as logical values. The logical *negation* operator is a unary operator. The single operand is taken to represent either logical true or logical false. The effect of applying these operators is shown in Table 6.2.

Table 6.2

P	Q	P && Q	P || Q	P	! P
false	false	false	false	false	true
false	true	false	true	true	false
true	false	false	true		
true	true	true	true		

The precedence and associativity of these logical operators is given in Appendix E.
Some expressions involving the negation operator are:

! 5	evaluates to 0
! 0	evaluates to 1
! 't'	evaluates to 0
3 + ! x	evaluates to 3 if x is non-zero, and
	evaluates to 4 if x is zero
! ! 5	evaluates to 1
! ! 0	evaluates to 0

The expression !5 evaluates to false since 5 is interpreted by the unary negation operator as the representation for true. The expression !'t' is somewhat unusual but also yields false since the ASCII encoding for character 't' is decimal 116, namely true. The expression !!5 has the equivalent form !(!5). With the integer value 5 interpreted as true, then, as above, !5 is false. Negating this value again delivers true.

In the context of the following declarations:

```
char c = 'x'
int i = 1, j = 3, k = 4;
```

Table 6.3 shows some example expressions involving the logical *and* and the logical *or* operators:

Table 6.3

Expression	Equivalent expression	Logical value	Derived value
i && j &&k	(i && j) && k	true	1
i && j || !c	(i && j) || (!c)	true	1
k < i && i < j	(k < i) && (i < j)	false	0
i == 2 || j == 1	(i == 2) || (j == 1)	false	0
i > 2 && !j	(i > 2) && (!j)	false	0

There is one subtlety about the logical *and* and the logical *or* operators. In the evaluation of subexpressions that are the operands of the operators && and ||, the evaluation process stops as soon as the outcome is determinable. Suppose that expression1 and expression2 are the expression operands. If expression1 has value zero (false), then in:

    expression1 && expression2

expression2 will not be evaluated because the value of the logical expression is already determined to be false. Similarly, if expression1 has a non-zero value (true), then in:

    expression1 || expression2

expression2 will not be evaluated since the value of the expression is already determined to be true.

In both instances the second expression may never be evaluated. If the second expression includes a side effect of its evaluation, then this will not be obtained if the expression is not evaluated. For example, using the above declarations, the expression:

    j < i && k += 2

is interpreted as:

    (j < i) && (k += 2)

and since the subexpression (j < i) is false, then variable k is not incremented. Statements or expressions that employ this kind of side effect can make programs very difficult to correct or to maintain and are actively discouraged.

6.4 The conditional operator

For completeness we discuss here the *conditional operator*. Strictly, this is not an operator that delivers a logical value. It does, however, include a logical expression and so we consider it here. The conditional operator consists of three expressions, with the first and second expression separated by the query symbol (?) and the second and third expressions separated by the colon symbol (:). The form is:

```
expression1 ? expression2 : expression3
```

The first operand is used to determine which of the other two operands should be evaluated. If the first expression delivers logical true (non-zero) then the result of the expression is expression2; if the first expression delivers logical false (zero) then the result of the expression is expression3.

To determine the least of two values we might use this operator. The minimum of the two values a and b can be obtained by:

```
min = a < b ? a : b
```

Like all operators, this operator has a precedence and an associativity. This is shown in Appendix E.

In Section 6.2 we noted that equality comparisons on two floating point values is best performed by determining if the two values are approximately equal. Thus instead of testing, if:

```
a == b
```

we should test if the absolute difference between a and b is negligible. Mathematically, we express this as:

```
| a - b | < epsilon
```

where, epsilon represents some small value and the notation $|x|$ means the positive value of x. To achieve this, we require a function to obtain the absolute value of some quantity. This function could be written using the conditional operator:

```
double absolute(double x)
{
    return ( x < 0 ? -x : x );
}
```

With this function, the original expression may be written using:

```
#define EPSILON     1.0E-4

absolute(a-b) < EPSILON
```

Note that the functions abs and fabs are members of the standard library and respectively obtain the absolute value of an integer and a floating point argument. For details, see Appendix F5.

6.5 The while statement

The fundamental means of constructing iterative clauses in C is the while statement. The syntax of the while statement is:

```
while (expression)
        statement
```

where while is a reserved keyword.

The while statemement is executed by first evaluating the control expression within the parentheses. If the result is non-zero, that is logical value true, then the statement is executed. The entire process is then repeated starting once again with evaluation of the expression. This looping continues until either because of the effect on the expression by execution of the statement or by a side effect of the expression itself, the expression now evaluates to zero. The value zero is the C representation for logical false. When the expression is zero, the loop terminates and the program continues execution with the next statement. A flow diagram for the while statement is shown in Figure 6.1.

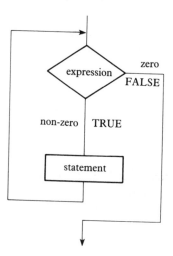

Figure 6.1

The principal feature of the while statement is that the control expression is first tested before deciding whether or not to execute the associated statement. This means that if the expression on first evaluation produces zero (logical false) then the loop is never obeyed. Because of this, a while statement is often described as causing the statement under its control to be obeyed *none or more times*.

Where the logic of a problem requires more than a single statement to be executed under control of the while, a compound statement may be used:

```
while (expression){
   statement 1;
   statement 2;
   _____;
   _____;
}
```

We are now ready to explore programs containing loops. As we shall note, problems with loops give rise to solutions with similar structures. By being able to recognize this, such programs are relatively straightforward to implement. We can then apply the same type of solution to most programs exhibiting this feature.

Program 6.1 reads single characters from the standard input, copying each character, as it is read, to the standard output. The copying continues until the first occurrence of a period (.) symbol is encountered in the data. The period is not copied and the program terminates. The use of a distinguishing data item to mark the end of the data set is a common programming device. This *sentinel* guards the end of the data. It is often referred to as the *end of file record*.

The use of an iterative statement in the solution to this program is suggested by the form of the data. The program data is a list or series of single character data items. Where the structure of the program's data has this form, the equivalent program structure is:

```
while(more data items)
      process data item
```

To generate the program design, we first extend our PDL with an iterative clause based on the while statement. The structure is:

```
WHILE some condition DO
   some statement(s)
ENDWHILE
```

As before, both the condition and the statement(s) are expressed as concise informal descriptions of the actions to be performed. Applying this to our programming problem, we arrive at the first-level solution:

```
read first character
WHILE this character is not the period symbol DO
   print this character
   read next character
ENDWHILE
```

Each action and expression is directly expressible in C. No further analysis is therefore necessary. We can immediately encode the solution as Program 6.1.

PROGRAM 6.1

```
/*
**      Read a sequence of characters from the standard input
**      and echo them to the standard output. Terminate the
**      program upon the first occurrence of a period (.)
**      symbol in the data set.
*/

#include <stdio.h>

#define PERIOD     '.'
```

```
main()
{
  char c;                 /* data item */

  c = getchar();          /* get first character */
  while (c != PERIOD){     /* test for end of data */
    putchar(c);           /* copy to standard output */
    c = getchar();        /* get next character */
  }
}
```

The program operates by first reading the initial data character. The character just read is then compared in the `while` control expression against the period symbol. Provided it is not the period, the character is copied to the output and the next data character is read. The looping continues until the period terminator appears in the data, at which point the loop and the program terminate. Notice, that if the first data character is a period, the loop is never entered. An initial period means that there are no characters to be copied, corresponding to non-execution of the `while` loop.

This and many other programs involving loops have the same solution pattern. First some initialization is performed before entering the loop. This includes, among other things, any initialization associated with the first iteration of the loop. In Program 6.1 the first character is read so that the loop condition can be evaluated. This is known as the *read ahead* mechanism. We must read the first data item, otherwise we cannot determine whether or not to obey the loop for the first time. Equally, the read ahead mechanism applies to all subsequent data items.

Second, the condition controlling repetition of the loop is expressed. This determines how the loop will be terminated. In the example program the required condition is that the current character is not the period symbol.

Third, some processing associated with the loop is executed. One or more statements will make up this processing logic. This often consists of processing one or more items of input data or of processing internally generated data. In the example, the processing is trivial. The data character previously read from the standard input is copied to the standard output.

Finally, the necessary actions are taken before determining whether the loop is to continue. This is the side effect which influences continuation of the loop. For our problem, the next data character is read from the input.

The shape of this solution in our PDL is:

```
initialize before entering loop
WHILE condition controlling execution of the loop DO
   processing logic
   set up for next iteration
ENDWHILE
```

We observe the same solution structure in Program 6.2. This program reads a series of positive floating point values. The data set terminates with a negative value sentinel. The program forms the sum of the positive values. The initialization consists of zeroising the summation and reading the first data item. The condition for loop continuation is that the current data value is positive. The processing logic consists of forming a running total and setting up for another iteration by reading the next data value. Expressed in our PDL we arrive at:

```
initialize the sum to zero
read first number
WHILE this number is positive DO
  add the number to the sum
  read next number
ENDWHILE
print the sum
```

PROGRAM 6.2

```
/*
**      Read a series of positive floating point numbers
**      and form their sum. The data is terminated with
**      a unique negative value.
*/

#include <stdio.h>

#define ZERO      0.0

main()
{
   float data, sum = ZERO;   /* data and running total */

   scanf("%f", &data);       /* get first data item */
   while (data >= ZERO){      /* data terminator? */
     sum += data;            /* form the sum */
     scanf("%f", &data);     /* get the next data item */
   }
   printf("The sum is %f\n", sum);
}
```

This same shape is also readily recognizable in the next program. The program operates on no input data. All the data is generated by the program itself. The program computes the sum of the first twenty integers: $1 + 2 + 3 + \ldots + 20$. Once again the program's data is an iteration of values. This time, they happen to be generated by the program and not provided as input data. The same analysis still applies – the program structure mirrors the data structure.

PROGRAM 6.3(a)

```
/*
**       Compute the total of the first 20 positive integers.
**       The program requires no data. All data values in the
**       program are self generated.
*/

#include <stdio.h>

#define INITIAL    1
#define MAX        20
#define ZERO       0

main()
{
   int data, sum = ZERO;   /* data and running total */

   data = INITIAL;         /* initial integer */
   while (data <= MAX)     /* terminate loop? */
     sum += data++;        /* form running total */
   printf("The sum of the first 20 integers is %d\n", sum);
}
```

The same result can be achieved by counting downward from 20 to 1. The major difference between the two program versions is the condition to terminate the loop.

PROGRAM 6.3(b)

```
/*
**       Form the sum of the first 20 positive integers.
**       Self generate the integer sequence 20, 19, ... ,2, 1
**       and simultaneously sum.
*/

#include <stdio.h>

#define MAX      20
#define ZERO     0

main()
{
   int data, sum = ZERO;   /* data and running total */

   data = MAX;             /* first integer value */
   while (data > ZERO)     /* loop control */
     sum += data--;        /* form running total */
   printf("The sum of the first 20 integers is %d\n", sum);
}
```

It is common practice when writing such fragments of a C program to incorporate all or part of the loop control into one place in the program. This unifies these related activities. The program is generally then more readable since control of the loop is no longer scattered among other processing statements.

Program 6.1 can be rewritten by incorporating the reading and testing of the single data character into the control expression. The solution is shown in Program 6.4.

PROGRAM 6.4

```
/*
**      Copy a character sequence from the standard input
**      to the standard output. The data is terminated by
**      the first occurrence of a period (.) symbol.
*/

#include <stdio.h>

#define PERIOD      '.'

main()
{
  char c;                                /* data character */

  while ((c = getchar()) != PERIOD)    /* read and test data */
    putchar(c);
}
```

Since the inequality operator has higher precedence than the assignment operator, it is necessary to ensure that the assignment is performed first. This we achieve with the additional parentheses. If we were to omit the extra parentheses, then the expression:

```
c = getchar() != PERIOD
```

evaluates to:

```
c = (getchar() != PERIOD)
```

First a character is read and compared with the symbolic constant ⱢERIOD. This evaluates to logical true (integer 1) or logical false (integer 0). The value 0 or 1 is then assigned to the character variable c.

In the program above, the strategy is to perform a combined assignment and conditional test in a single expression. The assignment is performed first, then the test. A similar approach can be taken when rewriting Program 6.2. The assignment is performed through a scanf function call. The condition is then tested. The sequencing of these two actions is achieved with the comma operator. The comma operator guarantees sequential execution of each expression. The returned value is that of the last executed expression – the required condition.

PROGRAM 6.5

```
/*
**      Sum a sequence of positive floating point values.
**      The series is of indeterminate length, but is
**      terminated with a negative number.
*/

#include <stdio.h>

#define ZERO      0.0

main()
{
   float data, sum = ZERO;      /* data and running total */

   while (scanf("%f", &data), data >= ZERO)   /* read and test */
      sum += data;                            /* processing */
   printf("The sum is %f\n", sum);
}
```

A final example illustrates how the unary decrement operator combines with the loop condition testing. We remember that the logical value false is represented by the value zero, while any non-zero value represents logical true. We can therefore establish a loop which counts downward from some initial positive value, terminating when the count reaches zero. While the count is not zero, the loop continues. In Program 6.6, the data consists of a single positive integer value followed by a series of floating point values. The integer specifies the number of supplied floating point values. The program calculates the mean (average) of the floating point numbers.

PROGRAM 6.6

```
/*
**      Compute the mean of a number of floating point values.
**      The program data consists of an integer N, followed
**      by N floats.
*/

#include <stdio.h>

#define ZERO      0.0
```

```
main()
{
    int count, number;         /* loop control, number of values */
    float data, sum = ZERO;    /* data and running total */

    scanf("%d", &number);      /* read how many floats */
    count = number;            /* initialise loop control */
    while (count--){           /* cycle number of times */
      scanf("%f", &data);      /* read data value */
      sum += data;             /* process it */
    }
    printf("Mean is %f\n", sum/number);
}
```

When developing software, we must endeavour to ensure its *robustness*. A robust program should, under all conditions, terminate in a controlled manner. If this last program is presented with the single data value 0, then no floating point numbers are to be averaged. The loop is therefore never executed, and the expression printed, i.e. sum/number, is evaluated as 0.0/0. Upon evaluation, the expression generates an overflow condition and the program abruptly terminates. To ensure that the program is more secure, this condition should be tested. Similarly, if the integer input value is negative, the program loops forever. A negative-valued count is interpreted as logical true. The value remains negative through decrementing. Ultimately, negative overflow occurs and the program dies. We introduce the statement to achieve this level of security later in this chapter.

There is no restriction on the statement or statements under control of a while statement. It is permissible to have while statements controlling other while statements. This gives rise to a construct known as nested while loops or, simply, *nested loops*. The operation of nested while statements is analogous to the hour and minute hands of a clock. The minute hand moves with rapidity from minute to minute. When the minute hand completes a cycle of sixty minutes, the hour hand advances by one hour. The minute hand then repeats the same rapid cycle. Similarly with nested while statements. The outer while statement progresses more slowly than the inner while statement. When the inner while statement completes one cycle, the outer while advances to the next iteration and the inner while restarts with a new inner loop.

Nested loops in a program arise from data sets which exhibit the same nested structure. A bank account program may process the accounts for a number of customers. The initial data analysis reveals that we have a series or iteration on customers. The resulting program outline is then:

```
WHILE more customers DO
  process one customer
ENDWHILE
```

Each customer, in turn, may hold a number of accounts. Again, an iteration on accounts for a given customer is required. We refine 'process one customer', replacing it with a loop over the customer's accounts:

```
WHILE more customers DO
   WHILE more accounts for this customer DO
     process customer's account
   ENDWHILE
ENDWHILE
```

These ideas are present in the next program, the output from which has a nested iterative structure.

Program 6.7 plots a solid isosceles triangle composed of asterisk (*) symbols. The first line contains a single asterisk. The second line contains three asterisks centred below the first, and so on. The full triangle spans five lines. The outer loop controls the number of lines to be displayed. Each line consists of a number of leading blanks and a number of asterisks. The number of blanks and the number of asterisks on any one line is dependent upon which line is being printed. Both the leading blanks and the asterisks are printed by two successive loops contained within the outer loop.

PROGRAM 6.7

```
/*
**      Form an isosceles triangle composed of asterisk
**      symbols. The first line contains a single * symbol.
**      The second line contains three asterisks centred
**      below the first, and so on. In all, the figure
**      spans five lines.
*/

#include <stdio.h>

#define NUMLINES    5
#define BLANK       ' '
#define ASTERISK    '*'
#define NEWLINE '\n'

main()
{
    int line;                       /* five line counter */
    int_leading blanks;             /* left margin counter */
    int stars;                      /* number of asterisks */

    line = 1;                       /* for each line */
    while (line <= NUMLINES){
      leading_blanks = 1;           /* margin */
      while (leading_blanks++       <= NUMLINES - line)
        putchar(BLANK);
```

```
       stars = 1;                    /* asterisks */
       while (stars++ <= 2 * line - 1)
         putchar(ASTERISK);

       putchar(NEWLINE);
       line++;
    }
}
```

The control expression in a while statement governs whether the loop is to be obeyed or to be terminated. Any non-zero expression value represents logical true and causes the loop to be obeyed one further time. A non-zero integer constant for this expression gives rise to what is known as an infinite loop. An infinite loop cycles indefinitely, never terminating:

```
#define TRUE     1
-----------
-----------

while (TRUE){
    -----------
    -----------
}
```

A program containing such a construct will run forever unless some action is taken to stop it or some statement embedded within the body of the loop is able to break the cycle. Section 6.9 introduces the appropriate statement. An infinite loop containing a statement to break the cycle at some prescribed junction can provide a natural way of expressing certain constructs.

6.6 The for statement

The for statement is closely related to the while statement. The syntax of the for statement is given by:

```
for(expression1; expression2; expression3)
     statement
```

with for a reserved keyword. Like the while statement, the statement under control of the for may be a single statement or a compound statement. Any of the statements controlled by the for may be another for statement, giving rise to nested for loops.

The for statement is semantically equivalent to:

```
expression1;
while (expression2){
```

```
        statement;
        expression3;
    }
```

The first expression is used to initialize the loop. Then `expression2` is evaluated and if it is non-zero (logical true) then the statement is executed. `Expression3` is evaluated, and control passes back to the loop beginning, to re-evaluate `expression2`. Normally, `expression2` is a logical expression used to control the iteration. Note that if this expression initially evaluates to zero (logical false), the loop is never entered. The third expression is frequently used to update some loop control variable before repeating the loop.

Two examples of the `for` statement are:

```
for(k = 1; k <= 10; k++)
        printf("The square of %d is %d\n", k, k * k);
```

and:

```
sum = 0;
for(i = 1; i <= m; i++)
    sum += i;
```

The first example generates and prints a table of the squares of the first ten integers. In the second example, the sum of the first m integers is computed. By employing the comma operator, the initialization of variable `sum` and the control variable i may both be accomplished in `expression1`. The second example may then be written as:

```
for(sum = 0, i = 1; i <= m; i++)
    sum += i;
```

The use of the comma operator is equally applicable to all three expressions in the `for` statement.

Any or all of the three expressions in a `for` statement may be omitted, but the two semicolon separators and the parentheses are mandatory. If `expression1` is missing, no initialization step is performed as part of the `for` loop. The last example might have been coded:

```
sum = 0;
i = 1;
for( ; i <= m; i++)
    sum += i;
```

Equally, we might have absorbed the increment to variable i into the assignment forming the running total for `sum`. In this case, the third expression can also be removed:

```
sum = 0;
i = 1;
for( ; i <= m; )
        sum += i++;
```

When `expression2` is missing, the condition always evaluates to logical true. Thus the loop in the code:

```
for( ; ; ){
    _____
    _____
}
```

is the infinite loop. It parallels the infinite `while` loop shown in the preceding section. One frequently finds the following #define used to establish an infinite loop:

```
#define FOREVER      for( ;; )

FOREVER{
    _____
    _____
}
```

The FOREVER explicitly indicates the nature of this specialized loop.

Since the `for` statement is semantically eqivalent to the `while` statement, it can equally well be used with iterative data structures. In certain instances, the `for` statement more naturally expresses the iterative processing logic than the `while` statement. For example, the loop in Program 6.3(a) is better represented by:

```
for(data = INITIAL; data <= MAX; data++) ....
```

when a known number of iterations is required.

We illustrate a simple example of the use of a `for` statement by repeating Program 6.1. The first and last expressions of the `for` are unused. The second expression controls the iteration.

PROGRAM 6.8

```
/*
**      Read a series of characters from the standard
**      input and echo them to the standard output. The
**      program finishes when the period symbol is
**      encountered in the data.
*/

#include <stdio.h>

#define PERIOD      '.'

main()
{
  char c;

  for (; (c = getchar()) != PERIOD; )
    putchar(c);
}
```

Working with the same data as Programs 6.1 and 6.8, we can develop a modified version which counts the number of data characters. The terminating period is omitted from the count. The first expression is used to initialize the count. The final expression is empty as nothing is to be done before advancing to the next iteration. The second expression again controls program looping. The statement under control of the loop increments the counter for each character read.

PROGRAM 6.9(a)

```
/*
**      Count the number of characters read from the standard
**      input. The character stream is terminated with the
**      first occurrence of the period symbol.
*/
#include <stdio.h>

#define PERIOD       '.'

main()
{
    char c;         /* data character */
    int  count;     /* character counter */

    for (count = 0; (c = getchar()) != PERIOD; )
        count++;
    printf("Number of characters is %d\n", count);
}
```

The third expression could also be the place to perform the increment to the counter. In that case there is now no statement to be controlled by the for statement. The program logic is completely encapsulated by the three for statement expressions. The statement consisting solely of the semicolon symbol is called the null statement. As the semicolon is easily 'lost' when reading the code, we annotate it with a comment.

PROGRAM 6.9(b)

```
/*
**      Count the number of characters read from the standard
**      input. The character stream is terminated with the
**      first occurrence of the period symbol.
*/

#include <stdio.h>

#define PERIOD     '.'
```

```
main()
{
  char c;          /* data character */
  int  count;      /* character counter */

  for (count = 0; (c = getchar()) != PERIOD; count++)
     /* do nothing */ ;
  printf("Number of characters is %d\n", count);
}
```

By using the comma operator in the three for statement expressions, very dense and cryptic C code can be produced. The code is both difficult to read and maintain if modification or correction is required. Because of this, the reader is not encouraged (at least initially) to indulge in this type of coding. This coding, however, may be experienced in others' programs. We illustrate with the following example.

A series of positive floating point values is given as data. The data set is terminated with a negative floating point number. Program 6.10 computes the mean of the positive data values. Note how all the processing and loop control logic is compacted into the three for statement expressions.

PROGRAM 6.10

```
/*
**      Compute the mean of a number of positive floating
**      point values. The data consists of a series of
**      positive values, terminated with a negative number.
*/

#include <stdio.h>

main()
{
  int  count;        /* count the positives */
  float data, sum;   /* data item, running total */

  for (count = 0, sum = 0.0;
    scanf("%f", &data), data >= 0.0;
    sum += data, count++)
           /* do nothing */ ;
  printf("The mean is %f\n", sum/count);
}
```

6.7 The do statement

As previously noted, the while statement tests the condition (expression) prior to obeying the loop. Since the for statement is semantically equivalent to the while, it too tests before entering the loop. In both cases if the condition is initially zero (logical false), then the loop is never obeyed at all.

Normally, iterative constructs are more logically coded using loops with initial condition checking (while and for). In a small number of cases, checking is required at the conclusion of the loop body. In these cases the do statement is the appropriate construct.

The do statement has the form:

```
do
   statement
while (expression)
```

The distinction between this statement and the while and for statements is that the conditional test is performed after executing the loop. The loop body is then guaranteed to be obeyed at least once. After first executing the statement, the expression is evaluated. If it is non-zero (logical true) then control passes back to the beginning of the do statement and the processing repeats. When the expression evaluates to zero (logical false), control passes to the next program statement.

The statement under control of the do may be a single statement or a compound statement. In the latter case, the form of the do statement is:

```
do {
   statement 1;
   statement 2;
   ----------

   ----------
} while(expression)
```

Consider a program to read a single positive integer value and to output the digits of that number in reverse sequence. For example, if the input value is 1234, then the output is 4321. The logic consists of repeatedly extracting the rightmost digit of the number and printing it. The digit is then removed from the number before continuing. The iteration stops when the number is reduced to zero. The solution, expressed in our extended PDL, is:

```
read the number
REPEAT
      obtain the rightmost digit
      print the digit
      remove the digit from the number
   WHILE number is non zero
```

and the program is Program 6.11.

PROGRAM 6.11

```
/*
**      Read a single positive integer value and output
**      the digits of that number in reverse sequence. For
**      example, if the input value is 1234, then the output
**      is 4321.
*/

#include <stdio.h>

main()
{
    int number, digit;         /* data value, rightmost digit */

    scanf("%d", &number);      /* input data item */
    do {
        digit = number % 10;   /* obtain rightmost digit .... */
        printf("%ld", digit);  /* .... and print it */
        number /= 10;          /* reduce the number */
    } while (number != 0);     /* repeat until nothing left */
    printf("\n");
}
```

We might have considered coding the problem with a `while` statement:

```
scanf("%d", &number);
while (number != 0){
    digit = number % 10;
    printf("%ld", digit);
    number /= 10;
}
```

The same input number 1234 produces the same output 4321. However, note what happens if the input value is 0 (zero). Since the do statement is obeyed once, the output is 0. However, when the solution is in terms of the while statement, which is obeyed none or more times, no output is produced as the loop is never entered. The do statement solution guarantees the display of at least one digit in all cases. This is the better solution since no output from a program can mislead the user into thinking that the program has somehow failed.

CASE STUDY   6.1 Reports

A student class is partitioned into a number of project groups. The number of students in each group is not necessarily always the same. Each student in the class is given an assessment and assigned a raw mark measured out of 80. A report is required showing the assessment for each student, for each group and for the entire class. The report format is shown below.

```
                                PROJECT REPORT
         PROJECT GROUP 1
                     IDENTIFICATION      RAW            PERCENTAGE
                     NUMBER              MARK (/80)     MARK
                     1234                40             50
                     5678                55             68
                     9012                30             37
                 GROUP 1 TOTAL                          155

         PROJECT GROUP 2
                     IDENTIFICATION      RAW            PERCENTAGE
                     NUMBER              MARK (/80)     MARK
                     3456                10             12
                     7890                20             25
                     9876                30             37
                     5432                40             50
                     1098                50             62
                     7654                60             75
                     3210                70             87
                 GROUP 2 TOTAL                          348

         GRAND TOTAL                                    503
```

No account is to be taken of page breaks in the report.

The program input consists of a series of records presented one per line. Each record gives the student's identification number and the raw assessment mark. The records are batched into project groupings with the group number prepended to each record. A trailer record containing all zeros terminates the groups, while another trailer record containing all nines terminates the data. The sample data set for the illustrated report above is:

```
         1      1234      40
         1      5678      55
         1      9012      30
         0      0000      00
         2      3456      10
         2      7890      20
         2      9876      30
         2      5432      40
         2      1098      50
         2      7654      60
         2      3210      70
         0      0000      00
         9      9999      99
```

Analysis of the data indicates that nested iteration is required. Two repeating groups are present in the data – a repetition over the project groups, and a repetition over the students in each group. The outer iteration cycles through each project group, with the inner iteration processing each student in that group. The outline logic for this processing is:

```
initialize grand total
produce class report heading
WHILE read next record; not the end of data record DO
   initialize project group total
   produce project group headings
   REPEAT
      process the current record
      read the next record
   WHILE not the end of group record
   produce project group summary
   add project group total to grand total
ENDWHILE
produce class report summary
```

The coding for the program is now relatively straightforward. The PDL is sufficiently close to the final version that we can convert to code directly.

```c
/*
**      A student class is partitioned into a number of project
**      groups, not necessarily of equal sizes. Each student
**      in the class is assigned an assessment mark measured
**      out of 80. Produce a report showing the assessment for
**      each student, for each project group and for the whole
**      class.
*/

#include <stdio.h>

#define GROUP_TRAILER    0
#define FILE_TRAILER     9

main()
{
   int grand_total;                /* percent mark */
   int group_total;                /* percent mark */
   int group_no, current_group_no; /* project groups */
   int identification;             /* student number */
   int raw, percent;               /* student assessment mark */

   grand_total = 0;
   printf("\t\t\tPROJECT REPORT\n\n");

   while (scanf("%d %d %d", &group_no, &identification, &raw),
            group_no != FILE_TRAILER){
      printf("PROJECT GROUP %2d\n", group_no);
      printf("\t\tIDENTIFICATION\tRAW\t\tPERCENTAGE\n");
      printf("\t\tNUMBER\t\tMARK (/80)\tMARK\n");
      current_group_no = group_no;
```

```
group_total = 0;
do {
   percent = raw * 100 / 80;
   printf("\t\t%4d\t\t%2d\t\t%3d\n", identification,
           raw, percent);
   group_total += percent;
   scanf("%d %d %d", &group_no, &identification, &raw);
} while (group_no != GROUP_TRAILER);
printf("\tGROUP %2d TOTAL\t\t\t    %6d\n\n",
          current_group_no, group_total);

   grand_total += group_total;
}
printf("GRAND TOTAL\t\t\t\t    %6d\n\n", grand total);
}
```

6.8 The if statement

The general form of the if statement is:

```
if(expression)
     statement 1;
else
     statement 2;
```

where if and else are reserved keywords. If the expression evaluates to non-zero
(logical value true), statement 1 is executed and control then passes to the next
program statement following the if statement. If the value of the expression is zero
(logical false), statement 2 is executed. Pictorially, the if statement can be
described by the flow diagram of Figure 6.2.

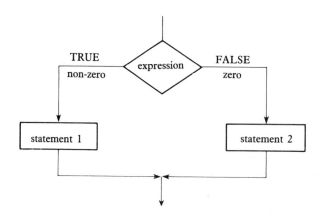

Figure 6.2

Both `statement 1` and `statement 2` may be single statements or compound statements. Some examples of valid `if` statements are:

(a)
```
if(count == 0)
   printf("The count is zero\n");
else
   printf("The count is not zero\n");
```

(b)
```
if(a < b)
   printf("Originally, a less than b\");
else {
   temp = a;
   a = b;
   b = a;
   printf("Interchange a and b\n");
}
```

(c)
```
if(ch == ' ' || ch == '\t' || ch == '\n') {
   whitespace++;
   printf("More whitespace characters\n");
} else
   others++;
```

We may also include another `if` statement as either or both of the statement parts. This gives rise to what is known as a *nested* `if` *statement*. Examples include:

(d)
```
if(expression 1)
   if(expression 2)
      statement 1;
   else
      statement 2;
else
   statement 3;
```

Semantically this is equivalent to:

```
if(expression 1){
   if(expression 2)
      statement 1;
   else
      statement 2;
} else
   statement 3;
```

In many instances it is better to incorporate the braces. Their presence highlights the structure of an otherwise complex statement. An actual example with explicit braces is:

```
if(number > 20){
   if(number < 30)
      printf("Number between 21 and 29 inclusive\n");
   else
      printf("Number exceeds 29\n");
} else
   printf("Number does not exceed 20\n");
```

Similarly, an `if` statement may be used in the `else` clause of another `if` statement:

```
(e)    if(expression 1)
         statement 1;
       else
         if(expression 2)
           statement 2;
         else
           statement 3;
```

Semantically, this is equivalent to:

```
       if(expression 1)
         statement 1;
       else {
         if(expression 2)
           statement 2;
         else
           statement 3;
       }
```

Again, the braces are often best included where it is felt the structure needs to be emphasized. An example of this form is:

```
       if(ch >= 'a' && ch <= 'z')
           printf("Lowercase letter\n");
       else {
         if(ch >= '0' && ch <= '9')
           printf("Digit symbol\n");
         else
           printf("Other symbol\n");
       }
```

In the present form the `if` statement provides a means of selecting one of two distinct logic paths. Sometimes we wish to select whether or not to obey some statement or statements. This is achieved through a shortened version of the `if` statement:

```
       if(expression)
           statement;
```

If the expression evaluates to logical true (non-zero) the statement is obeyed. Having obeyed the statement the program continues with the next instruction following this `if` statement. If the expression evaluates to logical false (zero) the statement is ignored and the program continues with the next statement. The statement part under control of this `if` statement may, as before, be a single statement or a compound statement.

When using this last form of `if` statement, an ambiguous construct can arise where the statement part is itself an `if` statement:

```
if(expression 1)
  if(expression 2)
    statement 1;
  else
    statement 2;
```

The ambiguity arises from the fact that we are unable to say whether the `else` part belongs with 'if(expression 1)' or with 'if(expression 2)'. Two possible interpretations are:

```
(a)  if(expression 1){        (b)  if(expression 1){
       if(expression 2)               if(expression 2)
         statement 1;                   statement 1;
       else                     } else
         statement 2;                 statement 2;
     }
```

In version (a) the `else` part associates with 'if(expression 2)'. In version (b) the `else` part associates with 'if(expression 1)'. This ambiguity, known as the 'dangling else problem', is resolved by the compiler always associating an `else` part with the nearest unresolved preceding `if`. Version (a) is therefore the correct interpretation. Explicit braces as shown in version (a) can often improve the readability of the code.

Various combinations of `if` statements can occur. The statement associated with the `else` clause may be another `if–else` statement. Equally, the next `else` clause may be yet another `if–else` statement, and so on. To illustrate, consider a program fragment to read an examination score and to assign a letter grade based on the score. The grading scheme that applies is shown by the following table:

Score	Grade
80–100	A
70–79	B
60–69	C
50–59	D
40–49	E
0–39	F

A single nested `if` statement can describe the necessary processing:

```
if(score >= 80)
  grade = 'A';
else
  if(score >= 70)
    grade = 'B';
  else
    if(score >= 60)
      grade = 'C';
```

```
    else
      if(score >= 50)
        grade = 'D';
      else
        if(score >= 40)
          grade = 'E';
        else
          grade = 'F';
```

The whole construct is a single statement forming a cascading chain of if statements. Suppose, for example, that the score is 65. The first two expressions evaluate to logical false and the corresponding two statements grade = 'A' and grade = 'B' are skipped. The third expression evaluates to logical true and the statement grade = 'C' is executed. Control then passes to the end of this statement.

The proper indentation for such a construct is shown as above. As can be seen, the structure rapidly tracks to the right. To avoid this situation, these statements are generally presented as:

```
if(score >= 80)
  grade = 'A';
else if(score >= 70)
  grade = 'B';
else if(score >= 60)
  grade = 'C';
else if(score >= 50)
  grade = 'D';
else if(score >= 40)
  grade = 'E';
else
  grade = 'F';
```

The if statement is used in programs in which the data offers a selection. If the program data offers a choice between, say, data item 1 and data item 2, then the corresponding program structure (expressed in our PDL) is a conditional:

```
IF data item 1
THEN
  process data item 1
ELSE
  process data item 2
ENDIF
```

Program 6.12 illustrates a simple use of an if statement. The program inputs two floating point numbers and outputs them in ascending order. The program data can either be already ordered or in descending order. These two alternatives are reflected in the solution structure:

```
read the two data values
IF first value less than second
THEN
```

```
    print first and second
ELSE
    print second and first
ENDIF
```

PROGRAM 6.12

```
/*
**      Read two floating point values and display them in
**      ascending order.
*/

#include <stdio.h>

main()
{
    float first, second;      /* data items */

    scanf("%f %f", &first, &second);
    if (first < second)
        printf("%f %f\n", first, second);
    else
        printf("%f %f\n", second, first);
}
```

The second program in this series operates on a sequence of characters of unknown length. The data set is terminated with a period symbol. The character sequence spans a number of lines and the program determines the number of text lines by enumerating the number of newline symbols. The program employs an if statement with no else part, used to detect the newline characters. The program data is an iteration of single characters. The corresponding program structure is then a loop. The PDL is:

```
WHILE read next character; character is not terminator DO
    process the character
ENDWHILE
```

The character processing is a selection. If the character is a newline symbol, the line counter is incremented. If the character is not a newline symbol it is ignored. The final PDL is:

```
initialize line counter
WHILE read next character; character is not terminator DO
    IF a newline symbol
    THEN
        increment line counter
    ENDIF
ENDWHILE
print final line counter value
```

PROGRAM 6.13

```
/*
**      Read a sequence of characters of indeterminate length
**      and count the number of lines of text by enumerating
**      the number of newline symbols. The data is terminated
**      by a period symbol.
*/

#include <stdio.h>

#define PERIOD     '.'
#define NEWLINE    '\n'

main()
{
  char c;              /* data character */
  int lines = 0;       /* line counter */

  while ((c = getchar()) != PERIOD)
    if (c == NEWLINE)
      lines++;
  printf("Number of lines is %d\n", lines);
}
```

Operating with the same data as in the program above, we develop a program to count the number of 'words' in the input character sequence. A word is defined to be any character sequence separated by whitespace characters (blanks, tabs and newlines).

Once again the data is a repetition of characters, giving rise to the same initial program structure:

```
WHILE read next character; character not the terminator DO
   process the character
ENDWHILE
```

The character processing must select from a whitespace character or a non-whitespace character. The former indicates that the input is no longer part of a word and a flag is set accordingly. For a non-whitespace character two possibilities exist. If the preceding data item was also a non-whitespace character, then we continue to be part of the same word. If the preceding symbol was a whitespace character, then we are processing the first character of a new word and the word counter is incremented. The overall PDL is:

```
initialize word count and set the in-word flag
WHILE read next character; character not the terminator DO
   IF a whitespace character
   THEN
      unset the in-word flag
```

```
    ELSE
      IF start of new word
      THEN
         increment word count
         set the in-word flag
      ENDIF
    ENDIF
ENDWHILE
print final word count
```

PROGRAM 6.14

```
/*
**      A piece of text consists of a character sequence
**      spanning a number of lines and terminated by a period
**      symbol. Count the number of "words" in the text.
**      A word is defined as any character string delimited
**      by whitespace (blank, tab and newline) symbols.
*/

#include <stdio.h>

#define PERIOD          '.'
#define BLANK           ' '
#define TAB             '\t'
#define NEWLINE         '\n'

#define FALSE           0
#define TRUE            1

main()
{
  char c;               /* data character */
  int  words = 0;       /* word counter */
  int  inword = FALSE;  /* word indicator */

  while ((c = getchar()) != PERIOD)
    if (c == BLANK || c == TAB || c == NEWLINE)
      inword = FALSE;
    else if (! inword){
      inword = TRUE;
      words++;
    }
  printf("Number of words is %d\n", words);
}
```

Once more with the same data, we count the number of occurrences of lower-case letters, upper-case letters, digits and other symbols. A nested if statement provides the necessary logic. The character handling operations are performed with the library macros islower, etc. See Appendix F.1 for details.

PROGRAM 6.15

```
/*
**      Enumerate the number of occurrences of lowercase
**      letters, uppercase letters, digits and other symbols
**      in a data set consisting of a character sequence
**      terminated with a period symbol.
*/

#include <stdio.h>
#include <ctype.h>

#define PERIOD      '.'

main()
{
  char c;                                   /* data character */
  int  lowercase, uppercase, digits, others;  /* counters */

  lowercase = uppercase = digits = others = 0;
  while ((c = getchar()) != PERIOD)
    if (islower(c))
      lowercase++;
    else if (isupper(c))
      uppercase++;
    else if (isdigit(c))
      digits++;
    else
      others++;

  printf("Number of lowercase letters %d\n", lowercase);
  printf("Number of uppercase letters %d\n", uppercase);
  printf("Number of decimal digits %d\n", digits);
  printf("Number of other symbols %d\n", others);
}
```

The final program in this section is a multi-function program making extensive use of the conditional if statement. The program accepts as input a date expressed in numerical form and verbalizes it. The input date appears in the international form:

```
DD/MM/YYYY
```

For example:

```
10/12/1985
```

The input date is assumed to be valid. The output from the program (for the above) is:

```
Tuesday 10 December 1985
```

To calculate the day of the week for a given date, Zeller's congruence can be employed. The algorithm computes for any valid date an integer in the range 0 to 6 inclusive, with 0 representing Sunday, 1 is Monday, and so on. The congruence is:

$$z = \{ \frac{26m - 2}{10} + k + D + \left[\frac{D}{4} \right] + \left[\frac{C}{4} \right] - 2C \} \bmod 7$$

The square brackets denote 'the greatest integer in', and mod 7 is the remainder (modulus) on dividing by 7. In the formula:

D = the year in the century
C = the century
k = the day of the month
m = month number, with January and February taken as
     months 11 and 12 respectively of the preceding
     year. March is then month 1, April is 2, ...,
     December is 10.

Thus for 10/12/1985, D = 85, C = 19, k = 10 and m = 10. For January 1, 1800, k = 1, m = 11, C = 17 and D = 99.

The congruence for 10/12/1985 is:

$$z = \{ \frac{26 * 10 - 2}{10} + 10 + 85 + \left[\frac{85}{4} \right] + \left[\frac{19}{4} \right] - 2 * 19 \} \bmod 7$$

$$= \{ 25 + 10 + 85 + 21 + 4 - 38 \} \bmod 7$$

$$= 107 \bmod 7$$

$$= 2$$

which, of course, is Tuesday. The program is as follows:

PROGRAM 6.16

```
/*
**      The program accepts as input a single date expressed
**      in the form DD/MM/YYYY and verbalizes it. For example,
**      the date 10/12/1985 produces the output:
**
**              Tuesday 10 December 1985
**
**      The input date is assumed to be valid and no checking
**      is performed.
*/

#include <stdio.h>

main()
{
```

```
    int  day, month, year;                        /* input date */
    int  zell;                                     /* congruence value */
    int  zeller(const int, const int, const int);
                                                   /* forward .... */
    void day_name(const int), month_name(const int);
                                                   /* .... references */

    printf("Enter the date as DD/MM/YYYY: ");  /* get the date */
    scanf("%2d/%2d/%4d", &day, &month, &year);
    zell = zeller(day, month, year);          /* apply congruence */
    day_name(zell);                           /* verbalize the day */
    printf("%2d", day);
    month_name(month);                        /* verbalize the month */
    printf("%4d\n", year);
}

/*
**      Apply Zeller's congruence to a date expressed in
**      the form 21/11/1985. The date given is assumed to
**      be valid.
*/

int zeller(const int day, const int month, const int year)
{
    int k, y, m, d, c;       /* formula variables */
    int z;                   /* computed value */

    k = day;                    /* initialize */
    y = year;

    if (month < 3){             /* formula month */
        m = month + 10;
        y = year - 1;
    } else
        m = month - 2;

    d = y % 100;             /* year and .... */
    c = y / 100;             /* .... century */

    z = (26 * m - 2)/10 + k + d + (d/4) + (c/4) - 2 * c;
    return (z % 7);
}

/*
**      Verbalize a day number, encoded according to Zeller's
**      congruence, into a variable length character string
**      surrounded by single blank characters.
*/

void day_name(const int d)
{
    if (d == 0)
```

```
      printf(" Sunday ");
   else if (d == 1)
      printf(" Monday ");
   else if (d == 2)
      printf(" Tuesday ");
   else if (d == 3)
      printf(" Wednesday ");
   else if (d == 4)
      printf(" Thursday ");
   else if (d == 5)
      printf(" Friday ");
   else
      printf(" Saturday ");
}


/*
**      Verbalize a month number in the range 1 to 12 inclusive
**      into a variable length character string surrounded
**      by single blank characters.
*/

void month_name(const int m)
{
   if (m == 1)
      printf(" January ");
   else if (m == 2)
      printf(" February ");
   else if (m == 3)
      printf(" March ");
   else if (m == 4)
      printf(" April ");
   else if (m == 5)
      printf(" May ");
   else if (m == 6)
      printf(" June ");
   else if (m == 7)
      printf(" July ");
   else if (m == 8)
      printf(" August ");
   else if (m == 9)
      printf(" September ");
   else if (m == 10)
      printf(" October ");
   else if (m == 11)
      printf(" November ");
   else
      printf(" December ");
}
```

CASE STUDY 6.2 Bank statement

A program is required to read details of transactions on a bank account and produce a statement summarizing these transactions. The program input consists of a sequence of integer values. The first value is a positive integer representing the bank account number. The second integer value is the initial balance of the account. The remaining integer values are either positive or negative and represent the transactions. The final transaction is the unique trailer value 0. A positive transaction represents a deposit (credit transaction) and a negative transaction represents a withdrawal (debit transaction).

For example, given the input data 1234, 847, − 150, − 35, + 30, − 249, − 172, + 55 and 0, the bank statement produced should appear as shown in Figure 6.3.

Bank Statement			
Account number: 1234 Transaction:	Credit	Debit	Balance
1			847
2		150	697
3		35	662
4	30		692
5		249	443
6		172	271
	55		326
Totals	85	606	326

Figure 6.3

The first-level design of the bank statement program is relatively straightforward. After the first two data values have been read, the statement headers and the initial balance line may be printed. Successive transactions are read and processed until the end of data trailer record is processed. Finally, the statement summary is generated. In outline, the program is:

```
read account number and initial balance
print statement headers and initial balance
initialize credit and debit totals
read the first transaction
initialize the transaction counter
WHILE not end of data value DO
   process and print this transaction
   read the next transaction
   increment the transaction counter
ENDWHILE
print the statement summary
```

Given this outline it is possible to be satisfied about its correctness. Using sample test data, such as that above, we can trace the program's behaviour. Only when this implementation has been fully tested do we progress to the next phase and continue with the refinement.

Printing the statement headers and producing the initial balance line is a self-contained task that should be isolated to a separate function. For it to operate correctly, the `main` function will need to provide this subsidiary function with the bank account number and the value of the initial balance.

The same analysis applies when we consider the statement summary. It, too, is programmed as a separate function. The summary is produced from the credit total, the debit total and the final balance. These values are communicated as arguments to the function.

Finally, we consider processing a single transaction. The transaction value is added to the current balance to produce the updated balance value. A positive transaction will increase the value of the balance when added to it. A negative transaction will reduce the value of the balance when added to it. Thus no special processing is required to update the balance other than by adding the transaction value.

If the transaction is positive, the total credit value is changed. If the transaction is negative, the total debit is changed. When all the computations are complete, the transaction print line can be presented. The processing and printing of one transaction is assigned to a secondary function.

From this analysis we can complete the coding of function `main`. Note how even the detailed coding still reflects the original program design. Details concerned with printing headers, processing transactions and printing summaries are not allowed to clutter the simple logic of the `main` function:

```
main()
{
    int account_number;                   /* identification */
    int number_of_transaction;            /* transaction counter */
    int credit_total, debit_total;        /* total credits/debits */
    int transaction_value;                /* value of transaction */
    int balance;                          /* balance of the account */
    void print_headers(const int, const int),
         process_transaction(const int, const int,
                             int *const, int *const, int *const),
         print_summary(const int, const int, const int);

    credit_total = debit_total = 0;       /* initialize totals */

    scanf("%d %d", &account_number, &balance);   /* initial data */
    print_headers(account_number, balance);      /* initial headers */

    scanf("%d", &transaction_value);      /* get first transaction */
    number_of_transaction = 1;            /* initialize count */
    while (transaction_value != 0){       /* end of data? */
        process_transaction(number_of_transaction, transaction_value,
            &credit_total, &debit_total, &balance);
```

```
        scanf("%d", &transaction_value);      /* next transaction */
        number_of_transaction++;              /* update count */
    }

    print_summary(credit_total, debit_total, balance);
}
```

Processing and printing one transaction is covered by the function `process_transaction`. This function receives the transaction number and the value of the transaction. The function is also supplied with the addresses of the credit and debit totals and the current balance. Through these addresses the current values can be obtained and new updated values assigned. The new assignations are returned to `main` for transmission to the next processing task.

Coding the functions `print_headers` and `print_summary` is trivial. We leave these for the final program listing. The major subproblem we must solve is the coding for function `process_transaction`. Like `main`, we start with an outline:

```
add value of transaction to current balance
IF a credit transaction
THEN
    update current credit total
    print a credit statement line
ELSE
    update current debit total
    print a debit statement line
ENDIF
```

A positive transaction (credit) is added to the current credit total. The credit total is initially set to zero and increases positively when a transaction is accumulated. A negative transaction (debit) is subtracted from the debit total. Subtracting a negative value equates to adding a positive value. The debit total, therefore, also increases positively when a transaction is accumulated. Thus, both the credit and debit totals remain positive throughout the program execution, as required.

The format of a transaction statement line is determined by whether the transaction is a credit or a debit. Two prints using different formats selected by the `if` statement simplify this problem. The function coding is:

```
void process_transaction(const int number, const int transaction,
        int *const credit, int *const debit, int *const balance)
{
    *balance = *balance + transaction;
    if (transaction > 0){
        *credit = *credit + transaction;
        printf("%8d\t%8d\t\t%8d\n", number, transaction, *balance);
    } else {
        *debit = *debit - transaction;
        printf("%8d\t\t%8d\t%8d\n", number, -transaction, *balance);
    }
}
```

The program listing follows.

```
/*
**      Read a series of transactions on a bank account and
**      produce a bank statement summarising these transactions.
**      The program input consists of a sequence of integers.
**      The first value is a positive integer representing
**      the bank account number. The second integer is the
**      initial balance of the account. The remaining data
**      values are either positive or negative. A positive
**      value represents a deposit and a negative value
**      represents a withdrawal. The end-of-data trailer
**      record is the value zero.
*/
#include <stdio.h>

#define LINE      "--------------------------------"\
                  "--------------------------------"


main()
{
   . . . . .
}


/*
**      Process a single transaction and produce a statement
**      line resulting from this. As a side effect, update
**      the balance and either the credit or debit totals.
*/

void process_transaction(const int number, const int transaction,
         int *const credit, int *const debit, int *const balance)
{
   . . . . .
}

void print_headers(const int number, const int balance)
{
   printf("\t\t\tBank Statement\n\n");
   printf("Account number: %6d\n\n", number);
   printf("Transaction     Credit     Debit        Balance\n");
   printf("%s\n", LINE);
   printf("\t\t\t\t\t\t%8d\n", balance);
}


void print_summary(const int credit, const int debit,
         const int balance)
{
   printf("%s\n", LINE);
   printf("Totals\t\t\t%8d\t%8d\t%8d\n", credit, debit, balance);
}
```

6.9 The `switch` statement

The `if-else` statement chain that we encountered in the last section (cf. Program 6.16), where the value of a variable is successively compared against different values, occurs so frequently that a special statement exists for this purpose. This is called the `switch` statement. Its format is:

```
switch(expression){
  case constant-expression-1 :
    statement 1a;
    statement 1b;
    -----------
    -----------
  case constant-expression-2 :
    statement 2a;
    statement 2b;
    -----------
    -----------
    ----
    ----
  case constant-expression-N :
    statement Na;
    statement Nb;
    -----------
    -----------
  default :
    statement Da;
    statement Db;
    -----------
    -----------
}
```

where `switch`, `case` and `default` are reserved keywords.

The control expression enclosed within parentheses is evaluated. The result must be of an integral type including char's. The constant expressions associated with each case keyword must also resolve to an integer. These expressions, called `case labels`, may be an integer constant, a character constant or an integer constant expression. When evaluated, each constant expression must deliver a unique integer value. Duplicates are not permitted.

During execution of the `switch` statement, the control expression is first evaluated. The resulting value is then compared with each `case` label in turn. If a case label value equals the value of the expression, control is passed to the first statement associated with that `case` label. All statements through to the end of the `switch` are then executed. For example:

```
n = 2;
switch(n){
  case  1 : printf("One\n");
  case  2 : printf("Two\n");
  case  3 : printf("Three\n");
```

```
      case  4 : printf("Four\n");
      default : printf("Default\n");
   }
   printf("End of switch\n");
```

The control expression is simply the value of the variable n. When evaluated it is compared against the integer literals 1, 2, 3 and 4. If a match is found, the corresponding statement and all subsequent statements in the switch are obeyed. If no match is found, the default statement(s) are obeyed. The output from the above example is:

```
   Two
   Three
   Four
   Default
   End of switch
```

The statement or statements associated with a case label may also include the null statement. The case label then associates with the statements on the next occurring case label. The following fragment illustrates:

```
   n = 2;
   switch(n){
     case  1 : printf("One\n");
     case  2 :
     case  3 : printf("Two or three\n");
     case  4 : printf("Four\n");
     default : printf("Default\n");
   }
   printf("End of switch\n");
```

and produces the output:

```
   Two or three
   Four
   Default
   End of switch
```

If no case constant expression evaluates to the same value as the control expression, then the statements associated with the default keyword are executed. Using the last program fragment above, but setting:

```
   n = 7;
```

before entering the switch statement, produces the output:

```
   Default
   End of switch
```

The default keyword and its associated group of statements is an optional component of the switch statement. In the illustrations it has been shown as the final element but this is not enforced by the language. If the value of the control expression does not equal any of the constant expressions, and no `default` is present, no statement in the body of the `switch` is executed. This is demonstrated by the example:

```
n = 7;
switch(n){
   case  1 : printf("One\n");
   case  2 :
   case  3 : printf("Two or three\n");
   case  4 : printf("Four\n");
}
printf("End of switch\n");
```

The output from this piece of code is:

```
End of switch
```

We have noted that after control is transferred to a `case` label or to the `default` label, execution continues through successive statements ignoring any additional `case` or `default` labels that are encountered until the end of the `switch` statement is reached. Generally, however, the switch statement is used as a multi-way selector. After transfer to a `case` label or to the `default` label, the group of associated statements is executed, then control is transferred to the end of the `switch` ignoring all other statement groups. This is achieved by making the last statement in each group the `break` statement. The `break` statement is fully discussed in the next section. In the context of a `switch` statement, the `break` statement is used to immediately terminate it. Consider now:

```
n = 3;
switch(n){
   case  1 : printf("One\n");              break;
   case  2 :
   case  3 : printf("Two or three\n");     break;
   case  4 : printf("Four\n");             break;
}
printf("End of switch\n");
```

which generates the output:

```
Two or three
End of switch
```

While the last break is logically unnecessary, it is a good thing to include it as a matter of style. It will help to prevent errors in the event that a fifth `case` label is later added to the `switch` during program maintenance.

The following program illustrates the use of the `switch` statement. The program operates on a character sequence of indeterminate length, terminated with the period symbol. The program counts the number of blanks, the number of tabs, the number of newline symbols and the number of all other symbols (cf. Program 6.15). The outline processing logic of this program is expressed by the PDL:

```
initialize all counters
WHILE read the next character; not the end of data character DO
   SWITCH this character TO
      WHEN (a blank)   increment blank counter
      WHEN (a tab)     increment tab counter
      WHEN (a newline) increment newline counter
      OTHERWISE        increment all other counter
   ENDSWITCH
ENDWHILE
```

PROGRAM 6.17

```
/*
**      A program to separately count the number of blank,
**      tab, newline and other characters. The input data
**      consists of a stream of characters terminated
**      by a period symbol.
*/

#include <stdio.h>

#define BLANK       ' '
#define TAB         '\t'
#define NEWLINE     '\n'
#define PERIOD      '.'

main()
{
   int nblank = 0, ntab = 0, nnewline = 0, nother = 0;
   char c;

   while ((c = getchar()) != PERIOD)
      switch (c){
         case BLANK   : nblank++;   break;
         case TAB     : ntab++;     break;
         case NEWLINE : nnewline++; break;
         default      : nother++;   break;
      }
   printf("%d %d %d %d\n", nblank, ntab, nnewline, nother);
}
```

Note the additional PDL construction used in the last example representing a multi-way `switch`. The structure used is:

```
SWITCH on-some-expression TO
     WHEN (this-value)          these-statements
     WHEN ( ........ )          ....
     ....                       ....
     ....                       ....
     OTHERWISE                  ....
ENDSWITCH
```

If the expression evaluates to a value which matches any of the WHEN clauses, the associated statements, and only these, are executed. The switch then terminates and the program logic continues with the following statement. If no match occurs, the escape mechanism is to the statements of the OTHERWISE clause. Note that our PDL avoids the need to specifically incorporate break statements. Our concern at this level is solely with the overall program design. Equally, no restrictions are placed on the expressions or values. We are allowed to say, for example:

```
SWITCH day-of-week TO
      WHEN (Mon, Tue, Wed, Thu, Fri)   working-days
      OTHERWISE                        weekend
ENDSWITCH
```

Program 6.18 also illustrates the use of the switch statement. The program is supplied with a date in the form of two integers representing the day and the month. The year is known not to be a leap year. The program calculates the date (day, month) of the day following the input date.

PROGRAM 6.18

```
/*
**      Determine tomorrow's date, given the date for
**      today. the year is known not to be a leap year,
**      and so only the day and month are provided as data.
*/

#include <stdio.h>

#define JAN   1
#define FEB   2
#define APR   4
#define JUN   6
#define SEP   9
#define NOV   11
#define DEC   12

main()
{
   int day, month;                            /* program data */
   void tomorrow(int *const, int *const);   /* ref. declaration */

   printf("Enter today's date: ");
   scanf("%d %d", &day, &month);
   tomorrow(&day, &month);
   printf("Tomorrow's date is %d %d\n", day, month);
}

void tomorrow(int *const d, int *const m)
                                      /* compute tomorrow's date */
```

```
{
  int_days_in_month;

  switch (*m){                        /* which month? */
    case APR :
    case JUN :
    case SEP :
    case NOV : days_in_month = 30; break;
    case FEB : days_in_month = 28; break;
    default : days_in_month = 31; break;
  }

  if (*d == days_in_month){     /* end of month? */
    *d = 1;                     /* yes, first day */
    if (*m == DEC)              /* end of year? */
      *m = JAN;
    else
      (*m)++;
  } else
    (*d)++;
}
```

CASE STUDY   6.3 Printing bank cheques

Computerized banking systems issue cheques to bank customers. The cheques include, among other things, the value of the cheque expressed numerically and as words. For example, the numerical sum of money 123:45 is expressed as:

```
ONE HUNDRED AND TWENTY THREE DOLLARS AND FORTY FIVE CENTS
```

A program is required to accept an indeterminate number of numerical monetary values and to output each value in both its numeric form and in its word equivalent form. Each monetary data value appears on a separate line and is represented by two integers separated by a colon symbol. The first integer is the number of dollars. The second integer is always given as two digits and represents the number of cents. All input values are less than 1000 dollars. The data is terminated with the zero monetary value 0:00.

The overall program structure is relatively simple. Each data value is read and processed. This iteration continues until the terminator is read. The program then stops. The PDL is:

```
read the first sum of money
WHILE not the terminating monetary value DO
  print the sum of money numerically
  print the sum of money in words
  read the next sum of money
ENDWHILE
```

Only the step 'print the sum of money in words' causes us any difficulty.

Further work is necessary to refine this stage. We can, in the meantime, relegate it to a subordinate function, passing the value of the dollars and cents as arguments. Armed with both these values the function can do its work. The `main` function is then immediately coded as:

```
main ()
{
  int dollars, cents;     /* input data */
  void do_conversion(const int, const int);

  scanf ("%d:%2d", &dollars, &cents);
  while ( !(dollars == 0 && cents == 0) ){
    printf ("%3d:%02d ", dollars, cents);
    do_conversion (dollars, cents);
    scanf ("%d:%2d", &dollars, &cents);
  }
}
```

The subordinate function, `do_conversion`, receives the monetary sum as two integer values – the number of dollars and the number of cents. The first value contributes to the first part of the alphabetical output as far as the word DOLLARS:

```
........ DOLLARS ....
```

The second value is responsible for the phrase starting AND:

```
.... AND ........
```

Care must be taken if either case is zero. If there are no dollars, the phrase up to and including the AND is omitted. Similarly, if there are no cents, the output stops at DOLLARS. The design for function `do_conversion` is:

```
IF non zero dollars
THEN
      convert dollars into words
      print "DOLLARS" or "DOLLAR"
ENDIF

IF non zero cents
THEN
      IF non zero dollars
      THEN
          print "AND"
      ENDIF
      convert cents into words
      print "CENTS" or "CENT"
ENDIF
```

and is programmed as:

```
void do_conversion (const int dollars, const int cents)
{
  void convert_to_words (const int);
```

```
    if (dollars > 0){
      convert_to_words (dollars);
      if(dollars > 1)
        printf(" DOLLARS");
      else
        printf(" DOLLAR");
    }

    if (cents > 0){
      if (dollars > 0)
        printf (" AND");
      convert_to_words (cents);
      if(cents > 1)
        printf(" CENTS");
      else
        printf(" CENT");
    }
    printf ("\n\n");
  }
```

The interesting feature of this function is that converting both the dollars and the cents into words is achieved with the same function (convert_to_words). The suffix DOLLARS and CENTS is the responsibility of the function do_conversion. Otherwise, the words produced are the same for both the dollars and the cents. The PDL for function convert_to_words is:

```
obtain the number of hundreds in the number
obtain the number of tens in the number
obtain the number of units in the number

IF non zero hundreds
THEN
     convert to words the number of hundreds
     print "HUNDREDS"
ENDIF

IF some tens or some units in the number
THEN
     print "AND"
     IF the tens and units is expressible as teens
     THEN
          convert to words the tens and units
     ELSE
          convert to words the number of tens
          convert to words the number of units
     ENDIF
ENDIF
```

The function convert_to_words is then:

```
void convert_to_words (const int number)
{
```

```
    int  hundreds, tens, units;
    void do_units(const int), do_teens(const int), do_tens(const int);

    hundreds = number / 100;
    tens     = (number % 100) / 10;
    units    = number % 10;

    if (hundreds > 0){
      do_units (hundreds);
      printf (" HUNDRED");
    }

    if (tens + units > 0){
      if (hundreds > 0)
        printf (" AND");
      if (tens == 1)
        do_teens (units);
      else {
        do_tens (tens);
        do_units (units);
      }
    }
}
```

The completed program is listed below, together with some sample input data and the resulting output:

```
/*
**      Accept as input an indeterminate number of monetary
**      values each less than 1000 dollars and output the sum
**      both numerically and in words. Each value is expressed
**      in the form PPP.pp, where PPP represents the dollars
**      and pp represents the cents. The data is terminated
**      with the value 0.00.
*/

#include <stdio.h>

main ()
{
    .....
}


/*
**      Convert a sum of money into words by first expressing
**      the dollars and then expressing the cents.
*/

void do_conversion (const int dollars, const int cents)
{
    .....
}
```

```
/*
**      Convert a numerical value into its equivalent expressed
**      in words.
*/

void convert_to_words (const int number)
{
  .....
}

/*
**      Routines to express selected values in words.
*/

void do_units (const int units)
{
  switch (units){
    case 0 : break;
    case 1 : printf (" ONE");        break;
    case 2 : printf (" TWO");        break;
    case 3 : printf (" THREE");      break;
    case 4 : printf (" FOUR");       break;
    case 5 : printf (" FIVE");       break;
    case 6 : printf (" SIX");        break;
    case 7 : printf (" SEVEN");      break;
    case 8 : printf (" EIGHT");      break;
    case 9 : printf (" NINE");       break;
  }
}


void do_teens (const int units)
{
  switch (units){
    case 0 : printf (" TEN");        break;
    case 1 : printf (" ELEVEN");     break;
    case 2 : printf (" TWELVE");     break;
    case 3 : printf (" THIRTEEN");   break;
    case 4 : printf (" FOURTEEN");   break;
    case 5 : printf (" FIFTEEN");    break;
    case 6 : printf (" SIXTEEN");    break;
    case 7 : printf (" SEVENTEEN");  break;
    case 8 : printf (" EIGHTEEN");   break;
    case 9 : printf (" NINETEEN");   break;
  }
}

void do_tens (const int tens)
{
  switch (tens){
    case 0 : break;
    case 1 : break;
```

```
      case 2 : printf (" TWENTY");      break;
      case 3 : printf (" THIRTY");      break;
      case 4 : printf (" FORTY");       break;
      case 5 : printf (" FIFTY");       break;
      case 6 : printf (" SIXTY");       break;
      case 7 : printf (" SEVENTY");     break;
      case 8 : printf (" EIGHTY");      break;
      case 9 : printf (" NINETY");      break;
    }
}
```

Sample data:

123:45
1:07
10:00
0:66
0:00

Program output:

123:45   ONE HUNDRED AND TWENTY THREE DOLLARS AND FORTY FIVE CENTS

  1:07   ONE DOLLAR AND SEVEN CENTS

 10:00   TEN DOLLARS

  0:66   SIXTY SIX CENTS

6.10 The break statement

The break statement is used to alter the flow of control inside loops and inside switch statements. We have already introduced the break statement in the preceding section, where it was used to cause immediate exit from within the nearest enclosing switch statement. The break statement can also be used with while, for and do statements. Execution of a break statement causes immediate termination of the innermost enclosing loop.

A break statement in loops is normally used in conjunction with an if statement. First, a loop is established to repeat some specified number of times or until some expected condition occurs. If, at any time, some abnormal situation occurs, the loop is terminated. The latter is achieved with a combination of if and break statements.

Program 6.19 illustrates this idea. Essentially, the program is a revised version of Program 6.13. An unknown number of single characters up to and including the period symbol are input. The number of lines in the text is enumerated by counting the number of occurrences of the newline symbol.

Instead of iterating until the terminator is discovered in the input, an infinite loop is established. The loop conveys the fact that an iteration is the major program construct. From within the loop we test for the end of data sentinel, and quit from the loop. The PDL is:

```
initialize the line counter
FOREVER DO
   read the next data character
   IF the terminator symbol
   THEN
      quit the loop
   ENDIF

   IF a newline symbol
   THEN
      increment the line counter
   ENDIF
ENDFOREVER
print the result
```

resulting in the program:

PROGRAM 6.19

```
/*
**      Input a stream of characters from the standard
**      input and count the number of lines of text by
**      enumerating the number of newline symbols. The
**      text is terminated by a period symbol.
*/

#include <stdio.h>

#define PERIOD     '.'
#define NEWLINE    '\n'

#define FOREVER    for (;;)

main()
{
   int  lines = 0;    /* line count */
   char c;            /* data character */

   FOREVER{
      c = getchar();
      if (c == PERIOD)
         break;
      if (c == NEWLINE)
         lines++;
   }

   printf("Number of lines is %d\n", lines);
}
```

The break statement can also reduce the complexity of the expression governing repetition of a loop. A simple description of the normal termination of the loop is handled by the loop test itself. The abnormal termination of the loop is the responsiblity of a break statement within the loop. Program 6.20(a) illustrates this use for the break statement. The program reads and forms the sum of 100 floating point data values. If at any time a negative floating point value is encountered in the data, the summation terminates. First, the PDL:

```
initialize the running total
FOR 100 times DO
  read the next data value
  IF a negative data item
  THEN
    quit the loop
  ENDIF
  add the data value to the running total
ENDFOR
print the result
```

PROGRAM 6.20(a)

```
/*
**      Read and form the sum of at most 100 positive
**      floating point numbers. If at any time a
**      negative value is encountered in the input
**      terminate with the sum thus formed.
*/

#include <stdio.h>

#define MAX      100

main()
{
  float data, sum = 0.0;   /* data, running total */
  int k;                    /* loop counter */

  for (k = 1; k <= MAX; k++){
    scanf("%f", &data);
    if (data < 0.0)
      break;
    sum += data;
  }

  printf("Sum is %f\n", sum);
}
```

Consider the above solution against the following version, Program 6.20(b). This second attempt is more complex and harder to understand since we have combined the tests for normal and abnormal loop termination. The increased complexity also lessens the likelihood that the program is correct.

PROGRAM 6.20(b)

```
/*
**      Read and form the sum of at most 100 positive
**      floating point numbers. If at any time a
**      negative value is encountered in the input
**      terminate with the sum thus formed.
*/

#include <stdio.h>

#define MAX     100
#define FALSE   0
#define TRUE    1

main()
{
  float data, sum = 0.0;   /* data, running total */
  int  k;                  /* loop counter */
  int  abort = FALSE;      /* abnormal termination */

  for (k = 1; k <= MAX && !abort; k++){
    scanf("%f", &data);
    if (data < 0.0)
      abort = TRUE;
    else
      sum += data;
  }

  printf("Sum is %f\n", sum);
}
```

6.11 The `continue` statement

The `continue` statement complements the `break` statement. Its use is restricted to `while`, `for` and `do` loops. When a `continue` statement is executed, control is immediately passed to the test condition of the nearest enclosing loop. All subsequent statements in the body of the loop are ignored for that particular loop iteration. The `continue` statement, like the `break` statement, is normally used in conjunction with an `if` statement. The syntax of the continue statement is simply:

```
continue;
```

The following short program demonstrates an application of the `continue` statement. The program reads ten floating point numbers, summing only the positive values. Negative data values are ignored by skipping the processing actions of the loop. First, the PDL:

```
initialize the running total
FOR 10 times DO
  read the next data value
  IF a negative data item
  THEN
    skip the loop
  ENDIF
  add data value to running total
ENDFOR
```

Then the program:

PROGRAM 6.21

```
/*
**      Input 10 floating point values, summing only
**      those values which are positive.
*/

#include <stdio.h>

#define MAX       10

main()
{
  float data, sum = 0.0;   /* data, running total */
  int  k;                  /* loop counter */

  for (k = 0; k < MAX; k++){
    scanf("%f", &data);
    if (data < 0.0)
      continue;
    sum += data;
  }

  printf("Sum of positive values is %f\n", sum);
}
```

6.12 Summary

1. The three principal program control structures are *sequence*, *selection* and *iteration*. The while, do and for statements provide the loop mechanism in C; selection is provided by the if and switch statements.

2. Logical expressions have an `int` value of 0 or 1, in which 0 represents logical *false* and 1 represents logical *true*. Further, any non-zero value is interpreted as logical true when evaluating a logical expression. Logical expressions are constructed from the relational operators (<, <=, etc.) and the logical operators (&&, ||, !), as well as the usual arithmetic operators.

3. The `while` statement is the fundamental loop construct in C. Since the control expression is tested prior to execution of each iteration, the statement(s) under control of the `while` may be executed zero or more times.

4. The `for` statement is semantically equivalent to the `while` statement, providing an abbreviated version of the latter. A `for` loop, therefore, executes zero or more times.

5. The `do` statement's control expression is computed following execution of the statement body. A `do` loop is therefore guaranteed to be obeyed one or more times.

6. The `if` statement provides a means of choosing whether or not to execute a statement. The `if-else` statement decides which of two statements to execute. In nested `if` statements, the compiler always associates an `else` part with the nearest unresolved preceding `if`.

7. The `switch` statement is a multiple-alternative control statement. It compares an integer expression against many possible values selected from `case` labels.

8. The `break` statement is used to alter flow of control inside loops and `switch` statements. The `break` statement when used with a loop (`while`, `for` and `do`), causes immediate termination of the innermost enclosing loop. When used with a `switch` statement, the `break` causes immediate exit from the enclosing `switch` clause.

9. The `continue` statement is used solely with `while`, `for` and `do` statements, and an execution causes control to pass immediately to the nearest enclosing loop's conditional expression for re-evaluation.

1,5,6,8,4,7,10

6.13 Exercises

1. Give equivalent logical expressions without using the negation operator:

```
!(a > b)                !(a <= b + 3)
!(a + 1 == b + 1)       !(a > 2 || b < 5)
!(a < b && c < d)
```

2. In the context of the following initialized declarations:

```
char c = 'X';
int  h = 2, i = -3, j = 7, k = -19;
```

Complete the following table:

Expression	Equivalent expression	Value
h && i && j	(h && i) && j	1 (true)
h && i || j		
h || i && j		
h || i && j || k		
!h && !j		
!h + !j		
h > j		
h <= j		
(j < k) || h		
j < (k || h)		

3. What is the difference between the two operators = and == ?

4. Is the following statement correct? If not, why not?

```
if (q >= r)
    printf("q is greater than or equal to r");
    a = b;
else
    printf("r is less than q");
    x = y;
```

5. We have already explained that:

```
while(1){
    ....
}
```

is an infinite loop. What happens when the following program is executed? If you are unsure, try it:

```
#include <stdio.h>
main()
{
  while(-22.55){
    printf("run forever, perhaps?");
  }
}
```

run forever
(-22.55 is not equal to 0)

6. What happens when you run the following program on your system? If it does not run as expected, change it so that it does:

```
#include <stdio.h>
main()
{
  float x, total = 0.0;
  for(x = 0.0; x != 0.9; x += 0.1){    /* bad test */
    total += x;
    printf("x= %f, running total= %f\n", x, total);
  }
}
```

< 1.0

7. Input three positive integers representing the sides of a triangle, and determine whether they form a valid triangle. (Hint: In a triangle, the sum of any two sides must always be greater than the third side.)

8. Write a program which computes the sum of the first ten integers. Modify the program to compute the sum of the first N integers, where N is given as a data value.

9. Prepare a function `quotient` which finds the quotient of two positive integers using only the operations of addition and subtraction:

```
int quotient(int numerator, int denominator)
```

Employ this function in a program which inputs two integers and outputs their `quotient`.

10. Prepare a function called `power` which computes a to the power b for two non-negative integer values a and b, using repeated multiplication:

```
long int power(const int a, const int b)
```

Then write a program to tabulate x, x^2 and x^3 for x = , 2, ... , 10.

11. Write a program that reads a single positive integer data value and extracts each digit from the integer and displays it as a word. For example, the input value 932 should display:

```
932: nine three two
```

12. Write a program that reads a number, then reads a single digit and determines how many times the digit occurs in the number.

13. Data to a program consists of a sequence of characters of unknown length. The data set is terminated with a unique period symbol. Write a program which counts the number of lines, the number of words and the number of characters in the input. Each input line is terminated by the newline symbol. A word is any sequence of characters that does not contain a blank, tab or newline symbol. The terminating period is not included in any count.

14. Using the data of Question 13, write a program which prints the words in the input one per line.

15. A prime number is one that is divisible only by 1 and by itself. Write a program to input a series of numbers and determine whether they are prime or not. Perhaps the simplest way to determine if a number is prime is to test whether the number is divisible by any value from 2 to one less than the number. The process can be shortened appreciably by performing the test from 2 to some lesser value than that given. How is this value obtained? Use it in your solution.

16. Write a program to display a multiplication table with the format shown below. The range of the table is given as program input:

```
X     1     2     3     4
----------------------------
1     1     2     3     4
2     2     4     6     8
3     3     6     9     12
4     4     8     12    16
```

17. Write a program to operate on the data of Question 13 and to compress repeated characters. The program copies its input to its output, replacing strings of repeating character sequences by [nX], where n is an integer count of the number of repetitions, and X is the character. Restrict the input not to include the characters [,] or digits. For example, the input:

```
ABCCCDEEFFFFG.
```

produces the output:

```
AB[3C]D[2E][4F]G.
```

Prepare a second program to expand the compressed text. Using the output of the first program, this second program should recreate the original input.

18. Input to a program is the monthly sales figures for a sales team. For each salesman, show his identification number, total sales, value of sales, profit (total sales − value of sales), and commission (= 10% of profit). The output to have the format:

NUMBER	TOTAL SALES(A)	VALUE(B)	PROFIT (A−B)	COMMISSION 10%(A−B)
1234	234.56	174.56	60.00	6.00
|	|	|	|	|
|	|	|	|	|
xxxx	xxx.xx	xxx.xx	xxx.xx	xx.xx
TOTALS	xxxx.xx	xxxx.xx	xxxx.xx	xxx.xx

19. Write a program which accepts a time expressed in hours, minutes and seconds and verbalizes that time as suggested by the following outputs:

```
09:10:00    ten past nine
10:45:00    quarter to eleven
11:15:00    quarter past eleven
17:30:00    half past five
19:50:00    ten to eight
06:12:29    just after ten past six
06:12:30    just before quarter past six
00:17:29    just after quarter past midnight
```

7

Programming in the large

WRITING LARGE PROGRAMS in C, as in any language, poses difficult problems of organization. Many modern programming languages contain constructs designed to help structure large systems. These constructs, variously known as *modules* or *packages*, make it possible to partition large software systems into reasonable sized components. Further, they usually support separate compilation of *program units* and make it possible to assemble libraries of shareable components. The use of such constructs to impose structure on large programs is often called 'programming in the large' in contrast to 'programming in the small', which is concerned with the detailed implementation of algorithms in terms of data items and program control structures.

When we design software we must endeavour to capture the structure of the design in a form that reflects our view of the real world problem. We have alluded to these issues in earlier chapters by having our program structures reflect the problem's data structures. Effective modifications to the system must honour the original and existing structures, otherwise; we apply fragmentary patches which destroy the original fabric of the software.

As we explore larger, even more complex problem domains, our difficulties increase and our software systems become unmanageably complex. Software engineering is concerned with building large software systems which are reliable, understandable, and easy to maintain and modify. These goals are achieved by applying a number of principles including abstraction, modularity, information hiding and localization.

Our inability to cope with complexity is at the root of all our programming problems. The basic tool we use to overcome complexity is *abstraction*. Abstraction is a conscious decision to ignore irrelevant details and to concentrate only on the relevant properties. Functional decomposition is a form of abstraction. At the highest problem and program levels we ignore details to concentrate on the original higher-level structures. Using a standard library routine such as `printf` is an application of functional abstraction. We are not concerned with the inner operations of this function, only how to use it. Equally, when we introduce our own functions, at the design stage the actual implementation details are ignored. The only relevant features are its operation and its interface. The implementation is detail to be considered later.

Ultimately our abstractions must be realized as program parts. This may involve

150

the definition of data types and variables to represent the abstract concept, and a set of functions to implement the applicable operations. For every abstraction in a program, a module is constructed. A module or program unit is a resource centre – a collection of data types, variables and functions for the particular abstraction. This way we can look upon the module in terms of *what* it does rather than *how* it does it. The details of implementation need not concern us, only the interface to the facilities supported by the module.

The C programming language supports independent compilation of program units. We shall use the term 'program unit' to emphasize our interest in program construction rather than separate compilation. A program unit is a collection of related resources – data and operations. Functions (operations) and data items may be *private* or *public* elements of a program unit. Public resources are accessible from other program units. Private members are inaccessible beyond the program unit in which they are declared and provide support for *information hiding.*

The aim of information hiding is to make inaccessible those details which do not concern other parts of the programming system. Information hiding also makes programs more secure. Hidden information may not be corrupted by a program unit which is not supposed to have access to that information. In certain circumstances, information hiding can also facilitate data independence – the data representation may be changed without recourse to the program units which make use of that data. The C program unit is thus the cornerstone of abstraction.

In the next two sections we shall consider abstraction through data design and through consideration of those language features necessary to support such an approach. The remainder of the chapter details the relevant language constructs. In subsequent chapters, particularly with the larger case studies, we will use these additional facilities to control the construction of the software.

7.1 Abstract data types

Much of the early work in software engineering and structured programming concentrated on procedural decomposition and upon the use of control structures in programming languages. An equally important area is data decomposition and the selection of appropriate logical and physical data structures in programs. *Abstract data types* provide a way of organizing and designing programs.

The essential idea behind an abstract data type is that it consists of a set of operators and an implementation. The former is visible and hence available to the user or client, while the latter is hidden. To use the data type it is not necessary to know the actual representation. Strictly, the crucial aspect of data abstraction is that knowledge about the implementation is not used in any user program.

As an example, suppose in our problem space we identify an object exhibiting the behaviour of a queue. The queue, therefore, may be considered as an (abstract) data object. The meaningful operations that may be applied to queues might include:

`createq(q)`	– create a new empty queue named q
`enterq(i, q)`	– data item i joins end of queue q
`serveq(q)`	– remove the item at the front of queue q
`emptyq(q)`	– test whether queue q is empty
`lengthq(q)`	– determine the number of items in queue q

The description of the abstract data structure `queue` and the operations upon the structure have been developed jointly without recourse to low-level program representations. The queue now becomes an abstract data structure with supporting operations which can be referred to in other parts of the system without requiring any knowledge of their implementation. The data objects and associated operations are packaged into a C program unit.

Identifying those program modules that must operate directly upon the logical data structures is an important activity during this design phase. This way, the *scope of effect* of individual data design decisions can be constrained (information hiding). The scope of effect concept may be used to measure the impact of changes to the system by quantifying the number of program modules that are affected by changes in a given module. By this means we are able to *decouple* one object from another.

One should attempt to minimize the scope of effect of design decisions by minimizing the number of modules that are aware of the representation chosen for any data object. As a consequence, only the basic operations upon an object need to be aware of the representation. Other parts of the software system can be constrained to use only the operations provided and can be prevented from modifying or even inspecting the physical representation.

As a result, one could change the actual representation without affecting other parts of the system. For example, in our queue we may initially realize it with an array (Chapters 11 and 12). We may subsequently rework the implementation as a linked list (Chapter 16). This is a consequence of our program design where changes are much more localized. With functional decomposition, a program's data is frequently global to the entire system, so that any representation changes affect all subordinate modules.

It is common to have multiple levels of abstraction in data design. If one particular physical representation for queues is chosen, and that concrete form is associated with another abstraction for which an implementation already exists, then the queue is built on this second abstraction. The queue operations use the subordinate operations as another instance of data abstraction without recourse to their representational detail.

The data decomposition is derived from our modelling of reality in terms of the objects and their operations present in the problem space. The result is that we structure our system around the objects that exist in our model. Further, we may also find that there are several similar objects in the problem and we would, therefore, establish a *class* of objects of which there are many instances, sharing common characteristics. From this we can derive general, reusable items of code.

7.2 Designing into C

In expressing our problem solution we require a language which provides sufficient tools so that our view of the problem space is directly expressible in that language. The language must provide facilities to express both the objects and operations on these objects of the real world problem. Only by having these capabilities will we be able to express our problem solution in terms of the structures of the problem space.

C is such a programming language. It provides a rich set of constructs for describing both data structures and operations upon these objects. Further, it offers a packaging facility by which we may build our abstractions of the problem into the program. The package or program unit is the cornerstone of abstraction, information hiding, visibility and locality.

We represent compileable program units as rectangular diagrams, annotated with the resources of the unit. The invisible features remain fully enclosed within the diagram. The *exportable* resources are shown in windows, accessible beyond the module. For example, in Figure 7.1 variable `length` and function `middle` are invisible outside the unit, while functions `left` and `right` are exportable, and hence may be used in other program units.

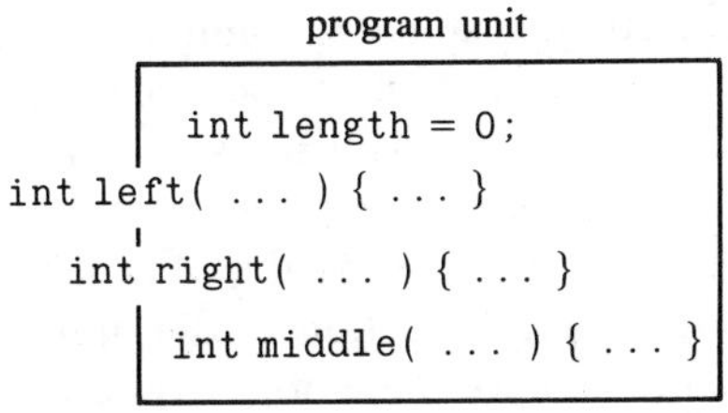

```
                        program unit

                  int length = 0;
        int left( ... ) { ... }
            int right( ... ) { ... }
                  int middle( ... ) { ... }
```

Figure 7.1

The provision of program units offer a number of advantages. These include:

1. Abstract data types, as described in the preceding section. The representation of the abstract data type is visible only within the module in which it is specified. Another application program module may manipulate the abstract data type through the provision of exportable primitive operations (external functions, Section 7.5). Furthermore, the representation of the abstract data type may be changed without affecting the higher-level program modules that employ these primitives.

2. Related operations may be grouped together, sharing variables in a controlled way. Data structures may be made private to a program unit and not exportable to other program units.

3. The module is a convenient unit for separate compilation. A module is constructed as a self-contained program unit. No references to its environment, other than external function calls, means that it can be compiled independent of other modules.

The C programming language is not the perfect vehicle on which to base our software engineering principles. It is incapable of enforcing strict rules upon the programmer. For example, it lacks the strong type checking required. Its packaging facility is only provided to support separate compilation. Nevertheless, the features of C should be fully exploited in the design of large scale software systems.

A programming principle is that the names of objects in a program should be introduced close to where they are used and only be accessible to those parts of the program where they are required. In C, this is achieved through the *scope* rules. The block structure of C permits the declaration of variables at any level.

The declaration of a variable within a block (automatic or local variables) restricts the scope of that variable to that block. Storage associated with the variable is allocated at run time when the block is entered and then released when the block is left. Blocks may be nested so that local variables can be introduced close to where they are required with access to variables in an outer block permitted from an inner block.

Multi-level locality contributes significantly to program readability. The characteristics of names are declared close to where they are used. The provision of local names also means that the temptation to use one variable for different tasks in different parts of a program can be avoided. This is normal practice in languages that do not support block structure and is a common source of error.

Block structure on its own is an inadequate mechanism for controlling the visibility of names. An additional mechanism is required to control which local names may be accessed from outside the program unit in which the names are declared. It should also be possible to specify that a variable local to a program unit should maintain its value from one activation of the unit to the next.

The constructs in C used to achieve these objectives are the *storage class*, the *scope* and the *linkage* of objects. The storage class determines the lifetime of the storage space associated with the object. A named object has a scope which is the region of the program over which it is known. Linkage determines whether the same name in different scopes refers to the same object

7.3 Storage classes

The Standard has regularized these related issues. There are only two storage classes: *automatic* and *static*. Section 5.3 introduced the storage class `auto`. Automatic variables are local to the function body in which they are declared. The scope of an identifier declared at the head of a block extends to the end of that block. Function parameters are treated similarly.

Static objects may be local to a block or external to all blocks. Unlike automatic variables, local static variables retain their value across function calls. Static objects are declared with the storage class keyword `static`.

External declarations introduce objects which are defined outside of functions. The scope of external declarations extends to the end of the program unit. The storage class for an externally declared object may be specified as `extern` or `static` or may be omitted.

If the first external declaration for a function or a variable includes the specifier `static`, then that identifier has *internal linkage*. Functions and data items declared in a program unit with storage class `static` are unique and private to that unit and are not exportable to other units.

Otherwise, the object is assumed to have *external linkage*, and every instance of the name of that object refers to the same object in every program unit. The storage class specifier `extern` is used to connect occurrences of the same name across separate program units. In this way functions and data items may be exported into one program unit from another.

7.4 Storage class `auto`

C is not a block structured programming language in the sense of Algol or Pascal. In these languages, functions may be declared nested within other functions. On the other hand, C does permit the declaration of variables in a block structured fashion. Variables declared in the body of a function have storage class `auto` (automatic). Automatic variables are internal to a function; they come into existence when a function is entered (called), and disappear when it returns. Arguments to functions are processed in a similar manner.

The term *scope* is used to define the region of the C program text over which a declaration is active. An identifier declared at the beginning of a function block has a scope that extends from its declaration to the end of the block. Formal arguments to a function also have the function block as their scope. In the function shown below, the variable `temp` has the storage class `auto` (as does the formal arguments a and b). The scope of the variable `temp` is the body of the function and cannot be accessed outside of this function.

```
void order(int *const a, int *const b)
    /* arrange a, b into ascending order */
{
    int temp;

    if(*a > *b){
        temp = *a;
        *a = *b;
        *b = temp;
    }
}
```

The declaration for variable `temp` explicitly specifies the type `int` and implicitly specifies the storage class `auto`. It is permissible to include the storage class explicitly with the reserved keyword `auto`, as in:

```
auto int temp;
```

though in practice it is usually omitted.

A function body is a *compound statement* – also called a *block*. A compound statement consists of a possibly empty sequence of declarations followed by a possibly empty sequence of statements, all enclosed in braces:

```
{
    optional-declaration-sequence
    optional-statement-sequence
}
```

Additionally, a compound statement may appear as a replacement for any single statement. When the compound statement has no declarations, it simply represents a group of statements. In the function `order`, a statement group is used with the `if` statement:

```
if(*a > *b){
    temp = *a;      /* compound statement */
    *a = *b;
    *b = temp;
}
```

When the compound statement includes declarations, it brings into existence a new scope. Recognizing that the variable `temp` is only required within the `if` statement, the function may be rewritten:

```
void order(int *const a, int *const b)
    /* arrange a, b into ascending order */
{
    if(*a > *b){
        int temp = *a;
        *a = *b;
        *b = temp;
    }
}
```

The scope of the variable `temp` is reduced to the inner compound statement which is part of the `if` statement. Any reference to the variable `temp` outwith this compound statement is illegal, even within the remainder of the function itself.

Compound statements that are nested may include declarations for identifiers with names the same as those in surrounding blocks. This introduces the concept of *visibility*. In the assignment:

```
*b = temp;
```

appearing in the function order, the use of the identifier `temp` is bound to the declaration:

```
int temp = *a;
```

in the compound statement in which they both appear. The declaration for this identifier is said to be visible since the use of the identifier is associated with that declaration.

A declaration for an identifier can become temporarily invisible when the declaration for an identifier with the same name appears in an enclosing inner compound statement. For example, in the following program the declaration for the integer variable sum is hidden by the declaration of sum as a floating point variable in the inner block. This loss of visibility is temporary. The integer variable sum reappears when the inner block terminates.

PROGRAM 7.1

```
/*
**      A program to demonstrate the concepts of scope
**      and visibility. Variables in an inner block with
**      the same name as those on an outer block
**      temporarily make invisible those outside the
**      block.
*/

#include <stdio.h>

main()
{
   int sum = 10;                   /* sum at the top level */

   {                              /* inner block */
     float sum = 3.1416;          /* outer sum hidden */
     printf("Inner sum (float): %6.4f\n", sum);
   }

   printf("Outer sum (int): %2d\n", sum);
}
```

The output from this program is:

```
Inner sum (float): 3.1416
Outer sum (int): 10
```

The declaration of an automatic variable may also be accompanied by an initializer. The initializer is any expression which specifies the initial value a variable may have at the beginning of its lifetime. An automatic variable comes into existence upon entry to the compound statement in which it is declared. The initial expression may employ any item having a valid run time value at the point of entry to the block. The following program illustrates these ideas.

PROGRAM 7.2

```
/*
**          Initialization of local variables by any known
**          run-time expression.
*/

#include <stdio.h>

main ()
{
  int  k;                          /* loop control */
  void square (const int);         /* referencing declaration */

  for (k = 1; k < 10; k++)
    square (k);
}


void square (const int d)
{
  int dsquared = d * d;     /* initialized expression */

  printf ("%2d squared is %3d\n". d, dsquared);
}
```

The automatic variable `dsquared` declared in the body of the function `square`, and local to it, has a perfectly valid initializer. The initializer is based on the formal argument d. When the function is executed an actual value for the argument will be available to initialize `dsquared`. The initialization takes place each time the automatic variable is established; that is, each time the function `square` is invoked. At each call a different actual argument value is provided and a different initial value computed. The program output is thus:

```
1 squared is  1
2 squared is  4
3 squared is  9
4 squared is 16
5 squared is 25
6 squared is 36
7 squared is 49
8 squared is 64
9 squared is 81
```

7.5 Storage class specifier `extern`

A C program consists of a collection of *external* objects. The adjective external is used in contrast to *internal* which describes the arguments and automatic variables defined in functions. External items are defined outside of functions. Functions themselves are external since C does not permit functions to be declared inside other functions. These external objects have external linkage.

In the programs that we have developed, it has been assumed that all the program source code resides in a single file. C actively supports the concept of modular programming in that it does not require that all the code for a program be contained in a single source file. These separate modules equate to our idea of a program unit.

To allow one function in one program unit to call another function in a second program unit, an *external referencing declaration* is required. The declaration informs the compiler that a function is to be called separately from its definition, that the function has a particular return type, and that the function's definition is in another program unit. These declarations are similar to prototype declarations but are preceded by the keyword `extern`.

Consider an application constructed from two program units `main.c` and `time.c`. The program determines the difference between two times both expressed as a twenty-four-hour clock time.

The `main` function resides in the program unit `main.c`. The problem solution is expressed in terms of the subordinate functions `hms_to_time` and `time_to_hms`. Both these complementary functions are contained in the second program unit. Function `hms_to_time` converts a twenty-four-hour clock time into its equivalent number of seconds. Function `time_to_hms` performs the inverse operation. Using our notation, the second program unit is shown by Figure 7.2.

```
                          time.c
         ┌─────────────────────────────────────────┐
         │ long int hms_to_time( ... ) { ... }      │
         │ void time_to_hms( ... ) { ... }          │
         └─────────────────────────────────────────┘
```

Figure 7.2

Both these functions are *exported from* this module and imported into the client program unit `main.c`. The latter thus contains two external referencing declarations for these subordinate functions. The coding for these two program units is then:

PROGRAM 7.3

```
/*
**      Determine the difference between two 24-hour
**      clock times. The input data and the result
**      are all expressed in the same 24-hour format.
*/

#include <stdio.h>
#include <stdlib.h>
```

```
main()
{
  int      hours1, minutes1, seconds1;   /* 1st time */
  int      hours2, minutes2, seconds2;   /* 2nd time */
  int      hours, minutes, seconds;      /* result */
  long int time1, time2;                 /* conversions */

                /* external referencing declarations */
  extern long int hms_to_time(const int, const int, const int);
  extern void time_to_hms(const long int,
                   int *const, int *const, int *const);

  scanf("%d %d %d", &hours1, &minutes1, &seconds1);
  scanf("%d %d %d", &hours2, &minutes2, &seconds2);

  time1 = hms_to_time(hours1, minutes1, seconds1);
  time2 = hms_to_time(hours2, minutes2, seconds2);

  time_to_hms(labs(time1-time2), &hours, &minutes, &seconds);
  printf("The difference is %d %d %d\n", hours, minutes, seconds);
}




/*
**        File:   time.c
**
**        Two functions to convert between a time measured
**        in a total number of seconds and a time expressed
**        in hours, minutes and seconds. Each function is
**        the complement of the other.
*/

#include <stdio.h>

#define SECS_IN_MIN             60
#define MINS_IN_HOUR            60

void time_to_hms (const long int t,
                   int *const h, int *const m, int *const s)
{
  int mins;

  mins = (int)(t / SECS_IN_MIN);
  *s   = (int)(t % SECS_IN_MIN);
  *m   = mins % MINS_IN_HOUR;
  *h   = mins / MINS_IN_HOUR;
}


long int hms_to_time (const int h, const int m, const int s)
{
```

```
      return(((long)h * MINS_IN_HOUR + m) * SECS_IN_MIN + s);
   }
```

Further, the C programmer who is the author of the program unit `time.c` minimizes the burden on the client by providing a header file containing all the necessary external declarations. We extend our notation by showing both the program unit and its associated header file with Figure 7.3.

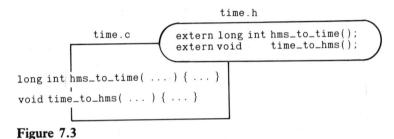

Figure 7.3

The actual content of this header file would contain:

```
/*
**    File:      time.h
**
**    Header file providing the specification of the
**    the two time conversion functions.
*/

extern long int hms_to_time(const int, const int, const int);
extern void time_to_hms(const long int,
                   int *const, int *const, int *const);
```

The two external referencing declarations in the application program unit (`main.c`) can then be replaced by a preprocessor `#include` statement:

```
#include "time.h"
```

The C programming language also supports external variables. An external variable is declared outside a function. Such variables are described as *global* since they may be referenced in the body of functions.

Because external variables are globally accessible, they provide an alternative to function arguments and return values as a means of communicating data between functions. An external variable has scope that extends from its declaration point to the end of the source program unit in which it appears. Any function declaration following this point may access the external variable by simply referring to its name.

We present these ideas by introducing a program unit for pseudo random number generation. The functions in the unit produce an apparently random sequence of integer values. A very simple generator is employed to reduce complexity. The sequence begins with an initial value provided as an argument to the function set_random. Successive values of the sequence are produced by the integer function random. Each new value is computed from the preceding value, which must, therefore, exist across successive calls of function random. Whereas automatic variables exist when a function is entered and disappear when it is left, external variables are *permanent*. Thus if two functions share data or one function is repeatedly called and uses the preceding value of some variable, then that variable has storage class extern. The program unit random.c has the signature shown in Figure 7.4.

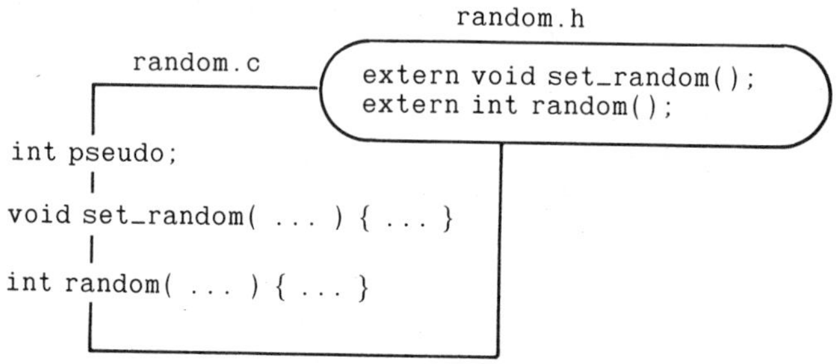

Figure 7.4

In the program unit random.c, the external variable pseudo can be referenced by both functions. This is as a consequence of its scope being from the point of declaration to the end of the source file in which it is declared. Thus, function set_random can assign to pseudo an initial value, while function random can use it to compute a new random value.

The implementation for this program unit is as follows:

```
/*
**      File:          random.c
**
**      Package of pseudo random number generating
**      code. Each random is generated from the
**      previous. The initial value is established
**      by the function set_random.
*/

#include <stdio.h>

#define MULTIPLIER      97
#define MODULUS         256
#define INCREMENT       59

int pseudo;                         /* permanent */

void set_random(const int seed)
{
```

```
    pseudo = seed;
}

int random(void)
{
    pseudo = (MULTIPLIER * pseudo + INCREMENT) % MODULUS;
    return (pseudo);
}
```

The associated header file for this program unit is given below. It is incorporated into an application program using an #include preprocessor statement, and provides the necessary external referencing declarations:

```
/*
**      File:          random.h
**
**      Specification of the exportable items from
**      the random number package
*/

extern void set_random(const int);
extern int  random(void);
```

We now complete our application program. A program simulates the throw of a six sided die. The program tabulates the number of occurrences of each of the six sides of the die which is thrown one hundred times.

PROGRAM 7.4

```
/*
**      Tabulate the number of occurrences of each
**      of the six sides of a die which is thrown
**      100 times.
*/

#include <stdio.h>
#include "random.h"

#define SIDES        6
#define TIMES        100
#define SEED         17

main()
{
    int throw, face;
    int one = 0, two = 0, three = 0,
        four = 0, five = 0, six = 0;

    set_random(SEED);
    for (throw = 1; throw <= TIMES; throw++){
        face = random() % SIDES + 1;    /* 1 to 6 inclusive */
```

```
    switch (face){
       case 1: one++;      break;
       case 2: two++;      break;
       case 3: three++;    break;
       case 4: four++;     break;
       case 5: five++;     break;
       case 6: six++;      break;
    }
}

    printf("Face distribution %d %d %d %d %d %d\n",
        one, two, three, four, five, six);
}
```

Note how the header file random.h is included at the topmost level. This means that these external references have global scope and can be referenced in any function in the program unit containing their declarations. Hence a function subordinate to main appearing in the same file may also use any of the randomizing functions.

The desire to make every program variable an external object, because it seems to simplify communication, must be resisted. First, it is difficult to modify such programs – there are too many functions using and modifying the values of these global variables. Second, the previous generality of functions programmed in terms of their arguments and local variables is, in this new version, now inextricably wired to the names of the external variables. Functions written with arguments are self-contained entities that could usefully be employed in other programs.

In the absence of explicit initialization, external variables are guaranteed to be set to zero. It is generally considered good programming practice, however, to show all initializations explicitly. To avoid any errors caused by the application programmer failing to initialize the random sequence, variable pseudo is explicitly initialized to 1 (see Figure 7.5).

The visibility of an external variable may be temporarily obscured by the declaration for an automatic variable within a function having the same name as the external variable. For example, consider Program 7.5.

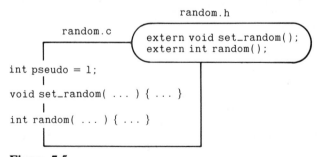

Figure 7.5

PROGRAM 7.5

```
/*
**        The visibility of external variables may be
**        temporarily obscured by the declaration for an
**        automatic variable in a function. Variable
**        sum in the program exhibits this feature.
*/

#include <stdio.h>

int sum;              /* defining declaration .... */
                      /* .... for external variable */

main()
{
   void subroutine(void);    /* forward reference */

   sum = 15;               /* the external variable */
   subroutine();           /* call the function */
   printf("External sum is %d\n", sum);
}


void subroutine(void)
{
   float sum = 1.234;       /* auto, shields external */

   printf("Local sum is %5.3f\n", sum);
}
```

The variable sum assigned the value 15 in the main function binds to the declaration for the external variable of type integer. However, within the function subroutine the variable sum appearing in the printf function call associates with the declaration for the local of type float. Thus the output from the program is:

```
Local sum is 1.234
External sum is 15
```

External variables are initialized conceptually at compile time. The initialization is performed once. The initial value may be any constant expression:

```
#define KILO              1024

int sum = 0;
long int memory = 64 * KILO;
char ampersand = '&';
```

Once again we emphasize the distinction between the *declaration* of an external variable and its *definition*. A declaration announces the properties of a variable (primarily its type). A definition additionally causes storage to be allocated. There must be only *one* definition of an external variable. There may be any number of `extern` declarations to access it. One may also appear in the program unit containing the definition. Only the definition may include an initializer.

7.6 Storage class static

We know that variables may be declared either within a function body or outside the body of a function. We refer to the former as local variables and to the latter as global variables. `Static` variables offer a new class of storage management. `Static` variables may be either local or global.

Local `static` variables are internal to the particular function in which they are declared, that is, they have local scope. Unlike automatic variables, `static` variables remain in existence, they do not come and go each time a function is called and they retain their values between function calls. Internal `static` variables provide *private* and *permanent* variable storage to a function.

`Static` variables, like externals, may be initialized with a constant expression. A `static` local variable is initialized once at the start of program execution. Thereafter, the value of a `static` variable when leaving a function is the same when the function is next entered. This is demonstrated by the following program.

PROGRAM 7.6

```
/*
**      Local static variables are initialized once
**      at compile time. Local variables, on the other
**      hand, are initialized each time the function
**      is entered.
*/

#include <stdio.h>

main()
{
  int i;                    /* loop counter */
  void subroutine(void);    /* forward reference */

  for (i = 0; i < 5; i++)
    subroutine();
}


void subroutine(void)
{
```

```
static int static_var = 0;     /* performed once */
int        auto_var   = 0;     /* for every function call */

printf("automatic = %d, static = %d\n", auto_var, static_var);

auto_var++;                     /* redundant operation */
static_var++;                   /* carried forward */
}
```

The function subroutine contains declarations for two local variables. The variable auto_var is an automatic of type int. The variable is initialized to zero at each function invocation. The increment performed on this variable, following the printf call, is lost on function termination. On the other hand, the initialization of the local static variable static_var is performed once at program invocation but the increment is executed on each function call. As a consequence, the output from the program is:

```
automatic = 0, static = 0
automatic = 0, static = 1
automatic = 0, static = 2
automatic = 0, static = 3
automatic = 0, static = 4
```

External static variables are also supported by C. An external static variable is known within the remainder of the source file in which it is declared, following the point of declaration, but not in any other program file. External static variables cannot be exported from a program unit. In C, static connotes not only permanence but also a degree of *privacy*. Internal static variables are known only inside the function in which they are declared; external static variables are known only within the source file in which they are declared. Their names do not interfere with variables or functions of the same name appearing in other files.

In the program unit random.c introduced in the preceding section, the external variable pseudo is used to hold successive values of the sequence of random numbers. The associated header file random.h provides the application program unit with the external references to the two exportable functions. There is nothing, however, to stop the application program from also including an external reference to the variable pseudo. If the application program contains the declaration:

```
extern int pseudo;
```

then this variable may now be referenced in any application program statement. In particular, it is capable of being erroneously assigned. The effect would be, of course, to corrupt the sequence of pseudo random numbers.

By giving this variable storage class static (strictly, external static), it will be global to the functions in the program unit in which it is declared, but not exportable to other program units. Controlled access to this variable is then provided by the exportable functions. Figure 7.6 illustrates how the program unit now reads.

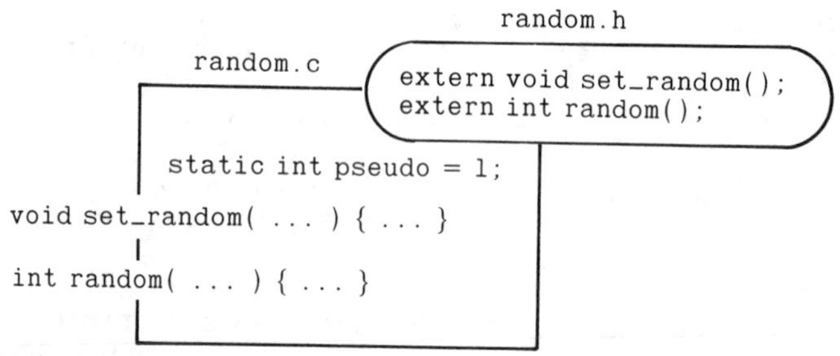

Figure 7.6

The application's programmer cannot now misuse the variable `pseudo`. Further, a link error would occur if the client program unit contained an explicit external referencing declaration to variable `pseudo`. The identifier `pseudo` may, however, be used in some other different context, for example, as a local or global variable in program unit `main.c`. It is not confused with the private variable with the same name in program unit `random.c`.

The storage class `static` can also be applied to functions. External `static` functions are known only within the source file in which they are declared. The concept of privacy equally well applies to functions as well as to `static` variables. External functions are exportable to other program units, whereas external `static` functions are not. This way the programmer of a module may select which functions in the module are to be accessible in other program units. External `static` functions can be considered as the building blocks of a module from which higher-level functions are constructed. These higher-level functions are exported to the application program, while the lower-level functions remain concealed. External `static` functions support the concept of information hiding.

7.7 Storage class specifier `register`

The final storage class specifier is called `register`. A `register` declaration informs the compiler that a variable will be referenced on numerous occassions and, where possible, such variables should use the CPU registers. The result may be a smaller and faster program.

The storage class `register` is only applicable to automatic variables and to function arguments. This storage class is indicated by prefixing a normal declaration with the reserved keyword `register`. A function to swap two integer values written in terms of `register` variables is:

```
void swap (register int *a, register int *b)
{
    register int temp = *a;
```

```
    *a = *b;
    *b = temp;
}
```

Register variables are restricted in a number of ways. First, most CPU's have a small number of registers available. Therefore, only a few variables in each function may be kept in registers. Where a C programmer names too many `register` class variables for the number of available CPU registers, the C compiler simply ignores the storage class `register` on the remaining declarations.

Storage class `register` is also restricted to certain types. This is very much machine-dependent. Often, the only supported types are int, char and pointer. The local system documentation needs to be consulted on this matter.

One is not allowed to take the address of a `register` variable. The address operator (&) is used to obtain the memory address of a variable. Where that variable resides in a CPU register, such an operation is meaningless.

None of the remaining examples in this book use `register` variables. Where some piece of logic is identified as time-critical, `register` storage class should be used. Unless specifically mentioned, we shall choose to ignore this storage class.

7.8 Storage classes, linkage and header files

We have shown that a C program consists of a collection of program units. They, in turn, consist of a set of external objects which are either functions or variables. By default, external objects with the same name must refer to the same thing. This is the property of *external linkage*. For example, consider the two files:

```
/* File1.c: */
    int x = 10;
    int f(void) { /* .. the body of function .. */ }

/* File2.c: */
    extern int x;
    extern int f(void);
    void g(void) { .. = f(); .. }
```

The variable x and the function f referenced in `File2.c` are the objects *defined* in `File1.c`.

An object may be made local to a program unit by use of the storage class specifier `static`. If the first external declaration for a function or variable includes the `static` specifier, the object has *internal linkage*. For example:

```
/* File1.c: */
    static int y = 20;
    static int h(void) { .... }

/* File2.c: */
    static int y = 30;
    extern int h(void);
```

Since each variable y is declared `static`, they are considered distinct objects sharing the same name. The definition for function h in `Filel.c` makes it private to this file. The external referencing declaration for h in `File2.c` will be accepted by the compiler, but will be reported as a linkage error by the linker.

A program spread across multiple files raises one further issue – shared definitions and declarations. Centralizing this information reduces the likelihood of introducing problems. We place all the common material in header files. In Program 7.3, for example, the author of the unit `time.c` also provides a header file containing the declarations for the exported functions. The header file centralizes these declarations for any program unit in an application program requiring these functions.

A header file typically contains:

macro definitions	`/* eg #define SECS_IN_MIN 60*/`
data declarations	`/* eg extern int x;        */`
function declarations	`/* eg extern int f(void);  */`
other include directives	`/* eg #include "defs.h"    */`
type definitions	`/*    see Chapter 9       */`
trivially, comments	`/*    such as this        */`

A header file would never contain the following items since they would result in duplicate definitions if the file was included into a number of program units for some application:

data definitions	`/* eg int sum = 0;        */`
function definitions	`/* eg void nothing(void){}*/`

7.9 Epilogue

We complete this chapter by reconsidering the program involving random number generation in terms of abstract data types. We have argued that the software architecture should be based on the objects in the problem space. In this example the random number is the principal object in the problem and is a candidate to become an abstract data type.

The specification for this data type is given not in terms of its implementation but in terms of the services available. A random number is seen as a data type on which the available services are (a) initialization (`set_random`); and (b) obtain the next random number in the sequence (`random`). The header files in C are used as the manifestation of this interface.

The implementation of an abstract data type consists of the representation and the algorithms. The representation specifies how values of the abstract data type are to be realized in the host language. The random number is represented by the single (hidden) integer variable pseudo. The separation between the use and the representation permit different implementations to exist in a way that does not affect the client program. We might, for example, choose to realize a random number as a pair of integers to provide a superior distribution of generated values.

7.10 Summary

1. Identifiers associate with some C object, such as a variable or a function, in a *declaration*. Declarations include both type and storage class. Storage classes may be given implicitly or explicitly in a declaration.

2. Declarations also have *scope* which determines the region of the C program over which that declaration is active. An identifier declared in a top level declaration has a scope that extends from the declaration point to the end of the source program unit. Such objects have external linkage and are described as *global*. Parameter declarations and declarations at the head of blocks have storage class auto, described as *local*.

3. A declaration is *visible* in some context if the use of the identifier in that context is bound to the declaration. A declaration might be visible throughout its scope, but may also be temporarily *hidden* by other overlapping declarations (see Program 7.5).

4. To permit the use of an identifier prior to its *defining* declaration, a *prototype declaration* is used. These declarations were introduced in Chapter 5 to permit a function to be called before its declaration.

5. Top level declarations are assumed to have *external linkage*. However, external linkage that is assumed and external linkage that is stated are usually reserved for two different meanings. Generally, the storage class specifier extern is explicitly included on all referencing declarations to objects defined in another program unit. The storage class extern is omitted for the (one) defining declaration for each external object.

6. Variables and functions have an existence at run time. The extent of these objects is the period of time for which storage is allocated to them. An object has static extent when it is allocated storage at the commencement of the program and remains allocated until program termination. Automatic variables and function arguments have local extent, are created upon entry to the block or function and are destroyed upon exit.

7. Static variables have static extent. Internal static variables have local scope. External static variables have scope which is limited to the program

unit in which they are declared. External `static` functions are also restricted to the unit in which they are declared. External `static` storage class provides privacy not inherent to `extern` storage class.

8. The `register` storage class specifier is only applicable to local variables and function arguments. The `register` storage class is a strong recomendation to the compiler that the associated variable be kept in a CPU register to improve program execution. Many restrictions, including type and maximum number of objects, usually apply to this class.

9. The declaration of variables may be accompanied by an initializer. Initializers for automatic variables may be arbitrary expressions which are evaluated at run time upon block entry. Variables with `static` extent can only be initialized with compile time (constant) expressions. Variables with `static` extent and no explicit initializers are guaranteed to be initialized to zero.

7.11 Exercises

1. Explain what is meant by the following terms:
    (a) abstraction   (b) program unit
    (c) information hiding   (d) localisation
    (e) exportable   (f) scope rules
    (g) private   (i) storage class
    (j) abstract data type

2. Distinguish between defining declarations and referencing declarations.

3. Why would an error occur at link time when the following two files are compiled and linked? Why is there no error at compile time?

```
        file1                        file2
    ------------------           ------------------
        . . . . .                    . . . . .
    extern int time;            static int time = 0;
        . . . . .                    . . . . .
```

4. What output is produced when the following three files are separately compiled then linked and run?

```
        file1                        file2
    ------------------           ------------------
    #include <stdio.h>          static int date = 10;
    extern int date;
```

```
main()
{
    printf("%d\n", date);
}
```

```
          file3
          ------------------
          int date = 20;
```

5.   A programmer has designed a screen handling program unit, an outline of which is provided below. In the package, a screen is identified as an abstract data type for which a representation and a number of operations are provided:

```
#include <stdio.h>
static int nrows, ncols;      /* screen dimensions */
static int row, col;          /* cursor coordinates */
static void loadcursor(int ro, int co)
        /* position cursor */
{
    .....
    row = ro;
    col = co;
}

void home(void)          /* cursor at top left */
{
    loadcursor(0, 0);
}

void atsay(int ro, int co, char ch)
    /* print ch at screen position ro, co */
{
    loadcursor(ro, co);
    putchar(ch);
}

etc.
```

(a) What are the resources in this program unit?

(b) What are the resources that represent the operations on the screen abstraction?

(c) Why do the integer variables `nrows`, `ncols`, `row` and `col` have storage class external `static`?
    What was the programmer's reasoning behind this decision?

(d) What are the exportable resources from this unit?
    What resources are hidden?
    Provide a suitable interface header file for this package.

(e) Suggest why the function `loadcursor` has storage class `static`.

6.   Rework the problem involving random number generation. The services available for this new version of the data type are initialization (set_random), obtain the current random value (random), and advance to the next random number in the sequence (next_random).

7.   Revisit exercise 12 of Chapter 5 treating a twenty-four-clock time as an abstract data type. The following services are to be provided on the data type:

```
void set_time(const int hours, const int minutes,
              const int seconds);
void print_time(void);
long int hms_time(void);
void set_long_time(const long int seconds);
void add_to_time(const long int seconds);
```

The function set_time establishes a clock time according to the given elements. The function set_long_time initializes the clock time according to the number of seconds that have elapsed since midnight. Function hms_time determines the number of seconds in a clock time. Function add_to_time advances the clock time by a number of seconds. Finally, print_time displays the time in the eight-character format HH:MM:SS.

8.   Repeat Program 16 in Chapter 6 treating a date as an abstract data type. The following services are to be provided:

```
void set_date(const int day, const int month,
              const int year);
```

to initialize a date, and:

```
void print_date(void)
```

to display a date in the same format as the original.

8

The C preprocessor

THE C PREPROCESSOR is a simple *macro processor* that conceptually processes the source text of a C program immediately before the compilation process. In some implementations, the preprocessor is actually a separate program which reads the program source file and produces a new intermediate file that is then used as input to the compiler proper. In other implementations a single program supports both the preprocessing and compiling phases, with no intermediate file produced.

The preprocessor is controlled by preprocessor *command lines* or *directives*, which are lines in the source program text beginning with the character '#'. The preprocessor removes all directives from the source file, and makes any necessary transformations to the source, as directed by these commands. The resultant text is then processed by the compiler.

The preprocessor operates on a line-at-a-time basis. The syntax of these preprocessor lines is independent of the other parts of the C language. The preprocessor also operates independent of the scope rules of C. Preprocessor directives such as #define remain in effect until the end of the program (translation) unit.

Preprocessor commands are program lines that start with a '#' symbol optionally preceded by whitespace characters. The '#' is followed by an identifier that is the *command name*. For example, #define is the command that defines a macro. Whitespace is also permitted betwen the '#' and the command name.

Operating line-at-a-time makes line boundaries significant to the preprocessor. Lines that terminate with the sequence backslash character followed immediately by the newline symbol is used to adjoin two adjacent lines. The lines are spliced together with the backslash and newline characters removed. The process may be repeated for two or more lines.

Finally, we note that the preprocessor replaces all C comments with a single space character. This occurs even in the absence of any preprocessor directives. Thus we may use comments to separate distinct lexical tokens.

8.1 Simple macro definitions

A macro definition (or simply a macro) is an identifier that symbolizes a defined string composed of one or more tokens. The preprocessor statement that establishes this association is the #define statement. The preprocessor then guarantees to textually replace occurrences of that identifier appearing in the remainder of the program file with the *token-string*. The token-string is frequently referred to as the *body* of the macro.

The string of tokens is not a string as defined in Section 3.4, but, rather, a character sequence terminated by a newline symbol. This character sequence without the newline symbol is the macro body.

There are two different forms for the #define statement. One for use in simple string replacement and the other to perform string replacement with argument passing. We shall consider the simple string replacement first.

A token-string is associated with an identifier by the #define statement. The form of this statement is:

```
#define identifier     token-string
```

The end of the identifier is taken as the first whitespace character to occur following the start of the identifier. The identifier is as defined in Section 3.5. The token-string is the remainder of the line. This simple form is frequently used to introduce named symbolic constants into a program. This way program constants such as the number of bits in a word or the number of days in a month, may be defined once in a program and then referred to elsewhere by name. This facilitates changing the value later if the need arises, providing a mechanism to isolate implementation-dependent values and assist program portability.

The following example illustrates the use of this preprocessor statement:

```
#define DAYS_IN_WEEK     7
```

From the point of definition throughout the remainder of the program source file, the preprocessor will replace all occurrences of DAYS_IN_WEEK with the token-string 7; leading and trailing whitespace characters around the token sequence is discarded. The replacement does not operate within strings. The program statements:

```
days = DAYS_IN_WEEK * weeks;
printf("%d weeks * DAYS_IN_WEEK is %d days\n", weeks, days);
```

would, after preprocessing, be compiled as:

```
days = 7 * weeks;
printf("%d weeks * DAYS_IN_WEEK is %d days\n", weeks, days);
```

Like all C preprocessor commands, a macro definition may be split cosmetically across a number of lines. Hence the macro:

```
#define BUFFER_SIZE     10\
24
```

is equivalent to:

```
#define BUFFER_SIZE     1024
```

After the preprocessor expands a macro name, the macro's definition body is appended to the front of the input and the check for macro calls continue. Therefore, the macro body can contain calls to other macros. For example, following:

```
#define BUFFER_SIZE     1024
#define TABLE_SIZE      BUFFER_SIZE
```

the name TABLE_SIZE expands in two stages to 1024. This technique is commonly used where some constant is dependent upon the value of another. For example:

```
#define BUFFER_SIZE         1024
#define BUFFER_CAPACITY     2 * BUFFER_SIZE
```

The name BUFFER_CAPACITY when used in a program expands into the string 2 * 1024.

The Standard includes a number of predefined macros. They may be used without giving definitions for them. Strictly, they may not be undefined or redefined. The names are:

__FILE__ The current source code file name as a string literal, e.g. "date.c".

__LINE__ The current source code file line number, a decimal integer.

__DATE__ A string literal containing the compilation date in the form "Mnn dd yyyy", e.g. "Apr 18 1989".

__TIME__ A string literal containing the compilation time in the form "hh:mm:ss", e.g. "20:12:34".

__STDC__ The integer constant 1 indicating that the compiler is standard conforming.

One possible way to use these predefined names is as in the following:

```
#define ASSERT(X)   if(!(X))\
    printf("ASSERT failed, line %d, file %s\n",
    __LINE__, __FILE__)
.....
ASSERT(b != 0);
.....
```

The following program illustrates a rather novel way of applying the #define statement. A criticism often labelled against C is that it is terse and cryptic. A C program may be made more verbose, and its structure highlighted, by flavouring it to resemble languages like Pascal. The flavouring is achieved by defining Pascal-like constructs using the #define statement. Program 8.1 repeats Problem 6.2.

PROGRAM 8.1

```
/*
**          Read a series of positive floating point values
**          terminated with a negative value and compute the
**          sum of the non-negative values.
*/

#include <stdio.h>

#define PROGRAM                 main()
#define FLOAT                   float
#define FORMATIN                "%f"
#define WHILE                   while (
#define DO                      )
#define BEGIN                   {
#define END                     }
#define FORMATOUT               "The sum is %8.2f\n"

PROGRAM
BEGIN
  FLOAT data, sum = 0.0;                    /* data and running total */

  scanf(FORMATIN, &data);
  WHILE data >= 0.0 DO
  BEGIN
    sum += data;
    scanf(FORMATIN, &data);
  END
  printf(FORMATOUT, sum);
END
```

8.2 Macro arguments

A #define preprocessor statement of the form:

```
#define identifier(identifier, identifier,.....) token-string
```

is a macro definition with arguments. The macro name is the identifier following the #define. The left parenthesis must immediately follow the macro name with no intervening whitespace. If whitespace separates the identifier and the left parenthesis then the definition is considered a simple definition with no arguments. The macro body is then taken to commence with the left parenthesis.

The comma separated list of identifiers (with optional whitespace) appearing between the parentheses are the *formal macro arguments*. The identifiers must be unique. Normally, the macro body is defined in terms of these formal arguments. The formal arguments appearing in the macro body act as templates for the actual arguments supplied when the macro is invoked.

Such a macro is invoked in a program by stating its name. The name need not be immediately followed by a left parenthesis as in its definition. After the left parenthesis is a comma separated list of actual arguments terminated by a right parenthesis. The number of actual arguments given must match the number of arguments the macro expects from the definition. The macro invocation is textually replaced with the body of the macro. Each formal argument appearing in the macro body is substituted by the corresponding actual argument.

```
For example:

#define READINT(I)      scanf("%d",&I)
```

Unlike a function, the type of argument I is not defined, since we are merely performing a textual substitution and not invoking a C function. With such a definition we can write a statement such as:

```
READINT(distance);
```

The preprocessor replaces this with:

```
scanf("%d",&distance);
```

Another example, this time with two arguments, is:

```
#define SWAPINT(X,Y)      {int temp = X; X = Y; Y = temp;}
```

By using block structure we introduce a local integer variable temp enabling us to provide a macro definition to interchange the values of the integer variables. A call is:

```
SWAPINT(low,high);
```

In all our examples, the token string extends to the end of the line. If the token-string extends over multiple lines, then each line, except the last, must terminate in a backslash symbol (\) followed immediately by a newline symbol. For example, a macro to determine whether a year is a leap year or not is:

```
#define IS_LEAP(Y)      Y % 4 == 0 && Y % 100 !=0 || \
                        Y % 400 == 0
```

With this definition we can write statements such as:

```
if (IS_LEAP(year)).....
```

evaluated as:

```
if (year % 4 == 0 && year % 100 !=0 || year % 400 == 0) ....
```

When using macros with arguments one must be careful to avoid a subtle pitfall. Consider the apparently innocent definition:

```
#define SQUARE(X)      X * X
```

The assignment:

```
bsquared = SQUARE(b);
```

behaves quite normally, being textually processed into:

```
bsquared = b * b;
```

However, the expression:

```
y = SQUARE(x+1);
```

expands to:

```
y = x+1 * x+1;
```

Because of the precedence rules for arithmetic operators, the expression is interpreted as:

```
y = x+ (1*x) + 1;
```

which does not produce the same as the intended result:

```
y = (x+1) * (x+1);
```

This last example is generally the required result. Its form gives us a clue for preparing the macro definition: all formal parameters appearing in a macro body should always be parenthesized. To avoid another obscure side effect of macro expansion, it is generally safer to enclose the whole macro body in parentheses if it is an expression. The definition for SQUARE is now:

```
#define SQUARE(X)      ((X) * (X))
```

The statement:

```
y = SQUARE(x+1);
```

now expands into:

```
y = ((x+1) * (x+1));
```

Commas that are part of an actual macro argument must be either quoted or parenthesized, otherwise they act as argument separators. Thus if we wish to call the macro SQUARE with the actual argument s = t + 1, s + 2 using the comma operator, then we are required to wrap it in parentheses as in:

```
SQUARE((s = t+1, s+2))
```

In Section 6.6 an infinite loop is symbolically defined by:

```
#define FOREVER      for (;;)
```

A variant is one of the most common for constructs. Frequently, a for statement is required in which a control variable is set to some initial value, then increments by one to some upper limit. We might define this with a macro employing arguments as shown in the following program.

PROGRAM 8.2
```
/*
**      Form the sum of the first 20 integers. The data to
**      this program is self-generated by the sequence
**      1, 2, 3, .... , 20.
*/

#include <stdio.h>

#define FOR(CONTROL, INIT, FINAL) for ((CONTROL) = (INIT);\
                                       (CONTROL) <= (FINAL);\
                                       (CONTROL)++)

main()
{
   int number, sum = 0;    /* number and running total */

   FOR(number, 1, 20)
     sum += number;
   printf("Sum of the first 20 integers is: %d\n", sum);
}
```

8.3 Macro expansion

The preprocessor operates by replacing the macro name (and any actual arguments if present) with the body of the macro. If the macro definition involves formal arguments, then each occurrence of a formal argument is replaced with the corresponding actual argument. The process is known as macro expansion.

In the macro replacement text, identifiers naming a macro formal parameter are replaced by the actual argument. Two special operators affect the replacement process. If in the macro body a formal parameter is immediately preceded by a # character, then the actual argument is enclosed in double quotes before replacement of the formal argument and its leading '#':

```
#define MESSAGE(X)      printf(#X)
```

and the call:

```
MESSAGE(Program error);
```

expands to:

```
printf("Program error");
```

This special treatment is known as *stringizing*.

The production of the quoted string involves replacing every occurrence of the symbol 'appearing in the actual argument by \'. Similarly, \ symbols are replaced with \\ combinations. These additional changes are necessary to ensure the resulting string is legally formed. Hence:

```
#define DEBUG(X)      printf(#X " = %f\n", X)
```

when invoked with:

```
DEBUG(a+b);
```

is expanded into:

```
printf("a+b" " = %f\n", a+b);
```

with the resulting adjacent strings coalesced.

An actual macro argument can be concatenated with another or with some fixed program text to produce a longer token. This token might be the name of a function, variable or type, or a C keyword; it may even be the name of another macro, in which case it will be expanded. Concatenation is achieved with the special preprocessor operator '##'. When a macro is called and following substitution of actual arguments, all '##' operators are deleted and any adjacent whitespace removed. The syntactic tokens on either side of the original '##' are then joined. After:

```
#define CAT(X, Y)      X ## Y
```

the call:

```
CAT(abc, 123)
```

yields:

```
abc123
```

For a more realistic example, consider a fragment of C that interprets commands selected from a numbered menu.

```
#define quit          1
#define help          2
     .....
scanf("%d", &selection);
switch(selection){
     case quit : quit_command();
     case help : help_command();
          .....
}
```

It would be clearer not to have to give each command name twice, once on the case label and once as part of the function name. Here is how it is done:

```
#define quit          1
#define help          2
     .....
#define command(NAME)    case NAME : NAME ## _command()
     .....
scanf("%d", &selection);
switch(selection){
```

```
        command(quit);
        command(help);
            .....
}
```

8.4 Redefining and undefining macros

It is not permissible to redefine a previously declared macro unless the redefinition is identical in the sense that the macro is of the same type and that the tokens of both definitions are identical. To avoid any difficulties it is best to remove a definition first before assigning a new one. A definition is removed (undefined) with the #undef preprocessor command. The command form is:

```
#undef identifier
```

This command causes the preprocessor to forget the macro definition with the given name. A completely new definition may then be given to the identifier using a #define command. If the identifier is currently not defined, then the #undef command is ignored:

```
#define TAX    10
#undef  TAX
#define TAX    15
```

would define TAX as 15.

8.5   File inclusion

The #include preprocessor statement causes the content of a named text file to be processed as if it had appeared in place of the #include command. There are three forms of the command:

```
#include "filename"
#include <filename>
```

and:

```
#include token-sequence
```

The first two forms differ in how the specified file is located in the computer's file store. If the filename is surrounded by double quotes then the file is expected in the same 'directory' as the file containing the #include command. Generally, this form is used to refer to other files written by the user. If the filename is delimited by diamond brackets < and >, the search for the file takes place in certain standard places. On UNIX systems, the files are expected in the directory /usr/include. This form is generally used to reference standard system files. In all our programs which perform input/output we have included the standard header <stdio.h>.

The final variant is a form of *computed include*. The token-sequence is interpreted and expanded by the preprocessor in the normal way. The result, then, must be one of the two original forms and is processed as described above.

An included file may itself contain other #include commands Nested #include is therefore supported. The depth of nesting is implementation dependent. Nesting to at least five or six levels is common.

8.6 Conditional compilation

The C preprocessor supports a facility known as *conditional compilation*. Conditional compilation features in a number of common programming problems. It is used to enhance program portability by establishing definitions which are themselves the subject of other definitions. Conditional compilation can also be used to selectively incorporate or omit a series of statements in a program. This is commonly used to activate or deactivate debugging statements.

The statement we use is:

```
#if constant-expression
     lines-1
#else
     lines-2
#end
```

The series of lines, denoted lines-1 and lines-2, is any number of lines of program text. The lines may be program declarations, program statements or even other preprocessor statements. The #else directive and its associated group of lines is optional and may be omitted. Either series of lines may also contain one or more sets of nested conditional compilation commands.

The preprocessor operates by first evaluating at compile time the constant-expression. If the expression evaluates to 0 (logical false), the first group of lines, lines-1, are discarded and the second group are passed on for compilation. If the expression evaluates to other than zero (logical true), lines-1 is passed on and lines-2 is discarded. The expression must be capable of being determined at compile time. That is, it may involve C operators but only with constants (literal or symbolic). No run time values such as a program variables may be used in these expressions.

This facility may be used to turn on and off debugging statements. When developing a program we might incorporate statements to trace a program's behaviour, for example statements to print messages or the values of program variables. During program development these statements are invaluable for detecting program errors. When the program is fully operational they are no longer required, or even desirable, and are compiled out of the code. Consider a function to convert a distance in yards, feet and inches to its equivalent distance in inches. The function behaviour is traced by including an additional printf function call. This is conditionally compiled into the code:

```
#define DEBUG               1

#define YARDS_TO_FEET       3
#define FEET_TO_INCHES      12

int distance (const int yards,
              const int feet, const int inches)
{
#if DEBUG
    printf("function distance\n");
    printf("arguments: %d yards, %d feet, %d inches\n",
     yards, feet, inches);
#endif
    return((YARDS_TO_FEET*yards+feet)*FEET_TO_INCHES+inches);
}
```

To turn of the tracing we merely have to redefine DEBUG to logical false:

```
#define DEBUG      0
```

As shown below, the whole operation may be controlled at compile time with the $-D$ option to the C compiler.

The constant expression in `#if` may take the form:

or: `defined identifier`
or: `defined ( identifier )`
             `! defined ( identifier)`

and are replaced by the long integer constant 1L if the identifier is defined to the preprocessor, and by 0L otherwise. The identifier need not be asociated with a macro body, but simply be known to the preprocessor. Hence the above illustration may also be expressed by:

```
#define DEBUG
     .....
#if defined(DEBUG)
     .....
#endif
```

In this and in preceding chapters we have shown how to use the `#define` statement to give symbolic names to constants as in:

```
#define INTSIZE     16
```

The latter might be used to specify the number of bits in an integer for a particular machine. Thereafter, the symbolic constant INTSIZE may be used throughout the program source text in place of 16. If the program had to be moved to a machine with a different number of bits in an integer, then this, and possibly other machine-dependent definitions, would have to be changed.

The problem of changing all the `#defines` when moving the program from one machine to another can be reduced by anticipating this likelihood and programming it by making use of the conditional compilation capabilities of the preprocessor:

```
#define INTSIZE          32
#define INTEL8086

#if defined(INTEL8086)
    #define INTSIZE      16
#endif

#if defined(VAX)
    #define INTSIZE      32
#endif

#if defined(MOTOROLA)
    #define INTSIZE      32
#endif
```

then INTSIZE is defined as 16 bits for an Intel 8086 microprocessor. To move to a different machine we can either replace #define INTEL8086 with, say:

```
#define VAX
```

or use the more convenient −D argument in the C compiler command line (see Appendix G). In this case we would not include definitions for the INTEL8086, VAX or MOTOROLA in the program source file. A single definition is established when the compiler is invoked.

The preprocessor conditional may also include nested #if using the #elif directive. The full form for an #if statement is then:

```
#if constant-expression-1
    lines-1
#elif constant-expression-2
    lines-2
#elif ...
    .....
#else
    .....
#endif
```

allowing us to express the last solution by:

```
#if defined(INTEL8086)
    #define INTSIZE      16
#elif defined(VAX)
    #define INTSIZE      32
#elif defined(MOTOROLA)
    #define INTSIZE      32
#else
    #define INTSIZE      32
#endif
```

Semantically, the control lines:

```
#if defined ( identifier )
#if ! defined ( identifier )
```

are equivalent to:

and:
```
#ifdef  identifier
#ifndef identifier
```

respectively.

Since the preprocessor supports nested include files, sequential dependencies lead to interminable conflicts during program integration. Each include file should be included only once during compilation, and if the includes are nested unconditionally, this property becomes hard to control. For example, consider the erroneous duplicate definition of INTSIZE during compilation of the program unit prog caused by the inclusion of local1.h and local2.h, the latter containing a nested inclusion of local1.h (Figure 8.1).

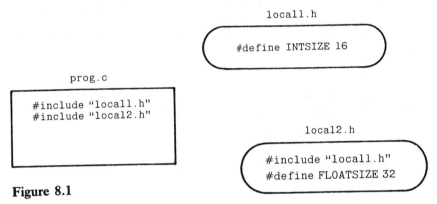

Figure 8.1

To avoid multiple inclusions of the same include file, each include file should begin with a #ifndef (or equivalent) that tests whether some #define'd symbol has already been defined (Figure 8.2).

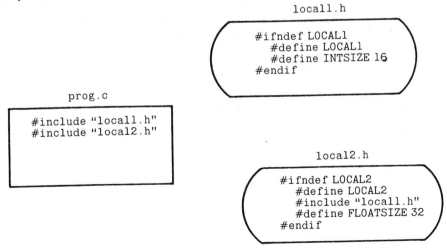

Figure 8.2

8.7 Line numbering, error generation, `pragmas` and `null`

Certain C tools that generate C source text as output use the #line preprocessor command so that compiler errors can reference the line number of the input file to the tool and not to the actual source text produced. The command:

or: ```
#line line-number "filename"
#line line-number
```

causes the compiler to treat subsequent lines in the program as if the program source file is named `filename`, and as if the line number begins at `line-number`. The `filename` is optional, and if omitted, then the last `filename` in the last #line is adopted or the name of the source file containing this #line is adopted if no name was previously specified. The #line command alters the results of the __FILE__ and __LINE__ predefined macros.

The #pragma command is specified in the ANSI standard to have an arbitrary implementation-defined effect. The control line form is:

```
#pragma token-sequence
```

and could be used, for example, to specify that the program is to be compiled to run on a MOTOROLA 68000 processor:

```
#pragma target 68000
```

Unrecognized pragmas are ignored.

A preprocessor line of the form:

```
#error token-sequence
```

causes the preprocessor to write a diagnostic message that includes the token-sequence. This directive would normally be used in conjunction with a preprocessor conditional which detects a combination of parameters which the program does not support properly. For example, if the program does not operate correctly on INTEL processors, one might write:

```
#if defined(INTEL)
    #error Does not support INTEL processors
#endif
```

The null directive consists of a preprocessor line consisting solely of the # symbol. The null command has no effect on the preprocessor, producing no output.

Generally, these preprocessor statements are not considered further in this book.

CASE STUDY   8.1 Date abstraction

This case study revisits Program 6.16 which verbalizes a date expressed in the input format DD/MM/YYYY. The enhancements made to this version are twofold. First,
```

we illustrate a number of uses of the C preprocessor; and, second, we look upon the date in the problem as an example of an abstract data type.

The problem naturally divides into two parts. The first is the actual application itself, inputting the data and directing the necessary conversions and printing. The second is concerned with the the implementation of the date as an abstract data type, and with the services available for that type. We choose, therefore, to package these two as program units called, respectively, main.c and date.c.

In any program unit resources (functions and data) are either private, exportable to other program units or are imported from program units. These three attributes are emphasized by the pseudo storage classes PRIVATE, IMPORT and EXPORT, equivalenced by the #define's in the header file visible.h:

```
/*
**      File:   visible.h
**
**      Symbolic names are defined for the terms EXPORT,
**      IMPORT and PRIVATE. A data item or function that
**      is labelled PRIVATE is synonymous with the storage
**      class static. An object that is IMPORTed from another
**      program unit is an extern object. Objects that are
**      EXPORTed from a module are implicitly global.
*/

#ifndef VISIBLE
  #define VISIBLE
  #define EXPORT
  #define IMPORT        extern
  #define PRIVATE       static
#endif
```

Throughout the text we have applied stepwise refinement in the analysis of our software. The problem pseudocode is expressed using a program design language. The header file pdl.h contains preprocessor constructs for this PDL so that we may use them directly in our program coding:

```
/*
**      File:   pdl.h
**
**      Provide all the necessary definitions to support
**      the program design language introduced in the text.
*/

#ifndef PDL
#define PDL
#define BEGIN           {
#define END             }
#define PROGRAM         main()

#define WHILE           while (
#define DO              ){
```

```
#define ENDWHILE            }
#define IF                  if (
#define THEN                ){
#define ELSE                } else {
#define ELIF                } else if (
#define ENDIF               }

#define SWITCH              switch (
#define TO                  ){
#define WHEN(LABEL)         case LABEL :
#define OTHERWISE           default :
#define ENDSWITCH           }

#define AND                 &&
#define OR                  ||
#define NOT                 !

#define PROCEDURE           void
#endif
```

We can implement a date as an abstract data type in the same manner as the random number of the preceding chapter. The implementation is dependent on there being at most one instance of the data type in use in the application program. Once again, the principal idea in defining a new data type is to separate the details of the implementation from its actual use. This is expressed by providing an interface consisting of a suite of functions to access and manipulate the data type.

Irrespective of how the date is represented, we will need to perform some basic operations in support of the application, such as initializing the date from the input data, verbalizing the day and the month, and printing the day and year numbers. These operations are expressed as functions set out in the header file date.h which provides the necessary specifications:

```
/*
**      File:           date.h
**
**      Header file for the date abstraction.
*/

#include "pdl.h"
#include "visible.h"

#ifndef DATE
  #define DATE

  IMPORT PROCEDURE set_date(const int d, const int m, const int y);
  IMPORT PROCEDURE print_day_name(void);
  IMPORT PROCEDURE print_day_number(void);
  IMPORT PROCEDURE print_month_name(void);
  IMPORT PROCEDURE print_year_number(void);
#endif
```

The actual representation for a date consists of three private integer variables in the program unit date.c. They are set by the application program using the operation set_date. The body of the program unit provides default initializations for the date. The individual elements of a date can be displayed by the print operations. Observe how printing the day name requires first determining Zeller's congruence then printing a day name from this value. The congruence is computed by a local private function since this is not required in the application. An alternative strategy would have been to export the Zeller function into the application and an associated function to print a day name given a congruence value for its argument:

```
/*
**       File:          date.c
**
**       Implementation of a date as an abstract date type.
**       This version is dependent on there being at most one
**       instance of the data type in the problem. The date is
**       realised by three concealed integer variables
**       representing the three components of a date.
*/

#include <stdio.h>
#include "pdl.h"
#include "visible.h"

PRIVATE int zeller(void);        /* forward reference */

                                 /* symbolic day names */

#define SUNDAY         0
#define MONDAY         1
#define TUESDAY        2
#define WEDNESDAY      3
#define THURSDAY       4
#define FRIDAY         5
#define SATURDAY       6

                                 /* symbolic month names */

#define JANUARY        1
#define FEBRUARY       2
#define MARCH          3
#define APRIL          4
#define MAY            5
#define JUNE           6
#define JULY           7
#define AUGUST         8
#define SEPTEMBER      9
#define OCTOBER        10
#define NOVEMBER       11
#define DECEMBER       12
```

```
                                        /* day name select and print */
    #define CASE(NAME)        WHEN(NAME) printf(" " #NAME); break

    PRIVATE int    day = 1;          /* date representation */
    PRIVATE int    month = 1;        /* with default initialization */
    PRIVATE int    year = 1;

    EXPORT PROCEDURE set_date(const int d, const int m, const int y)
    BEGIN
      day = d;
      month = m;
      year = y;
    END


    PRIVATE int zeller(void)
    BEGIN
      int    k = day;
      int    y = year;
      int    m, d, c;

      IF month < 3
      THEN
        m = month + 10;
        y = year - 1;
      ELSE
        m = month - 2;
      ENDIF

      d = y % 100;
      c = y / 100;
      return (((26 * m - 2) / 10 + k + d + (d/4) + (c/4) - 2 * c) % 7);
    END


    EXPORT PROCEDURE print_day_name(void)
    BEGIN
      int    zell = zeller();

      SWITCH zell TO
        CASE(SUNDAY);
        CASE(MONDAY);
        CASE(TUESDAY);
        CASE(WEDNESDAY);
        CASE(THURSDAY);
        CASE(FRIDAY);
        CASE(SATURDAY);
      ENDSWITCH
    END


    EXPORT PROCEDURE print_day_number(void)
    BEGIN
      printf(" %2d", day);
    END
```

```
EXPORT PROCEDURE print_month_name(void)
BEGIN
  SWITCH month TO
    CASE(JANUARY);
    CASE(FEBRUARY);
    CASE(MARCH);
    CASE(APRIL);
    CASE(MAY);
    CASE(JUNE);
    CASE(JULY);
    CASE(AUGUST);
    CASE(SEPTEMBER);
    CASE(OCTOBER);
    CASE(NOVEMBER);
    CASE(DECEMBER);
  ENDSWITCH
END

EXPORT PROCEDURE print_year_number(void)
BEGIN
  printf(" %4d", year);
END
```

Finally, we have the application program itself. Essentially the logic is unchanged from the original. The principal difference is organizational and the orchestration of the services of the data type:

```
/*
**       File:          case01.c
**
**       Input a date in the form DD/MM/YYYY and verbalise it
**       as, for example, TUESDAY 18 APRIL 1989. The date is
**       treated as an abstract data type and manipulated by
**       the services of the date program unit.
*/

#include <stdio.h>
#include "pdl.h"
#include "date.h"

PROGRAM
BEGIN
  int day, month, year;

  printf("Enter the date as DD/MM/YYYY: ");
  scanf("%2d/%2d/%4d", &day, &month, &year);

  set_date(day, month, year);
  print_day_name();
  print_day_number();
  print_month_name();
  print_year_number();
  printf("\n");
END
```

Do 1,2,3,4

8.8 Summary

1. The C preprocessor is a simple macro processor which conceptually processes the source text of a C program prior to compiling. The preprocessor is controlled by command lines, which are lines of the source program beginning with the character '#'.

2. The #define command introduces a macro definition. A macro is an identifier which symbolizes a token-string. The preprocessor replaces occurrences of that identifier with the token-string, possibly replacing any formal arguments appearing in the macro body with the actual arguments supplied when the macro is invoked. The #undef command removes a previous macro definition.

3. The #include preprocessor command line causes the content of a named file to be processed as if it appeared in place of the command. Two forms of file naming are provided, and differ in how the specified file is located in the computer's file store.

4. Conditional compilation is used to selectively incorporate or omit a series of program statements. The commands used are #if, #ifdef and #ifndef, as well as the associated #else, #elif and #end. Conditional compilation is used to enhance program portability and to embed debugging statements.

8.9 Exercises

1. Define a macro MIN that gives the minimum of two values, then write a program to test the definition.

2. Define a macro MAX3 that gives the maximum of three values. Test the definition in a program.

3. For an ASCII environment write macros IS_UPPER_CASE and IS_LOWER_CASE which, respectively, return a non-zero value if a single character argument is an upper case (lower case) alphabetic letter.

4. Write a macro IS_ALPHABETIC that gives non-zero if its argument is an alphabetic character. Have this macro use the two macros defined in the preceding example.

5. Enhance the date abstraction in the following ways:

   (a) Include a private function in date.c to validate the date, using it in the function set_date.

(b) Incorporate the Julian day service function `long int julian(void)` which computes the number of elapsed days from some epoch; the pseudo code is:

```
set baseyear to 0
set leapyear accordingly
calculate the day of the year
determine the number of leap years since the base year
calculate the julian day number from:
      365 * year + leapyears + dayofyear
```

(c) Include the function `void set_date_by_julian(long int julian)` which sets the date according to the julian day number given as the argument; the pseudo code is:

```
set baseyear to 0
estimate the year by:
        store quotient julian/365 to estyear
        store  estyear/4 − estyear/100 + estyear/400 to
            leapyears
        IF estyear − (estyear/400)*400 is 0
        THEN set leapyear to TRUE
        ELIF estyear − (estyear/100)*100 is 0
        THEN set leapyear to FALSE
        ELIF estyear − (estyear/4)*4 is 0
        THEN set leapyear to TRUE
        ELSE set leapyear to FALSE
        ENDIF
compute remaining days from:
        set remdays to julian − leapyears − 365*estyear
        IF leapyear is FALSE
        THEN reduce remdays by 1
        ENDIF
        WHILE remdays < 0 DO
              reduce estyear by 1
              store estyear/4 − estyear/100 + estyear/400
                        to leapyears
              IF estyear − (estyear/400)*400 is 0
              THEN set leapyear to TRUE
              ELIF estyear − (estyear/100)*100 is 0
              THEN set leapyear to FALSE
              ELIF estyear − (estyear/4)*4 is 0
              THEN set leapyear to TRUE
              ELSE set leapyear to FALSE
              ENDIF
              set remdays to julian − leapyears −
                    365*estyear
              IF leapyear is FALSE
              THEN reduce remdays by 1
              ENDIF
        ENDWHILE
```

```
calculate the month from remdays
calculate the day from remdays
set the year from the estyear
```

(d) Now add the service function void tomorrow(void) which advances the date by a single day. (Hint: use the solutions to parts (b) and (c).)

9

More on data types

WE HAVE ALREADY SEEN that the use of symbolic constants can improve program readability. By providing a suitable name (identifier) for a constant, as in the definition:

```
#define AUGUST    8
```

we can concentrate on the significance of the 'constant' AUGUST rather than on its specific 'value'. Should it be necessary to change this constant's value, only the definition need be changed, rather than scanning the whole program source file to locate and replace every occurrence of the literal 8.

For similar reasons, C provides the *type definition* whereby a programmer-defined name is given to a type. This facility is explored in the next section.

So far, we have met the fundamental data types provided by C. Sometimes we require a wider choice than this. For example, we might need a data type whose values are the days of the week. In this way we could naturally express the assignment:

```
day = MONDAY;
```

where MONDAY is a constant for this particular data type and day is a variable of the same type. C provides a means for us to specify our own data types. These features greatly enhance the ability to express programs in the abstract terms of the problem domain. We discuss these concepts in Section 9.2.

9.1 The typedef statement

The C programming language supports a number of fundamental data types such as char and int. A variable declaration for the fundamental types employs the *type-specifiers* char, int, etc. The declaration:

```
int hours, minutes;
```

specifies that the variables hours and minutes are of type int. The C language also provides the typedef declaration, which allows a type to be explicitly associated with an identifier. The statement:

```
typedef int    Time;
```

197

defines the type name `Time` to be equivalent to the C data type `int`. The named identifier can be used later to declare a variable or function in the usual way. The declaration:

```
Time hours, minutes;
```

declares the variables `hours` and `minutes` to be of type `Time`, equivalent to the type `int`.

The principal advantage of the use of the `typedef` in the above example is in the added readability that it lends to the definition of the variables. The declaration additionally incorporates the intended purpose of these variables in the program. Declaring them to be of type `int` in the normal way would not have made the intended use of these variables clear. A second advantage is that it allows abbreviations for long declarations. This will made apparent when arrays and structure declarations are introduced.

To define a new type name, the following procedure is applied. First, write a declaration as if a variable of the desired type were being declared. For example, to declare a variable `var` of type `int`, the declaration is:

```
int      var;
```

Second, substitute the variable name with the new type name:

```
int      Time;
```

Finally, prepend with the reserve keyword `typedef`:

```
typedef int      Time;
```

We illustrate the use of the `typedef` statement in Program 9.1. The program is supplied with a date represented as three positive integers, respectively the day, month and year. The program calculates the day number of the date for the given year. The 1 January for all years is day number 1. The 31 December is day number 365 for a non-leap year and day number 366 for a leap year.

PROGRAM 9.1

```
/*
**      Read a valid date in the form DD/MM/YYYY and determine
**      from it the day of the year. The 1 January for all years
**      is day number 1. The 25 December is day number 365 for
**      a non leap year and 366 for a leap year.
*/

#include <stdio.h>

#define FALSE           0
#define TRUE            1
#define ISLEAP(Y)       ((Y) % 4 == 0 && (Y) % 100 != 100 ||\
        (Y) % 400 == 0)
```

```
typedef int            Day;            /* type names */
typedef int            Month;
typedef int            Year;
typedef int            Daynumber;
typedef int            Daysinmonth;
typedef int            Boolean;

main ()
{
  Day         day;              /* supplied data value */
  Month       month, m;         /* m is month counter */
  Year        year;
  Daynumber   daynumber;        /* computed value */
  Daysinmonth daysinmonth (const Month, const Year);

  scanf ("%2d/%2d/%4d", &day, &month, &year);

  daynumber = 0;
  for (m = 1; m < month; m++)
    daynumber += daysinmonth (m, year);
  daynumber += day;

  printf ("%2d/%2d/%4d is daynumber %d\n",
        day, month, year, daynumber);
}

Daysinmonth daysinmonth (const Month month, const Year year)
{
  switch (month){
    case 4: case 6:            /* April, June, .... */
    case 9: case 11:           /* .... September, November */
      return (30);

    case 2:                    /* February -- special */
      if (ISLEAP(year))
        return (29);
      else
        return (28);
    default:
      return (31);
  }
}
```

A type name introduced by a typedef statement may clash with the names of other program variables and functions. This is known as name overloading. In the example above, we have used Day to represent a type name and day to represent a variable of that type. Since C is case sensitive, they are, of course, considered distinct by the C compiler. Name overloading, however, permits us to use the same identifier for both type names and variable or function names. Thus it would be perfectly acceptable to declare:

```
typedef int     day;
```

and:

```
day       holidays;
long int day;
```

The compiler resolves the ambiguity by employing contextual information. It does, of course, make the program more difficult to read and, perhaps, more difficult to debug if there are problems. It is better to use a different case for programmer defined type names, as above. If lower case type names are to be used then they should be distinct from other program names.

9.2 Enumeration types

The keyword `enum` is used to declare enumerated types. The enumeration type provides a means of naming (or enumerating) the elements of a finite set, and of declaring variables that take values which are elements of that set. The set of values is represented by identifiers called *enumeration constants*. For example, the declaration:

```
enum day { SUN, MON, TUE, WED, THU, FRI, SAT} d1, d2, d3;
```

creates a new enumeration type `enum day`, whose values are SUN, MON, . . ., SAT. It also declares three variables d1, d2 and d3 of the enumeration type `enum day`. These variables may be assigned values which are elements of the set:

```
d1 = MON;
```

We may also test the values of enumerated variables:

or
```
if (d1 == d2) ....
if ( !(d2 == SUN || d2 == SAT) ) ....
```

The *enumeration tag* day appearing in the declaration above is optional. The declaration is then equivalent to:

```
enum {SUN, MON, TUE, WED, THU, FRI, SAT} d1, d2, d3;
```

The enmumeration tag day, however, allows an enumeration type to be referenced after its definition. The single declaration:

```
enum day {SUN, MON, TUE, WED, THU, FRI, SAT} d1, d2, d3;
```

is exactly equivalent to the declarations:

```
enum day {SUN, MON, TUE, WED, THU, FRI, SAT};
enum day d1, d2, d3;
```

The first declaration does not allocate any storage, but a template is set up for the type `enum day`. This type may be used, as shown, in any subsequent declaration (including function argument declarations and function type specifiers).

From the preceding section, we may use a `typedef` statement to associate the type name Day with the enumerated `type enum day` as in:

```
enum day {SUN, MON, TUE, WED, THU, FRI, SAT};
typedef enum day        Day;
```

Based on these declarations we might imagine a program processing the days of the week. For a given day we may wish to compute what day is tomorrow. MON is the day after SUN, TUE is the day after MON, . . ., SUN is the day after SAT. The declaration for the function is:

```
Day tomorrow(const Day d)
{
  switch (d){
    case SUN: return MON;
    case MON: return TUE;
    case TUE: return WED;
    case WED: return THU;
    case THU: return FRI;
    case FRI: return SAT;
    case SAT: return SUN;
  }
}
```

By employing an enumerated type, the program meaning is enhanced as demonstrated in Program 9.2. This program computes an hourly employee's weekly pay, determined from the number of hours worked in each day of the week. Payment for Saturday is one-and-a-half times the basic rate and for Sunday is twice the basic rate.

PROGRAM 9.2

```
/*
**      Compute the week's pay for an hourly paid employee.
**      Overtime is applied for weekend working.
*/

#include <stdio.h>

#define SATADJUSTMENT        1.5
#define SUNADJUSTMENT        2.0

enum weekday {SUN, MON, TUE, WED, THU, FRI, SAT};
typedef enum weekday        Weekday;

typedef int        Hours;
typedef float      Rates;
typedef float      Wages;
```

```
main()
{
  Hours          hours;
  Rates          baserate, rate;
  Wages          wages;
  Weekday day;
  Weekday tomorrow(const Weekday);

  printf("Enter the basic hourly rate: ");
  scanf("%f", &baserate);

  wages = 0.0;
  printf("Enter the hours worked\n");
  printf("for Monday through Sunday: ");
  day = SUN;
  do {
    day = tomorrow(day);
    scanf("%d", &hours);

    switch (day){
      case MON: case TUE:
      case WED: case THU: case FRI:
        rate = baserate;                     break;

      case SAT:
        rate = SATADJUSTMENT * baserate;   break;

      case SUN:
        rate = SUNADJUSTMENT * baserate;   break;
    }

    wages += rate * hours;

  } while (day != SUN);

  printf("Total wages for the week: %8.2f\n", wages);
}


Weekday tomorrow(const Weekday d)
{
  switch (d){
    case SUN: return MON;
    case MON: return TUE;
    case TUE: return WED;
    case WED: return THU;
    case THU: return FRI;
    case FRI: return SAT;
    case SAT: return SUN;
  }
}
```

Strictly, the C compiler assigns an `int` value starting with 0 to each enumeration constant in a set. In the example:

```
enum day {SUN, MON, TUE, WED, THU, FRI, SAT};
```

SUN has value 0, MON has value 1, . . ., and SAT has value 6. These default assignations may be altered by assigning an explicit constant to an enumeration constant in the list. Successive elements from the list are then assigned subsequent values. Consider:

```
enum navigate {NORTH, EAST = 90, SOUTH = 180, WEST = 270};
```

The enumeration constant NORTH has default value 0; EAST has explicit value 90; SOUTH and WEST are, respectively, 180 and 270.

When writing programs with enumerated type variables, one should not rely on the fact that the enumeration constants are treated as integer constants. Instead, these variables should be treated as distinct variable types. The motive behind this segregation deals with one of the main strengths of the enumerated type, namely, safety. It is more difficult to accidently assign a variable the wrong value if proper mnemonics are used.

If it does prove necessary to mix enumerated types and, say, integer values, casts may be employed. The function `tomorrow`, shown earlier, may be written more succinctly as:

```
Day tomorrow(Day d)
{
    Day nextd;

    nextd = (Day) ((int) d+1)%7;
    return (nextd);
}
```

The assignment within function `tomorrow` makes use of two casts. First the formal argument d of type enum day is coerced to type int. If d is SUN the coerced value is 0, if d is MON, the coerced value is 1, and so on. To this value we then add 1 (moving on to tomorrow), then find the remainder on dividing by 7. The derived value is the integer constant associated with tomorrow. This is coerced back to the type enum day before assigning to the variable nextd.

9.3 Summary

1. The `typedef` statement associates a programmer-defined identifier with an existing type or with a programmer-defined type. Programmer-defined type names are used as abbreviations for longer type specifiers and to incorporate the intended purpose of the variables or functions in declarations.

2. An *enumeration* data type is defined by listing the identifiers by which the

values of the type are to be denoted. In most cases it is preferable to separate the type definition from the variable declaration, in which case the former does not allocate storage but simply acts as a template for the type. Unless assigned explicit integer values, the compiler assigns successive integer values to each enumeration constant starting with zero.

9.4 Exercises

1. Repeat Case Studies 6.3 and Program 7.4 using `typedef` statements as appropriate.

2. Prepare a function which verbalizes its single argument of type Day (as defined in Section 9.2).

3. Repeat Case Study 6.3 using an enumeration type for the decimal digits used in the functions `do_units`, `do_teens` and `do_tens`.

4. Prepare enumeration data type declarations for (a) the suits in a pack of cards, (b) the colours of the rainbow, (c) monetary denominations, and (d) the integer binary operators supported by C.

More on functions

CHAPTER 5 GAVE a comprehensive coverage of functions. In this chapter we consider three further aspects of functions: *recursive* functions, that is, functions that call themselves either directly or indirectly; function pointers; and functions with a variable number of arguments.

10.1 Recursive functions

Any function may invoke any other function, as we have already seen (Chapter 5). Programmers exploit this facility to build programs constructed hierarchically, in which the `main` function invokes subfunctions F1, F2,. . . to perform subsidiary tasks; these subfunctions in turn invoke further subfunctions G1, G2, . . . to perform simpler tasks, and so on (Chapters 5 and 7). A functionally decomposed program design can then be directly implemented through this language feature.

This is not the only way of exploiting the use of functions. In particular, a function may call or invoke itself. Such a function is said to be *recursive*. Many programming problems have solutions which are expressible directly or indirectly through recursion. The ability to map these solutions on to recursive functions leads to elegant and natural implementations.

Recursion is commonly used in applications in which the solution can be expressed in terms of successively applying the same solution to subsets of the problem. Common applications involve the searching and sorting of recursively defined data structures (Chapters 11, 12, 15 and 16). A recursive solution is frequently an alternative to using iteration.

To illustrate, consider a function to evaluate the factorial of a number. The factorial of a positive integer n, written n!, is defined as the product of the successive integers 1 through n inclusive. The factorial of zero is treated as a special case and is defined equal to 1. So:

```
n! = n*(n-1)*(n-2)*....*3*2*1     for n >= 1
```

and

```
0! = 1
```

It follows that:

```
5! = 5x4x3x2x1 = 120
```

The iterative solution is:

```
long int factorial(int n)
{
    int k;
    long product = 1L;

    if (n == 0)
        return (1L);
    else {
        for (k = n; k > 0; k--)
            product *= k;
        return (product);
    }
}
```

Customarily, the definition of factorial is given recursively. We observe that:

```
n! = n*(n-1)*(n-2)* .... *3*2*1
```

which we can group as:

```
n! = n*[(n-1)*(n-2)* .... *3*2*1]
```

The bracketed group is, of course, the definition for $(n - 1)$! Thus the recursive definition is:

```
n! = n*(n-1)!
```

with the special case:

```
0! = 1
```

We can now develop a function to calculate the factorial of an integer n according to this recursive definition. Such a function is illustrated in Program 10.1.

PROGRAM 10.1

```
/*
**      Tables of factorials for 0, 1, 2, . . . , 10. The
**      factorials are determined by a recursive function.
*/

#include <stdio.h>

main()
{
    int     j;
    long int factorial(const int);

    for (j = 0; j <= 10; j++)
```

```
      printf("%2d! is %ld\n", j, factorial(j));
}

long int factorial(const int n)
{
  if (n == 0)
    return (1L);
  else
    return (n * factorial(n-1));
}
```

The program's output is:

```
 0! is 1
 1! is 1
 2! is 2
 3! is 6
 4! is 24
 5! is 120
 6! is 720
 7! is 5040
 8! is 40320
 9! is 362880
10! is 3628800
```

The function factorial is recursive since it includes a call to itself. Let us see what happens in the case where the function is called to calculate the factorial of 5, for example. When the function is entered, the formal parameter n is set to 5. The conditional if statement determines that this n is not zero, and returns with the value obtained by evaluating n * factorial(n − 1), with n = 5, namely:

```
5 * factorial(4)
```

The expression specifies that the factorial function is to be called again, this time to obtain factorial(4). The multiplication of 5 by this value is left pending while factorial(4) is computed.

We call the factorial function again. This time, the actual argument is 4. Each time any C function is called it is allocated its own set of automatic variables and formal parameters with which to work. This applies equally to recursive or non-recursive functions. Therefore, the formal argument n that exists when the factorial function is called to calculate the factorial of 4 is distinct from the first call to calculate the factorial of 5.

With n = 4 this time, the function executes the return with the expression:

```
4 * factorial (3)
```

Once again, the multiplication by 4 is left pending while the factorial function is called to calculate the factorial of 3. The process continues in this manner until formal argument n has value 0. The situation is then as described by Table 10.1.

Table 10.1

factorial(n)	return (n * factorial(n-1))
5	5 * factorial (4) = 5 * ?
4	4 * factorial (3) = 4 * ?
3	3 * factorial (2) = 3 * ?
2	2 * factorial (1) = 2 * ?
1	1 * factorial (0) = 1 * ?

When the formal argument n is reduced to zero, the conditional `if` statement causes an immediate return with `long` value 1. The recursive descent can now start to unwind and all the pending multiplications can be evaluated in reverse order. Repeating the above table, but in reverse sequence, we obtain Table 10.2.

Table 10.2

factorial (n)	return (n * factorial (n-1))
1	1 * factorial (0) = 1 * 1 = 1
2	2 * factorial (1) = 2 * 1 = 2
3	3 * factorial (2) = 3 * 2 = 6
4	4 * factorial (3) = 4 * 4 = 24
5	5 * factorial (4) = 5 * 24 = 120

Lest it be argued that this last example is an artificial example, consider the Euclidean algorithm to determine the highest common factor of two positive integers n and m. The procedure can be written:

```
HCF(n,m) = if m > n then HCF (m,n)
              if m = 0 then n
              otherwise HCF(m, remainder when n is divided by m)
```

The resursive function can be written directly from the definition:

```
int hcf(int n,int m)
{
  if (m > n)
    return (hcf(m,n));
  else if (m == 0)
    return (n);
  else
    return (hcf(m, n % m));
}
```

On the other hand, the non-recursive form requires a certain amount of programmer skill. The implementation is also much less obvious:

```
int hcf(int n,int m)
{
  if (m > n)
  {
```

```
      int temp = m;
      m = n;
      n = m;
   }

   while (n % m ! = 0){
      int temp = m;
      m = n % m;
      n = temp;
   }

   return (m);
}
```

It is also possible to write a function which calls a second function which in turn calls the original function. This is known as *indirect recursion* and involves a circle of function calls. For example, function A calls function B, B calls C, and C calls A again. As usual, to permit a function call to precede the function declaration, a prototype declaration is employed. This is necessary with indirect recursion since it is impossible to textually rearrange the program so that every function definition precedes its use. For example, consider the mutually recursive functions A and B. Since A calls B, then we might consider placing the definition for B before A, but since B also calls A this is clearly impossible.

Recursion is not always the most efficient solution to a problem. Many problems which can be solved recursively can also be solved using iteration, as shown above. The solution may be less elegant but can be more efficient in terms of program execution time and memory requirements. For each recursive function call a separate region of memory is established to hold the values of the arguments and local variables. Hence, recursive algorithms are expensive in terms of memory space utilization. Further, for each recursive call, processor time is used to pass function arguments, establish the new memory area for that call, and to return its result upon completion.

The most persuasive argument in support of recursive functions is that they reflect recursively defined data structures and algorithms which are defined recursively. Further, some recursive algorithms are next to impossible to construct iteratively. Recursive functions which map recursive data structures are consistent with our philosophy of programs matching their data.

10.2 Pointers to functions

Objects of type function may be introduced in only one of two ways. First, a *function definition* creates a function object, defines the type of the arguments and return value, and provides the body of the function. For example, `square` is a function object:

```
int square(const int x)
{
```

```
        return (x * x);
    }
```

Second, a prototype function declaration is used to introduce a function declared elsewhere. A prototype for function `square` is:

```
    int square(const int);
```

The C language provides for values of one type to be automatically converted to values of other types in several circumstances. This unary conversion determines whether and how a single operand is converted before an operation is performed. An expression of type 'function returning T' for some type T is converted to value of type 'pointer to a function returning T' by substituting a pointer to the function for the function itself. The only expression that can have type 'function returning T' is the name of a function. A function identifier by itself and not in the context of a function call (the function identifier followed immediately by "(") is converted to the type 'pointer to function returning ... ". Thus, in the usual way, we may declare a variable of type 'pointer to a function returning ... ' and assign to it the name of a function. In the declaration:

```
    int (*fp)(const int);
```

the identifier `fp` is declared as a 'pointer to a function returning an int with a const int argument'. We may then assign to `fp` any 'pointer to a function returning an int with an argument of type const int'. The latter is delivered by the name of a suitably declared function. For example:

```
    fp = square;
```

Variable `fp` is a pointer to the function object known in the program as `square`. The function call:

```
    y = square(x);
```

can also be achieved indirectly with the indirection operator applied to an expression of type 'pointer to function returning int with a const int argument'. An equivalent call is:

```
    y = (*fp)(x);
```

It is especially useful to consider the declaration:

```
    int i, *pi, f(int), *fpi(int), (*fi)(int);
```

which declares an integer `i`, a pointer to an integer `pi`, a function returning an integer `f`, a function returning a pointer to an integer `fpi`, and a pointer to a function returning an integer `fi`. The declaration should be studied with some care. The construct:

```
    int .... , (*fi)(int);
```

says that `fi` is a pointer to a function returning an `int`. The first set of parentheses are necessary. Without them:

```
int .... , *fi(int);
```

would declare `fi` to be a function returning a pointer to an `int` (like `fpi`), which is quite different.

The use of `fp` in the statement:

```
y = (*fp)(x);
```

is consistent with the declaration. The variable `fp` is a pointer to a function, `*fp` is the function, and `(*fp)(x)` is the call to that function. The parentheses are necessary so that the components correctly associate.

Since this notation is unwieldy, the Standard permits a function call to have the form as introduced in Chapter 5. The designated function may be a function name or an identifier which is a pointer to a function. Hence we might present the last statement more clearly as:

```
y = fp(x);
```

Program 10.2 illustrates the use of this construct. The pointer to function variable `func` is first assigned to the function object `square` which in turn is called indirectly to determine 5 squared. The process is then repeated using the function `cube`.

PROGRAM 10.2

```
/*
**      Determine the square and the cube of the value 5.
**      The squaring and cubing functions are called
**      through indirect function calls.
*/

#include <stdio.h>
                                /* forward references */
int square(const int), cube(const int);

main()
{
  int y, x = 5;
  int (*func)(const int);      /* pointer to function */
  func = square;               /* not a call to square !! */
  y = func(x);                 /* indirect call on square */
  printf("Square of %d is %d\n", x, y);

  func = cube;
  y = func(x);
  printf("Cube of %d is %d\n", x, y);
}

int square(const int x)
{
```

```
    return (x * x);
}

int cube(const int x)
{
  return (x * x * x);
}
```

The syntax of the C language in handling function pointers makes the program text somewhat obscure. The `typedef` statement can improve matters by introducing a suitable type name. For example, the definition:

```
typedef int     (*Pfi)(int, float);
```

introduces `Pfi` as a pointer to a function returning an integer with an `int` and a `float` argument. The declaration for a variable of this type is then:

```
Pfi func;
```

Were it not for `typedef` statements, the obscurity can become much worse when we recognize that a 'pointer to a function returning ... ' object can be used as array types (Chapters 11 and 12), members of structures (Chapter 15) and even arguments to functions. For example, an array of pointers to functions returning integers is declared by:

```
int (*apfi[4])(int, float);
```

Using the `typedef` statement introduced above, we can increase the clarity of this declaration by:

```
Pfi apfi[4];
```

Thus `apfi` is an array, with each element of type `Pfi`. In turn, `Pfi` is a pointer to a function returning an `int`. Finally, `apfi` is an array of pointers to functions returning `int`'s.

In many programming problems we invoke one of a number of functions selected by the current value of some integer variable. For example, consider a program that displays a menu of options numbered 0, 1, 2 and 3. According to the value entered by the user, the program invokes a subsidiary function to service that choice. One possible program fragment might be:

```
display_menu();
scanf("%d", &choice);
switch (choice){
    case 0 : do_zero();   break;
    case 1 : do_one();    break;
    case 2 : do_two();    break;
    case 3 : do_three();  break;
   default : printf("Unknown selection\n");
}
```

Alternatively, we might consider establishing an array of pointers to these service functions, and activate the appropriate one by using the integer variable choice as an index into the array. The program constituents now are:

```
void do_zero(void), do_one(void),
     do_two(void), do_three(void);
typedef void          (*Pfv)(void);
Pfv do_choice[] = {do_zero, do_one, do_two, do_three};
```

```
display_menu();
scanf("%d", &choice);
if (0 <= choice && choice <= 3)
  do_choice[choice]();
else
  printf ("Unknown selection\n");
```

These concepts are demonstrated in Program 10.3. A menu of four options are available to the user. The choices are numbered 0 to 3 inclusive. Selection 1 invites the user to enter a date in the form DD/MM/YYYY. Selection 2 prints the date in the same format, and selection 3 prints the day of the week for the input date. After selecting 1, 2 or 3 the menu is redisplayed and the process repeats until the choice 0 is entered and the cycle terminates.

PROGRAM 10.3

```
/*
**      Demonstration of a menu driven program. Each
**      menu option is serviced by a function. The
**      selection made by the user is used to determine
**      the function to call. An array of function
**      pointers is indexed by the user choice to
**      invoke the support function.
*/

#include <stdio.h>

#define FOREVER          for(;;)
                                    /* pointer to a function ... */
                                    /* ... returning void */
typedef void          (*Pfv)(int *const, int *const, int *const);

void    stop(int *const, int *const, int *const),
        date_in(int *const, int *const, int *const),
        date_out(int *const, int *const, int *const),
        day_out(int *const, int *const, int *const);
int     menu(void);
int     zeller(const int, const int, const int);

Pfv selection[] = {stop, date_in, date_out, day_out};
```

```
main( )
{
  int            day, month, year;
  int            choice;

  FOREVER {
    choice = menu( );
    if (0 <= choice && choice <= 3)
      selection[choice](&day, &month, &year);
    else
      printf("\n\nUnknown selection\n");
  }
}

/*
**       Prompt the user and read the entered date.
*/

void date_in(int *const day, int *const month, int *const year)
{
  printf("\n\nEnter the date as DD/MM/YYYY: ");
  scanf("%d/%d/%d", day, month, year);
}

/*
**       Print the present value of the date.
*/

void date_out(int *const day, int *const month, int *const year)
{
  printf("\n\nEntered date is: %d/%d/%d\n", *day, *month, *year);
}

/*
**       Print the day name of the present date.
*/

void day_out(int *const day, int *const month, int *const year)
{
  static char *day_name[] = {
         "Sunday", "Monday", "Tuesday", "Wednesday",
         "Thursday", "Friday", "Saturday"
  };

  printf("\n\nDay is: %s\n", day_name[zeller(*day, *month, *year)]);
}

/*
**       Apply Zeller's congruence to a valid date
**       expressed as DD/MM/YYYY.
*/
```

```
int zeller(const int day, const int month, const int year)
{
  int k, y, m, d, c, z;

  k = day;
  y = year;
  if (month < 3){
    m = month + 10;
    y = year -1;
  } else
    m = month -2;
  d = y % 100;
  c = y / 100;

  z = (26 * m - 2)/10 + k + d + (d/4) + (c/4) - 2*c;
  return (z % 7);
}


/*
**        Terminate the program.
*/

void stop(int *const day, int *const month, int *const year)
{
  printf("\n\nProgram closing\n");
  exit(0);
}


/*
**        Main menu. A menu selection is displayed and
**        the user is invited to make a choice. The
**        selected value is returned to the main function,
**        validated, and the appropriate service
**        function called.
*/

int menu(void)
{
  int k, choice;

  for (k = 0; k < 24; k++)
    printf("\n");                /* clear screen */

  printf("\t\t\tMAIN MENU\n\n\n");
  printf("\t\t\t0 Exit\n");
  printf("\t\t\t1 Date in\n");
  printf("\t\t\t2 Date out\n");
  printf("\t\t\t3 Day out\n\n\n\n\n");

  printf("Enter selection: ");
  scanf("%d", &choice);
  return choice;
}
```

10.3 Functions as arguments

We have written programs in which one function invokes another. Indeed, without this facility, large programs would be very difficult to write. We sometimes encounter circumstances in which we wish to write a function that will invoke another function whose effect is not determined until program execution time. This is achieved by passing a pointer to a function as a formal *function argument*. The specification for this formal argument indicates a function pointer and the value returned by the function. For example, the declaration:

```
void ppp( ...., int (*f)(const int), ....)
. . . . .
{
  int x, y;
  . . . . .
  y = f(x);
  . . . . .
}
```

introduces a function ppp with a formal function argument f which returns an int and has an int argument. Within the body of ppp, f is used like any other pointer to a function returning an int. When the function ppp is called, the actual parameter corresponding to f must be the identifier of a function with the same argument requirements and the same result type. A legal call to ppp would be:

```
ppp( ...., square, ....);
```

with function square as defined in the preceding section.

Consider the function tabulate to generate a succession of values for x, as determined by the arguments lower, upper and increment, and to evaluate and print f(x). Function tabulate takes f as a function argument. The function declaration is:

```
void tabulate(double (*f)(const double),
    const double lower, const double upper, const double increment)
{
  double x;

  for(x = lower; x <= upper + 0.5 * increment; x += increment)
    printf("%6.2f %10.4f\n", x, f(x));
}
```

The function call:

```
tabulate(f1, 0.0, 1.0, 0.1);
```

would cause the values of x and f1(x) to be tabulated for x in the range 0.0 to 1.0 at intervals of 0.1. Function f1 should possess one const double argument and return a value of type double. Program 10.4 employs function tabulate to display x and x * x for x = 0.0, 0.1, 0.2, ..., 2.0.

PROGRAM 10.4

```
/*
**        Demonstration of a pointer to function argument.
**        A series of values are tabulated for some
**        given function. The tabulation function
**        receives the function as one of its arguments.
*/

#include <stdio.h>

                              /* forward references */
double square(const double);
void    tabulate(double (*)(const double),
                const double, const double, const double);

main()
{
  tabulate(square, 0.0, 2.0, 0.1);
}

void tabulate(double (*f)(const double),
      const double lower, const double upper, const double increment)
{
  double x;

  for(x = lower; x <= upper + 0.5 * increment; x += increment)
    printf("%6.2f %10.4f\n", x, f(x));
}

double square(const double x)
{
  return (x * x);
}
```

Functions as arguments are very useful for constructing general purpose functions, such as the function `tabulate` above. The facility must be used with great care since the effect of one function which receives another as an argument is not always immediately obvious. Programs using functions as arguments are often difficult both to understand and debug. Their strength, however, is in the functionality afforded by their use.

10.4 Functions with variable number of arguments

All the functions we have introduced have had a fixed number of arguments. The standard library function `printf` can, however, be called with a variable number of arguments. The new Standard mandates the provision of a set of *routines* to implement such *variadic* functions. The header `<stdarg.h>` provides facilities for stepping through the list of arguments of unknown number and type.

The following example shows the definition and prototype for such a function:

```
int sum(const int, ...);            /* prototype */

int sum(const int number, ...)      /* definition */
{
    ...
}
```

The ellipsis '...' appearing at the end of the argument list indicates that the function can take a variable number of arguments. To access the arguments within the function definition, a new type called va_list, and three functions (macros) that operate on objects of this type called va_start, va_arg and va_end are introduced from the header <stdarg.h>.

The type va_list is a typedef declared in <stdarg.h>. Its actual type is machine-dependent but is commonly an array or a pointer. We declare a variable of this type in the usual way:

```
va_list args;
```

Before any attempt is made to access a variable argument, list va_start must be called. It is effectively defined as:

```
void va_start(va_list ap, lastarg);
```

The macro initializes ap to point to the first unnamed argument. The initialization is performed by naming the last named argument in the function's formal argument list. Hence, we might have for function sum:

```
va_start(args, number);
```

Note that there must be at least one named argument in the function definition.

Following initialization, the actual arguments can be accessed sequentially by the va_arg macro. It is defined as:

```
type va_arg(va_list ap, type);
```

Note how the type returned by this 'function' is determined by its second argument. No real function could be defined this way. Each macro call delivers the next actual argument from the list of actual arguments as a value of the specified type. For example, to obtain the next argument as an integer, we write:

```
myint = va_arg(args, int);
```

Finally, when all the arguments have been processed, the function va_end should be called. It is defined as:

```
void va_end(va_list ap);
```

The function effectively implements a clean-up process. It is obligatory that this function should be called to ensure that the defined function performs a normal return.

We illustrate these issues with Program 10.5 which completes function sum to form the sum of the variable number of integer arguments for which the first named argument counts the number of variable arguments.

PROGRAM 10.5

```
/*
**      Form the sum of a variable number of integer
**      values presented as arguments to a variadic
**      function.
*/

#include <stdio.h>
#include <stdarg.h>

main()
{
  int sum(const int, ...);              /* prototype */

  printf("Sum of 10, 20, 30 and 40 is %d\n",
           sum(4, 10, 20, 30, 40));
}

int sum(const int number, ...)
{
  va_list      args;          /* list of arguments */
  int          arg;           /* individual argument */
  int          k, total = 0;

  va_start(args, number);
  for(k = 0; k < number; k++){
    arg = va arg(args, int);
    total += arg;
  }
  va_end(args);
  return total;
}
```

Note that the macro va_arg can only operate correctly if the *type* argument can be converted to a pointer to such an object by simply appending an asterisk '*'. Simple types such as int and char work without difficulty. If the argument is an array object say, int [ ], then the correct argument type is int * and not int [ ], since the latter is not a valid pointer type when we attach the asterisk.

In the case of variadic functions, the number of actual arguments must equal or exceed the number of formal arguments. The trailing arguments following the explicitly typed final argument suffer *default argument promotion* as follows: integral promotions (see Section 3.9) is performed on each integral argument (for example, short is promoted to int); each float argument is converted to double.

10.5 Summary

1.   Recursion is a powerful tool for solving particular categories of problems. The result is elegant and natural program solutions.

2.   A recursive function either calls itself directly or indirectly. Recursion usually consists of a general case and one or more base cases. It is vital in the program implementation that the recursive function can terminate through its base conditions.

3.   Recursive functions can be written in an equivalent iterative form. Due to system overheads, a recursive function may be less efficient than its iterative one.

4.   The C language supports the type 'pointer to function returning ...' which can be used as array elements, members of structures, function arguments, etc. Functions as arguments are useful for constructing general purpose functions whose effect is not determined until execution time.

5.   Where it is impossible to list the type and number of all the arguments to a function, the ellipsis '...' can be specified in the function signature. Their presence informs the compiler that zero or more arguments may follow and that their types are unknown.

10.6 Exercises

1.   Prepare a recursive function to form the sum of the first n positive integers using the recursive definition:

```
sum(n) = n + sum(n-1)
```

What is the base case for this definition?

2.   The following equations define the Fibonacci sequence of numbers:

```
Fib(1) = 1
Fib(2) = 1
Fib(n) = Fib(n-1) + Fib(n-2)        for n > 2
```

Produce a recursive C function directly from these definitions.

3.   Write a recursive function to calculate values of Ackermann's function, Ack(m, n), defined for m >= 0 and n >= 0 by:

```
Ack(0, n) = n + 1
Ack(m, 0) = Ack(m-1, 1)
Ack(m, n) = Ack(m - 1, Ack(m, n - 1))
                    for m > 0 and n > 0
```

What is the value for Ack(3, 2)?

4. Write a function, digit(n, k), that returns the value of the kth digit from the right of the number n. For example:

```
digit(234567, 2) = 6
digit(1234, 7)   = 0
```

5. Write a function, count(n, k), that returns a count of the number of occurrences of the digit k in the number n. For example:

```
count(4214, 4) = 2
count(73, 5)   = 0
```

6. Write a function, reverse(n), that returns a number that is the digits of the number n reversed. For example:

```
reverse(1234) = 4321
reverse(222)  = 222
```

7. A game called the Tower of Hanoi consists of a platform carrying three posts and a number of discs of different size. The object of the game is to move a tower of discs, arranged as a pyramid, from the left-hand rod to the right-hand rod using the middle rod. The conditions of the game are that only one disc may be moved at a time, and at no stage may a larger disc rest on a smaller disc.

8. Modify the random number generator package in Chapter 7 in the following way:

    (a) Incorporate the following declarations in the header file random.h:

```
typedef void    (*Pfv)(char *const s);
extern  void set handler(Pfv);
```

    where the type-specifier char *const indicates a character string.

    (b) Change the set_random function to perform error checking on its argument, which must be positive. On detecting an error, this function calls the error routine specified by the function pointer handler. This value is initialized to default_handler, but may be set by the package user through function set_handler:

```
static void default_handler (char *const s) {.....}
static Pfv handler = default_handler;
void set_handler (Pfv new) {.....}
```

11

Arrays and pointers

IN THE PROGRAMS written thus far, each variable was associated with a single data value. These variables are called simple variables. In this chapter we will begin the study of *aggregate types*. An aggregate type is a grouping of related data items. This class includes *arrays*, *structures* and *unions*.

The array is a data structure used to store a collection of data items that are all of the same type. By using an array, we can associate a single variable name with an entire collection of data. To process an individual item we need to specify the array name and indicate which array element is being referenced. Specific elements are distinguished by an *index* or *subscript*.

The motivation behind arrays is illustrated with the following problem. Suppose, for example, that we wish to construct a program which reads five integer values and prints them out in reverse order. To do so we might declare and use five integer variables as in:

```
main()
{
    int first, second, third, fourth, fifth;

    scanf("%d %d %d %d %d", &first, &second, &third,
        &fourth, &fifth);
    printf("%d %d %d %d %d\n", fifth, fourth, third,
        second, first);
}
```

If now, instead of five integer values to reverse we had, say, fifty, then manipulating the data by means of unique identifiers is an extraordinarily cumbersome approach.

11.1 Declaring and referencing arrays

In C, an array is declared just like any other variable. The syntax for an array declaration is:

```
type-specifier name[number-of-elements]
```

Type-specifier is any of the fundamental types of C which we have already met, including the enumeration type. The type `void` is not included in this permissible

223

set. The array size is specified as a constant expression representing the maximum number of elements. The array name is introduced as an identifer. An array called `table` with eight elements of type `integer` would be given by the declaration:

```
int table[8];
```

An array occupies a block of consecutive memory locations. Pictorially, the storage space reserved for the array table might appear as in Figure 11.1.

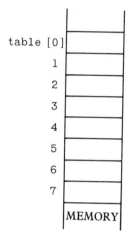

Figure 11.1

To process the data stored in an array, we must be able to reference each individual element. The array *subscript* is used to differentiate between different elements of the same array. A subscripted variable consists of an array name followed by an integer expression enclosed in square brackets. The subscripted variable `table[0]` refers to the first element of the array table, `table[1]` references the second element, and `table[7]` references the last element. Observe how the array declaration specifies the number of elements (eight), while the elements themselves are referenced by the subscripts 0, 1, 2, 3, 4, 5, 6 and 7.

A subscripted variable may be used in any expression in which a simple variable of the same type may be used. Examples of expressions involving subscripted variables include:

```
sum4 = table[0] + table[1] + table[2] + table[3];

table[7] = 7;

if (table[0] > table[7])
    printf("First is greater than last\n");
```

The expression used in a subscript is any generalized expression which yields an integer value. Thus we may write for simple integer variables i, j and k:

```
table[i+j] = 0;
for (k = 0; k < 8; k++) printf("%d\n", table[k]);
table[7 - table[j]] = j;
```

Like FORTRAN, C does not define support for any array bounds checking. The programmer must be especially diligent to ensure the code does not attempt to access an array element that is outwith the bounds of the array declaration when no bounds checking is implemented. In the context of the declaration for array table, the following statement is syntactically and semantically correct:

```
table[10] = 0;
```

It is anticipated, however, that the statement is not that required by the programmer. Nevertheless, the C compiler will accept the statement. The effect is that some area of memory is initialized to zero, possibly with disastrous effects if it is an area of memory assigned to another program variable.

We can now address and reprogram the original problem. Five integer values are read as input and printed in reverse order. An array is used in the solution, as shown in Program 11.1.

PROGRAM 11.1

```
/*
**        Read five integers from the standard input and
**        output them in reverse order.
*/

#include <stdio.h>

#define SIZE              5

main()
{
  int k;                        /* loop control */
  nt table[SIZE];               /* data values */

  for (k = 0; k < SIZE; k++)
    scanf("%d", &table[k]);     /* data input */

  for (k = SIZE - 1; k >= 0; k--)
    printf("%d\n", table[k]);
}
```

It was stated earlier that array elements may be of any of the fundamental types or enumeration types. Further valid array declarations include:

```
#define SIZE          10
#define NAMESIZE      20
#define ADDRSIZE      30
```

```
enum month {JAN, FEB, MAR, APR, MAY, JUN,
            JUL, AUG, SEP, OCT, NOV, DEC};
typedef enum month        Months;

int     age[TSIZE];
float   size[TSIZE+1];

Months date[8];
char    name[NAMESIZE], address[ADDRSIZE];
```

The array size has eleven elements of type float. The array date has eight elements, each of which is any of the enumeration constants JAN, FEB, . . ., DEC. In the last declaration, both name and address are character arrays. As a systems programming language, C is used extensively to process character arrays. Character arrays or strings are the subject of the next chapter.

The following program performs a simple *bubble sort* on an array of N integer values. The algorithm is one of many of the interchange sorts. The inner loop rearranges out of order adjacent pairs on each pass. At the end of the first pass, the largest element has been 'bubbled' to the end of the array, that is, to the element at index position N − 1. The outer loop repeats the process, each time decreasing the number of items to be sorted by one.

Data to our program consists of a single integer value followed by a number of integer data values. The first integer specifies the number of data items to follow.

PROGRAM 11.2

```
/*
**      Input a series of integer values, sort them, and
**      print them out. The ordering of the data into
**      ascending sequence is performed by a simple
**      bubble sort. The data set is preceded with an
**      integer count of the number of data items.
*/

#include <stdio.h>

#define TABLESIZE       100
#define SWAP(X,Y)       { int temp = (X); (X)=(Y); (Y)=temp; }

main()
{
    int size;                    /* number of data values */
    int i, j;                    /* loop counters */
    int table[TABLESIZE];        /* data set */

    printf("Enter the number of data values: ");
    scanf("%d", &size);
```

```
    if (size > TABLESIZE)
      printf("Too many elements, max is %d\n", TABLESIZE);
    else {
      for (i = 0; i < size; i++){ /* accept data */
        printf("data item %3d: ", i);
        scanf("%d", &table[i]);
      }

                                    /* bubble sort algorithm */
      for (i = size − 1; i > 0; i−−)
        for (j = 0; j <= i − 1; j++)
          if (table[j] > table[j+1])
            SWAP(table[j], table[j+1]);

                                    /* print sorted data */
      for (i = 0; i < size; i++)
        printf("data item %3d: %5d\n", i, table[i]);
    }
}
```

11.2 Multi-dimensional arrays

C provides for rectangular multi-dimensional arrays. In practice they are much less common than are one-dimensional arrays. Consider a table containing the marks scored by a class of students in each of several examination papers. The marks of one student could be stored in a one-dimensional array:

```
#define NUMBER_OF_PAPERS     5

int student[NUMBER_OF_PAPERS];
```

The complete marks table for all the students could be stored in array of such arrays, that is, in a two-dimensional array:

```
#define NUMBER_OF_PAPERS     5
#define NUMBER_OF_STUDENTS   50


int marks[NUMBER_OF_STUDENTS][NUMBER_OF_PAPERS];
```

We can visualize a two-dimensional array as having rows and columns. A row in this example would represent the marks obtained by a single student. A column represents the marks gained by all students in an individual examination paper. The intersection of a given row and column is the mark obtained by a student in a particular examination.

As suggested by the declaration for a two-dimensional array, C treats a two-dimensional array as really a one-dimensional array, each of whose elements is itself an array. Hence, a subscripted variable to reference the mark of an individual student in a single paper is written:

```
marks[row][column];
```

As an example of the use of multi-dimensional arrays, we present a program that measures the frequencies of pairs of adjacent letters in words. The program counts only within-word pairs, so that, given the input 'THE DOG.', it will count TH, HE, DO and OG, but not ED. The input stream is terminated by a period symbol as shown.

The counters are stored in a two-dimensional array whose declaration is:

```
#define ALPHABET    26
int counter[ALPHABET][ALPHABET];
```

The letter pair AA is recorded in `counter[0][0]`, the pair AZ in `counter[0][25]`, the pair ZZ in `counter[25][25]`, and so on. Note how the letter A results in an index value 0, the letter B index value 1, etc. We must, therefore, translate each letter into the correct index value. If ch is the variable representing an input character, then the conversion in an ASCII environment is readily achieved with the expression:

```
ch - 'A'
```

To process the text we use a two-character 'window'. The window moves through the input stream one character at a time, and whenever both characters in the window are letters, the corresponding element of `counter` is incremented.

PROGRAM 11.3

```
#include <stdio.h>
#include <ctype.h>

#define ALPHABET        26

#define BLANK           ' '
#define PERIOD          '.'
#define NEWLINE         '\n'

int counter[ALPHABET][ALPHABET];

main()
{
  void initialize(void), process(void),
      display(void);

  initialize();
  process();
  display();
}

void initialize(void)              /* counter array to zero */
{
```

```
    int row, col;

    for (row = 0; row < ALPHABET; row++)
      for (col = 0; col < ALPHABET; col++)
        counter[row][col] = 0;
}

void process(void)                    /* input stream */
{
    char thischar, prevchar;               /* input window */

    prevchar = BLANK;                      /* initialise */
    thischar = getchar();
    while (thischar != PERIOD){
      if (isupper(thischar) && isupper(prevchar))
        counter[prevchar-'A'][thischar-'A']++;
      prevchar = thischar;
      thischar = getchar();
    }
}

void display(void)
{
    int row, col;

    for (row = 0; row < ALPHABET; row++){
      for (col = 0; col < ALPHABET; col++)
        printf("%2d", counter[row][col]);
      putchar(NEWLINE);
    }
}
```

11.3 Arrays as function arguments

When an array name is passed to a function, what is passed is the location of the beginning of the array. Within the called function, this argument is truly a pointer, that is, a variable containing an address. The called function may then use this address to access an individual item of the array by employing the usual subscripting notation.

An array formal argument to a function is declared as:

```
void f(float t[], .... ){ ... }
```

which specifies that the argument t is an array of floats. The length of the array is not specified. The notation t[] indicates that t is an array. The actual array dimension will be established by the calling function. The prototype declaration would be presented as:

```
void f(float [], ..... );
```

If a two-dimensional array is to be passed to a function, the argument declaration in the function must include the column dimensions, that is, all but the first dimension. Thus if array `counter` in the last exercise was to be passed as an argument to the subordinate functions, the declaration for `initialize`, for example, would be:

```
initialize(int counter[][ALPHABET])
```

All but the first dimension of a formal array argument are required so that the compiler can determine the correct *storage mapping function*. Effectively, a two-dimensional array such as:

```
int table[3][4];
```

is stored in consecutive storage locations in row-order (Figure 11.2). To access, for example, element `table[1][3]` the storage mapping function determines that it is seven locations relative to the base of the array (element `table[0][0]`). In general, element `table[i][j]` is $4 * i + j$ locations relative to the array base. The storage mapping $4 * i + j$ is dependent upon 4, the number of elements in the second dimension. Hence the need to include this value in a formal array argument.

```
table[0][0]
table[0][1]
table[0][2]
table[0][3]
table[1][0]
table[1][1]
table[1][2]
table[1][3]
table[2][0]
table[2][1]
table[2][2]
table[2][3]
```
MEMORY

Figure 11.2

Program 11.2 performed a sort on a series of integer values using the bubble sort algorithm. We repeat the same problem on the same data, this time separating the task of reading, sorting and writing the array into three separate functions, passing the array between functions as an argument.

PROGRAM 11.4

```
/*
**        Input a sequence of integer values and sort them
**        into ascending order using the bubble sort
```

```
**        algorithm. The data set is preceded with an
**        integer count of the number of items.
*/

#include <stdio.h>

#define TABLESIZE        100

#define SWAP(X,Y)        { int temp = (X);\
        (X) = (Y); (Y) = temp; }

main()
{
  int  size;                        /* number of data items */
  int  table[TABLESIZE];            /* data values */
  int  input(int [], const int);    /* referencing .... */
  void sort(int [], const int),     /* .... declarations */
       output(const int [], const int);

  if ((size = input(table, TABLESIZE)) > TABLESIZE)
    printf("Too many elements, max is %d\n", TABLESIZE);
  else {
    sort(table, size);
    output(table, size);
  }
}

/*
**        Read a stream of integers from the standard input
**        and record in an array. The user is first prompted
**        for the number of data items. If this values exceeds
**        the maximum permissible value, then the program
**        terminates.
*/

int input(int table[], const int limit)
{
  int size;                        /* expected number */
  int k;                           /* loop control */

  printf("Enter number of data items:");
  scanf("%d", &size);

  if (size > limit)                /* sufficient room? */
    return (size);                 /* no, return error */

  for (k = 0; k < size; k++)
    scanf("%d", &table[k]);
```

```
/*
**        Sort an array of integers into ascending order
**        by application of the bubble sort algorithm.
**        Out of order pairs are repeatedly exchanged
**        'bubbling' the largest item to the end of the
**        array. The process repeats, with the second
**        largest element displaced into the penultimate
**        entry in the array, and so on.
*/

void sort(int table[], const int size)
{
  int i, j;

  for (i = size - 1; i > 0; i--)
    for (j = 0; j < i; j++)
      if (table[j] > table[j+1])
        SWAP(table[j], table[j+1]);
}


/*
**        Print the sorted array.
*/

void output(const int table[], const int size)
{
  int k;

  printf("Sorted list:\n");

  for (k = 0; k < size; k++)
    printf("%5d\n", table[k]);
}
```

The main advantage of the bubble sort is its simplicity. Its drawback, a serious one, is that it gets very slow as the number of elements to be sorted rises. Having constructed the program in a modular manner we can readily replace this sort routine with an improved version.

The Shell sort is much faster for large arrays. The basic idea is that in the early stages far-apart elements are compared and, if necessary, exchanged. This eliminates large amounts of disorder quickly, so later stages have less work to do. Gradually, the interval between compared elements is decreased, until it reaches one, at which point it effectively reduces to an adjacent interchange method. The replacement algorithm is given below. A full discussion of the Shell sort method is out of place here, but research has shown that the halving of intervals given in this implementation is not the optimal sequence (see Exercise 8):

```
/*
**      Sort an array of integers into ascending order
**      by application of the Shell sort algorithm.
**      In the early stages distant elements are
**      compared and, if necessary, exchanged. Gradually
**      the interval between compared elements is
**      reduced until adjacent elements are involved
**      in the comparison.
*/

void sort(int table[], const int size)
{
  int interval, i, j;

  for (interval = size/2; interval > 0; interval /= 2)
    for (i = interval; i < size; i++)
      for (j = i-interval;
           j >= 0 && table[j] > table[j+interval];
           j -= interval)
        SWAP(table[j], table[j+interval]);
}
```

11.4 Array initialization

It is permissible within C to initialize arrays. The array initializer consists of a brace-enclosed, comma separated list of constant expressions. For example, a six-element integer array may be initialized by:

```
int array [6] = { 0, 1, 2, 3, 4, 5};
```

Strictly, the bounds of the the array need not be given explicitly. In this case the C compiler counts the number of initializers and from it determines the array size. The above might also have been written:

```
int array [] = { 0, 1, 2, 3, 4, 5};
```

Where the array size is given explicitly and the number of items in the initializer is fewer than the number of elements, then the remaining elements are initialized to zero if the array is declared as external or as internal `static`, but are undefined for automatic arrays. Therefore:

```
static int array [6] = {0, 1, 2, 3};
```

is equivalent to:

```
static int array [6] = {0, 1, 2, 3, 0, 0};
```

If the number of initializers exceeds the number of elements in the array declaration, then the initializer is in error.

Multi-dimensional arrays may also be initialized. The initialization follows the same pattern. A multi-dimensional array with, say, N elements in the first dimension is initialized with an initializer appearing as:

```
int array [N] .... [...] = {I₀ , I₁ , ... I_{N-1} };
```

The initializers I apply the definition of an initializer recursively for the remaining array dimensions. Thus the two-dimensional integer array `rectangle[3][4]` has an initializer having the form:

```
int rectangle [3][4] = { I₀ , I₁ , I₂ };
```

Each initializer I is appropriate to an integer array now reduced to one dimension having four elements. Such an initializer would appear as:

```
{1, 2, 3, 4}
```

A complete initializer for `rectangle` is then:

```
int rectangle[3][4] = { {1,2,3,4},
                        {5,6,7,8},
                        {9,10,11,12} };
```

Again, where there are fewer than the required number of items, remaining elements are initialized to zero (but not automatic arrays). The initialization:

```
int rectangle[3][4] = { {1,2,3},
                        {5}
                                  };
```

is equivalent to:

```
int rectangle [3][4] = { {1,2,3,0},
                         {5,0,0,0},
                         {0,0,0,0} };
```

The following program unit supports two date conversion routines. Function `day_of_year` determines the day number within a year for a given date, taking account of possible leap years. Function `day_and_month` performs the complementary operation. Both functions employ the same (private) data, namely, a two-dimensional array in which the first row is the days in each month for a non-leap year, and the second row is the days in each month in a leap year. Note how the macro LEAP delivers the logical value TRUE (integer 1) or logical FALSE (integer 0), and how these provide the row index into the array.

```
/*
**      File:       date.c
**
**      Convert a date expressed as day, month and year into
**      the day number for that year; and the reverse
**      procedure.
*/

#define LEAP(Y)      ((Y)%4 ==0 && (Y)%100 != 0 || (Y)%400 == 0)

#define YEARS        2
#define MONTHS       13          /* Note extra month */

static int days_in[YEARS][MONTHS] =
      {    {0, 31, 28, 31, 30, 31, 30, 31, 31, 30, 31, 30, 31 },
           {0, 31, 29, 31, 30, 31, 30, 31, 31, 30, 31, 30, 31 }
      };

int day_of_year(const int day, const int month, const int year)
{
  int mon, leap;
  int days = 0;

  leap = LEAP(year);
  for (mon = 1; mon < months; mon++)
    days += days in[leap][mon];
  return (day + days);
}


void day_and_month(int *const day, int *const month,
      const int day_of_year, const int year)
{
  int mon, leap;

  leap = LEAP(year);
  for (mon = 1; day_of_year > days_in[leap][mon]; mon++)
    day_of_year -= days_in[leap][mon];
  *month = mon;
  *day = day_of_year;
}
```

11.5 Pointers and arrays

Chapter 5 introduced the concept of a pointer. Specifically it has been used to pass the address of a variable to a called function, enabling that function to obtain the variable's current value and, if necessary, to modify that value.

There is also a strong relationship between pointers and arrays in C. Pointers and arrays are used in almost the exact same way to access memory. However, there are subtle and important differences which, to the uninitiated, are somewhat hard to grasp. A pointer is a variable that takes addresses as values. An array name is also an address. The address associated with an array name is the initial location in memory in which the array is stored. Since an array name is an address, it is also, therefore, a pointer, but one which is fixed at compile time. Suppose we have the declaration:

```
#define     SIZE 8

int table[SIZE];
```

and that the compiler assigns the base address 400 to the array, then the memory image might appear as illustrated in Figure 11.3. In the diagram we are assuming that an integer occupies two storage locations (bytes).

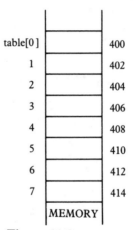

Figure 11.3

Figure 11.4

If `ptr` is a pointer to an integer, declared as:

```
int *ptr;
```

then the assignment:

```
ptr = &table[0];
```

sets `ptr` to point to the zeroth element of table. That is, `ptr` contains the address of `table[0]`, namely, address 400 (see Figure 11.4). By the usual notation, the assignment:

```
t = *ptr;
```

will copy the content of `table[0]` into `t`. Equally, the assignment:

```
*ptr = 0;
```

sets the value of `table[0]` to zero.

Since an array name is treated by the compiler as the base address of the array in memory, the name of an array is synonymous for the location of the zeroth element. Instead of writing:

```
ptr = &table[0];
```

we may also express it as:

```
ptr = table;
```

Pointer arithmetic is one of the most powerful features of C, providing an alternative to array indexing. If `ptr` is a pointer to a particular element of array `table`, then `ptr + 1` points to the next element. In general, for some integer `i`, `ptr + i` points `i` elements after `ptr`, and `ptr - i` points `i` elements before. Thus if `ptr` points to `table[0]` by:

```
ptr = table;
```

then `*(ptr + 1)` refers to the content of `table[1]`. Similarly, `*(ptr + i)` refers to the content of `table[i]`. Also, if `ptr` is the address of the base of the array, then `ptr + i` is the address of `table[i]`.

When we define a pointer that will be used to point to the elements of an array, we designate the pointer as pointing to the type of the elements contained in the array. Hence, `ptr` is declared as a pointer to an integer since it is used to access the integer array `table`. Had `table` been an array of floating point values, then `ptr` would have had to be declared:

```
float *ptr;
```

This base type is used in all pointer arithmetic. In `ptr + i`, `i` is first multiplied by the size of the objects of the base type to which `ptr` points, before being added to `ptr`. The value `i` is scaled according to the size of the object to which `ptr` points.

An array with an index expression and a pointer with an offset can be used interchangeably. Since C treats an array name as a (fixed) pointer to the base address of the array, then all expressions involving `table[i]` are immediately converted to the equivalent form, namely, `*(table + i)`. If `ptr` is a pointer to the zeroth element of the array `table`, `*(ptr + i)` references `table[i]`. Additionally, `ptr` may be subscripted: `ptr[i]` is identical to `*(ptr + i)`. This is allowable since both `table` and `ptr` are treated as pointers; one is fixed and the other is variable.

Finally, pointer expressions such as `ptr = table`, `ptr + i`, `ptr++` and `ptr -= i`, all make sense. If p and q are both pointing to elements of the one array, then p − q yields the integer value representing the number of array elements between p and q. The type of this result is implementation-dependent. The header file <stddef.h> defines a type ptrdiff_t that is a sufficiently large integral type for the signed difference of two pointer values.

The Standard endorses one exception with array pointers: it is permissible to use the address of the first element beyond the end of an array even though no such element exists. For the array table we may refer to &table[8]. This construction is used to determine when an array pointer no longer refers to an array element.

The one difference between an array name and a pointer is that the latter is a variable but the former is a constant. So ptr = table and ++ptr are valid operations, but constructs like table = ptr or table++ are illegal.

To set all the elements of the array table to zero we previously would have used:

```
for(i = 0; i < SIZE; i++)
   table[i] = 0;
```

Knowing that table[i] and *(table + i) are equivalent, we could also have used:

```
for(i = 0; i < SIZE; i++)
   *(table + i) = 0;
```

In fact, this conversion is automatically performed by the C compiler. Using a pointer variable, we express the same logic by:

```
for(ptr = table; ptr < &table[SIZE]; ptr++)
   *ptr = 0;
```

In this loop, the pointer variable ptr is initialized to the base address of the array table. Successive values of ptr, obtained from the operation ptr++, are equivalent to &table[0], &table[1], and so on. The loop continues provided the array elements are not all exhausted, and is determined when the pointer ptr no longer references an array element.

In a function definition a formal argument that is declared as an array is actually a pointer. When an array is passed, its base address is passed call by value. Hence the following two definitions are considered the same:

```
void f(float t[], ... )      void f(float *t, ... )
```

Reprogramming Problem 11.1 in terms of pointers, we have the alternative solution:

PROGRAM 11.5

```
/*
**      Read five integers and output them in reverse
**      order. Use an array to record the values, and
**      a pointer to reference the elements of the array.
*/

#include <stdio.h>

#define SIZE              5

main()
{
    int table[SIZE];      /* data values */
    int *ptr;             /* array access method */

    for (ptr = table; ptr < &table[SIZE]; ptr++)
        scanf("%d", ptr);

    for (ptr = &table[SIZE-1]; ptr >= table; ptr--)
        printf("%d\n", *ptr);
}
```

We previously noted that an array formal argument is actually a pointer. When an array argument is passed in a function call, the base address of the array is passed *call by value*. The array elements themselves are not copied. The formal argument operates as an initialized local variable whose value may be altered during function execution. The formal argument can then be used as a pointer to reference the elements of the array.

In Program 11.4, the function output cycles through successive elements of the array argument table, printing each value. A revised version expressed in terms of pointers is:

```
/*
**      Print the sorted array.
*/

void output(const int table[], const int size)
{
    int *base;

    printf("Sorted list:\n");

    for (base = table; table < base+size; table++)
        printf("%d\n", *table);
}
```

Incrementing table is perfectly legal, since it is a pointer variable; table++ has no effect on the actual array used in the function call to output. It is the private copy of that array's address that is incremented.

11.6   Functions returning pointers

A function processing an array and returning a reference to an array element can do so by returning the integer value of the array element subscript. Here, it is appropriate to describe the processing logic with subscripts. For example, consider a function called `smallest` that returns the integer index of the smallest item in an array of `floats`:

```
int smallest(const float array[], const int limit)
{
  int    index = 0, subscript;
  float least = array[index];

  for(subscript = 1; subscript < limit; subscript++)
    if (array[subscript] < least)
      least = array[index = subscript];

  return (index);
}
```

This function might then be invoked in some calling function to find the smallest element in an array `table` with `SIZE` elements:

```
printf("Smallest is %f\n", table[smallest(table, SIZE)]);
```

In some applications it is often more appropriate to describe the processing in terms of pointers. To achieve this, C supports *functions returning pointers* to data items. Reprogramming the preceding function with pointers:

```
float *smallest(float *const array, const int limit)
{
  float *index, *final, *subscript;
  float least;

  index = array;
  final = array + limit;
  least = *index;

  for (subscript = array + 1; subscript < final; subscript++)
    if (*subscript < least)
      least = *(index = subscript);

  return (index);
}
```

The declaration for function `smallest` now specifies that the returned value is a pointer to a `float`. This is indicated by the notation:

```
float *smallest( .... ) ....
```

The corresponding function call is now:

```
printf("Smallest is %f\n", *smallest(table, SIZE));
```

11.7 External array referencing

We have followed the principle that all objects in a C program must be declared before they are used. Where the defining declaration follows a reference to the item, then an explicit referencing declaration appears. This has been used in a number of cases: functions called before they are defined, references to data items declared in other program units, and so on.

The same principle applies to arrays. If a defining declaration for an array appears in a separate file or appears after it is to be referenced, then a referencing declaration must be used. Defining declarations are responsible for having actual storage allocated. For an array, a defining declaration might appear as:

```
int table[SIZE];
```

Referencing declarations act as compiler directives, informing the compiler of the attributes of the object. No space is allocated. An appropriate referencing declaration for array `table` is:

```
int table[];
```

indicating that `table` is an array of integers. The number of array elements is given in the corresponding defining declaration. Similar to formal array arguments, multi-dimensional arrays are referenced using declarations containing all but the first dimension. The referencing declaration for a two-dimensional array having four elements in the second dimension is:

```
float code[][4];
```

If the referencing declaration is to an array declared in another program unit then, as usual, the declaration is preceded with the storage class keyword `extern`:

```
extern float code[][4];
```

11.8 Arrays and `typedef` declarations

The `typedef` statement can be used to introduce synonyms for arrays. The declaration:

```
typedef char    String[80];
```

defines a type called `String` which is an array of eighty characters. Subsequently declaring variables to be of type `String` as in:

```
String text, line;
```

has the effect of defining the variables to be character arrays of size 80. The declaration for the variables `text` and `line` are equivalent to the definitions:

```
char text[80], line[80];
```

To define a type name involving arrays, the procedure introduced in Section 9.1 is used. First, we establish the form for a normal array declaration:

```
char      message[80];
```

Then replace the variable name, `message`, with the new type name, `String`:

```
char      String[80];
```

and finally prepend with the keyword `typedef`:

```
typedef char      String[80];
```

CASE STUDY   11.1 Quicksort

Of all the various sorting techniques, *quicksort* is perhaps the most widely used internal sort. An internal sort is one in which all the data to be sorted are held in primary memory.

Let us suppose that we want to sort an array of integers of size n into ascending order. The essential characteristic of the quicksort algorithm is to partition the original array by rearranging it into groups. The first group contains those elements less than some arbitrarily chosen value from the set, and the second group contains those elements greater than or equal to the value. The chosen value is known as the *pivot* element. Once the array has been rearranged with respect to the pivot, the same partitioning is then applied to each of the two subsets. When all subsets have been partitioned, the original array is sorted. Since the partitioning is applied in turn to the subsets, quicksort is best described recursively.

Suppose we wish to sort the elements a[lo], a[lo + 1], . . . , a[hi] of the integer array a into ascending order. We denote this task by:

```
rquick (a, lo, hi)
```

If, by some means, we are able to identify the pivotal element a[piv] and perform the rearrangement, then the problem divides into:

```
IF lo < hi
THEN
      partition the elements a[lo], .... a[hi] so that
      a[lo], a[lo+1], .... a[piv-1] < a[piv] <= a[piv+1],
      .... a[hi], where lo <= piv <= hi

      rquick (a, lo, piv-1)
      rquick (a, piv+1, hi)
ENDIF
```

Ideally, the pivot should be chosen so that at each step the array is partitioned into two sets with equal (or nearly equal) numbers of elements. This would then minimize the total amount of work performed by the quicksort algorithm. Since we do not know in advance what this value should be, we select for the pivot the first value that will provide a partition. Assuming that the array elements are randomly distributed, this is equivalent to choosing the pivot value randomly. We select as the pivot element the last in the set, a[hi]. The elements are rearranged entirely within the subset of a between a[lo] and a[hi]. An outline of the partitioning algorithm is:

```
low = lo
high = hi
pivot = a[hi]
REPEAT
     increase low until low >= high or a[low] > pivot
     decrease high until high <= low or a[high] < pivot
     IF low < high
     THEN
           exchange a[low] and a[high]
     ENDIF
UNTIL low >= high
exchange a[low] and a[hi]
```

Putting these elements together we arrive at a program to read a series of integer values, to sort them into ascending order using the quicksort algorithm, and then to print the sorted list. The data is preceded by an integer N representing the number of data items. The program is subdivided into three principal functions performing input, sorting and output respectively:

```
/*
**      Sort a sequence of integer values using the quicksort
**      algorithm. The set of integer data values is preceded
**      by the integer N representing the number of items.
*/

#include <stdio.h>

#define MAXTABLE        1000

#define SWAP(X,Y)      { int Z = (X);\
        (X) = (Y); (Y) = Z; }

                                /* prototype declarations: */
void    input(int [], int *const, const int),
        output(const int [], const int),
        quicksort(int [], const int),
        rquick(int [], const int, const int);
main()
{
   int table[MAXTABLE];               /* data items */
   int number;                        /* number of values */
```

```
    input(table, &number, MAXTABLE);    /* read the data */
    if (number <= MAXTABLE){            /* check sizes */
      quicksort(table, number);         /* apply algorithm */
      output(table, number);            /* print results */
    } else
      printf("Too many data items\n");
}

/*
**          --------------------------- oOo ---------------------------
**          --------------------------- oOo ---------------------------
*/

void input(int table[], int *const number, const int limit)
{
  int k;

  scanf("%d", number);
  if (*number > limit)
    return;

  for (k = 0; k < *number; k++)
    scanf("%d", &table[k]);
}

/*
**          --------------------------- oOo ---------------------------
**          --------------------------- oOo ---------------------------
*/

void output(const int table[], const int number)
{
  int k;

  for (k = 0; k < number; k++)
   printf("%d\n", table[k]);
}

/*
**          --------------------------- oOo ---------------------------
**          --------------------------- oOo ---------------------------
*/

void quicksort(int table[], const int number)
{
  rquick(table, 0, number-1); /* recursive quicksort */
}

/*
**          --------------------------- oOo ---------------------------
**          --------------------------- oOo ---------------------------
*/
```

```
void rquick(int table[], const int lo, const int hi)
{
  int low, high, pivot;

  low = lo;
  high = hi;
  if (low < high){
    pivot = table[high];
    do {
      while (low < high && table[low] <= pivot)
        low++;
      while (high > low && table[high] >= pivot)
        high--;
      if (low < high)                    /* out of order pair */
        SWAP(table[low], table[high]);
    } while (low < high);
    SWAP(table[low], table[hi]);    /* move pivot to low */
    rquick(table, lo, low-1);
    rquick(table, low+1, hi);
  }
}
```

CASE STUDY   11.2 Integer sets

In Chapters 5 and 6 we introduced a systematic approach to program construction based upon abstraction. In particular, functional decomposition or stepwise refinement described the program in terms of intermediate abstract actions. These abstractions reduce the complexity and details that must be considered at any stage during program development. The abstract operations identify the what is to be done, rather than the how it is to be done.

In Chapter 7 we encouraged the application of the same abstraction principle to the description of data. All data types in a program consist of a set of values and a set of operations upon these values. Abstract data types free the programmer from knowing how the values are actually represented by providing operators to manipulate them.

Consider, then, a program which manipulates sets of integers. The actual program will be defined presently. Irrespective of how the sets are implemented, we will need to perform basic set operations such as clearing a set to the empty set, inserting and removing elements of a set, and a test for set membership. Other possible operators include set union, set intersection and set difference. For our particular application the latter are not required and are ignored.

All of the operations are expressed as functions whose specifications are independent of the final representation for the sets. The implementation for the operators will have knowledge of the actual implementation, but this will not be evident in the calling sequence. This we achieve in C by encapsulating both the set data type and the operators in a program unit. The latter are exportable to the application program, while details of the former remain invisible. For instance, Figure 11.5 specifies the abstract data type integer set.

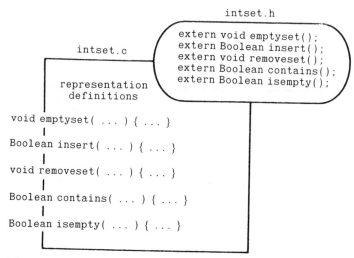

Figure 11.5

Strictly, the implementation developed allows only one instance of an integer set to be present. Our program units are used to partition the program text into manageable pieces. The program units are themselves `static`. We cannot create new program units or copies of existing units dynamically as programs execute.

The implementation details of the abstract data type integer set is private to the program unit `intset.c`. Several alternative implementations are possible. The packaging permits one representation to be substituted by another provided the operator interface remains unchanged.

Our implementation maintains a list of the members of a set using an array to hold the values. The implementation choice is reasonable if an upperbound, say SETMAX, can be placed on the number of members contained by the set. The set is then implemented by an array of `int`'s, together with a `size` variable indicating the number of present members in the set. The declarations are:

```
#define SETMAX              64

typedef int                 Set[SETMAX];     /* array representation */
typedef unsigned int        Members;         /* number of elements */

static Set                  set;
static Members              size = 0;        /* default size */
```

In this array version we choose the most convenient representation for set member insertion. Each new member is appended to the end of the existing set using the next available free array element without including duplicates. Set removal involves moving the later members towards array element 0 to fill the gap created by this operation. Both the remove and contains operators will use a linear search through the members to find the required value. By recording the members in ascending order in the array, a binary search algorithm might be employed. To do so, however, means the insert operator must now determine the correct position for insertion (see Exercise 7).

The header file for this package follows:

```
/*
**      File:           intset.h
**
**      Integer set abstract data type. The set abstraction
**      is defined by a representation-independent
**      specification. The specification consists of a
**      a set of operators for creating objects of the
**      type, retrieving certain information from the
**      objects, and updating the objects.
*/

#ifndef INTSET

    #define INTSET

    #include "boolean.h"

    extern void emptyset(void);
    extern Boolean insert(const int);
    extern void removeset(const int);
    extern Boolean contains(const int);
    extern Boolean isempty(void);

#endif
```

The implementation is provided by the associated program unit intset.c. To preserve the meaning of the variable size, we arrange that when the set contains, say, K members, variable size = K and the members are stored in array elements 1, 2, 3, ..., K. Array element 0 is unused. The listing for file intset.c now follows:

```
/*
**      File:           intset.c
**
**      Integer set abstract data type. The set abstraction
**      is defined by a representation-independent
**      specification. The specification consists of a
**      a set of operators for creating objects of the
**      type, retrieving certain information from the
**      objects, and updating the objects.
*/

#include <stdio.h>
#include "intset.h"
```

```
#define SETMAX        64

typedef int          Set[SETMAX];   /* array representation */
typedef unsigned int Members;       /* number of elements */

static Set           set;
static Members       size = 0;      /* default size */

/*
**      Operator EMPTYSET disposes of the records
**      representing any existing members of the set.
*/

void emptyset(void)
{
  size = 0;
}



/*
**      Private function LOCATE finds the position of the
**      first set element = MEMBER in the array, if one
**      is present; otherwise position = size+1.
*/

static Members locate(const int member)
{
  Members position = size;

  while (position)
    if (set[position] == member)
      break;
    else
      position--;

  return (position);
}

/*
**      The REMOVE operator searches the set for an
**      occurrence of the value to be removed. If one
**      is found, it is deleted from the array
**      representation and all successive elements
**      are brought forward one position.
*/

void removeset(const int member)
{
  Members      position, next;

  if (position = locate(member)){
    size--;
    for (next = position; next <= size; next++)
```

```
        set[next] = set[next+1];
    }
}

/*
**      Function CONTAINS searches the set members
**      and returns the appropriate logical value.
*/

Boolean contains(const int member)
{
   return locate(member);
}

/*
**      The order of the members of a set is unimportant.
**      The most convenient method to implement the
**      the operation INSERT is to perform a simple
**      append. Duplicates are ignored.
*/

Boolean insert(const int member)
{
   if (contains(member))
     return (TRUE);

   if (size < SETMAX − 1){
     set[++size] = member;
     return (TRUE);
   } else
     return (FALSE);
}

/*
**      Function ISEMPTY simply tests whether the set
**      contains no elements. If so, the logical value
**      TRUE is returned, otherwise FALSE.
*/

Boolean isempty(void)
{
   return size == 0;
}
```

And now for the problem itself. The classical algorithm for enumerating prime numbers is the Sieve of Eratosthenes. Suppose that we want to find all the prime numbers less than 12. We start by putting all the numbers from 2 to 12 inclusive on to the sieve:

2 3 4 5 6 7 8 9 10 11 12

We then repeat the following actions until the sieve is empty:

1.   Select and remove the lowest number from the sieve, claiming that it is a
     prime.
2.   Remove all multiples of that number from the sieve.

After step 1, we have 2 as a prime. From step 2, the sieve now contains the odd
numbers:

    3 5 7 9 11

Repeating the process, we know that 3 is the next prime and only 5, 7 and 11
remain on the sieve. The process continues until the sieve is empty. The identified
primes not exceeding 12 are then 2, 3, 5, 7, and 11.

    There are many ways to program this problem. One possibility is to employ the
integer set abstraction. The sieve is represented by a set and is initially established to
contain 2, 3, . . ., N for some data value N. Members are entered on to the sieve
with the insert operation and deleted with the remove operation. Since the set
abstraction does not guarantee any particular ordering of the members, a procedure
must be found to determine the lowest member of the set and those elements which
are multiples of this smallest value. In both cases this is done by cycling through all
the possible sieve values 2, 3, . . ., N seeking the desired condition. Because of
this the method we are applying is not the most efficient. The example is chosen for
pedagogic, rather than realistic, reasons.

    The problem domain is expressed in terms of a *sieve*. The solution we arrive at
will also be in terms of the sieve. In effect, the sieve is an abstract data object.
Ignoring the implementation for such an object, what are the operations performed
in association with it? Four operations have been alluded to in the problem
statement, and are:

1.   Initially establish a sieve containing the values 2, 3, . . ., N, for some N.
2.   Select and remove the smallest number in the sieve.
3.   Remove all multiples of the smallest from the sieve.
4.   Determine when the sieve is empty.

Using our usual notation, we develop the sieve package as shown in Figure 11.6.

    A hierarchy of abstractions is now present. The application program is expressed
in terms of the sieve abstract data type. For this, a package is established to define
the specification and implementation attributes of a sieve. The sieve operators
themselves are expressed in terms of the integer set abstraction. A suite of listings
for the sieve abstraction and the progam appear below.

```
/*
**        File :            sieve.h
**
**        Sieve abstraction. To obtain the prime numbers
**        less than some arbitrary value N, the classical
**        algorithm is the Sieve of Eratosthenes. The sieve
**        initially contains the numbers 2, 3, ... , N. The
**        lowest number is removed (the first prime) and
```

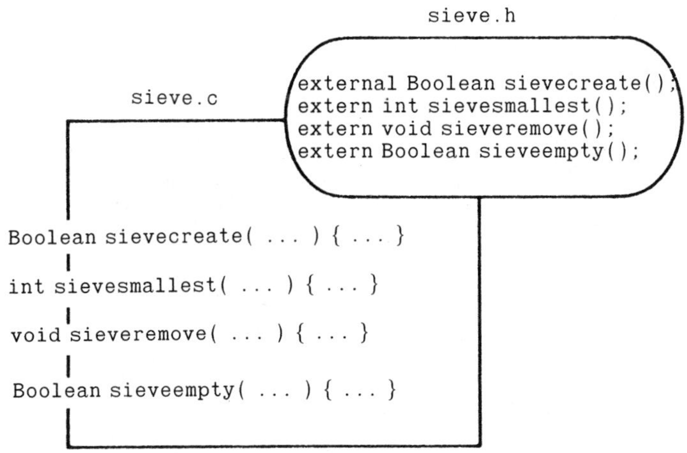

Figure 11.6

```
**        all numbers that are multiples of the lowest. The
**        process is repeated until the sieve is empty.
*/

#ifndef SIEVE

  #define SIEVE

  #include "boolean.h"

  extern Boolean sievecreate(const int);
  extern int sievesmallest(const int);
  extern void sieveremove(const int, const int);
  extern Boolean sieveempty(void);

#endif




/*
**        File :          sieve.c
**
**        Sieve abstraction. To obtain the prime numbers
**        less than some arbitrary value N, the classical
**        algorithm is the Sieve of Eratosthenes. The sieve
**        initially contains the numbers 2, 3, ... , N. The
**        lowest number is removed (the first prime) and
**        all numbers that are multiples of the lowest. The
**        process is repeated until the sieve is empty.
*/
```

```
#include <stdio.h>
#include "intset.h"
#include "sieve.h"

/*
**      Operation SIEVECREATE establishes the initial
**      condition for the sieve. A set representation for
**      the sieve is employed, and contains the values
**      2, 3, ..., N.
*/

Boolean sievecreate(const int n)
{
  int k;

  emptyset();                 /* start with an empty sieve */
  for (k = 2; k <= n; k++)/* generate the initial values */
    if (!insert(k))           /* set overflow? */
      return (FALSE);         /* then abort */

  return (TRUE);              /* all ok */
}

/*
**      Determine the lowest value in the sieve with
**      operation SIEVESMALLEST. All possible sieve values
**      are generated, tested for set membership, and
**      the least value determined.
*/
int sievesmallest(const int n)
{
  int k;
  if(isempty()) return 0;       /* special */
  for(k = 2; ; k++)
    if(contains(k)) return k;
}

/*
**      Remove the smallest member of the sieve and
**      all those values that are multiples of the
**      smallest.
*/

void sieveremove(const int smallest, const int n)
{
  int k;

  for(k = smallest; k <= n; k += smallest)
    removeset(k);
}
```

```
/*
**        Determine when there are no more sieve elements.
*/

Boolean sieveempty(void)
{
  return (isempty());
}
```

```
/*
**        File :          casell-2.c
**
**        Generate all the prime numbers less than
**        some value N using the Sieve of Eratosthenes
**        algorithm. The positive integer N is given as
**        program input.
*/

#include <stdio.h>
#include "sieve.h"

main()
{
  int size, lowest;

  printf("Enter the upper limit, N: ");
  scanf("%d", &size);

  if (!sievecreate(size))          /* initial sieve configuration */
    printf("Cannot create sieve of size %d\n", size);
  else {
    printf ("Prime numbers not exceeding %d:\n", size);
    while (!sieveempty()){          /* until no more elements */
      lowest = sievesmallest(size);          /* smallest = prime */
      printf("%d\n", lowest);
      sieveremove(lowest, size);  /* remove least and all multiples */
    }
  }
}
```

Observe how errors are dealt with in both packages. In the same way that integer division by zero generates the error condition overflow, the abstract data type operators should also detect error conditions. For example, in the integer set data type, it is an error to attempt to insert a new member into the set already containing the maximum permissible.

It is vital that the implementation of an abstract data type detects error situations. There are several ways to implement error handling. One strategy is to treat all errors as fatal errors, which immediately terminates program execution. The other strategy is to treat these error situations such that the user program may detect and react to them. It is this method used in both the integer set and the sieve data types. In both cases, error situations are handled by implementing certain functions to return Boolean values such that FALSE represents an error and TRUE represents success.

11.9 Summary

1. An *array* is an example of an aggregate type in which a collection of data items that are all of the same type are associated with a single name. An array declaration includes the type of the elements and the number of elements. Elements of an array are accessed by a *subscripted variable*, where the *subscript* or *index* is an integer expression. It is the programmer's responsibility to ensure that an array index is within bounds.

2. When an array name is passed as a function argument, a copy of the base address of the array is actually passed. In the header to a function definition, the declaration:

    ```
    int table[];
    ```

    is equivalent to:

    ```
    int *table;
    ```

    Within the function body either form can be indexed or used as a pointer. The declaration for a multi-dimensional array in a function definition must have all the dimensions specified except the first.

3. An array can be initialized with a list of compile time values. If an external or internal `static` array is not initialized, then all the elements are guaranteed to be set to zero.

11.10 Exercises

1. In the context of the declarations:

    ```
    float table[10];
    float *pt, *qt;
    ```

    what is the effect of the following statements:

    (a) pt = table;
         *pt = 0;
         *(pt + 2) = 3.14;

    (b) pt = table + 2;
         qt = pt;
         *qt = 2.718;

```
(c)  pt = table;                    (d)  pt = table;
     qt = table + 10;                    qt = table + 10;
     printf("%d\n",                      for(; pt < qt; pt++)
          qt - pt);                           *pt = 1.23;
```

2. A firm employs a group of twenty salesmen (with reference numbers 1–20 inclusive) who are paid commission on that portion of their sales which exceeds two-thirds of the average sales of the group. A program is required to read the sales value of each salesman and to print out the reference number of those who qualify for commission, together with their sales.

3. Data to a program consists of a sequence of positive integers terminated by a negative value. Determine if the number sequence is palindromic, reading the same both forwards and backwards.

4. Assume the number of rooms in a hotel is given by a constant NMBROFROOMS. Write (a) an array declaration suitable for keeping track of which rooms are free; and (b) a function to count how many rooms are free, given that appropriate values have been stored in the array.

5. A hospital patient's temperature is recorded four times a day for a week. Construct a program that will input the readings for each day, and:

    (a) output the data in a table as shown below:

```
          SUN MON TUE WED THU FRI SAT
   TEMP 1  X   X   X   X   X   X   X
        2  X   X   X   X   X   X   X
        3  X   X   X   X   X   X   X
        4  X   X   X   X   X   X   X
```

    (b) output the highest and lowest recorded temperatures together with the day and the number of the reading on which they occurred.

6. In Case Study 11.2 the number of members in a set is controlled by the integer 'size'. To permit a client program to determine this value, why is it considered bad programming practice to redeclare size with storage class 'extern'. How should it be done?

7. Reprogram program unit integer set (intset.c) in Case Study 11.2 such that the members of the set are recorded in ascending order. Rework the private function 'locate' to use a binary search algorithm.

    What are the effects of this change of representation on the sieve abstraction?

8.   Modify the Shell sort function of Section 11.3 by having the interval reduce by one-third on each pass. Initially the interval is determined from the recurrence relation:

```
interval₀ = 1
interval_{k+1} = 3 * interval_k + 1
```

until the value exceeds the number of items to be sorted.

9.   Using the data encapsulation concepts of Case Study 11.2, develop a program unit to support a table of integers. The interface to the unit is provided by the header file:

```
/*
**    File:    table.h
*/

#define FALSE     0
#define TRUE      1
typedef int       Boolean;

extern Boolean insert(const int x);
extern Boolean find(const int x);
```

where function `insert` returns FALSE if the table is full, otherwise it inserts x into the table and returns TRUE; and function `find` determines if the argument x is present in the table.

Develop a program that uses the *table* abstraction and reads a series of positive integers printing the duplicates as they are read. The data set terminates with a negative sentinel.

12

Character strings

STRINGS are one-dimensional character arrays. Normally, a string in C is terminated by an end-of-string sentinel consisting of the null character, '\0'. It is useful to think of strings as having variable length, but with a maximum allowable length determined by the size of the character array holding the string. The size of the array must be sufficient to include the end-of-string sentinel. As usual it is the programmer's responsibility to ensure that the array bounds are not exceeded.

String constants were defined in Section 3.4 as a character sequence enclosed in a matching pair of double quotes. The string "abc" is implemented as a character array of size 4. The final element of the array is the null character (see Figure 12.1). From Section 11.4, a character array may be initialized with these same values using the construct:

```
static char word [] = { 'a', 'b', 'c', '\0' };
```

C additionally permits a character array to be initialized with a string constant rather than having to list the individual characters. The above can also be expressed by:

```
static char word [] = "abc";
```

The latter is preferred since it is that much more readable.

A string constant such as:

```
"hello"
```

is an array of characters. The C compiler associates a pointer to the first character of the array. A variable declared of type pointer to char may be assigned the pointer to a character string. If variable greeting is declared as:

```
char *greeting;
```

then the statement:

```
greeting = "hello";
```

Figure 12.1

257

assigns to greeting a pointer to the actual character string. It must be emphasized that this is not a string copy; only pointers are involved. The declaration and assignation may be combined into:

```
char *greeting = "hello";
```

Care is required to distinguish between the declaration:

```
char word [] = "hello";
```

and:

```
char *greeting = "hello";
```

Superficially, both appear to achieve the same. The literal strings are treated as pointers to characters which then associate with the identifiers word and greeting. The difference is that the former is a constant pointer to a character, whilst the latter is a variable of type pointer to a char. All array names, such as word, are treated as constant pointers. On the other hand, greeting is a variable and may be subsequently assigned some new value, as in:

```
greeting = "Good morning";
```

As an illustration of how variable length character strings are used, let us develop a function to count the number of characters in a string. We shall call our function length and have it defined in terms of a single character array argument. The character array is terminated with the null character in the usual way. The null character is not included in the character count.

PROGRAM 12.1

```
/*
**      Implement a function to count the number of characters
**      in a character string. The count is enumerated by
**      searching through the string for the terminating
**      null character whilst maintaining the count. The null
**      character is not included in the count.
*/

#include <stdio.h>

main()
{
  static char word[] = { "abc" };
  static char *greeting = "hello";

  int length(const char []);                 /* prototype declaration */

  printf("Lengths %d and %d\n",
      length(word), length(greeting));
}
```

```
int length(const char string[])
{
  int count = 0;

  while (string[count] != NULL)
    count++;

  return (count);
}
```

In function `length`, the local variable `count` is declared and initialized to zero. The while loop sequences through the character array until the null character is reached. The null character signals the end of the string, the loop terminates and the value of the count returned as the function value. This value represents the number of characters in the string, excluding the null character. The program output is then:

```
Lengths 3 and 5
```

being the lengths of the two respective strings.

In practice, it is customary to express the control expression in the while statement in function `length` in another way. We observe that every non-null character in the string is counted. All non-null characters have a non-zero internal representation. Non-zero is interpreted in C as logical true. Only the null character has the internal value zero (logical false). The loop may therefore be written as:

```
while (string[count])
  count++;
```

A formal argument to a function that is an array is immediately converted by the C compiler into a pointer to the type of the array elements. The function `length` is treated as:

```
int length(char *const string)
```

This is still consistent with the function usage, since it is called with actual arguments `word` and `greeting` which are pointers to type char. Normally, the function would be coded in terms of pointers:

```
int length(char *const string)
{
  int count = 0;

  while (*string){
    count++;
    string++;
  }
  return (count);
}
```

Again, observe that the explicit comparison against null is redundant and, accordingly, is omitted.

One further revision is possible. The control expression in the `while` statement determines if the character pointed at is the null character. If it is not, both the counter and the pointer are incremented. The test and increment to the pointer may be combined using:

```
*string++
```

The value of `*string++` is the character that `string` pointed to before incrementing. The postfix operator `++` does not change `string` until after the character has been fetched. The final version for function `length` is:

```
int length(char *const string)
{
  int count = 0;

  while (*string++)
    count++;

  return (count);
}
```

This fragment of programming is a C idiom. It should be rehearsed and understood. Many subsequent programs are fashioned this way.

12.1 String comparisons

It is not possible in C to perform direct comparison of two strings. Statements such as:

```
if (string1 < string2) ....
```

and:

```
while (string1 != string2) ....
```

are not permissible since the relational and equality operators can only be applied to simple data types such as `int`, `char` and `float`. To determine if two strings are equal, say, we must perform a character by character comparison of the two strings under discussion. If we simultaneously exhaust both strings, and all the characters to that point are identical, then the strings are equal, otherwise they are unequal.

We develop a function called `equal` with two character string arguments. If the strings are identical, function `equal` returns the logical constant TRUE, otherwise it returns FALSE. This way, the function may be used in tests:

```
if (equal (string1, string2)) ....
```

and:

```
while (! equal (string1, string2)) ....
```

The function and driver program is shown in Program 12.2. The while loop in the body of function equal compares corresponding character elements of the two strings. Provided the characters are the same, the scanning continues. When they differ, or when the end of one string is obtained, the loop terminates. One of three possible conditions now exist – the end of both strings has occurred, in which case the strings are identical; one or other string has terminated and they now differ from this point; or the two corresponding characters are not the same. From this the correct return code is determined.

PROGRAM 12.2

```
/*
**      Determine if two strings are equal. Direct string
**      comparisons are not implemented in C. The function
**      'equal' compares two strings and if they are
**      identical, returns the value TRUE, otherwise
**      returns FALSE. The equality test is implemented by
**      a character by character comparison.
*/

#include <stdio.h>

#define FALSE            0
#define TRUE             1

typedef int              Boolean;
typedef char             *String;

Boolean equal (String, String);

main ()
{
  static char str1 [] = { "Programming in C" };
  static char str2 [] = { "Programming is fun" };

  if (equal (str1, str2))
    printf ("Equal\n");
  else
    printf ("Unequal\n");

  if (equal (str2, "Programming is fun"))
    printf ("Equal\n");
  else
    printf ("Unequal\n");
}


Boolean equal (String stringa, String stringb)
{
```

```
    while (*stringa == *stringb++)
      if (*stringa++ == '\0')
        return (TRUE);

    return (FALSE);
}
```

12.2 Character string input

The standard I/O library function `scanf` can be used with the %s conversion to read a string of characters (see Appendix F4). The declaration and statement:

```
char message[80];
scanf ("%s", message);
```

have the effect of reading a character string from the standard input and storing it in the character array `message`. Note that unlike previous `scanf` calls, the address operator & is not required before an array of character variable name. The operator is not necessary since the C compiler has already equivalenced `message` into a pointer to type `char`. Variable `message`, therefore, is already treated as an address.

If the above `scanf` call were executed and the following characters entered at the terminal:

```
Hello
```

then the null-terminated string "Hello" is read by `scanf` and stored in the character array `message`. If instead, the following line of text were supplied:

```
Good morning
```

then only the string "Good" is stored in the array `message`, since any whitespace character terminates the %s conversion. If the same `scanf` call were executed a second time, then the string "morning" is stored in the array.

Program 12.3 illustrates the use of `scanf` with the %s conversion to read three strings.

PROGRAM 12.3

```
/*
**      Program to illustrate character string input
**      through use of the standard function 'scanf'.
*/

#include <stdio.h>

#define SIZE              80
```

```
main()
{
  char wordl[SIZE], word2[SIZE], word3[SIZE];

  printf("Enter the text: ");
  scanf("%s %s %s", wordl, word2, word3);
  printf("wordl = %s\nword2 = %s\nword3 = %s\n",
      wordl, word2, word3);
}
```

The program operates by first issuing the prompt "Enter the text: ". If, in response, the user were to enter two character strings separated by a space, then the first is assigned to variable wordl and the second to variable word2. The space acts as a separator between each string, terminating the first string and discarded as leading whitespace preceding the second string. If the second string is terminated by a newline, it too is discarded when reading the third string.

The program was tested with the following dialogue. User input is underlined to distinguish it from program output:

```
Enter the text: Programming in
C
wordl = Programming
word2 = in
word3 = C
```

Many text processing applications require that an entire line of text be read from the terminal before processing can commence. To use scanf and the %s conversion we would need to know in advance the number of individual strings appearing on a single line. Commonly this is not always available. Lines of text often contain different number of words or strings.

To support line at a time reading, we implement a function called read_line. This function reads a line of text up to and including the newline symbol. All the text characters, but excluding the newline character, are stored in the character array s. The string is null terminated in the usual manner. The integer argument limit denotes the length of the array. If more characters appear in the input line than can be successfully stored in the array, the input continues to the newline, but all excess characters are ignored.

```
typedef char              *String;
void read_line (String s, int limit)
{
  char c;                     /* input character */
  int count = 0;              /* character count */

                              /* read until end of line */
  while ((c = getchar ()) != NEWLINE){
    count++;
```

```
      if (count < limit)       /* room in string? */
         *s++ = c;             /* then record */
   }
   *s = '\0';
}
```

We are now in a position to develop a string handling program to read a series of lines of text from the standard input and to echo each line to the standard output with the characters of the line reversed. The input is terminated with a line consisting of the string "ZZZ". The text lines are input using the function read_line. Each input line is compared (using function equal) against the terminator. Upon discovering the unique terminator, the program stops. Otherwise, an in-place reversal of the character strings in the line is performed, and the line echoed to the standard output.

PROGRAM 12.4(a)

```
/*
**        Read a series of lines from the standard input
**        and write each line to the standard output with
**        the characters reversed. The input terminates
**        with the line ZZZ.
*/

#include <stdio.h>

#define FALSE           0
#define TRUE            1
typedef int             Boolean;

#define SIZE            132
#define TERMINATOR      "ZZZ"
#define NEWLINE         '\n'
#define NOT             !

typedef char            Line[SIZE];
typedef char            *String;

void    read_line(String, int);
void    reverse(String);
Boolean equal(String, String);
int     length(String);

main ()
{
   Line          line;

      read_line (line, SIZE);                    /* first data line */
      while (NOT equal (line, TERMINATOR)){ /* end of data? */
         reverse (line);                       /* reverse it, then .. */
```

```
      printf ("%s\n", line);           /* .. print it */
      read_line (line, SIZE);          /* next data line */
}
  }


  void read_line (String s, int limit)
  {
    char c;                    /* input character */
    int count = 0;             /* character count */

                         /* read until end of line */
    while ((c = getchar ()) != NEWLINE){
      count++;
      if (count < limit)        /* room in string? */
        *s++ = c;               /* then record */
    }
     *s = '\0';
  }


  Boolean equal (String stra, String strb)
  {
    while (*stra == *strb++)
      if (*stra++ == '\0')
        return (TRUE);

    return (FALSE);
  }


  void reverse (String s)
  {
    char c, *t;

    t = s + length (s) - 1;    /* end of string */
    while (s < t){             /* two ends approaching centre */
      c = *s;                  /* exchange */
      *s++ = *t;
      *t-- = c;
  }
  }


  int length (String s)
  {
    int count = 0;

    while (*s++)
      count++;

    return (count);
  }
```

12.3 Standard library string handling functions

The standard C library contains many useful string handling functions. They are fully documented in Appendix F.2. A number of the more common examples are illustrated below.

Two character strings s1 and s2 may be compared using the function strcmp:

```
int strcmp(char *s1, char *s2)
```

An integer is returned which is less than, equal to, or greater than zero depending on whether s1 is lexicographically less than, equal to, or greater than s2. The character-by-character comparison is performed in terms of the implementation character set, for example ASCII.

This function could have been used in place of function equal in the last example. The test:

```
while (NOT equal(line, TERMINATOR)) ....
```

would be replaced by the equivalent:

```
while (strcmp(line, TERMINATOR) != 0) ....
```

since a non-zero returned by function strcmp implies that the two string arguments line and TERMINATOR are unequal.

In particular, to emphasize that function strcmp does not alter either of its two string arguments, the prototype is:

```
int strcmp(const char *s1, const char *s2)
```

A count of the number of characters in a null-terminated string is performed by the function strlen. The prototype for this function is:

```
int strlen(const char *s)
```

Again, in the last example, strlen could be used as a direct replacement for function length.

The function strcpy copies the content of string s2 to string s1, overwriting the old content of s1. The entire content of s2 is copied, including the terminating null character. A pointer to the first character of s1 is returned as the function value. The function header is:

```
char *strcpy(char *s1, const char *s2)
```

Thus to copy the content of a string called oldname to a second string called newname, we use:

```
strcpy(newname, oldname);
```

When using strcpy, the destination string must be large enough to receive the copied string.

The function strcat appends the content of string s2 to the end of string s1.

The pointer to the first character string s1 is returned as the function value. The null character that terminates s1 initially and the characters that follow it are overwritten with the characters from s2, including a new terminating null character. The function header is:

```
char *strcat(char *s1, const char *s2)
```

Consider three strings called prefix, name and suffix which are to be concatenated together to produce a string called filename. The effect is achieved by copying the prefix string into the destination, and then concatenating the other two strings to the destination. The coding is:

```
strcpy(filename, prefix);
strcat(filename, name);
strcat(filename, suffix);
```

Using appropriate functions from the standard library, Program 12.4(a) is rewritten below. In particular, functions length and equal are replaced by strlen and strcmp respectively. Also from the standard library, function gets (see Appendix F4) replicates the role of function read_line in the original program. The function prototype for gets is in <stdio.h>, and the prototypes for all the string handling functions are in <string.h>. A more secure variant of gets is the library function fgets (see Appendix F.4).

PROGRAM 12.4(b)

```
/*
**      Read a series of lines from the standard input
**      and write each line to the standard output with
**      the characters reversed. The input terminates
**      with the line ZZZ.
*/

#include <stdio.h>
#include <string.h>

#define SIZE            132
#define TERMINATOR      "ZZZ"

typedef char            Line[SIZE];
typedef char            *String;

void    reverse(String);

main ()
{
  Line          line;
```

```
      gets (line);                           /* first data line */
      while (strcmp (line, TERMINATOR) != 0){   /* end of data? */
        reverse (line);                      /* reverse it, then .. */
        printf ("%s\n", line);               /* .. print it */
        gets (line);                         /* next data line */
      }
    }


    void reverse(String s)
    {
      char c, *t;

      t = s + strlen (s) - 1;    /* end of string */
      while (s < t){             /* two ends approaching centre */
        c = *s;                  /* exchange */
        *s++ = *t;
        *t-- = c;
      }
    }
```

CASE STUDY   12.1 Word concordance

A program is required to examine a piece of text and produce a list, in alphabetical order, of all the distinct words which appear in the text. It may be assumed that no word is more than twenty characters long, that the words are separated by one or more whitespace characters, that the text contains no punctuation symbols (hyphens, commas, apostrophes, etc.) and that the text terminates with the unique word 'ZZZ'. The sample input:

```
the quick brown fox jumped
over the lazy dog
ZZZ
```

would produce the corresponding output:

```
brown
dog
fox
jumped
lazy
over
quick
the
```

The overall form of the program to solve the problem can be as follows:

```
initialize the list of words
get the first word from the input text
WHILE not the end of text
DO
```

```
        record the word in the list
        get the next word from the input text
    ENDWHILE
    print the words in the list
```

At this stage we identify two abstractions involved:

(a) a stream of words extracted from the input text, one at a time;
(b) a list of the words.

For the present, we shall ignore the input stream abstraction and concentrate on the list of words. To implement the program, the word list abstraction must allow operations to:

(a) record a word in the list;
(b) print the entire list content in dictionary order;
(c) initialize an empty list.

The number of words in the list is unpredictable. However, since we shall represent the list as an array of words of some fixed size, then we also require an operation to:

(d) determine when the capacity of the list is exhausted.

A representation-independent version of the word list abstraction is achieved by packaging the data structures and operations in a program unit wordlist.c. The features of the word list abstraction required by the application program are the operations to initialize the list, insert a word into the list, print the list of words in alphabetical order, and determine if the list is full. Details of the list are otherwise hidden from the client program. Using our usual notation, the package outline is shown by Figure 12.2.

The word list is implemented as an array of words. Defining the type Word as a character string of length 21 (maximum of twenty characters plus the null character), provides a suitable data representation for a word:

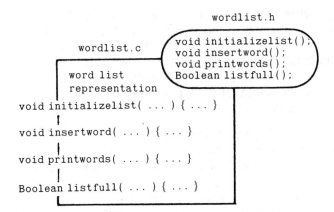

Figure 12.2

```
#define WORDSIZE      21
typedef char          Word[WORDSIZE];
```

Setting the word list table to be of length 256, say, then the implementation is an array of this size, each element of type `Word`:

```
#define LISTSIZE      256
typedef Word          WordList[LISTSIZE];
```

The program output is to be an alphabetically ordered list of the words occurring in the input text. We may approach this problem in two ways: construct an unsorted list as the text is input then perform a sort immediately before outputting the list; or, construct the list in such a way that its content are always in alphabetical order. We shall choose the latter method since it is more efficient. To do so, each new entry inserted into the list must maintain the ordering of the list.

The complete word list is then represented as a variable of type `WordList`. In addition, an integer variable is maintained as the current length of the list, i.e. the actual number of words presently in the list. This variable is called `listlen`. The variable declarations are then:

```
static WordList       wordlist;
static int            listlen;
```

Note that both have storage class `static` and are hence private to the program unit.

An empty list is trivially represented by initializing the variable `listlen` to zero, so we have:

```
listlen = 0;
```

Recording a new word read from the input text into the word list can be expressed as an operation described by the function header:

```
void insertword(Word word)
```

The procedure takes a new word and searches the current list to determine whether or not that word has already occurred in the text. If it has, it already appears in the list and the duplicate is discarded. If not, the new word is inserted in its correct position in the list, maintaining the alphabetical ordering of the list.

We shall perform a linear search of the list in looking for duplicates. Beginning the search at the first element of the list, we inspect successive elements until one of three possibilities occurs:

1. An entry in the list matches the new word; the duplicate is ignored and no further processing is performed on the list.
2. The list is exhausted with no match found; the new word is introduced at the end of the list.
3. A word alphabetically greater than the new word is found in the list; the located word and all successive words are displaced down the list by one place and the new word introduced into the vacated location.

This action may be expressed as:

```
initialize index to the first word in the list
WHILE the list is not exhausted DO
        IF the new word is alphabetically after
           the referenced word in the list
        THEN
                advance the index to the next word in the list
        ELSE
                terminate the search on a match
        ENDIF
ENDWHILE
IF not a duplicate word
THEN
        displace all words in list from reference point
        insert new word into available location
ENDIF
```

The list is maintained by recording the number of words currently held. If there are listlen words in the list, they are indexed as 0, 1, 2, ... , listlen − 1. This value is used to control the search:

```
for index = 0; index < listlen; index++ DO
        IF the new word is alphabetically after
           the referenced word in the list
        THEN
                advance the index to the next word in the list
        ELSE
                terminate the search on a match
        ENDIF
ENDFOR
```

Upon completion of the loop, the integer variable index refers to the entry in the list containing a word that either matches the new word or is alphabetically after the new word. For example, if the new word to be entered into the list is GOAT, and the list is of length 5 and contains the information shown in Figure 12.3, then the index value is 2, as shown.

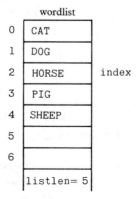

Figure 12.3

To add a new word to the list, we increase the word list length by 1, and move all the words alphabetically greater than the new word down the list by one position, inserting the new word in the vacated slot. This repositioning must begin at the end of the list, otherwise the entries in the list will be overwritten. The procedure in outline is:

```
listlen++;
for (shift = listlen; shift > index; shift--)
    copy list element [shift-1] into list element [shift]
copy new word into list element [index]
```

After increasing the length of the list and moving the entries from the index position the list now appears as shown in Figure 12.4 with the new word to be entered into the vacated location in the list. The final configuration for the list after copying the new word into the correct position is shown in Figure 12.5.

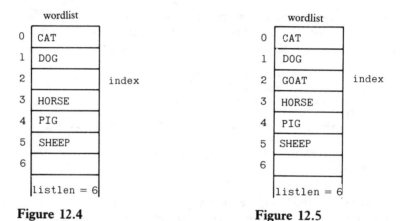

Figure 12.4   Figure 12.5

Printing the ordered list of words is straightforward. The operation is implemented by cycling through each word in the list in turn, and printing it:

```
FOR each word in the list DO
    print the word
ENDFOR
```

The word list is exhausted if there is no more room in the table. This is determined if the variable listlen equals the table size (256). If the capacity of the word list is exhausted before all the input text is read, no more entries are made in the table. Reading the input continues until the terminator is input. The table is then displayed.

The second abstraction in this problem is the stream of input words. The single operation upon this abstraction delivers the next word from the input text. Recollect that the library function scanf with the conversion operator %s will read a string of non-whitespace characters into a character array. Further, any leading whitespace is discarded. Thus reading the next word from the input is implemented with the built-in:

```
scanf("%s", word)
```

where word is an array of characters.

The completed program is listed below:

```
/*
**        Examine a piece of text and produce a list, in
**        alphabetical order, of all the distinct words
**        which appear in the text. The text is read from
**        the standard input, terminates with the unique
**        word 'zzz', contains no punctuation symbols, and
**        has no word with more than 20 characters.
**
**        The word list is maintained by an array. Each new
**        word is compared with those words presently in the
**        list. A duplicate word is discarded, and a new
**        word is correctly inserted into the list.
*/

#include <stdio.h>
#include "wordlist.h"

main ()
{
  Word          word;           /* next data word */

  initializelist();
  scanf ("%s", word);           /* read first word */
  while (strcmp (word, TERMINATOR) != 0){  /* end of data? */
    if (! listfull ())          /* room in table? */
      insertword (word);
    scanf ("%s", word);         /* read next word */
  }

  printwords ();                /* tabulate */
}




/*
**        File:   wordlist.h
**
**        Header file for the word list abstraction. This file
**        defines a series of manifest constants, a word list
**        table, and a set of associated operators.
*/
```

```
#define FALSE          0
#define TRUE           1
typedef int            Boolean;

#define WORDSIZE       21
typedef char           Word[WORDSIZE];
#define TERMINATOR     "ZZZ"

extern void initializelist(void);
extern void insertword(Word);
extern void printwords(void);
extern Boolean listfull(void);
```

```
/*
**       File:   wordlist.c
**
**       Word list abstraction implementation. The abstraction
**       is realised using an array of WORDs. The number of
**       words presently in the list is maintained by 'listlen'.
*/

#include <stdio.h>
#include <string.h>
#include "wordlist.h"

#define LISTSIZE        256
typedef Word            WordList[LISTSIZE];

static int      listlen = 0;     /* list initially empty */
static WordList wordlist;        /* word list realisation */


void initializelist(void)
{
  listlen = 0;
}


void printwords(void)
{
  int        index;                      /* list index */

  for (index = 0; index < listlen; index++)
    printf ("%s\n", wordlist[index]);
}


void insertword (Word word)
{
```

```
int          index, shift;      /* table indices */
int          comp;              /* comparison flag */
Boolean found;                  /* search indicator */

found = FALSE;                  /* look for word in list */
for (index = 0; index < listlen; index++)
  if ((comp = strcmp (wordlist[index], word)) > 0){
                                /* insert here? */
    found = TRUE;               /* new word position .... */
    break;                      /* .... is 'index' */
  } else if (comp == 0)         /* if duplicate word .... */
    return;                     /* .... discard */

if (! found)                    /* insert new word at .... */
  index = listlen;              /* .... end of list */

for (shift = listlen; shift > index; shift--)
                                /* move each .. */
  strcpy (wordlist[shift], wordlist[shift - 1]);
                                /* .. word down .. */
strcpy (wordlist[index], word);
                                /* .. list and .. */
listlen++;                      /* .. insert and update list length */
}


Boolean listfull(void)
{
  return (listlen == LISTSIZE);
}
```

12.4 Conversions between strings and numerics

Many string handling programs require conversions from both string to number and number to string. Programs are required to read a string of characters and to extract from that string a sequence of decimal digits and convert them to their equivalent numerical value.

As an example, here is a simple version of a function called atoi (ASCII to integer conversion) for converting a string of digits to its numeric equivalent.

```
int atoi(char s[])
{
  int i, n;

  for(n = 0, i = 0; s[i] >= '0' && s[i] <= '9'; i++)
    n = 10 * n + s[i] - '0';
  return n;
}
```

The header file <stdlib.h> declares functions for number conversions. It contains, among other things:

```
int atoi(const char *s)
```

which converts an optionally signed string s to its integer value (leading whitespace is ignored); and

```
long int atol(const char *s)
double atof(const char *s)
```

to convert a string to, respectively, a `long` and a `double`.

The same effect can be achieved by an alternative route. The standard library function `scanf` performs a parse of the stream of characters from the standard input, placing the converted characters into memory locations. For example, the function call:

```
scanf("%d", &number)
```

reads and converts a stream of input characters into a decimal integer value, storing the result at the address of the integer variable `number`. The form of this function call is:

```
scanf(format, argument1, argument2, .... )
```

A variant of this function is known as `sscanf`. Its function call is:

```
sscanf(string, format, argument1, argument2, .... )
```

This function is like `scanf` in operation. The only difference is that `sscanf` takes input characters from a string, while `scanf` always takes its input from the standard input. In the context of the declarations:

```
int number;
char *p = " 123 is an integer";
```

the statements:

```
number = atoi(p)
```

and:

```
sscanf(p, "%d", &number)
```

achieve the same effect – the decimal value 123 is assigned to the integer variable `number`.

Equally, a numerical value may be converted to a null-terminated character string by employing the function `sprintf`:

```
sprintf(string, format, expression1, expression2, .... )
```

The function performs output formatting, writing the output characters to the string specified as the first actual argument. Operationally, the function behaves like `printf`. Given the declaration:

```
char numeric[10];
```

then the statement:

```
sprintf(numeric, "%d", number)
```

reconverts the value 123 in the integer variable number back into a null-terminated string called numeric (see Figure 12.6).

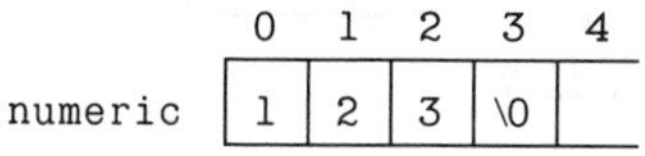

```
           0   1   2   3   4
numeric  | 1 | 2 | 3 | \0 |   |
```

Figure 12.6

12.5 Arrays of pointers

Since pointers are themselves variables, it is possible to construct arrays of pointers. That is, each array element is a pointer to some object. In the declaration:

```
int *ptr[4];
```

variable ptr is an array of four elements of pointers to integers. If x and t are integer variables, then the assignment:

```
ptr[3] = &x;
```

sets the last element of the array to the address of the variable x. By the usual notation, the assignment:

```
t = *ptr[3];
```

copies the content of x into the variable t.

Equally, any element of the array ptr may address any element of an integer array. Given the declarations:

```
int v4[4], v7[7], v2[2], v3[3];
```

we may set the zeroth element of ptr to address the first item in integer array v4 by the assignment:

```
ptr[0] = &v4[0];
```

or, more commmonly, by:

```
ptr[0] = v4;
```

If we were to assign successive elements of the array ptr to the base address of arrays v4, v7, v2 and v3, then in effect we have constructed a two-dimensional *jagged* array. The rows of this array have varying number of elements. The array is no longer the conventional rectangular shape. Pictorially, the two-dimensional array may be viewed as shown in Figure 12.7. The necessary assignments are:

ptr

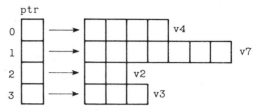

Figure 12.7

```
ptr[0] = v4;
ptr[1] = v7;
ptr[2] = v2;
ptr[3] = v3;
```

The array v7 may be printed with the function call:

```
print_row(ptr[1], 7);
```

where function `print_row` has been programmed as:

```
void print_row(int *pt, int n)
{
   int   k;                    /* loop counter */

   for (k = 0; k < n; k++)     /* for every element */
      printf("%d\n", *pt++);   /* print and advance */
}
```

More commonly, arrays of pointers are used with strings. We illustrate by designing a program that sorts a series of text lines into alphabetical order.

Program 11.3 sorted an array of integers by the Shell sort method. In this example we shall employ the same algorithm to sort lines of text. For this, we need a suitable data representation that will operate efficiently and conveniently with lines of text of varying length.

One solution is to refer to the lines indirectly by pointers. Since there is likely to be more than one line of text, an array of pointers is required. A large array called linebuffer holds the lines that are to be sorted in an end-to-end fashion. A second array, linepointer, contains pointers to where in linebuffer the corresponding line begins. That is, linepointer[k] is the position in linebuffer for the beginning of the kth line, for k >= 0. Figure 12.8 illustrates this organization.

When the sort algorithm calls for an exchange of out-of-order line pairs, only the points are exchanged, not the text lines themselves. This eliminates the high overhead associated with moving large quantities of data. Further, it simplifies the storage management where the lines being swapped are of different lengths.

The sort program reads lines of text into the data structure, sorts them (by rearranging the pointers) then prints them. Since the array linepointer will be of some fixed size, this dictates the maximum number of lines that can be stored.

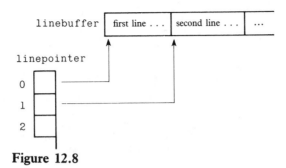

Figure 12.8

Another maximum is the total amount of space available in linebuffer. If this space is exceeded when reading the data lines, this too is an error condition. The function responsible for performing the input returns an appropriate status code to indicate if the input was successful or whether either of the limits had been exceeded. The text lines of input are terminated with the end of data trailer "ZZZ".

The preceding version of Shell sort must be modified to accommodate string and string pointers instead of integers. The only changes necessary to the sort function is where values are compared and values are exchanged. String comparisons are performed by the standard library function strcmp. The exchanging of two integer values is replaced with an exchange of two string pointers, implemented with a macro.

PROGRAM 12.5

```
/*
**      Input a series of lines of text and outputs them
**      in alphabetical order. The lines are first recorded
**      then sorted using the Shell sort algorithm. The
**      input is terminated with the unique line 'zzz'.
*/

#include <stdio.h>
#include <string.h>

#define MAXCHARS        10000
#define MAXLINES        200
#define MAXTEXT         128

#define TERMINATOR      "ZZZ"

enum status{ OFLOLINES, OFLOCHARS, SUCCESS };
typedef enum status     Status;


Status  read_lines(char *[], char [], int *);
void    shell_sort(char *[], int);
void    print_lines(char *[], int);
```

```
#define SWAP(X, Y)        { char *P; P = (X); (X) = (Y); (Y) = P; }

main ()
{
  char          linebuffer[MAXCHARS];     /* lines of text */
  char          *linepointer[MAXLINES];   /* indices to lines */
  int           numlines;                 /* number of input lines */

  switch (read_lines (linepointer, linebuffer, &numlines)){
    case SUCCESS   :     shell_sort (linepointer, numlines);
                         print_lines (linepointer, numlines);
                         break;
     case OFLOLINES :     printf ("Too many lines\n");     break;
     case OFLOCHARS :     printf ("Too many chars\n");     break;
  }
}


Status read_lines(char *linepointer[],
        char linebuffer[], int *numlines)
{
  char *buffer, *endbuffer;               /* next space, end of space */
  char line[MAXTEXT];                     /* single line of text */

  buffer = linebuffer;         /* initialize next space pointer */
  endbuffer = linebuffer + MAXCHARS;
                               /* char beyond available space */

  *numlines = 0;
  while (gets (line), strcmp (line, TERMINATOR) != 0)
    if (*numlines == MAXLINES)          /* too many lines? */
      return (OFLOLINES);
    else if (buffer + strlen (line) + 1 >= endbuffer)
                                  /* enough store? */
      return (OFLOCHARS);
    else {
      linepointer[(*numlines)++] = buffer;  /* establish index */
      strcpy (buffer, line);              /* copy into line buffer */
      buffer += strlen (line) + 1;    /* update buffer pointer */
    }

  return (SUCCESS);
}


void shell_sort(char *linepointer[], int numlines)
{
  int interval, i, j;                    /* interval and counters */
```

```
    for (interval = numlines/2; interval > 0; interval /= 2)
      for (i = interval; i < numlines; i++)
        for (j = i - interval; j >= 0; j -= interval){
          if (strcmp (linepointer[j], linepointer[j+interval]) <= 0)
            break;
          SWAP(linepointer[j], linepointer[j+interval]);
        }
}


void print_lines(char *linepointer[], int numlines)
{
  int k;

  for (k = 0; k < numlines; k++)
    printf ("%s\n", linepointer[k]);
}
```

12.6 Pointers to pointers

A formal argument of a function declared to be of type 'array of T' where T is some arbitrary type, is treated as if it were declared to be of type 'pointer to T'. Because of the equivalence of pointers and arrays (see Section 11.5), this change is invisible to the programmer and performed automatically by the C compiler. For example, in the function:

```
int sumarray(int a[], int n)
{
  int sum, k;          /* running total and counter */

  sum = 0;
  for (k = 0; k < n; k++)
    sum += a[k];

  return (sum);
}
```

the argument a could have been declared by the programmer as:

```
int *a
```

This, in fact, is what the C compiler does.

Where a function argument is declared to be of type 'array of T' and T is of type 'pointer to S' for some arbitrary type S, it is equivalenced to type 'pointer to pointer to S'. For example, the function print_lines in Program 12.6 which has the declaration:

```
void print_lines(char *linepointer[], int numlines)
{
      _____
      _____
}
```

is converted to:

```
void print_lines(char **linepointer, int numlines)
{
      _____
      _____
}
```

That is, linepointer has as its value the base address for a series of memory locations (i.e. an array), each of which is the address of the first character of a null-terminated array of characters (a string). Pictorially the arrangement appears as shown in Figure 12.9. The object referred to as linepointer possesses the value that is the address of the array of addresses. The object referred to as *linepointer is the first address contained in that array, and is therefore the address of the first character in the first string. The object referred to as **linepointer is the first character in the first string.

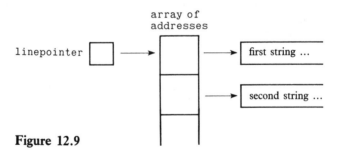

Figure 12.9

The precedence and associativity of the indirection operator * and the other operators must be carefully noted. Particular attention should be paid to the operators * (indirection), ++ (increment) and -- (decrement), all having equal precedence and all associating right to left. Thus *(*linepointer+1) references the second character of the first string; **linepointer++ references the first character of the first string (and advances linepointer by one); while **++linepointer references the first character of the second string (having first advanced linepointer by one).

From this discussion, we could remodel function print_lines in terms of these multi-level indirections:

```
void print_lines(char **linepointer, int numlines)
{
```

```
    int    k;
    for (k = 0; k < numlines; k++)
      printf("%s\n", *linepointer++);
}
```

12.7 Command line arguments

Normally a C program exists in an environment established by the resident operating system. The environment usually supports passing command line arguments to a program when it begins execution. For example, consider a program called sum which is invoked with two arguments on the command line. These arguments are an integer pair which are summed and printed by the program. The program might be activated by:

```
    sum 123 456
```

The output from the program is, of course, 579.

Function main of a program is often defined with two formal arguments conventionally called argc and argv. The first argument, argc, is the number of command line arguments. Since the program name is always included in the count, argc always exceeds 0. In the example call of program sum, argc is 3. The second argument, argv, is an array of pointers to char, pointers to the first character in the null-terminated array of characters that represent the argument strings. By convention, argv[0] is the program name. In the example, argv[0], argv[1] and argv[2] are respectively 'sum', '123' and '456'. The first argument proper is argv[1]. The last argument is argv[argc − 1]. One posssible version for this program follows.

PROGRAM 12.6

```
/*
**      Form the sum of two integers given as command
**      line arguments.
*/

#include <stdio.h>
#include <stdlib.h>

main(int argc, char *argv[])
{
  int first, second;

  if (argc != 3)         /* check number of arguments */
    printf("Usage: %s number number\n", argv[0]);
  else
    printf("%d\n", atoi(argv[1]) + atoi(argv[2]));
}
```

Another simple illustration of command line arguments is the program `echo`, which echoes its arguments to the standard output, with each string separated by a single blank character. That is, if the command is:

```
echo My first      program
```

the output is:

```
My first program
```

In this example, `argc` is 4, and `argv[0]`, `argv[1]`, `argv[2]` and `argv[3]` are `'echo'`, `'My'`, `'first'` and `'program'` respectively. Note how all leading whitespace characters are not included in the arguments. Their appearance in the command line serves only to act as separators. The program is:

PROGRAM 12.7(a)

```
/*
**      Echo all command line arguments each separated
**      by a single blank character.
*/

#include <stdio.h>

#define NEWLINE          '\n'

main(int argc, char *argv[])
{
  int k;

  for (k = 1; k < argc; k++)              /* for each argument */
    printf("%s%c", argv[k], k != argc-1 ? ' ' : '\n');
}
```

Since `argv` is a pointer to an array of pointers, there are several ways to implement this program, manipulating the pointer rather than indexing an array. One variation is given in Program 12.7(b).

PROGRAM 12.7(b)

```
/*
**      Echo all command line arguments each separated
**      by a single blank character.
*/

#include <stdio.h>

#define NEWLINE          '\n'
```

```
main(int argc, char **argv)
{
  --argc;
  while (--argc >= 0)
    printf("%s%c", *++argv, argc ? ' ' : '\n');
}
```

Since `argv` is a pointer to the beginning of the array of pointers (to the command line argument strings), incrementing it by 1 (`++argv`) makes it point to `argv[1]`. Each successive increment moves to the next argument address; `*argv` is then the pointer to that string. At the same time, `argc` is simultaneously decremented and when it becomes zero there are no more arguments to print.

Many C programs are supplied with arguments in this manner. Often, the arguments are the names of files to be processed by the program, permitting the program to be constructed such that these filenames are run time arguments. In some instances, these arguments are supplemented with options used to further vary the effect of the program. Options are frequently introduced as single or multiple characters preceded by a leading hyphen (–) symbol.

One possible variation of the `echo` program might support the option 'r'. If the option is present as the first command line argument, then the remaining arguments are printed in reverse order. If the option is omitted, the echo program behaves as before. Any other option appearing with the leading hyphen is flagged as an error. For example:

```
echo -r my     first     program
```

would produce the output:

```
program first my
```

PROGRAM 12.8

```
/*
**      Echo all command line arguments to the standard
**      output. Each argument is separated by a space.
**      If the first argument is the option '-r' then
**      the arguments are echoed in reverse order. All
**      other options are illegal.
*/

#include <stdio.h>

#define NEWLINE        '\n'
#define HYPHEN         '-'
#define LETTERR        'r'

main(int argc, char *argv[])
{
  int k;
```

```
          if (argv[1][0] == HYPHEN)          /* first argument option? */
            if (argv[1][1] == LETTERR)       /* permissible option? */
              for (k = argc - 1; k > 1; k--) /* reverse printing */
                printf("%s ", argv[k]);
            else
              printf("%s: illegal option\n", argv[0]);
          else
            for (k = 1; k < argc; k++;        /* normal printing */
              printf("%s ", argv[k]);

        putchar(NEWLINE);
      }
```

Optional arguments should be permitted in any order if more than one is supported by the program. The program should also be insensitive to the actual number present. Where there is more than one option given, it is often convenient for the user if they can be concatenated. The final version of program echo which we shall develop supports the arguments '−r' and '−n'. As before, the '−r' option reverses the printed arguments. The '−n' option causes no newline symbol to be printed at the end of the output. In this way, the echoed arguments appear as a prompt, with the cursor immediately following the output. The command:

```
    echo -n -r date: the Enter
```

produces the output:

```
    Enter the date:
```

which is not terminated with a newline. Concatenating the two options so that they appear:

```
    echo -nr date: the Enter
```

or:

```
    echo -rn date: the Enter
```

produces the same results as in the first example. An option which is duplicated has the same effect if it only appeared once. The same output is produced by:

```
    echo -nr -r date: the Enter
```

where the additional option '−r' is redundant. All other options are illegal and are flagged accordingly. Here is the program:

PROGRAM 12.9

```
/*
**      Echo command line arguments to the standard
**      output. The two supported options are '-r' (reverse)
**      and '-n' (newline).
*/
```

```
#include <stdio.h>

#define NEWLINE        '\n'
#define HYPHEN         '_'
#define LETTERR        'r'
#define LETTERN        'n'

#define FALSE          0
#define TRUE           1
typedef int            Boolean;

main (int argc, char *argv[])
{
  Boolean    reverse = FALSE, newline = TRUE;   /* option flags */
  char       *s;                                /* string pointer */
  int        k;

  while (--argc > 0 && **++argv == HYPHEN)  /* for every option */
    for (s = *argv+1; *s != '\0'; s++)      /* compounded options */
      switch (*s){
        case LETTERR :     reverse = TRUE;       break;
        case LETTERN :     newline = FALSE;      break;
        default      :
          printf ("Echo: illegal option %c\n", *s);
          argc = 0;                              /* force termination */
          break;
      }

  if (reverse)                                /* order? */
    for (k = argc - 1; k >= 0; k-)
      printf ("%s ", argv[k]);
  else
    for (k = 0; k < argc; k++)
      printf ("%s ", argv[k]);

  if (newline)
    putchar (NEWLINE);
}
```

12.8 Initializing pointer arrays

In Program 6.16 we encountered a function called day_name which printed the day
of the week when given Zeller's congruence for that day. Consider the problem
rewriting this function to return a pointer to a character string containing the name
of the nth day of the week (n is 0 – 6 inclusive, representing Sunday, Monday,
. . . Saturday). The function operates by having a private array of character
strings containing the day names, and returns a pointer to the correct one when
called. The function is:

```
char *day name(int n)
{
  static char *name[] =
    { "Sunday", "Monday", "Tuesday", "Wednesday",
      "Thursday", "Friday", "Saturday", "Illegal day" };

  if (n < 0 || n > 6)
    return (name[7]);
  else
    return (name[n]);
}
```

The declaration for name, which is an array of character pointers, is the same as for linepointer in Program 12.6. The initializer is a list of character strings, each assigned the correct position in the array. Note how a measure of robustness is maintained by filtering out the special case. The characters in the kth string are stored somewhere in memory and a pointer to them is stored in name[k].

12.9 Summary

1. *Strings* are one-dimensional arrays of type char. The null character \0 is used to delimit a string. System functions such as strcmp will only work on properly null-terminated strings.

2. The standard library I/O function scanf can be used to read a sequence of non-white space characters using the %s formatter. On completion, the input string is automatically null terminated.

3. Arrays of pointers to type char (i.e. pointer to pointers) are used to process lists of strings. The second argument to function main is of this type, allowing a program access to its command line arguments.

4. External and static strings may be initialized. Initializations of the form:

    ```
    char s[] = { 'a', 'b', 'c', '\0' };
    char s[] = "abc";
    ```

    are considered identical by the compiler. A list of strings can be used to initialize an array of character pointers:

    ```
    char *list[] = { "Programming", "in", "C" };
    ```

12.10 Exercises

1. Prepare a function to capitalize every lower case alphabetic character in the string argument s. All other characters remain untouched. The function header is:

```
void capitalise(char *s)
```

(Hint: use the macros in `ctype.h`.)

2. Prepare a function to shift the characters of the string argument s one place to the left, overwriting the original initial character. Develop the complementary function to shift the characters of a string one place to the right, padding with a single blank (space) character on the left.

3. Write a function called 'left_rotate' with the following header, to rotate cyclicly the characters of the argument string s, n character places to the left:

```
void left_rotate(char *s, int n)
```

Write the corresponding function 'right_rotate'.

4. With suitable definitions, write a Boolean function 'less' which returns TRUE if the string s is lexicographically less than the string t, and FALSE otherwise. The function header is:

```
Boolean less(char *s, char *t)
```

Design the corresponding functions 'less than or equal', 'equal', 'not equal', 'greater than' and 'greater than or equal'. Each function may employ any previously written function in this suite.

5. Write a function that accepts strings of any length and determines whether they are palindromes. Additionally, allow the function to accept a sentence string containing spaces which are to be ignored when determining if the sentence is palindromic.

6. Write a function called 'substring' to extract a portion of a character string. The function header is:

```
void substring(char *source, int start,
    int count, char *result)
```

where source is the character string from which we are extracting the substring; result is the array of characters which receives the extracted string; start is an index into the source string and is the position of the first character in the source string (start >= 0); and count is the number of characters to be extracted (count >= 0). Ensure that the function performs all the necessary checks and operates correctly under all circumstances.

7. Write a function called 'remove string' to remove a specified number of characters from a character string. The function header is:

```
void remove_string(char *source,
    int start, int count)
```

where source is the character string from which we are removing the substring; start is an index into the source string and is the position of the first character in the source string (start >= 0); and count is the number of characters to be removed (count >= 0). The resulting string is returned through source.

8. Write a function called 'insert_string' which inserts one character string into another. The function header is:

```
void insert_string(char *source,
    char *text, int start)
```

where source is the source string; text is the string to be inserted; and start is the position in the source string where the text string is to be inserted.

9. Input to a program represents the text of a telegram. The input consists of one or more lines containing a number of words each separated by a number of spaces. The unique word 'END' terminates the input. Produce a bill for this telegram with each word costing 10 cents and an additional charge of 5 cents for every word over eight letters long. The output to appear as:

```
Number of words            : 23
Number of normal sized words : 19 at 10 is 1.90
Number of oversized words   :  4 at 15 is 0.60
TOTAL                       :          2.50
```

10. Modify the concordance program to optionally print the word list in reverse alphabetical order. The option is indicated by the command line argument '-r'.

11. Extend the last question to support the optional command line argument '-f', where the words are printed in order of increasing frequency.

13

Storage management

A *VARIABLE-SIZED* DATA STRUCTURE is one in which the number of components may change *dynamically* during program execution. The major types of variable sized data structures include *lists*, *stacks*, *queues* and *trees*, and are the subjects of Chapters 15 and 16.

Variable sized data objects are used when the amount of data in a problem is not known in advance. Use of fixed sized arrays requires that large amounts of storage are reserved in advance for the maximum size of data that might be encountered. Variable sized data structures allow storage to be allocated incrementally during program execution.

There are two fundamentally different approaches to these dynamic data structures. In some languages they are provided directly. In others, a pointer data type is provided, with facilities for the dynamic allocation of storage explicitly by the programmer. This is the approach taken in C. Several language features are then necessary to make this possible:

1. An elementary data type *pointer*. A pointer data object contains the location of another data object, or it may contain the special null pointer, NULL. Pointers are ordinary objects that may be simple variables or components of arrays (or structures; see Chapter 16). Pointers were the subject of Chapters 5, 11 and 12.

2. A *creation operation* for data objects of fixed size, such as elementary types or arrays. The creation operation both allocates a block of storage for the data object and returns a pointer to its location, which may then be stored as the value of a pointer variable. The creation operator differs in two ways from the ordinary creation of variables caused by declarations:

    (a) The data objects created have no names, their values are accessed through pointers; and

    (b) Data objects may be created in this way at any point during program execution, not just on entry to a function.

3. A *selection operation* for pointer values that allow the data object to which it points to be accessed.

4. A *deletion operator* to recover blocks of storage.

13.1 Implementation

The creation operator both allocates storage for a fixed-sized data object and also delivers a pointer to the new data object. In C this operation is provided by a number of standard library functions. Function `malloc` allocates a contiguous region of memory of `size` bytes, and returns a pointer to the beginning of the allocated block. The function prototype for `malloc` is:

```
void *malloc(size_t size)
```

contained in the standard header file `<stdlib.h>`. The region of memory is not specially initialized in any way; the caller must assume that it contains garbage. As shown, the value returned by `malloc` is a pointer to type `void`. The interpretation of void * pointers is of an *untyped pointer*. An untyped pointer in C is used as a *generic* pointer. Any pointer may be converted to type `void` * without loss of information. Further, if the result is converted back to the original pointer type, then the original pointer is restored. If `ptr` and `pt` are variables declared as:

```
char *ptr, *pt;
```

then:

```
ptr = malloc(20);
```

establishes a region of memory of 20 bytes with `ptr` a pointer to the beginning of this area. The block of memory is anonymous. No variable name associates with it. The variable `ptr` provides a pointer to this unnamed area. Using `ptr` as shown in the preceding two chapters, we can reference any of the allocated 20 bytes. For example, to fill the region with 20 letter B symbols, we might use:

```
for (pt = ptr, k = 0; k < 20; k++)
    *pt++ = 'B'
```

If it is impossible for some reason to perform the requested allocation, `malloc` returns the null pointer, NULL, as defined in the standard I/O header, `<stdio.h>`. The last illustration may be shown incorporating the additional check:

```
if ((ptr = malloc(20)) == NULL)
    printf("Cannot allocate\n");
else
    for (pt = ptr, k = 0; k < 20; k++)
        *pt++ = 'B';
```

When a region of memory is allocated in response to a request, a pointer to the region is returned to the caller. This pointer will be of pointer type `void` * and is guaranteed to be properly aligned for *any* data type. The caller may then use a cast operator to convert this pointer to another pointer type or use the fact that no information loss occurs when using `void` * pointers as described above. If it is known, for example, that for a particular implementation an integer occupies 2 bytes, then:

```
int *px;

px  = malloc(2);
*px = 15;
```

allocates an area of memory sufficient to store a single integer using `malloc`, with the return address assigned to `px`. This anonymous integer location is then assigned the value 15.

In this last illustration, we needed to know the size of an `int` object. The number of bytes occupied by an `int` is machine-dependent and this reduces the portability of the code presented. This problem is removed by employing the `sizeof` operator.

The `sizeof` operator is used to obtain the size of a type or a data object. The `sizeof` expression has the form:

```
sizeof( type-name )
```

or:

```
sizeof expression
```

Applying this operator to a parenthesized type name yields the size of an object of the specified type; that is, the number of storage units (bytes) that would be occupied by an object of that type. The type name may be any of the fundamental types, or an array, the size of which is the total number of bytes in the array. The result is an unsigned integral constant and is implementation-defined. The standard header `<stddef.h>` defines the type as `size_t`. The portability problem of the preceding example is removed by using:

```
px = malloc(sizeof(int));
```

Applying the `sizeof` operator to an expression yields the same result as if it had been applied to the name of the type of the expression. Although a generalized expression is permitted, more commonly this form is used with a variable name as the expression. Clarity is improved if the expression is parenthesized. Given the declaration:

```
int x, *px;
```

an area sufficient to store an `int` may be established with:

```
px = malloc(sizeof(x));
```

The operator `sizeof` is described as a compile time operator in so far as the result of applying this operator to an expression can always be deduced at compile time by examining the type of the objects in the expression. The result of `sizeof` is not dependent on the particular values of any run time objects. When `sizeof` is applied to an expression, the expression is analysed at compile time to determine its type. This means that any side effects as a result of execution of the expression are not a matter for compile time determination. For example, compilation of the declaration:

```
int obj1 = 1, obj2 = sizeof(obj1++);
```

results in some initial value assigned to obj2 (the number of bytes for an int, since obj1++ is an expression of type int), but will not increment obj1.

The following program demonstrates one use of the library function malloc. The program inputs two integer data values and outputs them in reverse order. Instead of declaring two integer variables to represent the data items, pointers are employed. Space for two integers is created dynamically (by malloc) and pointers assigned to the space. The program then operates in terms of the pointers rather than in terms of integer variables. The example is intended merely to illustrate dynamic storage. It is not recommended as the solution to this problem. The conventional solution is given in Program 5.3.

PROGRAM 13.1

```
/*
**      This program reads two integer values from the
**      standard input, and outputs them in reverse order.
**      The locations for the two integers are created
**      dynamically using the library function "malloc".
*/

#include <stdio.h>
#include <stdlib.h>

main()
{
  int *first, *second;      /* pointers to the data values */

  if ((first = malloc(sizeof(int))) == NULL)
    printf("Cannot create first\n");
  else if ((second = malloc(sizeof(int))) == NULL)
    printf("Cannot create second\n");
  else {
    printf("Enter the data: ");
    scanf("%d %d", first, second);
    printf("Reversed data: %d %d\n", *second, *first);
  }
}
```

Since memory is frequently a critical resource, available in limited quantities, it is desirable that the storage allocated by a call to malloc is returned to the system for later reuse. The function free allows the programmer to deallocate a region of memory previously allocated by malloc. The prototype declaration for this function is:

```
void free(void *pointer)
```

The argument to free is a pointer to a void previously returned by malloc. Once a region of memory has been freed, it should no longer be referenced by the program. The storage manager recycles the memory region for use with subsequent calls to malloc.

Program 13.2 repeats the preceding example but, additionally, explicitly frees the region of memory dynamically established by malloc. Once again, the example is merely for illustrative purposes. Practical uses of free will be shown in later chapters.

PROGRAM 13.2

```
/*
**        This program reads two integer values from the
**        standard input, and outputs them in reverse order.
**        The locations for the two integers are created
**        dynamically using the library function "malloc".
*/

#include <stdio.h>
#include <stdlib.h>

main()
{
    int *first, *second;      /* pointers to the data values */

    if ((first = malloc(sizeof(int))) == NULL)
        printf("Cannot create first\n");
    else if ((second = malloc(sizeof(int))) == NULL)
        printf("Cannot create second\n");
    else {
        printf("Enter the data: ");
        scanf("%d %d", first, second);
        printf("Reversed data: %d %d\n", *second, *first);
        free(first);
        free(second);
    }
}
```

When the region of memory to be allocated represents an array of N elements each of type T, then the call to function malloc represents the total number of bytes required by the storage structure, namely:

```
int *ptr, table[100];
```

or:
```
ptr = malloc(100 * sizeof(int));
ptr = malloc(sizeof(table));
```

Alternatively, we can employ the related library function calloc. The heading is:

```
void *calloc(size_t count, size_t size)
```

which allocates memory sufficient to hold an array with count elements each requiring size bytes of storage. A pointer to the first byte is returned, or NULL if the request is impossible. The example above can also be expressed by:

```
ptr = calloc(100, sizeof(int));
```

The space allocated is guaranteed to be initialized to zero.

Data to a program consists of a single integer followed by a series of floating point values, the number of which is given by the leading integer. The floating point values are read and printed in reverse order by the program. The values are stored in an array during input. The array is dynamically created and the size is determined by the initial data item.

PROGRAM 13.3

```
/*
**      Read a series of floats from the standard input and
**      write them to the standard output in reverse order.
**      The values are preceded by an integer count of the
**      number of data items. This value is used to
**      dynamically create an array to store the data.
*/

#include <stdio.h>
#include <stdlib.h>

main()
{
  int n, k;                  /* count and loop control */
 float *base, *ptr;          /* array base and index */

  scanf("%d", &n);
  if ((base = calloc(n, sizeof(float))) == NULL)
    printf("Unable to create the array\n");
  else {
    for (ptr = base, k = 0; k < n; k++)
      scanf("%f", ptr++);
    for (ptr = base + n, k = 0; k < n; k++)
      printf("%f\n", *(--ptr));
    free(base);
  }
}
```

Program 12.5 produced an alphabetical sort of a number of lines of text. To operate efficiently and conveniently with lines of text of varying lengths, a suitable data structure was devised. The implementation consisted of a large array called linebuffer holding the lines to be sorted in an end-to-end fashion, and a second array, linepointer, containing pointers to where (in linebuffer) the corresponding lines begin. Both these arrays must be reserved (declared) in advance for the maximum size of data that might be encountered. Robustness in the program is ensured by including array bounds checking in function read_lines where the input is read and stored in the arrays.

For many programs this form of static allocation is satisfactory. However, it is incompatible with data structures whose size is dependent on input data. In the application, the size of both linepointer and linebuffer is dependent upon the number of lines of text and the total number of characters in the text respectively.

In Chapter 16 we will introduce a method for making both structures grow dynamically. For the present, dynamic storage allocation is applied to linebuffer only. Provided storage can be created dynamically without restriction, no limit is imposed upon the total number of characters in the text.

Whereas in Program 12.5 storage is drawn from a fixed sized pool (linebuffer), Program 13.4 obtains space for each input line by a call on malloc (through function strdup). Function strdup copies the string argument into a safe place, obtained through a call on malloc. The function returns a pointer to the allocated storage area.

PROGRAM 13.4

```
/*
**      Input a series of lines of text and outputs them
**      in alphabetical order. The lines are first recorded
**      then sorted using the Shell sort algorithm. The
**      input is terminated with the unique line 'ZZZ'.
*/

#include <stdio.h>
#include <stdlib.h>
#include <string.h>

#define MAXLINES            200
#define MAXTEXT             128

#define TERMINATOR          "ZZZ"
                        /* status codes after reading input */
enum status{ OFLOLINES, OFLOCHARS, SUCCESS };
typedef enum status        Status;
                        /* forward references */
Status  read_lines (char *[], int *const);
void    shell_sort (char *[], const int);
void    print_lines (char *[], const int);

#define SWAP(X, Y)         { char *P = (X); (X) = (Y); (Y) = P; }
```

```
main ()
{
  char        *linepointer[MAXLINES];    /* indices to lines */
  int         numlines;                  /* number of input lines */

  switch(read_lines (linepointer, &numlines)){
    case SUCCESS    :    shell_sort (linepointer, numlines);
                         print_lines (linepointer, numlines);
                         break;
    case OFLOLINES :    printf ("Too many lines\n");    break;
    case OFLOCHARS :    printf ("Too many chars\n");    break;
  }
}


Status read_lines (char *linepointer[], int *const numlines)
{
  char line[MAXTEXT], *ps;              /* single line of text */

  *numlines = 0;
  while (gets (line), strcmp (line, TERMINATOR) != 0)
    if (*numlines == MAXLINES)          /* too many lines? */
      return (OFLOLINES);
    else if ((ps = strdup(line)) == NULL)   /* enough store? */
      return (OFLOCHARS);
    else
      linepointer[(*numlines)++] = ps;       /* establish index */

  return (SUCCESS);
}


void shell_sort (char *linepointer[], const int numlines)
{
  int interval, i, j;         /* interval and counters */

  for (interval = numlines/2; interval > 0; interval /= 2)
    for (i = interval; i < numlines; i++)
      for (j = i - interval; j >= 0; j -= interval){
        if (strcmp (linepointer[j], linepointer[j+interval]) <= 0)
          break;
        SWAP(linepointer[j], linepointer[j+interval]);
      }
}


void print_lines (char *linepointer[], const int numlines)
{
  int k;

  for (k = 0; k < numlines; k++)
    printf ("%s\n", linepointer[k]);
}
```

This same approach, namely, an array of pointers to character strings can also be applied to the word concordance problem of Case Study 12.1. There, an array of characters of some fixed, arbitrary size realized a word, while an array of such words implemented the concordance. Now the concordance can be represented by an array of pointers to the strings that are the words. The latter are dynamically allocated and hence not subject to the restriction. Further, when we insert a word into its correct alphabetical position in the concordance, our new implementation involves moving pointers rather than strings, reducing the run time overhead.

CASE STUDY   13.1 Queues

The C program unit is used to put resources in one place because they are logically related. In the preceding examples of abstract data types, the variables and functions associated with the data type are grouped together in one program unit. In these examples, only one instance of the data type is used. In this and the next case study multiple instances of the data type are supported using dynamic storage allocation.

A city centre car park has room for N vehicles. Cars enter the garage from the in gate and exit from the out gate. The cars are garaged in a queue-like discipline. New arrivals join the end of the garage queue. Departures, however, can be from anywhere in the queue. When a vehicle leaves the queue, the original ordering is maintained. If the garage is full, new arrivals join a waiting queue outside the garage facility. When a vacancy occurs in the car park, the vehicle at the front of the waiting queue (if any) enters the garage.

A queue is a data structure in which all insertions take place at one end, the rear, and all removals are from the other end, the front. Conceptually, we visualize a queue as:

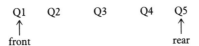

The vehicles awaiting entry to the garage are ordered and maintained as a queue. When the garage is full new arrivals join the end of this waiting queue. A car may leave this waiting queue without having entered the garage. A departure from this queue may also be from any position.

The two principal operations associated with a queue are the insertion and removal of items. The insertion operation adds a new item to the rear of the queue. A check must be performed to ensure that there is room in the queue. If the queue is not empty, the removal operation takes an item from the front of the queue. Operations are also available to obtain statistics about the queue, e.g. is the queue full?

We now formulate an abstract specification of a queue of items (of type int) as a package of queue operators and data structures. In addition to the operators mentioned above, we define a `createq` operation which establishes a new `queue` of some given maximum size. The abstraction is provided through the header file `queue.h`:

```
/*
**      File :          queue.h
**
**      Implementation of a queue of integers using an
**      array. The functions are parameterized to permit
**      a number of arrays to be processed. Arrays are
**      dynamically created by operation "createq" for
**      some given queue length, N. The queue itself is
**      indexed by 1 to N inclusive. Array element 0
**      contains the queue size N, element N+1 is the
**      present queue length, element N+2 is the queue
**      front, and element N+3 is the queue rear. The
**      queue is organized cyclicly around the array.
*/

#include "boolean.h"

typedef int             *Queue;

extern Queue createq(const int size);
extern void appendq(Queue queue, const int item);
extern void removeq(Queue queue, int *const item);
extern Boolean isfullq(Queue queue);
extern Boolean isemptyq(Queue queue);
extern int lengthq(Queue queue);


with:


/*
**      File:           boolean.h
*/

#ifndef FALSE
   #define FALSE        0
   #define TRUE         1
   typedef int          Boolean;
#endif
```

The data to the parking program consists of a series of records, one per line. Each record consists of a four-digit license plate number, and the single character 'A' or 'D' representing, respectively, arrival and departure. The data set terminates with the unique sentinel 0000Z. Every departure is guaranteed to correspond to a previous arrival. For the sample data:

```
1234A
2345A
3456A
4567A
3456D
5678A
6789A
```

and a garage queue of length N = 4, the garage and waiting queues appear as in Figure 13.1.

Figure 13.1

The further data items:

```
4567D
7890A
8901A
1234D
```

leaves the two queues as shown in Figure 13.2.

Figure 13.2

The program is required to produce a snapshot of both queues for every arrival and departure. We assume in the program that the garage has a capacity of 4, and that a safe upperbound for the waiting queue is 100. The program, expressed in terms of arrivals and departures, is listed below:

```
/*
**      File :          case01.c
**
**      Implement the city centre car park. The two
**      queue abstractions in the problem are
**      provided by the Queue data type and the
**      associated operations.
*/

#include <stdio.h>
#include "queue.h"
                        /* forward references */
void    arrival(Queue, Queue, const int);
void    departure(Queue, Queue, const int);
void    report(Queue, Queue);
```

```
main()
{
  int   plate;                      /* license number */
  char  code;                       /* arrival/departure */
  Queue garage, waiting;            /* the two queues */

  if ((garage = createq(4)) == NULL)
                                    /* establish the garage */
    printf("Cannot create the garage\n");
  else if ((waiting = createq(100)) == NULL)
                                    /* establish waiting queue */
    printf("Cannot create the waiting queue\n");
  else {
    while (scanf("%4d%c", &plate, &code), plate != 0){
                                    /* more data? */
      switch (code){
        case 'A' : arrival(garage, waiting, plate);   break;
        case 'D' : departure(garage, waiting, plate); break;
      }
      report(garage, waiting);
    }
  }
}
```

If the garage is not already full, then a new arrival enters the garage queue. If the maximum number of vehicles is already in the garage, the new arrival joins the waiting queue which is assumed to have sufficient capacity to holds any number of cars. The procedure for function arrival then becomes:

```
/*
**      A new ARRIVAL enters the garage if it is not
**      already full; otherwise it joins the waiting
**      queue.
*/

void arrival(Queue garage, Queue waiting, const int plate)
{
  if (! isfullq(garage))           /* room in garage? */
    appendq(garage, plate);        /* yes - no checks reqd. */
  else
    appendq(waiting, plate);       /* no - join waiting */
}
```

A vehicle can leave from either of the two queues. If the departing vehicle is not in the garage, it can be safely assumed to be in the waiting queue. In either case, whichever queue the car is deleted from, queue discipline is maintained.

The removal of an entry from a queue can be expressed in terms of the queue operators. A queue can be cyclicly rotated by repeatedly removing an item from the front of the queue and reinserting it at the rear of the same queue. The reinserting can be made conditional, so that if the removed item matches that to be deleted, then it is not reinserted.

First, we build the function `member` which determines if a given search key item is a member of a queue. The function is implemented using the cyclic rotate algorithm:

```
/*
**      Rotate cyclicly all the items in the queue
**      such that the queue is undisturbed. The full
**      rotation is achieved by removing and then
**      reinserting. If any item matches the search key
**      TRUE is returned, otherwise FALSE is returned.
*/

Boolean ismember(Queue queue, const int key)
{
  int     k, lngth, item;
  Boolean found = FALSE;

  lngth = lengthq(queue);
  for (k = 0; k < lngth; k++){
    removeq(queue, &item);
    if (key == item)
      found = TRUE;
    appendq(queue, item);
  }
  return (found);
}
```

The implementation for this (and other) operations on vehicle queues reflect weaknesses in the primitives to manipulate `queues`. It is representative of a poorly designed interface to the `queue` data type. Operation `ismember` must dequeue an item off the `queue`, then immediately enqueue it. While off the `queue`, the item is compared against the search key. Had the `queue` data type supported the operation `isinq`, to search for an item in the `queue`, then the implementation of `ismember` would have been facile. We shall have more to say on interface design later in the text.

A departure operation nominates a vehicle guaranteed to be in either the garage or the waiting queue. If the car is in the waiting queue, it is simply deleted. If the vehicle is in the garage queue, it is removed and the first car in the waiting queue (if any) joins the garage. Function `delete` implements the removal of a single item from the `queue`; a departure is implemented by a similarly named function:

```
/*
**      Rotate all the items in the queue by removing
**      and then reinserting. If any item removed
**      matches the item to be deleted, it is not
**      inserted back on to the queue.
*/

void delete(Queue queue, const int key)
{
  int k, lngth, item;
```

```
  lngth = lengthq(queue);
  for (k = 0; k < lngth; k++){
    removeq(queue, &item);
    if (item != key)
      appendq(queue, item);
  }
}


/*
**      The vehicle next to depart is either in the
**      garage or in the waiting queue. If the car is
**      in the waiting queue it is simply removed.
**      If the car is not in the waiting queue, it is
**      guaranteed to be in the garage. The car is then
**      removed from the garage and the first of any
**      waiting vehicles now enters the garage.
*/

void departure(Queue garage, Queue waiting, const int plate)
{
  int item;

  if (ismember(waiting, plate))     /* in waiting queue? */
    delete(waiting, plate);         /* yes - remove it */
  else {
    delete(garage, plate);          /* no - remove from garage */
    if (! isemptyq(waiting)){        /* any waiting? */
      removeq(waiting, &item);      /* first in waiting queue ... */
      appendq(garage, item);        /* ... enters garage */
    }
  }
}
```

Finally, two functions implement the queue reporting. The primitive function qreport produces a labelled report listing each entry in a nominated queue. Function report invokes this primitive for the two problem queues:

```
/*
**      Produce a report on the members of a single
**      queue.
*/

void qreport(char *const name, Queue queue)
{
  int k, lngth, item;

  printf("%s", name);
  lngth = lengthq(queue);
  for (k = 0; k < lngth; k++){
    removeq(queue, &item);
    printf("%6d", item);
    appendq(queue, item);
```

```
  }
  printf("\n");
}

/*
**      Produce reports on the two queues - the garage
**      queue and the waiting queue.
*/

void report(Queue garage, Queue waiting)
{
  qreport("garage :", garage);
  qreport("waiting:", waiting);
}
```

We now consider the representation of a queue. An array of some fixed length is used to hold the items in the queue. Two variables front and rear are required to define the limits of the queue within the array. Variable front references the array element containing the first item in the queue. Variable rear indicates the array element in which is stored the next item to be added to the queue, i.e. immediately following the last queue item.

Using this representation, the queue drifts down the array as items are added and then removed from the queue. Ultimately, the rear of the queue reaches the end of the array. Further, as items are removed from the front of the queue, some free space exists at the beginning of the array. To utilize this area, the array is considered to be circular, with the end of the array wrapping around to the beginning.

The queue is initialized with both front and rear assigned the values 1. These values denote an empty queue. However, if repeated insertions are applied to the queue until it becomes full, front and rear will both have the values 1 again, since rear will be cyclicly reassigned. In fact, when front and rear are the same values, it is impossible to distinguish between a full queue and an empty queue. To rectify this, we introduce a third variable called length, the number of items presently in the queue. For an empty queue, length = 0, and for a full queue length = N, where N is the maximum queue size.

Since the program must support two queues, the abstraction must be capable of creating two (or more) unique queues. This is achieved dynamically using the storage management function calloc within the queue operation createq. Each queue has the parameters size, length, front and rear associated with it. This we achieve by creating an array with size + 4 integer elements having the configuration shown in Figure 13.3. This representation is possible since the queue (or array) has base type int. The value size is supplied as an argument to the constructor operation createq. The initialization of the queue parameters takes the form:

```
    length = 0     front = 1     rear = 1
```

Using the functions getq and putq (see the final listing, below) to retrieve and store the queue parameters, function createq is programmed as:

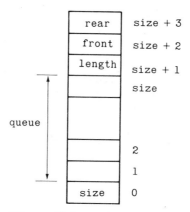

Figure 13.3

```
/*
**      Establish a new queue with a capacity for size
**      items using the CREATEQ operator. Return NULL if
**      not successful.
*/

Queue createq(const int size)
{
  Queue queue;

  if ((queue = calloc(size+4, sizeof(int))) == NULL)
    return (NULL);
  else {
    putq(queue, size, 0, 1, 1);
    return (queue);
  }
}
```

The operation `lengthq` is implemented by inspecting the value of the `length` parameter. Functions `isemptyq` and `isfullq` are also expressed in terms of `length`. For example:

```
/*
**      Operation ISFULLQ determines if the queue is full
**      or not. The logical values TRUE or FALSE are
**      returned.
*/

Boolean isfullq(Queue queue)
{
  int       size, length, front, rear;

  getq(queue, &size, &length, &front, &rear);
  return (size == length);
}
```

Provided the `queue` is not already full, the `appendq` function places the new item in the array as indexed by `rear`, then increments both `rear` and `length`. The increment to `rear` must be cyclic to reflect the `queue` organization. This can be expressed by:

```
rear = rear == size ? 1 : rear + 1
```

or more concisely by:

```
rear = rear % size + 1
```

The function `appendq` becomes:

```
/*
**      The APPENDQ procedure (provided the queue is not
**      full) places the new item in the array element
**      indicated by rear, and then increments both
**      length and rear.
*/

void appendq(Queue queue, const int item)
{
   int          size, length, front, rear;

   getq(queue, &size, &length, &front, &rear);
   *(queue + rear) = item;
   rear = rear % size + 1;
   length++;
   putq(queue, size, length, front, rear);
}
```

Function `removeq` takes an item from the front of the `queue`, then increments `front` and decrements `length`. The coding is otherwise similar to `appendq`.

The listing below provides the complete implementation for the `queue` abstraction:

```
/*
**      File :           queue.c
**
**      Implementation of a queue of integers using an
**      array. The functions are parameterized to permit
**      a number of arrays to be processed. Arrays are
**      dynamically created by operation "createq" for
**      some given queue length, N. The queue itself is
**      indexed by 1 to N inclusive. Array element 0
**      contains the queue size N, element N+1 is the
**      present queue length, element N+2 is the queue
**      front, and element N+3 is the queue rear. The
**      queue is organised cyclicly around the array.
*/

#include <stdio.h>
#include <stdlib.h>
#include "queue.h"
```

```
/*
**        Obtain the statistics of the given queue.
*/

static void getq(Queue queue, int *const size,
    int *const length, int *const front, int *const rear)
{
  *size   = *queue;
  *length = *(queue + (*size) + 1);
  *front  = *(queue + (*size) + 2);
  *rear   = *(queue + (*size) + 3);
}


/*
**        Establish new parameters for the given queue.
*/

static void putq(Queue queue,
    const int size, const int length, const int front, const int rear)
{
  *queue             = size;
  *(queue + size + 1) = length;
  *(queue + size + 2) = front;
  *(queue + size + 3) = rear;
}

/*
**        Establish a new queue with a capacity for size
**        items using the CREATEQ operator. Return NULL if
**        not successful.
*/

Queue createq(const int size)
{
  .....
}


/*
**        The APPENDQ procedure (provided the queue is not
**        full) places the new item in the array element
**        indicated by rear, and then increments both
**        length and rear.
*/

void appendq(Queue queue, const int item)
{
  .....
}

/*
**        Providing the queue is not already empty, operation
**        REMOVEQ takes the item from the front of the queue.
*/
```

```
void removeq(Queue queue, int *const item)
{
  int          size, length, front, rear;

  getq(queue, &size, &length, &front, &rear);
  *item = *(queue + front);
  front = front % size + 1;
  length--;
  putq(queue, size, length, front, rear);
}

/*
**      Operation ISFULLQ determines if the queue is full
**      or not. The logical values TRUE or FALSE are
**      returned.
*/

Boolean isfullq(Queue queue)
{
  .....
}

/*
**      The logical value TRUE is returned if operation
**      ISEMPTYQ determines that there are no items in
**      the queue; FALSE otherwise.
*/

Boolean isemptyq(Queue queue)
{
  int          size, length, front, rear;

  getq(queue, &size, &length, &front, &rear);
  return (length == 0);
}

/*
**      Determine the present number of items in
**      the queue.
*/

int lengthq(Queue queue)
{
  int          size, length, front, rear;

  getq(queue, &size, &length, &front, &rear);
  return (length);
}
```

CASE STUDY   **13.2 Vectors**

An array in C is specified of fixed constant size, has bounds starting at zero, and is
not subject to any array bound checking at run time. Using techniques borrowed
from the preceding case study, we can construct vectors of our own design
incorporating features which remove these constraints.

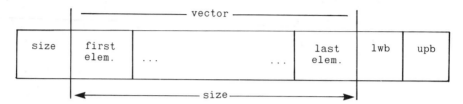

Figure 13.4

Once again, the idea is to have a structure allocated dynamically using the free
storage allocator calloc. This structure includes both the vector itself and its
attributes, namely, the lower and upper vector bounds and the vector size. The
arrangement is shown in Figure 13.4. The first component (size) records the
actual number of elements in the vector and the final two store the lower (lwb) and
upper (upb) bounds of the vector. Hence if v represents the vector, then the first
element is effectively indexed as v[lwb] and is at position 2 in the structure (or
offset 1 from the size component); the second element is v[lwb + 1] at
position 3 (offset 2); the last element is v[upb] at position size + 1 (offset
size).

The representation structure is established by the vector constructor function
vec. The function arguments are the bounds of the vector. The function value is a
pointer to an int (with synonym Vector) addressing the dynamically allocated
structure initialized with the appropriate values:

```
typedef int     *Vector;

Vector vec(int lwb, int upb)
{
  Vector new;
  int size = upb - lwb + 1;

  if(size <= 0){
    printf("Bad vector limits (default to vec(1, 1))\n");
    lwb = upb = size = 1;
  }
```

```
new = calloc(size+3, sizeof(int));
*new = size;
*(new+size+1) = lwb;
*(new+size+2) = upb;

return new;
}
```

Objects of type `Vector` can now be declared and passed around in the usual ways. Vectors can be both function arguments and function results. Automatic variables of type `Vector` can be declared and initialized by function `vec`. The dimensions of the vector can now be run time values as illustrated by the following code fragment:

```
int max;
scanf("%d", &max);
{
    Vector table = vec(1, max);
    . . . . .
}
```

As usual, when we exit from the inner block the storage space for the automatic variable `table` is released. This does not relinquish the representation structure; only the variable `table` which points to that structure is released. We have no way of deallocating dynamic storage at block exit so we must provide it as a service function. This function will be called at block exit when the storage is no longer referenced:

```
void dvec(Vector v)
{
    free(v);
}
```

We have explained how indexing a vector is translated into a position (or offset) in the representation structure. Two functions are provided for this purpose – one to `access` the value of the item in the vector, and one to `assign` a new value:

```
int access(Vector v, const int index)
{
    if(index < LWB(v) || index > UPB(v)){
        printf("Bad index (access) %d\n", index);
        return 0;
    } else
        return *(v + 1 + (index - LWB(v)));
}


void assign(Vector v, const int index, const int value)
{
    if(index < LWB(v) || index > UPB(v))
        printf("Bad index (assign) %d\n", index);
    else
        *(v + 1 + (index - LWB(v))) = value;
}
```

Packaging this up in the usual way into a program unit we arrive at the following:

```
/*
**         File:             vector.h
*/

typedef int                *Vector;

extern Vector    vec(int, int);              /* constructor */
extern void      dvec(Vector);               /* destructor */
extern int       access(Vector, const int);
extern void      assign(Vector, const int, const int);


/*
**         File:             vector.c
*/

#include <stdio.h>
#include <stdlib.h>
#include "vector.h"

#define LWB(V)             (*((V) + 1 + (*(V))))
#define UPB(V)             (*((V) + 2 + (*(V))))


/*
**         Function VEC is the vector constructor. The function
**         arguments represent the vector bounds. These limits
**         are checked and defaulted if in error. The representation
**         structure is then dynamically allocated and initialised.
*/

Vector vec(int lwb, int upb)
{
  .....
}

/*
**         Function DVEC is the vector destructor.
*/

void dvec(Vector v)
{
  .....
}


/*
**         Function ACCESS delivers the value of the vector
**         element at subscript value index, ie effectively
**         v[index]. The bounds are checked and zero returned
**         if in error.
*/
```

```
int access(Vector v, const int index)
{
    .....
}


/*
**      Function ASSIGN effectively performs the operation
**      v[index] = value. Bound checking is enforced and no
**      assignation performed if in error.
*/

void assign(Vector v, const int index, const int value)
{
    .....
}
```

Finally, we illustrate with a simple example. A program reads a sequence of integers and prints them in reverse order. The sequence is preceded with an integer counter specifying the number of values in the sequence. A vector of the required size is allocated for this purpose:

```
/*
**      File:           case02.c
*/

#include <stdio.h>
#include "vector.h"

main()
{
    int number;

    printf("Enter the number of data values: ");
    scanf("%d", &number);
    if(number > 0){
        Vector table = vec(1, number);
        int     k, data;

        printf("Enter data values:\n");
        for(k = 1; k <= number; k++){
            scanf("%d", &data);
            assign(table, k, data);
        }

        printf("Reversed data values:\n");
        for(k = number; k >= 1; k--)
            printf("%d\n", access(table, k));

        dvec(table);
    }
    printf("Program stop\n");
}
```

13.2 Summary

1. *Variable sized* data objects are used when the amount of data is not known in advance. In C, a *pointer* data type is provided and standard library functions for the dynamic allocation of storage.

2. The function `malloc` takes an argument of type `unsigned` integer and returns a pointer to a `void` that is the base of the allocated storage. Storage allocated by `malloc` is returned to the system for subsequent recycling by the library function `free`. It is the programmer's responsibility to ensure that the `malloc` operation is successful, and that memory that has been freed is not referenced.

13.3 Exercises

1. Develop a function called `concat` to concatenate multiple strings into a common allocated string and return the string's address. The function's prototype declaration is:

```
char *concat(const int n, ...)
```

where n is the number of strings to be concatenated. The remaining arguments are of type `char *const` representing the individual strings.

2. Reimplement the Sieve of Eratosthenes (Case Study 11.2), using the `Vector` data type as the concrete representation of the sieve.

3. Implement an `IntStack` (integer stack) data type using the `Vector` data type as the underlying representation. A `stack` is a last-in-first-out store, with operations applied to the top item in the `stack`. The interface for the IntStack is given by the header file:

```
/*
**      File:      intstack.h
*/
#ifndef INTSTACK
  #define INTSTACK

  #include "boolean.h"

  typedef int          *IntStack;

  extern IntStack newstack(const int size);
  extern IntStack push(const int item, IntStack stack);
  extern IntStack pop(IntStack stack);
```

```
    extern int top(IntStack stack);
    extern Boolean isfull(IntStack stack);
    extern Boolean isempty(IntStack stack);
#endif
```

Using only the stack operations, prepare a program to read a series of positive integers (with a negative sentinel) and to determine if the data is palindromic, that is, reads the same both forward and backward.

4. Following Exercise 3, develop a program unit IntQueue, for a queue of integers, with a Vector as the concrete representation. Repeat the exercise using one stack and one queue in the solution.

14

Files

THE PROGRAMS we have studied have all produced some output, and in the majority of cases accepted some input. This has been achieved by using the standard files' standard input and standard output. These simple programs are unrepresentative of the majority of computer applications. Most applications involve the storage of very large volumes of permanent data. To retain the data between program execution, they are held in computer *files* on some auxiliary storage medium, for example, magnetic disc. In this chapter we consider the standard files and other files in some detail.

A computer file is a set of data values which is either produced by a program or is the input to a program. In general, a file is a collection of *records*. A record is the basic unit for processing. Generally, programs read and write single records from/to files. According to the application, a record may consist of a single character, or a line of text, or some other organization. Records usually consist of a number of data items known as *fields*. A record consisting of a line of text may have the words of the text as the fields. The fields themselves may be further subdivided into subordinate fields, for example the individual letters of the words.

File organization methods define how the records of a file are arranged. Four common types of file organization are:

   serial/sequential random
   indexed   inverted

In this chapter we shall consider applications employing the first two methods.

Serial files are organized such that each record in the file, except the last, has a unique successor; and each record, except the first, has a unique predecessor. This ordering is a consequence of the order in which the records are written to the file when the file is created.

Sequential files are organized so that the records maintain some ordering. A given field of the record, called the *key* field, is used to establish this ordering. Figure 14.1 shows an excerpt of a student file, where the fields of each record are the student identification number, student name, subject and grade. The file is organized sequentially and is maintained in ascending sequence of the identification number. Any addition or deletion of records to/from this file must maintain the key ordering of the sequence. A new record for a student with number 45 must be inserted immediately before the record for student Jones.

```
ID
NUMBER    NAME      SUBJECT    GRADE
12        Brown     C          4
23        Smith     C++        3
34        Black     ML         3
56        Jones     C          7
67        Thomson   ML         5
```

Figure 14.1

Random file organization is applicable only to files held on direct access storage media. This method of access is used when the records are processed randomly with respect to their key field. Associated applications use this method to provide very fast access to the records of the file.

A random file is a set of records each identified by a unique *relative record number*. If there are N records in the file, each is distinguished by a unique integer 1, 2, 3, . . . , N. When a record is stored in a random file, its location is determined by an *addressing algorithm* which transforms the record key into an integer in the range 1 to N inclusive. Retrieval of the same record from the file for the given key value employs the same addressing algorithm and computes the same relative record number. Figure 14.2 shows the records from the preceding example of a sequential file held as a random file. The file contains at most thirty-seven records (the chosen maximum number of students in a class) and the addressing algorithm is:

```
student-identification-number mod 37 + 1
```

where mod is the modulus operator.

```
RELATIVE
RECORD
NUMBER    NUMBER    NAME       SUBJECT    GRADE

1
2
. . .
13        12        Brown      C          4
. . .
20        56        Jones      C          7
. . .
24        23        Smith      C++        3
. . .
31        67        Thomson    ML         5
. . .
35        34        Black      ML         3
36
37
```

Figure 14.2

File processing in a high-level programming language is supported by various operations performed on the file and its records. A new file is established with zero records using a *create* operator. Before processing of a file can begin, it must first be *opened*. When processing is completed, a file must be *closed* properly. Files may be opened in one of a number of *modes*, e.g. input mode (the file is read but remains unchanged), output mode (new records are written to the file) and input/output mode (records are both read from and written to the file).

There are essentially two operations that apply to records of a file. A single record is retrieved from the file with a *read* operation. For a sequentially organized file, this operation causes the next record of the sequence to be read. With a random file, the record retrieved is determined by the given key value and hence the relative record number. A new record value is incorporated into a file with the *write* operation. For a sequential file, the record written to the file is the successor of the preceding record written to the file. The record key determines where in a random file a record is written.

Reading a sequential file will ultimately cause the file to be exhausted. To determine this condition, an *end of file* operator is also required.

The standard C library contains all the functions necessary to implement these file operations. Functions `fopen` and `fclose`, respectively, open and close files. Variants of the functions which perform input/output to the standard input and standard output operate on files. Functions performing input from a file also return an end of file indicator. The position where the next input/output operation is performed on a file is achieved with the function `fseek`. The remainder of this chapter is concerned with applications employing these file handling functions.

14.1 File access

Before a file can be read or written it must first be opened. This is performed by the standard library function `fopen`. The function `fopen` takes two arguments. The first argument is the name of the file to be opened, presented as a null-terminated string. The second argument denotes how the file is to be opened and is also given as a character string. This second argument is known as the *open mode*. A number of possible modes are supported including:

   `"r"` open an existing file for reading.

   `"w"` create a new file, or truncate an existing one for writing.

   `"a"` create a new file, or append to an existing one for writing.

   `"r+"` open an existing file for update (both reading and writing), starting at the beginning of the file.

   `"w+"` create a new file, or truncate an existing one, for update (both reading and writing).

   `"a+"` create a new file, or append to an existing one, for update (both reading and writing).

Opening a file may cause an error indicator to be set. This might arise for a number of reasons. For example, opening a file in *read-only* (`"r"` or `"r+"`) mode presupposes that the named file already exists in the file store. If it does not exist, fopen returns an error.

If a file does not exist and is opened for *writing* ("w" or "w+") or *appending* ("a" or "a+"), then it is automatically created. If it already exists, then its original content is irretrievably lost when opened.

Some systems distinguish between text and binary files. For the latter type of file, a "b" must be appended to the mode string.

Once fopen has opened the specified file in the prescribed mode, it returns an internal name which is then used in subsequent input/output operations on that file. This internal name is called a *file pointer*. The data type FILE is used to hold information about a file or, more generally, a *stream*. The actual details of the data type FILE need not concern us. All the necessary definitions are provided in the standard input/output header <stdio.h>. The declaration for a file pointer is:

```
FILE *fp;
```

and specifies that the variable fp is a pointer to the derived type FILE. Notice that FILE is a type name (established through a typedef statement in <stdio.h>) like any other type name.

The prototype declaration for the function fopen in <stdio.h> is:

```
FILE *fopen(char *filename, char *mode)
```

An actual call to fopen to open for reading a file called data is:

```
fp = fopen("data", "r");
```

If there is no error when opening the file, fopen returns a file pointer assigned to the file pointer variable fp. Subsequent input operations performed on the file are in terms of fp. If there is any error, fopen returns the null pointer NULL. An error on opening a file is normally trapped with a conditional of the form:

```
if((fp = fopen("data", "r")) == NULL)
    printf("Cannot open data file\n");
else
    . . . . . .
```

When the processing performed upon a file is complete, it must be closed. The file or stream must be closed in an orderly fashion including the emptying of any *internal buffers* held by the system. This is achieved with the function fclose:

```
int fclose(FILE *fp)
```

The function fclose takes the single argument fp, which should be the file pointer of a previously successfully opened file as performed by fopen. If any error is detected, fclose returns EOF, otherwise it return zero. The value EOF is conventionally used to denote end of file.

The following program opens, then immediatedly closes a file, the name of which is given as the single command line argument. The file is not assumed to exist in the file store and should, therefore, open in write only mode. Checks are performed to ensure the opening and closing operations are successful.

PROGRAM 14.1

```
/*
**      Program to demonstrate the operators fopen and
**      fclose. A file whose name is given as the command
**      line argument is first opened and then immediately
**      closed. The return codes from these file primitives
**      are checked.
*/

#include <stdio.h>

#define WRITEONLY       "w"

main(int argc, char *argv[])
{
  FILE *fp;

  if(argc != 2)
    printf("Usage: %s filename\n", argv[0]);
  else if((fp = fopen(argv[1], WRITEONLY)) == NULL)
    printf("%s: cannot open %s\n", argv[0], argv[1]);
  else {
    printf("%s successfully opened\n", argv[1]);
    if(fclose(fp) == EOF)
      printf("%s: cannot close %s\n", argv[0], argv[1]);
    else
      printf("%s now closed\n", argv[1]);
  }
}
```

14.2 The functions `fgetc`, `fputc` and `feof`

The function `fgetc` reads a single character from a file. This function's behaviour is identical to the function `getchar` which we have previously encountered. The prototype declaration for the function `fgetc` is:

```
int fgetc(FILE *fp)
```

where `fp` is a file pointer as returned by a previous call to function `fopen`. Execution of the statement:

```
c = fgetc(fp);
```

has the effect of reading a single character from the stream denoted by `fp`. Subsequent characters are read from the same stream by making further calls to `fgetc`.

The function `fgetc` returns the value EOF when the end of file is reached. This non-existent character can be used, for example, in a loop control condition to read and process sequentially the characters in a file:

```
while((c = fgetc(fp)) != EOF) .....
```

Care is required to ensure that the variable c used to represent the data character returned by fgetc is of type int. This is necessary to ensure that the loop operates correctly. To illustrate the difficulties, assume we are operating on a machine with 16-bit integers, and the EOF value is − 1. The representation for EOF is:

```
-1 (decimal) = 1111111111111111 (binary)
```

If fgetc returns EOF and this is assigned to the variable c which is erroneously declared as a character variable of, say, 8 bits, then c is assigned the low order 8 bits returned by fgetc (EOF), namely:

```
c = 11111111 (binary)
```

The inequality test (! =) will then fail to recognize the EOF value, since:

```
11111111 != 1111111111111111
```

evaluates to logical TRUE. The loop would thus cycle indefinitely.

To explicitly indicate that a variable is to operate as a character variable, but is represented as an integer to correctly handle detection of EOF, we recommend the type name Character be introduced. The name implies the variable type but conceals its representation as an int:

```
typedef int        Character;

Character c;

while((c = fgetc(fp)) != EOF) .....
```

Strictly, function fgetc returns EOF either when the end of file has been detected or when an error has occurred. The function feof should be used to determine if the end of file has been truly reached. The function prototype for feof is:

```
int feof(FILE *fp)
```

If end of file has been detected on the specified stream, feof returns a non-zero value (representing logical TRUE), otherwise zero (logical FALSE) is returned. Thus we may loop through a file character by character until the end of file is reached or until an error has occurred with the following code outline:

```
while((c = fgetc(fp)) != EOF){
  .....
  /* process character c */
  .....
}
```

then determine whether we have an error or the true end of file:

```
if(! feof(fp))
  printf("Read error\n");
```

```
else
    /* ..... final processing ..... */
```

Function getchar, used to read a single character from the standard input, also returns the same EOF status code. So all preceding programs that processed single characters read from the standard input, and searched for an explicit file terminating character, might alternatively have detected EOF. Program 6.1 echoed characters from the standard input to the standard output. The program employed the period symbol as the unique terminator. Rewriting the program in terms of EOF and releasing the period character so that it may be a member of the input data, we arrive at Program 14.2.

PROGRAM 14.2

```
/*
**        Copy a stream of characters from the standard
**        input to the standard output. The copying
**        process terminates upon reading the end-of-file
**        on the standard input.
*/

#include <stdio.h>

typedef int              Character;

main ()
{
  Character c;

  while((c = getchar()) != EOF)
    putchar(c);
}
```

To terminate this program we must enter at the keyboard the character which corresponds to EOF. This character is very much system-dependent. On most UNIX systems, EOF is represented by the control-D character. On MSDOS environments it is control-Z.

The function fputc writes a single character to a file. The function's behaviour is otherwise identical to the function putchar which we have used extensively. The prototype declaration for function fputc is:

```
int fputc(int c, FILE *fp)
```

If fputc is successful in writing the character to the nominated stream it returns the character as a value of type int. If an error occurs, fputc returns EOF.

With these preliminaries complete, we can now write a program called copy to copy the content of one file to a second file. The two file names are supplied as command line arguments with the source file named first. Note how the majority of the program consists of error checking. We shall have more to say on this subject shortly.

PROGRAM 14.3

```
/*
**      Copy the content of a source file to a destination
**      file. The two file names are given as command line
**      arguments. Full validation is performed upon
**      the file handling primitives.
*/

#include <stdio.h>

typedef int             Character;

#define READONLY        "r"
#define WRITEONLY       "w"

main(int argc, char *argv[])
{
  FILE       *fpsource, *fpdestination;
  Character c;

  if(argc != 3)
    printf("Usage: %s file1 file2\n", argv[0]);
  else if((fpsource = fopen(argv[1], READONLY)) == NULL)
    printf("%s: cannot open %s\n", argv[0], argv[1]);
  else if((fpdestination = fopen(argv[2], WRITEONLY)) == NULL){
    printf("%s: cannot open %s\n", argv[0], argv[2]);
    if(fclose(fpsource) == EOF)
      printf("%s: %s is not closed correctly\n", argv[0], argv[1]);
  } else {
    while((c = fgetc(fpsource)) != EOF)
      if(fputc(c, fpdestination) == EOF){
        printf("%s: error in writing to %s\n", argv[0], argv[2]);
        break;
      }

    if(! feof(fpsource))
      printf("%s: error in reading %s\n", argv[0], argv[1]);

    if(fclose(fpsource) == EOF)
      printf("%s: %s incorrectly closed\n", argv[0], argv[1]);
    if(fclose(fpdestination) == EOF)
      printf("%s: %s incorrectly closed\n", argv[0], argv[2]);
  }
}
```

14.3 The functions `fscanf` and `fprintf`

The functions `fscanf` and `fprintf` perform analogous operations to the `scanf` and `printf` functions on a file. These new functions each take an additional argument, which is the file pointer to the required file. The prototype declarations are:

```
int fscanf(FILE *fp, char *format, ... )
```

and:

```
int fprintf(FILE *fp, char *format, ... )
```

When executing `fscanf` the input operation may terminate prematurely. This may be due to reading end of file on the specified stream or because there is a conflict between the control string (`format`) and an input character. If the input reaches end of file before any conflict has occurred, then `fscanf` returns EOF. If the operation is terminated, `fscanf` returns the number of successful assignments.

A fragment of code to read two integer values from a file and perform the necessary error checking to ensure that the correct number of data items has been read and that the end of file has not been detected is:

```
status = fscanf(fpin, "%d %d", &first, &second);
if(status != 2){
  if(status == EOF)
    printf("Unexpected end of file\n");
  else
    printf("Failure reading from file\n");
} else {
  .....
  /* process the input data values */
  .....
}
```

When executing `fprintf`, the value returned is negative if any error occurs; otherwise, the return value is the number of characters written. Thus, the two values read from a file by the code above may then be written to a second file by the following additions:

```
status = fscanf(fpin, "%d %d", &first, &second);
if(status != 2){
  if(status == EOF)
    printf("Unexpected end of file\n");
  else
    printf("Failure reading from file\n");
} else if(fprintf(fpout, "%d %d\n", first, second) < 0)
printf("Failure writing to file\n");
```

The error codes returned by `fscanf` and `fprintf` also apply to the functions `scanf` and `printf` respectively. The same status checking shown in the example above can also be applied to the standard input and to the standard output.

The following program is based on the preceding one. This time, a file of integers is copied to a second file. The source and destination file names are given as command line arguments. To avoid including checks on correct file closure, we have discarded the returned int value from fclose.

PROGRAM 14.4

```
/*
**      Copy a series of integers from a source file to
**      a destination file. The file names are given as
**      command line arguments. The copy process
**      terminates upon reading the end of file condition
**      on the source file.
*/

#include <stdio.h>

#define READONLY      "r"
#define WRITEONLY     "w"

main(int argc, char *argv[])
{
  FILE *fpin, *fpout;
  int  data, status;

  if(argc != 3)
    printf("Usage: %s file1 file2\n", argv[0]);
  else if((fpin = fopen(argv[1], READONLY)) == NULL)
    printf("%s: cannot open %s\n", argv[0], argv[1]);
  else if((fpout = fopen(argv[2], WRITEONLY)) == NULL){
    printf("%s: cannot open %s\n", argv[0], argv[1]);
    fclose(fpin);
  } else {
    while((status = fscanf(fpin, "%d", &data)) != EOF){
      if(status != 1){
        printf("Failure on file read\n");
        break;
      }
      if(fprintf(fpout, "%d\n", data) < 0){
        printf("Failure on file write\n");
        break;
      }
    }
    fclose(fpin);
    fclose(fpout);
  }
}
```

14.4 The functions `fgets` and `fputs`

To read and write entire lines of data from and to files the functions `fgets` and `fputs` can be used. The function `fgets` takes three arguments: a string `s`, a count `n`, and a stream `fp` which must be opened for input:

```
char *fgets(char *s, int n, FILE *fp)
```

The argument `s` is assumed to point to the beginning of a character array. Characters are read from the specified stream and are stored in successive locations of the array. The reading continues until an end of file is reached, until a newline is encountered, or while the number of input characters does not exceed n. When the input is complete, an additional terminating null character is appended to the stored characters.

If the input is successful, a pointer to the array `s` is returned. If an error occurs during the input or the end of file is encountered, then the null pointer, NULL, is returned. Errors are therefore trapped in the usual way:

```
if(fgets(line, SIZE, fpin) == NULL) .....
```

The prototype declaration for function `fputs` is:

```
int fputs(char *s, FILE *fp)
```

Function `fputs` writes the null-terminated string `s` to the stream denoted by `fp`, which must be opened for output. If any errors occur during the writing operation, `fputs` returns EOF.

We have used the `#include` facility of the C preprocessor to assemble most of the programs in this book. In the following example we demonstrate how we might actually implement this useful facility. The general outline of our version of `include` is:

```
WHILE get one line of the source file; not the end of file DO
    IF the line starts with #include
    THEN
        include this new file
    ELSE
        output the line to the destination file
    ENDIF
ENDWHILE
```

If the included file contains further `#include`'s, this naturally leads to a recursive solution. Nested `#include`'s are useful and readily implemented in C with a recursive implementation of the appropriate function.

The program is invoked with the command line:

```
include source-file-name destination-file-name
```

As described by the PDL, the lines of text are copied from the source file to the destination file. If at any time a line from the source file consisting of:

```
#include file-name
```

is met, then the include operation applies to this new source file, continuing to send
the output to the same destination file as the first. When the new source file is
exhausted, the copying continues with the original file or the program terminates if
it is the first file.

PROGRAM 14.5

```
/*
**      Copy the content of a source file to a
**      destination file. The two file names are given
**      as command line arguments. A line of text of the
**      form:
**
**              #include filename
**
**      appearing in the source file is replaced with
**      the content of the named file. Nested include
**      statements is supported to the depth permitted
**      by the maximum number of open files allowed by
**      the host operating system.
*/

#include <stdio.h>
#include <string.h>

#define READONLY        "r"
#define WRITEONLY       "w"

#define LINESIZE        256
#define INCLUDE         "#include"

void    file_include(FILE *, FILE *);

main(int argc, char *argv[])
{
    FILE        *fpsource, *fpdestination;

    if(argc != 3)
        printf("Usage: %s file1 file2\n", argv[0]);
    else if((fpsource = fopen(argv[1], READONLY)) ==.NULL)
        printf("%s: cannot open %s\n", argv[0], argv[1]);
    else if((fpdestination = fopen(argv[2], WRITEONLY)) == NULL){
        printf("%s: cannot open %s\n", argv[0], argv[2]);
        fclose(fpsource);
    } else {
        file_include(fpsource, fpdestination);
        fclose(fpsource);
        fclose(fpdestination);
    }
}
```

```
/*
**          Perform a line by line copy of the source file
**          to the destination file. Expand all #include
**          lines. Permit nested #include's.
*/

void file_include(FILE *fpin, FILE *fpout)
{
    char line[LINESIZE], word1[LINESIZE], word2[LINESIZE];
    FILE *fp;

    while(fgets(line, LINESIZE, fpin) != NULL)       /* eof input? */
        if(sscanf(line, "%s %s", word1, word2) != 2)  /* two words? */
            fputs(line, fpout);                        /* simple copy */
        else if(strcmp(word1, INCLUDE) != 0)          /* #include line? */
            fputs(line, fpout);                        /* no, copy */
        else if((fp = fopen(word2, READONLY)) == NULL)
            printf("Cannot open %s -- ignored\n", word2);
        else {
            file_include(fp, fpout);                   /* nested include */
            fclose(fp);
        }
}
```

14.5 Stdin, stdout **and** stderr

When a C program executes, three 'files' are automatically opened by the system and file pointers provided for them. The files are the standard input, the standard output and the standard error output. The respective file pointers are called stdin, stdout and stderr. These file pointers are predefined in the standard input/output header <stdio.h>. They are constants not variables. It is, therefore, not permissible to assign values to them.

Normally, these files associate with the user's terminal. All standard I/O functions that perform input and do not take a file pointer as an argument (getchar, gets and scanf) take their input from stdin. So the example call:

```
fscanf(stdin, "%d", &number);
```

will read the next integer value from the standard input, and is equivalent to the call:

```
scanf("%d", &number);
```

All standard I/O functions that perform output and do not have a file pointer argument (putchar, puts and printf) deliver their output to stdout. So:

```
fprintf(stdout, "My first program\n");
```

is equivalent to:

```
printf("My first program\n");
```

The 'functions' which perform single character transfers on the standard input and the standard output are generally implemented as macros. The macros `putc` and `getc` are equivalent in operation to the true functions `fputc` and `fgetc` respectively. Although written as macros, they can be considered to have the following declarations:

```
int putc(int c, FILE *fp)    int getc(FILE *fp)
```

The 'functions' `getchar` and `putchar` can be defined in terms of `getc`, `putc`, `stdin` and `stdout` as follows:

```
#define getchar()    getc(stdin)
#define putchar(C)   putc((C), stdout)
```

Finally, there is the file pointer `stderr`. It is intended that any error messages produced by a program be written to this 'standard error' stream. In an interactive environment, this stream is associated with the user's terminal. `Stderr` exists so that error messages can be logged to a device or file other than where the normal output is written. This is particularly desirable when the program's output is *redirected* to a file or sent down a *pipe* by the operating system. In the programs in this chapter, error messages should therefore have been delivered by statements of the form:

```
if((fp = fopen(argv[1], READONLY)) == NULL)
    fprintf(stderr, "%s: cannot open %s\n", argv[0], argv[1]);
```

using `fprintf` and `stderr` instead of `printf` and `stdout`.

14.6 The function `exit` and error treatment

A program automatically terminates whenever the last statement in function `main` is executed. At times it may be desireable to force program termination when an error condition is detected. To explicitly abort a program, the function `exit` can be called. The function call:

```
exit(n);
```

has the effect of terminating the current program, flushing and closing any open files, and making the value of the integer n available to whatever process in the system was responsible for activating this program (for example, the operating system). Under UNIX, the integer value 0 conventionally denotes a successful program, and non-zero for a program that terminates due to some detected error condition. The symbolic values EXIT_FAILURE and EXIT_SUCCESS may be used as the function argument. These macros are defined in `<stdlib.h>`.

All the programs of this chapter included extensive error checking which had the effect of concealing the program logic somewhat. We can go someway towards

cleaning up the code by relegating the error diagnostics to a function called
syserr. When this function is called, an error message is delivered, all open files
are closed and the program abandoned. Revisiting Program 14.3 we have the
following version.

PROGRAM 14.6

```
/*
**       Copy the content of a source file to a destination
**       file. The copy process is performed character by
**       character. The source and destination file names
**       are given as command line arguments.
*/

#include <stdio.h>
#include <stdlib.h>

typedef int          Character;       /* character input */

#define READONLY       "r"
#define WRITEONLY      "w"

void    syserr(const int , char *const, char *const);

char    *programname;

main(int argc, char *argv[])
{
  FILE *fpsource, *fpdestination;
  Character c;

  programname = argv[0];

  if(argc != 3)
    syserr(1, "Usage: %s file1 file2\n", programname);
  else if((fpsource = fopen(argv[1], READONLY)) == NULL)
    syserr(2, "Cannot open %s\n", argv[1]);
  else if((fpdestination = fopen(argv[2], WRITEONLY)) == NULL)
    syserr(3, "cannot open %s\n", argv[2]);
  else {
    while((c = fgetc(fpsource)) != EOF)    /* loop until done */
      if(fputc(c, fpdestination) == EOF)
        syserr(4, "error in writing to %s\n", argv[2]);

    if(! feof(fpsource))                    /* all done? */
      syserr(5, "error in reading %s\n", argv[1]);

    exit (EXIT_SUCCESS);
  }
}
```

```
/*
**         ------------------------------ oOo ------------------------------
**         ------------------------------ oOo ------------------------------
*/

void syserr(const int errcode, char *const message,
            char *const argument)
{
  fprintf(stderr, "%s [%2d]: ", programname, errcode);
  fprintf(stderr, message, argument);

  exit(EXIT_FAILURE);
}
```

14.7 Direct access

A number of different file structures are possible and supported by functions in the
standard library. The simplest file organization is the serial file and is the type of file
we have processed so far. A serial file is constructed by writing new records to the
end of the file. When the file is subsequently read, the components are input in the
same order as they were originally written to the file.

A different file structure, one which permits direct access to a specified
component of the file, is also supported by the standard I/O library. A *direct access*
file can be interpreted as a number of data blocks or *record areas*. Each record area is
of some fixed size measured as a number of bytes. To read (or write) a record, we
must first position the reading (writing) head at the first byte of the record area. The
required number of bytes is then transferred to (from) memory (Figure 14.3).

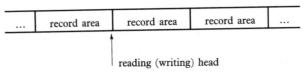

Figure 14.3

The function fseek allows random access within a file. The header for function
fseek is:

```
int fseek(FILE *fp, long offset, int origin)
```

The first argument must be a file pointer to a file opened for input, output or both.
The third argument must have the value SEEK_SET, SEEK_CUR or SEEK_END
(defined in <stdio.h>). If it is SEEK_SET, then the position in the file is set
equal to the value of the second argument considered as a byte count. The first byte
of the file is numbered 0. The origin value SEEK_SET is used when we wish to
locate the read/write head at some *absolute* position in the file. In particular, the call:

```
fseek(fp, 0L, SEEK_SET)
```

will rewind the file to the beginning.

If the third argument is SEEK_CUR, then the position in the file is set equal to the current position plus the signed offset. A positive offset will advance the position away from the beginning of the file, while a negative offset moves towards the beginning of the file. The origin value SEEK_CUR is used for *relative* positioning within the file.

If the third argument is SEEK_END, then the position is set to the end of the file plus the signed offset. This functionality is often used to extend a file. To seek to the end of the file before, say, writing, the call is:

```
fseek(fp, 0L, SEEK_END)
```

If the operation succeeds, then fseek returns 0, otherwise it returns a non-zero value. It is usual to check this condition with a clause of the form:

```
if(fseek(fp, offset, origin) != 0)
    fprintf(stderr, "Seek error\n");
else
    . . . . .
```

Once the required location in the file has been obtained with a call to fseek, subsequent reading and writing will begin at that position. The input and output can either be performed by the file I/O functions such as fscanf, fprint or by two additional functions called fread and fwrite.

The function fread reads a block of *binary* data into a specified memory buffer. The function header is:

```
size_t fread(void *buffer, size_t size,
                    size_t count, FILE *fp)
```

The first argument is a pointer to the buffer into which the input is read. The second argument is the size of the items in the buffer (size_t is an unsigned integer value defined in <stddef.h>); if the first argument is of arbitrary type T, then the second argument is generally computed by the expression sizeof(T). The third argument is the number of items of type T to be read. Thus the total number of bytes read from the file is size * count. The fourth argument is a file pointer that is opened for input.

For example, to input twenty characters into an array, the call is:

```
char table[20];

fread(table, sizeof(char), 20, fp);
```

The second example reads twenty integers into an array:

```
int    stack[20];

fread(stack, sizeof(int), 20, fp);
```

The actual number of items read is returned by function `fread`. Generally, this value is tested to determine if the operation has been successful. If the return value is less than the number of items in `count`, the functions `foef` and `ferror` must be used to determine the status. Typically, `fread` is used as in:

```
if((nread = fread(stack, sizeof(int), 20, fp)) != 20){
  if(feof(fp))
    fprintf(stderr, "End of file detected\n");
  else
    fprintf(stderr, "Read error\n");
  . . . . .
  . . . . .
}
```

The counterpart to `fread`, writing a block of binary data from a memory buffer to a file is called `fwrite`. The header is:

```
size_t fwrite(void *buffer, size_t size,
              size_t count, FILE *fp)
```

The actual number of items written to the file is returned by `fwrite`. If an error occurs, the value returned is less than `count`.

The following program illustrates a simple use of these functions. A file, named in the command line argument to the program, consists of a number of text characters. All but the first ten characters of the file are to be copied by the program to a second file, also given in the command line. Skipping the first ten characters could be accomplished by simply calling `fgetc` ten times and discarding the result. The method would be inefficient, however, if we had to skip, say, the first 1000 characters of a large file. The `fseek` function need only be called once to position the file at the desired point to allow copying to commence. To fully utilize the system buffering, the `fread` and `fwrite` operations are performed on the default buffer size BUFSIZ, defined in `<stdio.h>`.

PROGRAM 14.7

```
/*
**      Copy the content of one file to a second file,
**      discarding the first 10 characters in a header
**      of the source file. The file names are given as
**      command line arguments. The characters which are
**      removed are done so by skipping using direct
**      access operations.
*/

#include <stdio.h>
#include <stdlib.h>

#define READONLY        "r"
#define WRITEONLY       "w"
#define SKIP            10L
```

```
char    *programname;

void    syserr(const int, char *const, char *const);

main(int argc, char *argv[])
{
  FILE         *fpsource, *fpdestination;
  char         buff[BUFSIZ];
  int           nread;

  programname = argv[0];
  if(argc != 3)
    syserr(1, "Usage: %s file1 file2\n", programname);

  if((fpsource = fopen(argv[1], READONLY)) == NULL)
    syserr(2, "cannot open %s\n", argv[1]);
  if((fpdestination = fopen(argv[2], WRITEONLY)) == NULL)
    syserr(3, "cannot open %s\n", argv[2]);

  if(fseek(fpsource, SKIP, SEEK_SET) != 0)
    syserr(4, "fail on header in %s\n", argv[1]);

  while((nread = fread(buff, sizeof(char), BUFSIZ, fpsource)) != 0)
    if(fwrite(buff, sizeof(char), nread, fpdestination) != nread)
      syserr(5, "fail on write to %s\n", argv[2]);

  if(! feof(fpsource))
    syserr(6, "fail on read from %s\n", argv[1]);

  fclose(fpsource);
  fclose(fpdestination);
  exit(EXIT_SUCCESS);
}

void    syserr(const errcode, char *const message,
                  char *const argument)
{
  fprintf(stderr, "%s [%2d]: ", programname, errcode);
  fprintf(stderr, message, argument);
  exit(EXIT_FAILURE);
}
```

Two additional functions associated with direct access files are rewind and ftell. The function headings are:

```
void rewind(FILE *fp)      and      long ftell(FILE *fp)
```

Function rewind resets a file to its beginning. The argument must be a file pointer to a file that is opened for input or output. From our preceding discussion of fseek, rewind (fp) is equivalent to:

```
fseek(fp, 0L, SEEK_SET)
```

The function ftell takes a file pointer for a file that is currently open and returns the byte position in the stream. Thus:

```
fseek(fp, OL, SEEK_END);
size = ftell(fp);
```

will determine the number of bytes currently in the file identified by the file pointer fp.

14.8 Summary

1. A *file* is a collection of records of some base type. File organization methods determine how the records of a file are processed, and include *serial* and *random* access. A serial file is constructed by writing new records to the end of the file. When the file is subsequently read, the elements are input in the same order as they were originally written. A *direct access* file can be written or read to/from any position within the file.

2. Before a file can be read or written it must first be opened. This operation is performed by the library function fopen, which returns an internal name (file pointer) that is then used in subsequent I/O operations. When the processing of a file is complete it must be closed in an orderly manner using the function fclose. The library function exit flushes and closes any open files before terminating a program.

3. Serial processing of a file is provided by the library functions fgetc, fputc, fscanf, etc. Random access within a file is provided by the functions fseek and rewind.

4. Three files automatically provided in all C programs are known by the file pointers stdin, stdout and stderr. Thus, for example, the function getchar reads a single character from the standard input and is effectively the call fgetc(stdin).

14.9 Exercises

1. Implement your own version of the library functions fgets and fputs.

2. Use the file handling functions of the standard library to double space a text file. The names of the files are given as command line arguments, with the source file named first and the target file named second.

3. Write a program to copy one file to another, removing any blank lines in the source file. The file names are given as command line arguments.

4. Write a program to number the lines in a text file. The input file name should be passed as a command line argument. The program should write to `stdout`.

5. Write a program called `concat`, which concatenates a set of named input files on to the standard output. One or more file names are given as command line arguments.

6. Write a program to display the content of a text file on to the standard output, twenty lines at a time. The input file is given as a command line argument. Each twenty lines are displayed following a return character entered from the standard input.

7. Given two files of integers sorted into ascending order, write a program to merge the files into a third file of sorted integers. All three file names are given as command line arguments.

8. Write a program called find that searches for patterns. If the command:

```
find pattern filename
```

is given, then the string pattern is searched in the named file. All lines containing the pattern are printed.

Modify this program to support the command line option −n which, if present, requests that the line number should be printed as well.

9. Write a program which operates as a file printer. The program print is invoked with one or more file names as arguments. It prints the files with top and bottom margins on each page, and, at the top of each page the file name and the page number.

15

Structures, unions and bit fields

IN CHAPTERS 11 AND 12 we introduced the array – an aggregate of values all of the same type. To reference an individual array element we require the name of the array and a subscript.

The C programming language also supports a second aggregate type known as a *structure*. The structure is a composite of components which are distinct and, perhaps, also of different types. Many programs in this book process calendar dates. A date may be considered as the composition of three values – the day number, the month number and the year number. We can define a structure called `date` consisting of the three components by:

```
struct date { /* date template: */
    int    day;
    int    month;
    int    year;
};
```

The reserved keyword `struct` introduces a structure declaration, which is a list of declarations enclosed in braces. An optional name called a *structure tag* may follow the word `struct` (as with `date` here). A structure declaration, such as the one above, which is not followed by a list of variables does not allocate variable storage, but acts as a *template* for the named structured type. The tag acts to name this definition, which can then be used in the declaration of variables, as in:

```
struct date today, holiday;
```

This declaration introduces two variables `today` and `holiday`, both structures of type `date`. The structure tag `date` appearing in the declaration of the variables may be substituted by the full declaration. The variable declaration is then equivalent to:

```
struct { /* date template: */
    int    day;
    int    month;
    int    year;
} today, holiday;
```

By not tagging the structure with a name, we cannot employ the structure elsewhere in the program. This is somewhat less useful and is relatively uncommon in programs.

337

Further examples of structure declarations include:

(a)
```
struct complex {    /* complex numbers: */
   double  real;
   double  imaginary;
};
```

a structure for manipulating complex numbers in a mathematical/engineering application.

(b)
```
enum suit { CLUBS, DIAMONDS, HEARTS, SPADES };
struct card {  /* card description: */
  enum suit  soot;
  int        rank;
};
```

for use in a card playing program.

15.1 Members

The elements named in a structure declaration are called *members* of the structure. For example, the members of the date structure, introduced in the preceding section, are called day, month and year. Like arrays, a notation is required to reference a member of a structured variable. To refer to one component of a structured variable, the variable is qualified by the member name in a construct of the form:

```
variable-name.member-name
```

To identify the year component of the variable today, we use:

```
today.year
```

From the structure declaration this member is of type int and can be used in any expression in which a simple integer variable might appear. For example, to set the value of member day in the variable holiday to 25, the statement is:

```
holiday.day = 25;
```

To test the value of members we can use constructs such as:

```
if (today.day == 25 && today.month == 12)
   printf("Merry Xmas\n");
```

In the construct:

```
variable-name.member-name
```

the period symbol is known as the *selection operator*. The left-hand operand is a structured variable and the right-hand operand is a member name. The selection operator has the highest (equal) priority among the operators. The precedence and associativity of the selection operator is shown in Appendix E.

The above discussions are incorporated into the following C program. In function main, the structure called date is established and a declaration is made for the variable today of this type. The program then proceeds to assign individual values to each member of the variable before displaying today's date with an appropriate printf function call.

PROGRAM 15.1

```
/*
**      Assign and print a date. The program demonstrates
**      simple handling of structured values. The date
**      is represented as a three member structure.
*/

#include <stdio.h>

main()
{
  struct date { /* template for a date: */
    int         day;
    int         month;
    int         year;
  };
  struct date today;              /* variable */

  today.day = 27;                 /* assign */
  today.month = 9;
  today.year = 1985;

  printf("Today\'s date is %2d/%2d/%4d\n",
      today.day, today.month, today.year);
}
```

The usual scope rules of C apply. In particular, the structured type date is local to the main function. This means that we may not declare variables as structures of type date outside function main. For structure type date to be globally available, an external declaration is necessary.

The programmer can achieve a high degree of modularity and portability by using typedef declarations to name these derived types. This is a consequence of the abstraction of these data types through tag names and typedef statements. Applying typedef declarations to structure types can be done in a number of ways. Following a structure template such as:

```
struct date { /* date template: */
  int       day;
  int       month;
  int       year;
};
```

the type name `Date` can be associated with this structure through the declaration:

```
typedef struct date     Date;
```

Thereafter, structure variables of type `struct date` may be declared as:

```
Date     today;
```

When using `typedef` declarations to name a structured type, the tag name is irrelevant. The structure's template and the type name are then introduced in a single unified declaration. The two-stage process above may also be achieved by:

```
typedef struct date {     /* template and name: */
    int     day;
    int     month;
    int     year;
} Date;
```

The type name `Date` now serves in place of the structure type. The declaration for the structured variable `today` appears as before. But note how the tag name `date` is no longer employed. The normal declaration for the above is then:

```
typedef struct {     /* no tag name introduced */
    int     day;
    int     month;
    int     year;
} Date;
```

Two dates are given to a program representing, respectively, the date of birth of a person and today's date. The program computes that person's age expressed as a number of years.

PROGRAM 15.2

```
/*
**      Compute a person's age expressed as a number of years
**      given the date of birth of that person and today's
**      date.
*/

#include <stdio.h>

struct date { /* template: */
  int         day;
  int         month;
  int         year;
  };
typedef struct date             Date;

main ()
{
  Date        dateofbirth, today;
  int         age;
```

```
printf ("Date of birth?: ");
scanf ("%d/%d/%d",
    &dateofbirth.day, &dateofbirth.month, &dateofbirth.year);

printf ("Today\'s date?: ");
scanf ("%d/%d/%d", &today.day, &today.month, &today.year);

if (today.month > dateofbirth.month ||
    (today.month == dateofbirth.month &&
                    today.day >= dateofbirth.day))
  age = today.year - dateofbirth.year;
else
  age = today.year - dateofbirth.year - 1;

printf ("Age: %d\n", age);
}
```

15.2 Name overloading

The names of structure members are defined in a special overloading class associated with the structure type. Member names within a structure must be distinct, but they may be the same as member names in other structures and may be the same as variable, function, type names and enumerated constants. For example, consider the following sequence of declarations:

```
int    a;
struct x { int a; double b; } b;
struct y { int b; double a; } c;
```

The identifier a has three non-conflicting declarations; it is an integer variable, an integer member of structure x, and a double member of structure y. These three declarations are used respectively in the expressions:

```
a
b.a
c.a
```

The compiler determines from the context in which the name is used the association that is required.

15.3 Internal storage of structures

Structure members are stored in memory in the same order in which they are declared. However, since structures are often composed of members of different types, and since different data types often have different address alignment requirements, 'holes' may be imbedded in the actual memory space. For some hardware many multi-byte data items must be located at an address that is exactly divisible by 2 or by 4.

Consider the structure declaration:

```
struct alignment { /* storage alignment example: */
    int    numb1;
    char   ch;
    int    numb2;
} example;
```

Assume that `int`'s require alignment on a double byte boundary address (i.e. an even address), while `char`'s can be placed at any address. The structure variable `example` then occupies memory as shown in Figure 15.1, assuming that an `int` occupies two bytes. The second integer `numb2` cannot immediately follow `ch` because the next location is not an even byte number. Therefore, an additional byte is inserted to align `numb2` as required.

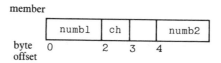

Figure 15.1

From this example we see that the actual memory layout of a structure is machine-dependent. Portable code should not depend on the actual numeric values of the offsets of the structure members. Always let the compiler keep track of them.

15.4 Structures and functions

Structured items may also be taken as arguments to functions and as values returned from functions. To illustrate the use of structures with functions, consider the construction of a package of operations to be performed on *rational* numbers. A rational number is a fractional value expressed as the quotient of two positive integer values. Examples of rational numbers include 1/2, 3/4 and 7/8. The elements of a rational number are the *numerator* and the *denominator*. The rational number 3/4 has numerator 3 and denominator 4. An appropriate type is:

```
typedef struct {    /* rational number: */
    unsigned int    numerator;
    unsigned int    denominator;
} Rational;
```

In Standard C structures can be passed as arguments and returned as function values. So, if two integer values `num` and `den` are to be composed into a rational value, we might employ the function `assign`:

```
#define NUM(R)    ((R).numerator)
#define DEN(R)    ((R).denominator)
```

```
Rational assign(unsigned int num, unsigned int den)
{
  Rational rat;

  NUM(rat) = num/gcd;
  DEN(rat) = den/gcd;
  return rat;
}
```

The function uses the local variable `rat` of type `Rational` and assigns the two arguments to its member values. This is explicitly returned to the calling function and may be assigned there to a variable of type `Rational`.

We want the rational value always expressed in its simplest form. Thus, if the integer arguments given to function `assign` are 8 and 6 (i.e. 8/6), we wish the function to effectively deliver the reduced rational number 4/3. To do so we must determine the highest common factor of the two arguments and divide this value into both. This is implemented with the recursive function `hcf`. Since we are to construct a package of rationals, we choose to conceal the local function `hcf` by giving it storage class `static`:

```
static unsigned int hcf(unsigned int n, unsigned int m)
{
  if(m > n)
    return hcf(m, n);
  else if (m == 0)
    return n;
  else
    return hcf(m, n % m);
}

Rational assign(unsigned int num, unsigned int den)
{
  unsigned int gcd;
  Rational rat;

  gcd = hcf(num, den);
  NUM(rat) = num/gcd;
  DEN(rat) = den/gcd;
  return rat;
}
```

The final revision we must make to function `assign` is to trap the error condition where the denominator has value zero. The rational number a/0 does not exist. The final version is then:

```
Rational assign(unsigned int num, unsigned int den)
{
  unsigned int gcd;
  Rational rat;
```

```
if(den == 0){
  fprintf(stderr, "Error: assign(%d, %d)\n", num, den);
  exit(1);
}

gcd = hcf(num, den);
NUM(rat) = num/gcd;
DEN(rat) = den/gcd;
return rat;
}
```

If the floating point equivalent of the elements of a fractional number are divided, then the real value of the rational number is delivered. The rational 3/4 then reduces to 0.75. We can express this with a function having a single rational argument:

```
float real(Rational rat)
{
  return (float) NUM(rat)/DEN(rat);
}
```

Two rational values a/b and c/d are added by performing the following arithmetic and then reducing the result to the simplest form:

$$\frac{a}{b} + \frac{c}{d} = \frac{ad + bc}{bd}$$

```
Rational add(Rational rat1, Rational rat2)
{
  unsigned int num, den;

  num = NUM(rat1) * DEN(rat2) + NUM(rat2) * DEN(rat1);
  den = DEN(rat1) * DEN(rat2);
  return assign(num, den);
}
```

A sample package and the complementary header appears below. The package supports those already defined, together with `multiply` (two rational numbers), `ratzero` (generate rational zero: 0/1), `ratunit` (generate rational unity: 1/1), and a series of functions to perform relational tests on pairs of rational values:

```
/*
**      File:             rational.h
**
**      Specification for the package of rational numbers.
*/

#include "boolean.h"

typedef struct { /* template and name: */
  unsigned int      numerator;
  unsigned int      denominator;
} Rational;
```

```
#define NUM(R)          ((R).numerator)
#define DEN(R)          ((R).denominator)

#define ratzero()       assign(0, 1)
#define ratunit()       assign(1, 1)

extern float    real(Rational);
extern Rational assign(unsigned int, unsigned int);
extern Rational add(Rational, Rational);
extern Rational multiply(Rational, Rational);
extern Boolean  less(Rational, Rational);
extern Boolean  equal(Rational, Rational);

#define greater(X, Y)        (less(Y, X))
#define unequal(X, Y)        (!equal(X, Y))
#define lessorequal(X, Y)    (!less(Y, X))
#define greaterorequal(X, Y) (!less(X, Y))



/*
**      File:           rational.c
**
**      Implementation package for the rational numbers.
**      Supported are the operations for assignment,
**      addition, multiplication and the relational
**      operator less.
*/

#include <stdio.h>
#include "rational.h"

float real(Rational rat)
{
  .....
}

static unsigned int hcf(unsigned int n, unsigned int m)
{
  .....
}

Rational assign(unsigned int num, unsigned int den)
{
  .....
}

Rational add(Rational rat1, Rational rat2)
{
  .....
}
```

```
Rational multiply(Rational rat1, Rational rat2)
{
  unsigned int num, den;

  num = NUM(rat1) * NUM(rat2);
  den = DEN(rat1) * DEN(rat2);
  return assign(num, den);
}

Boolean less(Rational rat1, Rational rat2)
{
  return NUM(rat1) * DEN(rat2) < NUM(rat2) * DEN(rat1);
}

Boolean equal(Rational rat1, Rational rat2)
{
  return NUM(rat1) * DEN(rat2) == NUM(rat2) * DEN(rat1);
}
```

We will use this package of rational numbers to develop a program to compute the partial sums of the harmonic series. The program will evaluate $H(n)$ for various values of n, where:

$$H(n) = 1 + \frac{1}{2} + \frac{1}{3} + \ldots + \frac{1}{n}$$

The result of the calculation is to be expressed in the form of a rational number. The program is invoked with the command line:

```
harmonic n
```

where the integer value n is given as the argument. For example, the call:

```
harmonic 8
```

produces the output:

```
2: 3/2
3: 11/6
4: 25/12
5: 137/60
6: 49/20
7: 363/140
8: 761/280
```

PROGRAM 15.3

```
/*
**      Compute the partial sums of the harmonic series H(n)
**      for various values of n, where:
**
**      H(n) = 1 + 1/2 + 1/3 + 1/4 + ... + 1/n
**
```

```
**          The integer value n is given as a command line argument.
*/

#include <stdio.h>
#include "rational.h"

main(int argc, char *argv[])
{
   int          k, n;
   Rational     sum, term;

   if (argc != 2)
     fprintf(stderr, "Usage: %s number\n", argv[0]);
   else {
     sscanf(argv[1], "%d", &n);          /* obtain n */

     sum = ratunit();                    /* sum = 1, initially */
     for (k = 2; k <= n; k++){           /* remaining terms */
       term = assign(1, k);
       sum = add(sum, term);
       printf("%2d: %d/%d\n", k, NUM(sum), DEN(sum));
     }
   }
}
```

15.5 Pointers to structures

We have shown how a pointer can be defined to point to a fundamental data type such as an int or a char. Pointers can also be defined to point to structures. Using the date structure introduced earlier and defining a type name Date through a type definition we may proceed to declare a variable today of type Date by:

```
Date       today;
```

A variable declared as a pointer to a Date variable is established in the usual way:

```
Date       *ptrdate;
```

or, by firstly introducing a type name for an object of type pointer to Date through:

```
typedef Date      *PtrDate;
```

and then declaring variable ptrdate by:

```
PtrDate       ptrdate;
```

The variable ptrdate can then be used in the expected fashion. We can, for example, set it to point to the Date variable today, with the assignment:

```
ptrdate = &today;
```

Having performed the assignment, we can indirectly access any member of the date structure pointed to by `ptrdate`. If `p` is a pointer to some structured object, then the notation:

```
p -> member-name
```

refers to the particular member name. Strictly, the symbol `->` is another C operator known as the *structure pointer operator* and has precedence and associativity as shown in Appendix E. Using the pointer variable `ptrdate`, we may set the member `day` of the `date` structure to, say, 7 with the statement:

```
ptrdate -> day = 7;
```

To test if `today` is the last day of the year, the statement:

```
if (ptrdate -> day == 31 &&
        ptrdate -> month == 12) ....
```

can be used. To read an integer value from the standard input and assign it to the member `year` of the object of type `Date` pointed to by `ptrdate`, the statement is:

```
scanf("%d", &ptrdate -> year);
```

These three illustrative statements contain a mixture of operators. The assignment statement employs both the structure and assignment operators; the `if` statement uses the structure and equality operators and the logical and operator; the `scanf` function call employs both the address operator and the structure operator.

As always, the C programmer must be vigilant about operator precedence and operator associativity. The structure pointer operator (`->`) and structure member reference operator (`.`) have highest priorities. In the assignment:

```
ptrdate -> day = 7;
```

the stucture operator having precedence over the assignment operator first delivers the object to receive the value before the assignment is performed. In the `if` statement, the operators are, in decreasing order of precedence: the structure operator, the equality operator and the logical and operator. The conditional expression is effectively evaluated as:

```
if (((ptrdate -> day) == 31) &&
        ((ptrdate -> month) == 12)) ....
```

In the final example:

```
scanf("%d", &ptrdate -> year);
```

the address operator has low priority relative to the stucture operator. Thus the object delivered by the structure pointer has its address taken and passed to `scanf` so that an input value may be placed at that location.

While not really a sensible way to do things, we could write Program 15.1 in terms of pointers. We include this as Program 15.4 only for illustration.

PROGRAM 15.4

```
/*
**       Assign values to the members of a structured date,
**       then print them. The structured date value is
**       manipulated through pointers to illustrate.
*/

#include <stdio.h>

struct date { /* date template: */
  int                                           day;
  int                                           month;
  int                                           year;
};
typedef struct date    Date;            /* variable and . . . */
typedef Date           *Ptrdate;        /* ... pointer types */

main ()
{
  Date          today;
  Ptrdate       ptrdate;

  ptrdate = &today;
  ptrdate -> day       = 27;
  ptrdate -> month     = 9;
  ptrdate -> year      = 1985;

  printf ("Today\'s date is %2d/%2d/%4d\n",
      ptrdate -> day, ptrdate -> month, ptrdate -> year);
}
```

The notation:

```
ptrdate -> day
```

refers to the member `day` of the date structure to which the pointer variable `ptrdate` points. Since `ptrdate` points to a structure, the `day` member could also be referred to by:

```
(*ptrdate).day
```

but pointers to structures are so frequently used that the `->` notation is provided as a convenient shorthand. The parentheses are necessary in `(*ptrdate).day` because the structure member operator '.' has higher precedence than the indirection operator '*'. The parentheses guarantee to first deliver the structured object from which the member `day` is obtained.

15.6 Initializing structures

Initialization of structures is similar to initialization of arrays – the values of the members are listed within a pair of matching braces, with each element separated from the next by a comma symbol. To initialize the structure Date variable xmas to 25 December 1986, the declaration is:

```
Date xmas = {25, 12, 1986 };
```

Initialization of all variables, including structure variables, can only be performed with constant values or constant expressions or by expressions delivering a value of the required type.

If fewer values are listed than there are members of the structure, the remaining members are assigned the default value zero for external or static structures and are undefined for automatic structured objects. So the external declaration:

```
Date beginning = { 1, 1 };
```

sets beginning.day and beginning.month to 1, but provides no explicit initializer for beginning.year. By default, its initial value is then 0.

15.7 Array members of structures

It is possible to define structures that contain arrays as members. In many applications, arrays of characters are used. For example, we might define a record type to describe the details of a person as follows:

```
enum gender { FEMALE, MALE };
typedef enum gender         Gender;

struct person {     /* single individual: */
    char        surname[NAMEMAX];
    char        forename[NAMEMAX];
    Gender      sex;
    int         age;
};
typedef struct person       Person;
```

A value of type Person consists of four members – a surname which is an array of characters, a forename similarly defined, a component sex which is either FEMALE or MALE, and an integer age.

If we have the declaration:

```
Person      employee;
```

then:

```
employee                    denotes a variable of type Person.
employee.forename           denotes a string of characters which might be
```

assigned, compared, or output using the usual string operations.

`employee.surname[0]`   denotes the first character of the employee's surname and may be used in any way appropriate to a character variable.

The following are all permissible operations upon the structure variable employee:

```
employee.sex = FEMALE;
if (employee.age > 60) ....
strcpy(employee.surname, "Smith");
if (employee.forename[0] == 'A') ....
```

From the preceding section, initialization of structure variables is permissible. Those members that are character arrays are initialized as shown in Section 12.1. Then we might initialize structure variable `employee` with:

```
Person employee =
    { "Bloggs", "Joe", MALE, 21 };
```

15.8 Arrays of structures

A structure may occur as a component of other aggregate types. In particular, an array type may be defined whose elements are structures. Thus, the C programming language supports both members of structures which are arrays and arrays of structures. For example:

```
typedef enum { FEMALE, MALE } Gender;

typedef struct {     /* single individual: */
    char    surname[NAMEMAX];
    char    forename[NAMEMAX];
    Gender  sex;
    int     age;
} Person;

Person      staff[STAFFSIZE];
```

defines an array called `staff`. Each element of the array is defined to be of type `Person`. For this declaration:

`staff`   denotes the complete array.

`staff[i]`   denotes a variable of type Person.

`staff[i].forename`   denotes an array of characters which may be assigned, compared, or output using the usual string operators.

`staff[i].surname[j]`   denotes a single character value.

Further, if a function called, say, `print_person` exists and prints the details of an employee, then the call:

```
print_person(staff[k]);
```

is correct, assuming the function prototype is:

```
void print person(Person employee)
```

Equally, if a function called `sort`, arranges the `staff` into alphabetical order based on the `surname`, the call:

```
sort(staff, STAFFSIZE);
```

would be appropriate for the function prototype:

```
void sort(Person staff[], int size)
```

Initialization of arrays of structures is similar to the initialization of multi-dimensional arrays. The declaration:

```
Person staff[] =
    { { "Bloggs", "Joe",  MALE,    21 },
      { "Smith",  "John", MALE,    30 },
      { "Black",  "Mary", FEMALE, 25 } };
```

declares an array of size 3. Each element is of type `Person`, and establishes a workforce consisting of Joe Bloggs, John Smith and Mary Black is established.

The `sort` function when applied to this workforce could be invoked with the call:

```
sort(staff, NSTAFF);
```

The quantity NSTAFF is the number of employees in staff. Although we could enumerate this explicitly with:

```
#define NSTAFF    3
```

it is easier and much safer to do it within the program, especially if the list is subject to change. If the size of the array and the size of an individual element is determinable, then the number of entries is:

```
size-of-array / size-of-array-element
```

We have already met the compile time unary operator `sizeof`, used to compute the size of any object. The computation can then be expressed in terms of this operator and used in a #define statement to set the value of NSTAFF:

```
#define    NSTAFF    (sizeof(staff)) / sizeof(Person))
```

Let us apply all these new concepts to the following problem. A program is required to count the number of occurrences of each C keyword appearing in a program text. Keywords appearing in strings and comments are included in the count.

The keyword counting program is invoked with a single command line argument being the name of the program text file to be processed. After checking this argument, the `main` function reads the input one 'word' at a time. Each word is compared against a list of all the C keywords. If no match is found, the word is ignored. If a match is found, the associated keyword `counter` is incremented. This action is relegated to the subsidiary function `count`.

PROGRAM 15.5

```
/*
**      A program to count the occurrences of each C keyword.
**      The name of the text file containing the program is
**      given as a command line argument. This program listing
**      is used as the test input.
*/

#include <stdio.h>
#include <stdlib.h>
#include <ctype.h>
#include "boolean.h"

struct wordcount{ /* template: */
    char        *keyword;
    int         keycount;
};
typedef struct wordcount        WordCount;

static WordCount keytable[] = {
        "auto",         0,      "break",        0,
        "case",         0,      "char",         0,
        "const",        0,      "continue",     0,
        "default",      0,      "do",           0,
        "double",       0,      "else",         0,
        "enum",         0,      "extern",       0,
        "float",        0,      "for",          0,
        "goto",         0,      "if",           0,
        "int",          0,      "long",         0,
        "register",     0,      "return",       0,
        "short",        0,      "signed",       0,
        "sizeof",       0,      "static",       0,
        "struct",       0,      "switch",       0,
        "typedef",      0,      "union",        0,
        "unsigned",     0,      "void",         0,
        "volatile",     0,      "while",        0
};

#define NKEYS           (sizeof(keytable) / sizeof(WordCount))
#define READONLY        "r"
#define WORDSIZE        128
```

```
char      *programname;

Boolean  nextword(FILE *, char *);
void      count(char *, WordCount [], int);
void      print(WordCount [], int);
void      syserr (int, char *, char *);

typedef int      Character;

main (int argc, char *argv[])
{
  FILE        *fp;
  char        word[WORDSIZE];
  int         n;

  programname = argv[0];

  if(argc != 2)
    syserr(1, "Usage: %s filename\n", programname);
  else if((fp = fopen(argv[1], READONLY)) == NULL)
    syserr(2, "Cannot open %s\n", argv[1]);
  else{
    while(nextword(fp, word))
      count(word, keytable, NKEYS);
    print(keytable, NKEYS);
    exit(EXIT_SUCCESS);
  }
}


void count(char *word, WordCount table[] , int size)
{
  int         n;

  for(n = 0; n < size ; n++)
    if(strcmp(word, table[n].keyword) == 0){
      table[n].keycount++;
      return;
    }
}

void print(WordCount table[], int size)
{
  int n ;

  for(n = 0; n < size; n++)
    printf("\t%-15s %4d\n", table[n].keyword, table[n].keycount);
}


Boolean nextword(FILE *fp, char *word)
{
  Character ch;
```

```
  while(ch = getc(fp), ! isalpha(ch))
    if(ch == EOF) break;
  if(ch == EOF) return FALSE;

  *word++ = ch;
  while(ch = getc(fp), isalpha(ch))
    *word++ = ch;
  *word = '\0';
  ungetc(ch, fp);
  return TRUE;
}


void syserr(int errcode, char *message, char *argument)
{
  fprintf(stderr, "%s [%2d]: ", programname, errcode);
  fprintf(stderr, message, argument);

  exit(EXIT_FAILURE);
}
```

When this program text file is processed by itself, the output is:

```
auto        1
break       2
case        1
char        13
const       1
continue    1
default     1
do          1
double      1
else        3
enum        1
extern      1
float       1
for         3
goto        1
if          6
int         13
long        1
register    1
return      4
short       1
signed      1
sizeof      3
static      2
struct      3
switch      1
typedef     3
union       1
```

```
unsigned      1
void          7
volatile      1
while         4
```

15.9 Nested structures

Structures are allowed to occur as components of other aggregate types, including structures. It is therefore possible to define structures that contain another structure as one or more of their members. An application might, for instance, process details of the book stock held in a library. For each book the following information is maintained: the ISBN (International Standard Book Number), the author, the title, the publisher, the edition and the date of publication. In the context of this data, the last item is considered a single entity. In reality it is, of course, composed of three parts – a day, a month and a year. Thus we have a nested structure based on the following declarations:

```
typedef struct {      /* template and name: */
     int      day;
     int      month;
     int      year;
} Date;

typedef struct {      /* contains substructure: */
     char     isbn[ISBNSIZE];
     char     author[AUTHORSIZE];
     char     title[TITLESIZE];
     char     publisher[PUBLISHERSIZE];
     int      edition;
     Date     dateofpublication;
} Book;
```

A stock of 100 books can be established and the first two entries made with the following declaration plus initialization:

```
Book stock [100] =
     { { "0131101633", "Kernighan and Ritchie",
         "The C Programming Language", "Prentice Hall",
         1, {1, 1, 1978}},
       { "0131155105", "K Barclay",
         "C Problem Solving and Programming",
         "Prentice Hall",
         1, {1, 2, 1989}}
     };
```

For this declaration:

stock	denotes the complete array.
stock[i]	denotes a variable of type Book.

```
stock[i].dateofpublication
```
denotes a variable of type Date.

```
stock[i].dateofpublication.year
```
denotes a variable of type int.

15.10 Files of structures

The file handling primitives `fread`, `fwrite` and `fseek` consider a file as an unstructured series of byte values. The programmer may superimpose some arbitrary data structure so that the file becomes a sequence of records of some given type. Recall the structured data type `Person` introduced in Section 15.7. A variable of type `Person` called, say, `employee` may be written to a file by the statement:

```
fwrite(&employee, sizeof(Person), 1, fp)
```

The first actual argument to `fwrite` is the address of a character buffer. The number of bytes transferred in the operation is the number of bytes in the employee record and is determined by the compile time operator `sizeof(Person)`. If the same number of bytes is read from the same position in the file into a `Person` structure, then the original data is recovered. The file can now be interpreted as a file of `Person` records.

CASE STUDY   15.1 Integer sets

In Case Study 11.2 a set of integers was realized by an array of integers with associated counters. In that example the integer set was viewed as an abstract data type and, where only one instance of the data type is required, the representation structure can be hidden within the program unit. In Case Study 13.1 multiple instances of a data type were implemented using dynamic storage allocation and pointers. In this example we consider having multiple instances of the data type combining structures and dynamic storage.

Once again we implement an integer set data type. In the application program two instances of the data type are required. The program accepts two positive integer data values and displays a list of the prime factors common to both numbers, together with a list of the prime factors of each number excluding the common values. The program operates by finding the prime factors of each number as a set of integers, then determines the common values using the set `intersection` operation. The distinct values are found using set `difference`.

The following fragment of a header file specifies the abstract data type `IntegerSet` with some possible operators:

```
/*
**      File:   intset.h
**
```

```
**          The set of integers is realized with a structure
**          containing all the set attributes, namely, its maximum
**          permissible size, its current size, a dynamically
**          allocated block of storage for the set elements, and
**          an iterator.
*/

typedef ...        IntegerSet;

extern IntegerSet integerset(int max);          /* constructor */
extern void        dintegerset(IntegerSet set);  /* destructor */
extern IntegerSet insert(int item, IntegerSet set);
extern IntegerSet intersection(IntegerSet set1, IntegerSet set2);
extern IntegerSet difference(IntegerSet set1, IntegerSet set2);
extern Boolean     ismember(int ietm, IntegerSet set);
extern Boolean     isfull(IntegerSet);
```

The problem solution is straightforward and is implemented in terms of our set abstract data type:

```
/*
**          File:          case01.c
*/

#include <stdio.h>
#include "intset.h"

IntegerSet primes(int);
void        printset(char *, IntegerSet);

main()
{
  IntegerSet primes1, primes2;
  IntegerSet commonprimes;
  IntegerSet primes1only, primes2only;
  int        number1, number2;

  printf("Enter the two numbers: ");
  scanf("%d %d", &number1, &number2);

  primes1 = primes(number1);     /* find the primes of .. */
  primes2 = primes(number2);     /* .. the data values */

  commonprimes = intersection(primes1, primes2);
  primes1only  = difference(primes1, primes2);
  primes2only  = difference(primes2, primes1);

  printset("Common primes:", commonprimes);
  printset("Primes unique to first number:", primes1only);
  printset("Primes unique to second number:", primes2only);
```

```
  dintegerset(primes1);
  dintegerset(primes2);
  dintegerset(commonprimes);
  dintegerset(primes1only);
  dintegerset(primes2only);
}


/*
**       Determine the primes for the given argument.
*/

IntegerSet primes(int number)
{
  IntegerSet set = integerset(number);   /* log2(number) better */
  int        test= 2;                     /* trial value */

  while(number != 1){
    if(number % test == 0){
      set = insert(test, set);
      number /= test;
    } else
      test++;
  }

  return set;
}

/*
**       Display the content of a set 5 values per line.
**       The set is traversed using the iterators.
*/

void printset(char *mess, IntegerSet set)
{
  .....
}
```

This problem gives rise to an associated abstraction mechanism called the *iteration abstraction* or *iterator* for short. Iterators generalize the iteration facilities available in programming languages. They allow client programs to iterate over arbitrary data types. For example, an obvious requirement of this problem is to perform a print of each element in a given set:

```
FOR all elements of the set DO
      print the element
ENDFOR
```

Such a loop processes each element of the set. Alternatively, in some other problem it may be necessary to search for an element in the set that satisfies some criterion.

Integer sets as we have defined them provide no convenient way to perform such loops. If `printset` were provided as an `IntegerSet` operation, we could implement it efficiently using an array index where the set is represented by an array. However, `printset` is not an obvious `IntegerSet` operation. Even if it were, in what manner is the set to be formatted? Even if we could answer this and other similar questions about the formatting, what about other similar operations we might require? For example, we may need to form the sum of the elements of a set. The data type must provide operations to implement this and other procedures.

To support iteration we need access to the elements of the set. This we provide by operations to initialize the iteration (`inititer`), to obtain the current element of the set (`getiter`), to advance to the next item in the set (`nextiter`), and to determine when the processing is complete (`moreiter`).

Each operation is implemented as a function in the `IntegerSet` package. The structure representing the set is enhanced with an additional integer field called `iter` used to index the array which realizes the set. The operations initialize and update this variable:

```
/*
**        File:   intset.h
**
**        The set of integers is realized with a structure
**        containing all the set attributes, namely, its maximum
**        permissible size, its current size, a dynamically
**        allocated block of storage for the set elements, and
**        an iterator.
*/

#include "boolean.h"

typedef struct{          /* set of integers: */
   int          maxsize;          /* overall set capacity */
   int          size;             /* present number of elements */
   int          *set;             /* the set elements */
   int          iter;             /* iterator */
} IntegerSet;

extern IntegerSet integerset(int max);          /* constructor */
extern void       dintegerset(IntegerSet set);  /* destructor */
extern IntegerSet insert(int item, IntegerSet set);
extern IntegerSet intersection(IntegerSet set1, IntegerSet set2);
extern IntegerSet difference(IntegerSet set1, IntegerSet set2);
extern Boolean    ismember(int ietm, IntegerSet set);
extern Boolean    isfull(IntegerSet);

                    /* Iterator operations: */

extern IntegerSet inititer(IntegerSet);
extern Boolean    moreiter(IntegerSet);
extern int        getiter(IntegerSet);
extern IntegerSet nextiter(IntegerSet);
```

We can now complete the `printset` function:

```
void printset(char *mess, IntegerSet set)
{
  int count = 0;

  printf("%s\n", mess);
  set = inititer(set);
  while(moreiter(set)){
    printf("%6d", getiter(set));
    if(++count == 5)
      count = 0, putchar('\n');
    set = nextiter(set);
  }
  putchar('\n');
}
```

The program is completed by implementing the program unit intset.c:

```
/*
**        File:              intset.c
*/

#include <stdio.h>
#include <stdlib.h>
#include "intset.h"

#define MIN(A, B)        ((A) < (B) ? (A) : (B))


/*
**        Function INTEGERSET acts the constructor operation
**        for sets of integers. Dynamic storage is set aside
**        for the required amount, and the attributes initialised.
*/

IntegerSet integerset(int max)
{
  IntegerSet intset;
  int        *new;

  new = calloc(max, sizeof(int));
  if(new == NULL){
    fprintf(stderr, "No space (integerset)\n");
    exit(1);
  }

  intset.maxsize = max;
  intset.size = 0;
  intset.set = new;

  return intset;
}
```

```
/*
**      Function DINTEGERSET is the destructor operation. It
**      should be called on block exit when the dynamic storage
**      is to be relinquished.
*/

void dintegerset(IntegerSet set)
{
  free(set.set);
}


/*
**      Function INSERT enters a new integer value into the
**      named set, providing that value is not already present
**      and that there is space.
*/

IntegerSet insert(int item, IntegerSet set)
{
  if(isfull(set))
    return set;
  else if(ismember(item, set))
    return set;
  else {
    set.set[set.size++] = item;
    return set;
  }
}


/*
**      Two predicates ISFULL and ISMEMBER perform the
**      appropriate checks.
*/

Boolean isfull(IntegerSet set)
{
  return set.maxsize == set.size ? TRUE : FALSE;
}

Boolean ismember(int item, IntegerSet set)
{
  int k;

  for(k = 0; k < set.size; k++)
    if(set.set[k] == item)
      return TRUE;

  return FALSE;
}


/*
**      Function INTERSECTION implements the corresponding set
**      operation. Since the resulting set will be no greater
```

```
**      than the smaller of the two sets, storage of this size
**      is allocated.
*/

IntegerSet intersection(IntegerSet set1, IntegerSet set2)
{
  int        set1size = set1.size;
  int        set2size = set2.size;
  IntegerSet set = integerset(MIN(set1size, set2size));
  int        k;

  for(k = 0; k < set1size; k++)
    if(ismember(set1.set[k], set2))
      set = insert(set1.set[k], set);

  return set;
}


/*
**      Function DIFFERENCE implements the corresponding set
**      operation. The resulting set can be no larger than the
**      first operand.
*/

IntegerSet difference(IntegerSet set1, IntegerSet set2)
{
  int        set1size = set1.size;
  IntegerSet set = integerset(set1size);
  int        k;

  for(k = 0; k < set1size; k++)
    if( ! ismember(set1.set[k], set2))
      set = insert(set1.set[k], set);

  return set;
}

/*
**      Iterators:
*/

IntegerSet inititer(IntegerSet set)
{
  set.iter = 0;
  return set;
}


Boolean moreiter(IntegerSet set)
{
  return (set.iter < set.size);
}
```

```
int getiter(IntegerSet set)
{
  return set.set[set.iter];
}


IntegerSet nextiter(IntegerSet set)
{
  set.iter++;
  return set;
}
```

15.11 Unions

The union data type in C is similar to *variant records* in other programming languages. The union data type is similar to the structure data type in that both can contain members of different types and sizes. Unlike structures, however, a union can hold at most one of its components at a time. Effectively, the members are overlaid in the storage allocated for the union. The compiler allocates sufficient storage to accommodate the largest of the specified members.

A union is a variable which can legitimately hold any one of several types. We demonstrate this in the following illustration. The notation used to declare and access members of a union is identical to that used with structures, with the keyword union replacing struct. Consider:

```
union number {      /* members are overlaid: */
    int       integer;
    float     decimal;
};
typedef union number    Number;

Number    data;
```

The variable data will be large enough to hold the larger of the two types (int or float), regardless of the machine it is compiled on. Provided the usage is consistent, either of the types may be assigned to data and used in expressions. It is the responsiblity of the programmer to maintain consistency and keep track of what type is currently stored in a union. If something is stored as one type and extracted as another, then the results are machine-dependent. This is illustrated in Program 15.6.

PROGRAM 15.6

```
/*
**      A program to illustrate how a system overlays an int
**      and a float. The program also shows how in C it is
**      the programmer's responsibility to maintain
**      consistency.
*/
```

```
#include <stdio.h>

union number {
  int      integer;
  float    decimal;
};
typedef union number      Number;

main ()
{
  Number        data;

  data.integer = 20000;
  printf ("int: %6d, float: %f10.4\n", data.integer, data.decimal);

  data.decimal = 123.0;
  printf ("int: %6d, float: %f10.4\n", data.integer, data.decimal);
}
```

The program demonstrates how a system overlays an int and a float. The program output, which is dependent upon the computer system in which it is run, might be:

```
20000        0.0000
31553      123.0000
```

Members of unions are accessed just as for structures. Syntactically, we use:

```
union-variable.member-name
```

or:

```
union-pointer -> member-name
```

when using a pointer to a union variable. Unions may occur within structures and arrays and vice versa. The notation for accessing a member of a union in a structure (or for a structure in a union) is the same as that for nested structures. For example, in the structure array staff defined by:

```
#define WORDSIZE            20
#define NAMESIZE            25
#define STAFFSIZE          120

typedef union {
     char          word[WORDSIZE];
     int           number;
} WordNumber;

typedef struct {
     WordNumber  day;
     WordNumber  month;
     int         year;
} Date;
```

```
typedef struct {
    char        surname[NAMESIZE];
    char        forename[NAMESIZE];
    Date        birthday;
} Person;

Person          staff[STAFFSIZE];
```

in which both day and month may be expressed as either an integer or as character string, the member number for component day is referred to as:

```
staff[k].birthday.day.number
```

and the first character of the string word for member month by:

```
staff[k].birthday.month.word[0]
```

The ANS definition of C places the same restrictions on unions as on structures. The only operations on unions supported are to take its address, to access one of its members, assignment to unions, and passing unions as function arguments and as return values from functions.

There is no provision in C to enquire which component of a union was last assigned. The programmer can, however, enclose a union in a structure that includes a tag component to indicate which member of a union is active. For example, we might add to the union Number:

```
typedef enum { INT, FLOAT } Tag;

typedef union {
    int        integer;
    float      decimal;
} Number;

typedef struct {
    Tag        tagged;
    Number     value;
} Pair;

Pair        data;
```

To assign to the union, we write either:

```
data.tagged       = INT;
data.value.integer = 123;
```

or:

```
data.tagged       = FLOAT;
data.value.decimal = 123.0;
```

We can then write portable functions that can discriminate among the possible values of the union. For example, we repeat the last program, including the above definitions and a function to print a Pair value, whatever it may contain.

PROGRAM 15.7

```
/*
**        Associate a tag value with a union to permit
**        discrimination among possible values of the union.
*/

#include <stdio.h>

typedef enum { INT, FLOAT } Tag;

union number { /* number pair template: */
  int           integer;
  float         decimal;
};
typedef union number     Number;

struct pair { /* tagged number pairs: */
  Tag           tagged;
  Number        value;
};
typedef struct pair      Pair;

void print_pair (Pair);

main ()
{
  Pair          data;

  data.tagged        = INT;
  data.value.integer = 20000;
  print_pair (data);

  data.tagged        = FLOAT;
  data.value.decimal = 123.0;
  print_pair (data);
}


void print_pair(Pair d)
{
  switch (d.tagged){
    case INT:       printf ("Integer: %d\n", d.value.integer);
                    break;
    case FLOAT:     printf ("Decimal: %f\n", d.value.decimal);
                    break;
  }
}
```

The output from this program is:

```
20000
123.000000
```

The print_pair function correctly discriminates between the fields integer and decimal according to the value assigned to the tag.

C unions may be initialized using either an expression delivering a value of the same type or by a brace-enclosed initializer. When using the latter, however, only the first member can be set in this way. Thus in the union Number of Program 15.6, only the field member integer may be assigned.

15.12 Bit fields

Systems programming activities are often required to manipulate data not only at the byte level, but also at the bit level. Bit fields are typically used in machine-dependent programs which require data structures to correspond to some fixed hardware representation. For example, data formats for interfaces to hardware devices often require the ability to access individual bits.

The C compiler allows integer numbers to be packed into spaces smaller than that ordinarily allowed. These components are called *bit fields* and are specified by following the member declarator with a colon symbol and a constant integer expression specifying the width of the field in bits:

```
struct packed {
unsigned int          a : 2;
unsigned int          b : 4, c : 7;
} bits = { 1, 7, 33 };
```

The intent is that member a is allocated the first 2 bits of the structure, member b the next 4 bits, and finally member c the next 7 bits. The 2-bit field a is capable of representing the four values 0 to 3 inclusive; b is capable of storing the values 0, 1, 2, ... , 15; and the 7-bit field c may represent the values 0 to 127 inclusive.

The compiler assigns in either a left-to-right or a right-to-left order of the bits in a machine word needed to store the fields. The internal representation of bit fields, therefore, is machine-dependent. A machine word usually equates with the data type int, and the memory allocation for int's differs among machines. Further, while the majority of machines store fields left-to-right, some store right-to-left. Assuming a two-byte int and a left-to-right storage format, the memory representation for variable bits as declared and initialized above is shown in Figure 15.2.

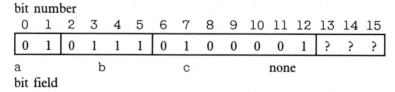

Figure 15.2

A field may not overlap an `int` boundary. If the bit field width would cause this to happen, the field is aligned at the next int boundary. Thus the declaration:

```
struct filled {
      unsigned int     a : 4;
      unsigned int     b : 10;
      unsigned int     c : 10;
};
```

would require two 16-bit words with the fields a and b in the first word and field c in the second word.

Without qualification, bit fields must be considered as highly-machine dependent. For example, the Standard permits an implementation to choose to use a `long` in place of an `int` when a bit field is defined with more bits than a single precision `int`.

Field members are restricted to type `int`. Arrays of fields are not allowed. Fields cannot be addressed directly by pointers, and the address operator cannot be applied to a bit field member.

The use of bit fields is likely to be non-portable and therefore should only be used in situations where memory is a scarce resource. The following program is a repeat of Program 15.2. In a date the day number has (maximum) range 1 to 31 inclusive, month number is 1 to 12 inclusive, and the year is 0 to 99 if we discount the century. If memory is at a premium, we may choose to pack the day, month and year into respectively 5 bits (0 to 31 inclusive), 4 bits (0 to 15 inclusive) and 7 bits (0 to 127 inclusive) fields. The resulting program is as follows.

PROGRAM 15.8

```
/*
**      Program illustrating bit fields. The program
**      determines a person's age measured in years
**      given that person's date of birth and today's
**      date. The dates are packed into bit fields
**      of a 16-bit integer.
*/

#include <stdio.h>

struct date { /* packed date template: */
   unsigned int    day : 5;
   unsigned int    month : 4;
   unsigned int    year : 7;
            };
typedef struct date              Date;

void    askfordate (char *, Date *);

main ()
{
```

```
    Date          dateofbirth, today;
    int           age;

    askfordate ("Date of birth?: ", &dateofbirth);
    askfordate ("Today\'s date?: ", &today);

    if(today.month > dateofbirth.month ||
        (today.month == dateofbirth.month &&
          today.day > dateofbirth.day))
        age = today.year - dateofbirth.year;
    else
      age = today.year - dateofbirth.year - 1;

    printf ("Age: %d years\n", age);
}

void askfordate (char *prompt, Date *date)
{
    unsigned int          d, m, y;

    printf("%s", prompt);
    scanf("%d/%d/%d", &d, &m, &y);

    date -> day = d;
    date -> month = m;
    date -> year = y;
}
```

15.13 Summary

1. A *structure* is an example of an *aggregate type* consisting of a collection of subcomponents treated as a single entity. The subcomponents are called the *members* of a structure and are not necessarily of the same type.

2. Members of a structure are accessed by the *structure member* operator '.' or by the *pointer to structure member operator* '->'. If s is a structure variable and m is a member of s, then 's.m' refers to the member m of s. If p is a pointer to s, then '(*p).m', or better 'p->m', refer to the member m of s.

3. If s and t are structure variables of the same type, then the assignment s = t is supported. Also, a structure is permissible as an argument to a function and as the value returned by a function.

4. Structures may contain array members, and arrays of structure elements are supported. Additionally, structures may be members of other structures.

5. *Unions* have the same syntactic form as structured objects. Union members share the same storage overlaid upon each other.

6. *Bit fields* are members of a structure packed into a machine word. The internal representation of bit fields is highly machine-dependent.

15.14 Exercises

1. Define an array of structures that could be used for a telephone directory. Include the name, area code and phone number for a maximum of forty records.

2. Define a file of records containing information on computer science courses. The first field of the record contains the course name. The second field contains the course number. The third field is an array of module numbers. Write a program to read this file and and to print the course names which include a given module.

3. Write a program that uses bit fields to display the bit representation of the simple type `int`. The program is to operate upon a series of positive data values.

4. Develop the program unit for the associated header file given below. The `String` data type has a pointer to a null terminated array of characters as the underlying data structure. In addition, a length counter is maintained:

```
/*
**      File:      strings.h
*/

#ifndef STRINGS
  #define STRINGS

    typedef struct {  /* strings template: */
       char       *string;    /* dynamic, null terminated */
       int        size;       /* of string */
    } String;

    extern String string(char *);        /* constructor */
    extern void   dstring(String);       /* destructor */
    extern int    slength(String);       /* length? */
    extern String scopy(String);         /* duplicate */
    extern int    sless(String, String); /* less than? */
    extern void   sprint(String);        /* display */
  #endif
```

The constructor operator `string` dynamically creates storage for the given null-terminated character array and sets the size value. The destructor `dstring` releases the dynamic storage space. Operation `scopy` returns a copy of the given argument, duplicating the dynamic string space.

Prepare an application program to enter a series of `strings` into an array of `Strings`, to sort the array, and to display the result.

5. Develop a program unit for handling the real and imaginary parts of a complex number. The header file is:

```
#ifndef COMPLEX
  #define COMPLEX
  #include <math.h>

  typedef struct {  /* complex number template: */
    double real;    /* real part */
    double imag;    /* imaginary part */
  } Complex;

  extern Complex complex(double, double);  /* constructor */
  extern Complex cadd(Complex, Complex);   /* addition */
  extern Complex cmul(Complex, Complex);   /* multiply */
  extern Complex cdiv(Complex, Complex);   /* divide */
  extern void    cprint(Complex);          /* display */

  #define PI        (4.0 * atan(1.0))
#endif
```

A program that calculates the voltage of an AC electrical circuit containing a conductor, a resistor and a capacitor employs the formulae:

$$Z = R + jwL + 1/(jwC)$$
$$V = ZI$$
$$w = 2 * PI * F$$

where

R = resistance (double)
L = inductance (double)
C = capacitance (double)
F = frequency (double)
I = current (double)
w = frequency in rads/sec (double)
j = imaginary 1 ie (0, 1) (Complex)
Z = impedance (Complex)
V = voltage (Complex)

6. Rework Exercise 5 of Chapter 8 using a structure to represent dates.

7.   An input stream consists of a mixture of alphabetic character strings, integers (strings of decimal digits), and punctuation symbols (such as `,` `;` `[` `}`, etc.). A program is required to display only the integers in the input.

The problem can be tackled by using a lexical analyser to separate the input into a sequence of tokens. The analyser and associated declarations are provided by the header file:

```
/*
**       File:     lex.h
*/

#ifndef LEX
  #define LEX

  #define MAX        128

  typedef enum { INTSY, STRSY, PUNCSY, EOFSY } TokenTag;

  typedef union {
    int        integer;        /* integer or punctuation */
    char       string[MAX];
  } TokenValue;

  typedef struct {
    TokenTag   tag;
    TokenValue value;
  } Token;

  extern Token lex(void);

  #define TAG(T)     ((T).tag)
  #define INT(T)     ((T).value.integer)
  #define STRING(T)  ((T).value.string)
#endif
```

Dynamic data structures

THE AGGREGATE TYPES of array and structure permit the description of data structures whose form and size are fixed. These various *data structures* or *information structures* are accompanied by a set of algorithms that can be used for their access and manipulation, for example sorting an array.

The data structures we shall now consider are different in that they use storage or memory dynamically. The amount of storage in use is directly proportional to the amount of information stored at a given stage in the computation.

The static data structures have a role to play in the creation of these dynamic data structures. The aggregates array and structure form the basic unit of storage for dynamic data structures. These basic units are commonly referred to as *nodes* of the data structure. These nodes are linked together in some way to form the structure, with the *linkage* information contained within each node. A given data structure is characterized by the structure imposed on the data by these linkages. Generally, there are three classes : *linear*, *hierarchical* and *graph* structures.

The *linear linked list* is the simplest of these categories. Normally each node has associated with it a data field and a single *link* field. The link associates one node with the next node in the list. The result is a chain-like structure, logically appearing as shown in Figure 16.1.

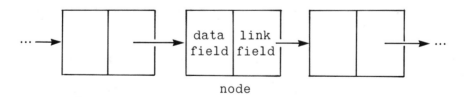

node

Figure 16.1

Probably the most widely used structure from the hierarchical class is the *binary tree*. Each node in the structure can have one *predecessor* or *ancestor* and as many as two *successors* or *descendants*. Thus each node contains data and the links to its two ancestors, as shown by Figure 16.2.

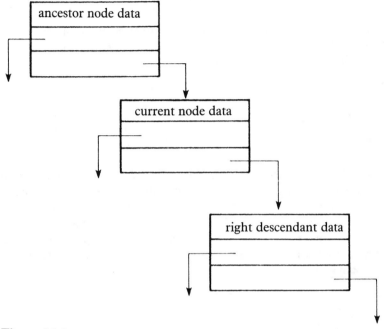

Figure 16.2

The *graph* is a generalization of the tree structure which allows loops. Each node of a graph links to one or more other nodes as shown by Figure 16.3.

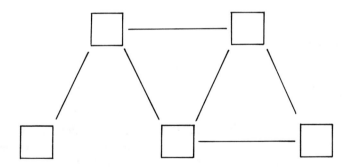

Figure 16.3

We shall not consider graphs in this book.

16.1 The linear linked list

A structure in which a member is a pointer to other such structures is known as a *self-referential structure*. The type declarations that will be needed to implement the linear linked list data structure are of the form:

```
struct node {       /* singly-chained linked list: */
   int          data;
   struct node *link;
};
typedef struct node         Node;
typedef Node                *PtrNode;
```

It is perfectly legal for a structure to contain a pointer to an instance of itself. These structures are conveniently displayed pictorially, with the links represented by arrows (see Figure 16.4). A `typedef` declaration introduces programmer-defined type names. Thereafter a `typedef` name is the syntactic equivalent of the associated type. Hence in the example of Figure 16.4 we may choose to introduce the `typedef` declarations before the structure declaration. The latter may then use these type names as in:

```
typedef struct node         Node;
typedef Node                *PtrNode;
struct node {
   int          data;
   PtrNode      link;
};
```

The member `data` is, in this example, a data item of type `int`. It can, of course, be any valid C type, including aggregate types array and structure. Using nested structures, a node can be made to carry a large quantity of associated data. For example, information in a node may be represented by the declaration:

```
struct info { ----- };
typedef struct info     Info;
```

and then the node by:

```
struct node {     /* aggregate data in list: */
   Info          data;
   struct node   *link;
};
```

The member `link` is a pointer variable containing the address of another node. As a special case, this member may be the value NULL which is defined in <stdio.h>. The pointer value NULL is used to represent the end of the list. Assigning or comparing a pointer to NULL is a valid pointer operation.

Let us now declare some variables of type `Node` with integer data items:

```
Node     first, second, third;
```

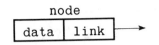

Figure 16.4

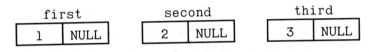

Figure 16.5

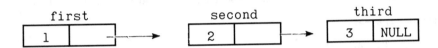

Figure 16.6

and perform some assignments on these structures:

```
first.data    = 1;
second.data   = 2;
third.data    = 3;

first.link = second.link = third.link = NULL;
```

The result of this coding is as shown in Figure 16.5. A chain-like structure can be established by having the `link` member of `first` address the node `second`, and for its link in turn to address the node `third`. The statements are:

```
first.link  = &second;
second.link = &third;
```

These pointer assignments result in linking `first` to `second` and `second` to `third`. We now have a linear linked list (see Figure 16.6). To reference the data items on this linked list there are a number of equivalent expressions. To retrieve the data item '1', the expression is:

```
first.data
```

The expression:

```
first.link
```

is an object of type pointer to a `struct node`. It does, of course, point to the `struct node` object called `second`. From Section 15.5, a pointer to a structure permits a member of that structure to be accessed by:

```
structure-pointer -> member-name
```

The expression to reference the data value '2' is:

```
second.data
```

or, indirectly:

```
first.link -> data
```

The two operators, pointer to structure member reference (->) and structure member reference (.) are of equal precedence and associate left to right. Therefore, the link member of first will be determined, and then the member data of the structure addressed by this pointer.

Similarly, the member link of the object second can be referenced through:

```
first.link -> link
```

and, in turn, the data item '3' by:

```
first.link -> link -> data
```

The essential feature here is that the members of the objects second, third and any more which may be linked into this list are accessible not only by their name (e.g. second.data) but also through the pointers which refer to them (first.link -> data). Excepting first, the nodes in the linked list may be treated *anonymously*. Location first can also be treated this way if we have an additional variable of type PtrNode called head, declared and initialized by:

```
PtrNode head = &first;
```

to act as a pointer to the head (or first node) of the list. We then have Figure 16.7.

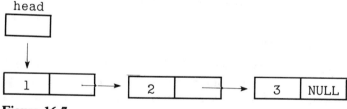

Figure 16.7

One of the most fundamental operations on a list is list traversal in which every node of the list is visited exactly once. For each node visited, some action, such as printing the data item associated with the node, is performed. Using the list established above, Program 16.1 prints each integer in the list. List traversal is achieved by setting a pointer to the head of the list, then advancing through the list via the link pointer until the value NULL is determined, denoting the end of the list.

PROGRAM 16.1

```
/*
**      Manually establish a linear linked list then
**      perform a list traversal. Initialize a pointer
**      to the first list node, then cycle through the
**      nodes via the link member until the end of list
**      is recognized.
*/

#include <stdio.h>

typedef struct node          Node;
typedef Node                 *PtrNode;

struct node {  /* singly chained linked list: */
   int         data;
   PtrNode     link;
};

main()
{
   Node    first, second, third;
   PtrNode head, ptr;
                                        /* build a list: */
   first.data = 1;     first.link = &second;
   second.data = 2;    second.link = &third;
   third.data = 3;     third.link = NULL;
   head = &first;

   ptr = head;                          /* list traversal */
   while (ptr != NULL){                 /* more nodes? */
      printf("%d\n", ptr -> data);      /* access data */
      ptr = ptr -> link;                /* advance to next node */
   }
}
```

Anonymous locations can be created dynamically while the program is executing. These dynamic data structures can expand and contract freely as required. The linked list offers the advantage that it can be made just as long as necessary – no more and no less. The array, by comparison, has its size fixed in advance and an arbitrary limit on the number of elements must be imposed.

We can dispense completely with the named nodes and operate solely with anonymous nodes if each node can be created dynamically. A new region of memory can be allocated using the storage management function `malloc`. The function allocates a region of memory and returns a pointer to the first byte. Using the `sizeof` operator applied to the type name representing the dynamic data structure elements (Node) yields the number of bytes in the Node:

```
sizeof(Node)
```

This, in turn, is given as the argument to `malloc` to create space for one Node:

```
malloc(sizeof(Node))
```

Again, the value returned by `malloc` is a generic pointer. For this address to be assigned to a variable of type `PtrNode`, we can simply perform an assignment, or we can explicitly coerce the returned pointer into the desired type with a cast to make our intention explicit. That is, if variable `ptrnode` is declared as:

```
PtrNode      ptrnode;
```

then:

```
ptrnode = (PtrNode) malloc(sizeof(Node));
```

causes space for one Node to be dynamically created and for the variable `ptrnode` to point to it. Pictorially, we have Figure 16.8. The members of this dynamically created node can be assigned values with expressions of the form:

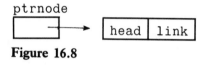

Figure 16.8

```
ptrnode -> data = ....;
ptrnode -> link = ....;
```

We combine this idea and list traversal in Program 16.2. Data to the program consists of a series of positive integers of unknown length and a negative terminator. The program reads the data and prints the values in reverse order. Each data value is entered on to a dynamically created linked list. Since the `head` object provides access to the front of the list, inserting a new node on to the list is most easily achieved at that point. The new node has its data field filled, and its link field is set to the value referenced by `head`, i.e. the first node. The `head` is then set to point to the new node, incorporating it into the front of the list.

PROGRAM 16.2

```
/*
**      Read a series of positive integers terminated
**      with a negative sentinel. Enter each data value
**      on to the front of a dynamically created linked
**      list. Print the values in reverse order by removing
**      from the front of the list.
*/

#include <stdio.h>
#include <stdlib.h>
```

```
typedef struct node        Node;
typedef Node               *PtrNode;

struct node {   /* singly chained linked list: */
  int          Data;
  PtrNode      link;
};

main()
{
  int          data;
  PtrNode      head = NULL;
  PtrNode      new, ptr;

  printf("Input data:\n");
  while(scanf("%d", &data), data >= 0){
    if((new = (PtrNode)malloc(sizeof(Node))) == NULL){
      fprintf(stderr, "No space\n");
      exit(1);
    }
    new -> data = data;
    new -> link = head;
    head        = new;
  }

  printf("\n\nReversed data:\n");
  ptr = head;
  while(ptr != NULL){
    printf("%d\n", ptr -> data);
    ptr = ptr -> link;
  }
}
```

16.2 List processing

With static data structures it is always known where the current item should be retrieved or inserted. For example, with an array some index variable would be used to refer to the particular array element. In general, list processing applications require retrievals and insertions anywhere within a list. The list abstraction which we now develop provides the characteristics generally associated with lists.

cursor

Figure 16.9

Let us consider the range of operations to manipulate a list of items of some arbitrary type. An abstraction for a list is an ordered sequence L1, L2, L3, . . . ,

Ln (see Figure 16.9). At present, we ignore the fact that the list is realized through pointers and concentrate on the operations. Later we shall consider the implementation details.

At any instance, only one item of the list can be under inspection. We identify this as the list item under the *cursor*. Effectively, we have a window through which the cursor item may be viewed, and no other is visible. This we depict by labelling the item cursor as shown in Figure 16.9.

To access all the list items a number of cursor positioning operations will be provided. Two obvious candidates are the operations forward and backward which, respectively, position the cursor on the next (previous) list item. To scan the list in order L1, L2, L3, ... we should first locate the cursor at item L1 then repeatedly apply forward. Operation sethead positions the cursor on item L1. Similarly, operation settail positions the cursor on list item Ln.

All these cursor positioning operators may result in the cursor falling off either end of the list. For example, if the cursor is on list item Ln, then the operation forward effectively moves the cursor on to the non-existent item immediately to the right of the list. We define an operation isinlist which returns the logical value FALSE when the cursor is in either of these two off-list positions. Otherwise, it returns TRUE.

The simple list enquiry operations are isnil and length. Operation isnil determines if a list is empty or not, returning the respective values TRUE or FALSE. Operation length supplies a count of the number of list items. Clearly, if isnil is TRUE then length is zero. Equally, if isnil is TRUE then isinlist is FALSE. If isnil is FALSE, then isinlist can be either TRUE or FALSE according to the position of the cursor in a non-empty list.

The value of the list item in the cursor window may be obtained with the operator content. If this operator is used when isinlist is FALSE then an execution error occurs and the program halts.

Inserting and deleting a list item is also defined in terms of the cursor window concept. Insertion takes place immediately before or immediately following the cursor item with the operators insertbefore and insertafter. For example, given the list shown in Figure 16.9, then the result of inserting the new list item Lk using (a) insertbefore and (b) insertafter is shown in Figure 16.10.

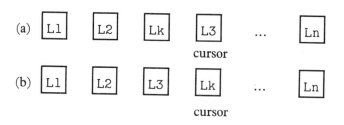

Figure 16.10

Both these operators have an additional argument which determines where to place the cursor following the insertion. We can either choose to retain the cursor window on its existing list item or reposition the cursor on the inserted item. Example (a) of Figure 16.10 shows the final destination of the cursor if we have selected not to move the cursor. Example (b) shows the outcome if we move to the new item.

If isinlist is FALSE when executing either of these insertion operators, then we need to define their behaviour at this boundary condition. Operation isinlist does not specify whether the cursor is to the left or to the right of the list. If insertbefore places the new item immediately before that in the cursor window, then it does not make sense to interpret the cursor off the left of the list, since the insertion operation would effectively place the new item ahead of the non-existent item, as shown in Figure 16.11. If, however, we interpret the cursor off the right of the list, then the semantics of insertbefore is to append an item on to the tail of the list, as shown in Figure 16.12.

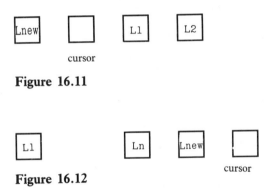

Figure 16.11

Figure 16.12

The cursor is then either on this new item or remains off the list as given by the positioning parameter. Following a similar argument, we shall interpret insertafter as an operation which prepends an item on to the head of the list when isinlist is FALSE.

Inserting an item into a list can only follow once a list has been initialized. An empty list is established with the operation nil. Following this operation, isnil is TRUE, isinlist is FALSE, and length has value zero.

Deleting the item currently in the cursor window is provided by the remove operation. Upon deletion, the cursor moves to the following list item if one exists. If one does not exist then the cursor is off the list and isinlist becomes FALSE. If isinlist is FALSE when remove is executed, the result is a null operation and nothing is deleted.

As noted in the preceding section, traversing a list applying some operation to all the list items is a common list processing feature. We complete our consideration of typical list processing operations with the operator traverse, which visits each list item applying a given operation to the item.

16.3 List representation

As shown earlier in the chapter, a list of objects may be represented by a singly-chained structure with pointers which follow from the first item through to the last item. The list itself is represented by a pointer to the first item. To represent the cursor window we should additionally associate two further pointers with the list: one to refer to the list item in the cursor and one to refer to its immediate predecessor. The latter is required to permit the adjustment of pointers when implementing the `insertbefore` operation. For example, a list with its three pointers is shown in Figure 16.13. Then to insert a new item before the cursor the pointer field of the new node links to the cursor node and the predecessor links to the new item, as in Figure 16.14.

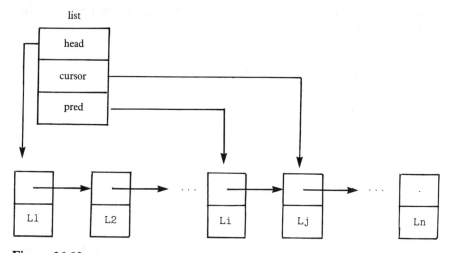

Figure 16.13

The singly chained representation does not permit efficient implementation of backward movement operations. Nor can we readily set the cursor on the tail of the list without traversing all or parts of the list. An alternative approach is to use a *doubly linked list* in which each node contains two links, one to the next node in the list and one to the preceding node. This greatly simplifies the cursor window representation. First, the cursor is representable by a single pointer. The preceding and the following items are accessible through the two pointers of the node in the cursor. Movement in either direction is readily implemented. With a doubly linked list traversals in either direction, insertions and deletions from arbitrary positions in the list are implemented without difficulty. The cost of using a doubly linked list is the additional space required for a second pointer.

One further variation to this implementation avoids the boundary problem of the first and last list element. By introducing a *sentinel* node and connecting the nodes

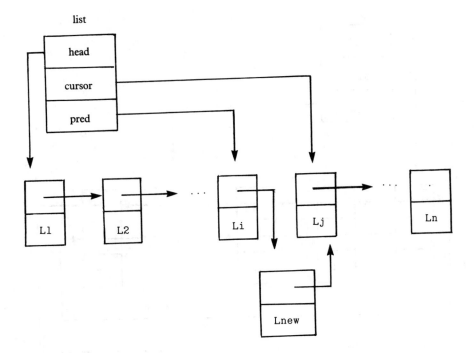

Figure 16.14

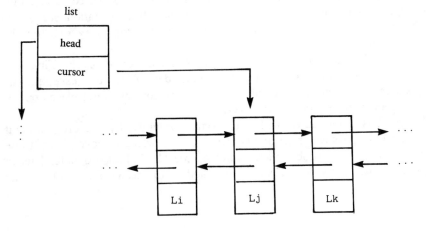

Figure 16.15

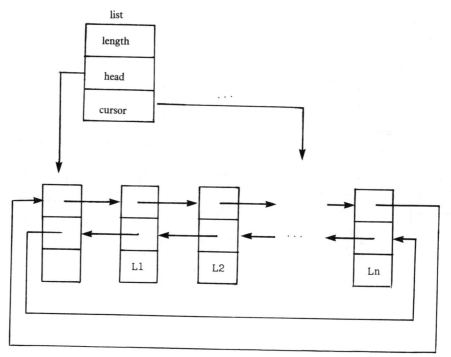

Figure 16.16

together in a circular fashion removes the difficulty. The head of the list is a pointer to this sentinel node. The successor of the sentinel is the first item in the list, while the predecessor of the sentinel is the last item. Operation isinlist will only return FALSE if the cursor addresses this sentinel.

One minor enhancement incorporates the list length into the list cell and avoids having to repeatedly count the number of list items each time operation length is called. For every insertion the counter is incremented. For every deletion the counter is decremented.

Let us revisit Program 16.1, embellishing it in a number of places. First, the integer values placed on the list are given as program data. All values, excepting the last, are positive. The final negative value is the terminator and is not placed on the list. The program then prints the list of values.

The list itself is manipulated with the services provided by the program unit intlist.c. This package implements the list as described above. Only those operations required by the problem are implemented. The full set is detailed later in this chapter. The necessary definitions are supplied by the header file intlist.h:

```
/*
**      File:           intlist.h
**
**      Interface to a circular/doubly linked list of
**      integers. The specification provides an explicit
**      interface to the representation and a series of
**      service routines.
*/

#include "boolean.h"

typedef enum{ NOMOVE, MOVE}     Where;

typedef struct intlist          IntList;
typedef struct intnode          IntNode;

struct intlist {        /* header for list: */
  int           length;
  IntNode       *head;          /* addresses sentinel node */
  IntNode       *cursor;        /* data node in the window */
};

struct intnode {        /* doubly linked node: */
  int           data;
  intNode       *predecessor;
  IntNode       *successor;
};


extern IntList nil(void);
extern Boolean isinlist(IntList);
extern IntList sethead(IntList);
extern IntList forward(IntList);
extern int     content(IntList);
extern IntList insertafter(int, IntList, Where);




/*
**      File:           intlist.c
**
**      implementation of the service routines for a
**      circular/doubly linked list of integers.
*/
```

```
#include <stdio.h>
#include <stdlib.h>
#include "intlist.h"


static void error(char *mess)
{
  fprintf(stderr, "%s\?n", mess);
  exit(1);
}

IntList nil(void)
{
  IntList list;
  IntNode *node = (IntNode *) malloc(sizeof(IntNode));

  if(node == NULL) error("No space (nil)");
  node -> data = 0;
  node -> predecessor = node -> successor = node;
  list.length = 0;
  list.head = list.cursor = node;
  return list;
}


Boolean isinlist(IntList list)
{
  return (list.head == list.cursor) ? FALSE : TRUE;
}

IntList sethead(IntList list)
{
  list.cursor = list.head -> successor;
  return list;
}

IntList forward(IntList list)
{
  if(list.head == list.cursor)
    return list;
  else {
    list.cursor = list.cursor -> successor;
    return list;
  }
}
```

```
int content(IntList list)
{
  if(list.head == list.cursor)
    error("Access violation (content)");
  else
    return list.cursor -> data;
}


IntList insertafter(int data, IntList list, Where where)
{
  IntNode *next = list.cursor -> successor;
  IntNode *node = (IntNode *) malloc(sizeof(IntNode));

  if(node == NULL) error("No space (insertafter)");
  list.length++;
  node -> data = data;
  node -> successor = next;
  node -> predecessor = list.cursor;
  list.cursor -> successor = node;
  next -> predecessor = node;
  if(where == MOVE) list.cursor = node;
  return list;
}
```

The application program itself is relatively straightforward. Each data value is placed on the list with the operator insertafter, with the cursor following the new list item. Initially, the list is set up as the empty list using nil. Once the list is constructed, the cursor is positioned on the first item using sethead. Subsequent items are accessed by repeatedly calling forward. The process continues until the end of the list when operation isinlist returns FALSE.

```
/*
**       Read a series of positive integers and print them
**       in order. The data set is terminated with a
**       negative sentinel. The data values are stored in
**       a list and retrieved from this list for printing.
*/

#include <stdio.h>
#include "intlist.h"

main()
{
  int          data;
  IntList       list;
```

```
   list = nil();
   printf("Input the data:\n");
   while(scanf("%d", &data), data >= 0)
     list = insertafter(data, list, MOVE);

   printf("\n\nList content:\n");
   list = sethead(list);
   while(isinlist(list)){
     printf("%d\n", content(list));
     list = forward(list);
   }
 }
```

16.4 Privacy

In the last program the header file presented a specification of the services provided on the data type. The type itself is introduced with the name IntList, visible in the header as a structure containing, among other things, a pointer to a series of objects of type IntNode whose construction is also available. We have not fully concealed the implementation allowing a client program direct access to the underlying structure. The solution in C is to move the definition for an IntNode and an IntList into the program unit, and present an untyped pointer in the header. This way, any client reading the header cannot determine the nature of IntList and hence the implementation strategy. The relevant changes are:

```
/*
**      File:            pintlist.h
**
**      Interface to a circular/doubly linked list of
**      integers. The specification provides an explicit
**      interface to the series of service routines. The
**      representation is made private to clients through
**      the use of untyped pointers.
*/

#include "boolean.h"

typedef enum{ NOMOVE, MOVE}     Where;

typedef void                    *IntList;

extern IntList nil(void);
     /* ... etc ... */
```

and:

```
/*
**        File:              pintlist.c
**
**        implementation of the service routines for a
**        circular/doubly linked list of integers.
*/

        /* ... etc ... */

typedef struct list              List;
typedef struct node              Node;

struct list {    /* header for list: */
   int          length;
   Node         *head;           /* addresses sentinel node */
   Node         *cursor;         /* data node in the window */
};

struct node {    /* doubly linked node: */
   int          data;
   Node         *predecessor;
   Node         *successor;
};

        /* ... etc . . . */

IntList nil(void)
{
   List *list = (List *) malloc(sizeof(List));
   Node *node = (Node *) malloc(sizeof(Node));

   if(list == NULL) error("No space (nil)");
   if(node == NULL) error("No space (nil)");
   node -> data = 0;
   node -> predecessor = node -> successor = node;
   list -> length = 0;
   list -> head = list -> cursor = node;
   return list;
}

        /* ... etc ... */
```

16.5 Levels of abstraction

Data type IntList is relatively general. Restricted forms of IntList, such as
IntStack (a stack of integers) or IntQueue (a queue of integers, see Case Study
13.1) are more common than the list itself.

It will, of course, be commonplace to define new data types in terms of older ones
(see Case Study 11.2). In such cases the *derived* data type is based on its *antecedent*
data type. In the case of both IntStack and IntQueue the antecedent is only

relevant to their implementation and not to their use. By not declaring the antecedent data type publicly, we can engineer new data types in terms of others. For example, a stack of integers can be defined like this:

```
/*
**      File:           intstack.h
**
**      Integer stack derived from integer list.
*/

#ifndef INTSTACK

  #define INTSTACK

  #include "boolean.h"

  typedef void          *IntStack;

  extern IntStack newstack(void);
  extern IntStack push(int, IntStack);
  extern int      top(IntStack);
  extern IntStack pop(IntStack);
  extern Boolean  isnewstack(IntStack);

#endif
```

and:

```
/*
**      File:           intstack.c
**
**      Integer stack implementation based on a list
**      of integers.
*/

#include "intstack.h"
#include "pintlist.h"

IntStack newstack(void)
{
  return nil();
}

IntStack push(int data, IntStack stack)
{                                          /* assuming a fully .. */
  stack = sethead(stack);                  /* populated intlist .. */
  return insertbefore(data, stack, NOMOVE);
}                                          /* package */

int top(IntStack stack)
{
```

```
    stack = sethead(stack);
    return content(stack);
}

IntStack pop(IntStack stack)
{
    stack = sethead(stack);
    stack = remove(stack);     /* assuming remove in intlist package */
}

Boolean isnewstack(IntStack stack)
{
    return isnil(stack);       /* assuming isnil in intlist package */
}
```

16.6 Generic lists

Clearly one could define lists of other types (char *, double, etc.) in the same
way as IntList was defined. The process is both trivial and tedious, and, to a
certain extent, subject to error. In this section we consider how the process might be
simplified.

Consider developing a data type GList for linked lists in such a way for it to be
used as the antecedent for creating lists of objects of all types. First we define a type
GType capable of holding a pointer:

```
typedef void    *GType;
```

Then we define a Node and a List in the usual way:

```
/*
**      File:           glist.h
*/

#ifndef GLIST

  #define GLIST

  #include "boolean.h"

  typedef enum{ NOMOVE, MOVE}    Where;
  typedef void                   *GType;
  typedef void                   *GList;

      /* ... others ... */

  extern GList        gnil(void);
  extern Boolean      gisinlist(GList);
  extern GType        gcontent(GList);
  extern GList        gsethead(GList);
  extern GList        gforward(GList);
  extern GList        ginsertafter(GType, GList, Where);
```

```
        /* ... others ... */

#endif

and:

/*
**      File:           glist.c
*/

#include <stdio.h>
#include <stdlib.h>
#include "glist.h"

typedef struct list     List;
typedef struct node     Node;

struct list{
  int           length;
  Node          *head;
  Node          *cursor;
};

struct node{
  GType         data;
  Node          *predecessor;
  Node          *successor;
};

        /* ... function definitions ... */
```

Our GList exhibits all the usual behaviour associated with a list. Excepting one small detail, it is surely a list abstraction. The issue is that what we have is a list of void * pointers (GType) which are all but useless. To make this base list practical we derive a new list, say an IntList, from it. Pointers to integers, rather than the integer objects themselves, are put into the list. Here is the definition of IntList trivially derived from GList:

```
/*
**      File:           dintlist.h
**
**      Integer list derived from a generic list.
*/

#ifndef DINTLIST

  #define DINTLIST

  #include "glist.h"

  typedef void          *IntList;
```

```
      #define nil()          gnil()
      #define isinlist(L)    gisinlist(L)
      #define sethead(L)     gsethead(L)
      #define forward(L)     gforward(L)
        /* ... others ... */

      extern IntList insertafter(int, IntList, Where);
      extern int     content(IntList);
          /* ... others ... */

  #endif
```

and:

```
  /*
  **      File:            dintlist.c
  */

  #include <stdio.h>
  #include <stdlib.h>
  #include "dintlist.h"

  static void error(char *mess)
  {
    fprintf(stderr, "%s\n", mess);
    exit(1);
  }

    IntList insertafter(int data, IntList list, Where where)
  {
    int *new = (int *) malloc(sizeof(int));

    if(new == NULL) error("No space (insertafter)");
    *new = data;
    return ginsertafter(new, list, where);
  }

  int content(IntList list)
  {
    return (int) (*gcontent(list));
  }

        /* ... others ... */
```

With these conventions the circular/doubly linked representation of our list abstraction may be programmed as shown below. The new feature to note is that function `gremove` is given an argument which describes how the data item space is to be released. The `GList` abstraction is a list of pointers to the data items and not the data items themselves. The space referred to by the pointer is freed according to the second argument to `gremove`. This complexity is necessary since the objects pointed to may themselves have complex structures and the simple use of the standard library function `free` may be inappropriate. For example, if we have a list of integers, then to remove one item involves freeing the space occupied by an integer. However, if the list item is itself some complex structure, say a list of integers, then we need to know how such an item is to be released:

```
/*
**      File:           list.h
*/

#ifndef GLIST

   #define GLIST

   #include "boolean.h"

   typedef enum{ NOMOVE, MOVE}    Where;
   typedef void                   *GType;
   typedef void                   *GList;
   typedef void                   (*Delete)(GType);
   typedef void                   (*Operation)(GType);

   extern GList        gnil(void);
   extern int          glength(GList);
   extern Boolean      gisnil(GList);
   extern Boolean      gisinlist(GList);
   extern GType        gcontent(GList);
   extern GList        gsethead(GList);
   extern GList        gsettail(GList);
   extern GList        gforward(GList);
   extern GList        gbackward(GList);
   extern GList        ginsertbefore(GType, GList, Where);
   extern GList        ginsertafter(GType, GList, Where);
   extern GList        gremove(GList, Delete);
   extern void         gtraverse(GList, Operation);

#endif
```

and:

```
/*
**      File:           glist.c
*/

#include <stdio.h>
#include <stdlib.h>
#include "glist.h"

typedef struct list     List;
typedef struct node     Node;
```

```
struct list{
  int          length;
  Node         *head;
  Node         *cursor;
};

struct node{
  GType        data;
  Node         *predecessor;
  Node         *successor;
};

static void error(char *mess)
{
  fprintf(stderr, "%s\n", mess);
  exit(1);
}

GList gnil(void)
{
  List   *list = (List *) malloc(sizeof(List));
  Node   *node = (Node *) malloc(sizeof(Node));

  if(list == NULL) error("No space (nil)");
  if(node == NULL) error("No space (nil)");
  node -> data = NULL;
  node -> predecessor = node -> successor = node;
  list -> length = 0;
  list -> head = list -> cursor = node;
  return list;
}

int glength(GList list)
{
  return ((List *)list) -> length;
}

Boolean gisnil(GList list)
{
  return (((List *)list) -> length == 0) ? TRUE : FALSE;
}

Boolean gisinlist(GList list)
{
  return (((List *)list) -> head == ((List *)list) -> cursor) ?
    FALSE : TRUE;
}

GType gcontent(GList list)
{
  if(((List *)list) -> head == ((List *)list) -> cursor)
    error("Access violation (content)");
  return ((List *)list) -> cursor -> data;
}
```

```
GList gsethead(GList list)
{
  ((List *)list) -> cursor = ((List *)list) -> head -> successor;
  return list;
}

GList gsettail(GList list)
{
  ((List *)list) -> cursor = ((List *)list) -> head -> predecessor;
  return list;
}

GList gforward(GList list)
{
  if(((List *)list) -> head == ((List *)list) -> cursor)
    return list;
  else {
    ((List *)list) -> cursor = ((List *)list) -> cursor -> successor;
    return list;
  }
}

GList gbackward(GList list)
{
  if(((List *)list) -> head == ((List *)list) -> cursor)
    return list;
  else {
    ((List *)list) -> cursor =
      ((List *)list) -> cursor -> predecessor;
    return list;
  }
}

GList ginsertbefore(GType data, GList list, Where where)
{
  Node  *previous = ((List *)list) -> cursor -> predecessor;
  Node  *node     = (Node *) malloc(sizeof(Node));

  if(node == NULL) error("No space (insertbefore)");
  ((List *)list) -> length++;
  node -> data = data;
  node -> successor = ((List *)list) -> cursor;
  node -> predecessor = previous;
  previous -> successor = node;
  ((List *)list) -> cursor -> predecessor = node;
  if(where == MOVE) ((List *)list) -> cursor = node;
  return list;
}

GList ginsertafter(GType data, GList list, Where where)
{
  Node  *next = ((List *)list) -> cursor -> successor;
  Node  *node = (Node *) malloc(sizeof(Node));
```

```
    if(node == NULL) error("No space (insertafter)");
    ((List *)list) -> length++;
    node -> data = data;
    node -> successor = next;
    node -> predecessor = ((List *)list) -> cursor;
    ((List *)list) -> cursor -> successor = node;
    next -> predecessor = node;
    if(where == MOVE) ((List *)list) -> cursor = node;
    return list;
}

GList gremove(GList list, Delete delete)
{
  Node   *previous = ((List *)list) -> cursor -> predecessor;
  Node   *next     = ((List *)list) -> cursor -> successor;

  if((((List *)list) -> head == ((List *)list) -> cursor) return list;

  previous -> successor = next;
  next -> predecessor = previous;
  delete(((List *)list) -> cursor -> data);
  free(((List *)list) -> cursor);
  ((List *)list) -> cursor = next;
  ((List *)list) -> length-;
  return list;
}

void gtraverse(GList list, Operation operation)
{
  list = gsethead(list);
  while(gisinlist(list)){
    operation(gcontent(list));
    list = gforward(list);
  }
}
```

16.7 Sorting lists

The order in which items appear in a list is determined by the use of the insertion
operators, the location of the cursor, and the requirements of the application. In
certain circumstances it may be necessary to establish an ordering of the values in
the list. In some examples there may be several possible orderings. For example, a
list of students having the attributes:

```
typedef struct {    /* student details: */
  char          *name;
  int           age;
     /* ... others ... */
} Student;
```

may be ordered by name or by age. To achieve this we need to `sort` the items in the list into the order required.

We therefore include a `sort` operator in our generic list abstraction. The operator must be supplied with a means to determine the ordering of two list items since the abstraction makes no assumption about the types of the items in the list. The `sort` operator is specified in the header file `gslist.h` of which the relevant modifications are:

```
/*
**  File:              gslist.h
*/

#ifndef GSLIST

    /* ... others ... */

    typedef int                 (*Order)(GType, GType);

    /* ... others ... */

    extern GList       gsort(GList, Order);

#endif
```

The `gsort` function is called with the second parameter used to compare a pair of list items. The function delivers -1 (0 or $+1$) if the first argument is less (equal or greater) than the second argument. To illustrate the use of this function, consider sorting a list of strings. Here we can use the standard library function for the second argument to `gsort`:

```
namelist = gsort(namelist, (Order)strcmp);
```

Note how we assure the compiler that all is well by casting the second actual argument. Equally, to sort a list of integers, the usage is:

```
intlist = gsort(intlist, (Order)intcmp);
```

with the auxiliary function `intcmp` defined as:

```
int intcmp(int *num1, int *num2)
{
  if(*num1 < *num2)
    return -1;
  else if(*num1 > *num2)
    return +1;
  else
    return 0;
}
```

Any of the standard sort techniques may be applied to lists. However, the representation structure also makes possible a scheme in which the sorted list is produced by rearrangement of the pointers connecting the nodes. A sorted list can be produced by removing one item at a time from the unsorted list and relinking it into the sorted list at the appropriate position:

```
GList gsort(GList list, Order order)
{
  Node *unode, *pnode;        /* unsorted list nodes */
  Node *snode;                /* sorted list node */
  Node *sentinel;             /* address of sentinel */

  if(gisnil(list)) return list; /* ignore empty list */

  sentinel = ((List *)list) -> head;
  snode = sentinel -> successor;   /* first node is sorted */
  unode = snode -> successor;      /* second node is unsorted */
  snode -> successor = sentinel;   /* complete the sorted .. */
  sentinel -> predecessor = snode; /* .. list of one item */

  while(unode != sentinel){        /* plough through unsorted list */
    pnode = unode -> successor;    /* what is next */
    snode = sentinel -> successor; /* first item in sort list */
    while(snode != sentinel)       /* compare all sort list items */
      if(order(unode -> data, snode -> data) > 0)
        snode = snode -> successor;    /* advance to next */
      else {
        unode -> successor = snode;    /* insert new node .. */
        unode -> predecessor = snode -> predecessor;
        snode -> predecessor -> successor = unode;
        snode -> predecessor = unode;  /* .. ahead of sort item */
        break;
      }
    if(snode != sentinel)          /* more sort items? */
      unode = pnode;               /* yes - advance */
    else {
      unode -> successor = sentinel;
      unode -> predecessor = sentinel -> predecessor;
      sentinel -> predecessor -> successor = unode;
      sentinel -> predecessor = unode;
    }
  }
  ((List *)list) -> cursor = ((List *)list) -> head;
  return list;
}
```

Program 16.4 illustrates the use of the general list abstraction supporting the sort operator. Input to the program consists of a series of names terminated with the unique name ZZZ. The program forms a list of these names, sorts them into alphabetical order, then prints the list. The names are recorded in a NameList derived from the generic list GList.

PROGRAM 16.4

```
/*
**        Input a series of names and form a list. Sort
**        the list, then print the result.
*/

#include <stdio.h>
#include <string.h>
#include "namelist.h"

#define NAMESIZE        30
#define TERMINATOR      "ZZZ"

main()
{
  char          name[NAMESIZE];
  NameList      namelist = nilnames();

  printf("Input the names:\n");
  while(scanf("%s", name), strcmp(name, TERMINATOR) != 0)
    namelist = appendname(name, namelist);

  printf("\n\nSorted name list:\n");
  namelist = sortnames(namelist);
  printnames(namelist);
}




/*
**        File:           namelist.h
**
**        Name list derived from a general list.
*/

#ifndef NAMELIST

  #define NAMELIST

  typedef char          *Name;
  typedef void          *NameList;

  extern NameList nilnames(void);
  extern NameList appendname(Name, NameList);
  extern NameList sortnames(NameList);
  extern void     printnames(NameList);

#endif
```

```
/*
**        File:           namelist.c
*/

#include <stdio.h>
#include <stdlib.h>
#include <string.h>
#include "gslist.h"
#include "namelist.h"

static void error(char *mess)
{
  fprintf(stderr, "%s\n", mess);
  exit(1);
}

static Name namedup(Name name)
{
  Name new = (Name) malloc(strlen(name)+1);

  if(new == NULL) error("No space (namedup)");
  return strcpy(new, name);
}

NameList nilnames(void)
{
  return gnil();
}

NameList appendname(Name name, NameList list)
{
  return ginsertafter(namedup(name), list, MOVE);
}

NameList sortnames(NameList list)
{
  return gsort(list, (Order)strcmp);
}

static void printname(Name name)
{
  printf("%s\n", name);
}

void printnames(NameList list)
{
  gtraverse(list, (Operation)printname);
}
```

16.8 Sorted list abstraction

It is common to have to construct a list in some sort order. This removes the overhead of having to perform a sort operation on the list. We can respecify our list abstraction to maintain ordering among the elements of the list. The principal change to the specification of the unordered list is the replacement of the insert operators (insertbefore and insertafter) by a single insert operation. The data item is placed in its correct position in the list, determined by an ordering function.

Many of the remaining unordered list operators are not applicable to an ordered list. A limited ordered list abstraction might then appear as:

```
/*
**      File:           golist.h
**
**      A general sorted list abstraction based upon
**      the general list abstraction.
*/

#ifndef GOLIST

  #define GOLIST

  #include "boolean.h"

  typedef void        *GOType;
  typedef void        *GOList;
  typedef void        (*GOperation)(GOType);
  typedef int         (*GOrder)(GOType, GOType);

  extern GOList  gonil(void);
  extern Boolean goisnil(GOList);
  extern int     golength(GOList);
  extern GOList  goinsert(GOType, GOList, GOrder);
  extern void    gotraverse(GOList, GOperation);

#endif
```

The ordered list is a higher-level abstraction than the general list. Its simpler interface reflects reduced programmer control over the abstraction. In return, the programmer is relieved of the burden of maintaining sorted lists.

The ordered list abstraction is readily derived from the general list. The implementation is shown below. To reduce function call overhead, the first four functions in the program unit may be replaced with macro definitions in the header file:

```
/*
**      File:           golist.c
*/
```

```
#include "glist.h"
#include "golist.h"

GOList gonil(void)
{
  return gnil();
}

Boolean goisnil(GOList list)
{
  return gisnil(list);
}

int golength(GOList list)
{
  return glength(list);
}

void gotraverse(GOList list, GOperation operation)
{
  gtraverse(list, (Operation)operation);
}

GOList goinsert(GOType data, GOList list, GOrder order)
{
  list = gsethead(list);
  while(gisinlist(list))
    if(order(data, gcontent(list)) <= 0)
      return ginsertbefore(data, list, NOMOVE);
    else
      list = gforward(list);

  return ginsertbefore(data, list, NOMOVE);
}
```

CASE STUDY 16.1   Word Concordance (revisited)

Case Study 12.1 produced a word concordance for some input text. The concordance consisted of an alphabetical list of all the distinct words in the text. In that implementation, the word list is realized using an array of words. A significant characteristic of this particular implementation is that movement of existing list elements is required when a new word is inserted into its correct alphabetical position in the array. Further, some predetermined limit on the number of list elements must be established at compile time.

The limitations of the array representation may be overcome by using a linked list representation. Inserting items in the list is effected by adjustments to pointers. Subject to the amount of available dynamic memory, no set limit is imposed on the length of the list.

In the original concordance program, an ordered list was maintained. In this way, the overhead of performing a sort is avoided. Ordered lists can be maintained using our ordered list abstraction.

From the generic ordered list abstraction, as specified by the header file golist.h, a derived version for an ordered list of words is obtained. The associated header file owordlist.h specifies the type names for a word (Word) and for a list of words (WordList), and prototype declarations for the services provided by the abstraction:

```
/*
**        File:             owordlist.h
**
**        Ordered word list abstraction derived from
**        the generic ordered list abstraction.
*/

#ifndef OWORDLIST

   #define OWORDLIST

   typedef char      *Word;
   typedef void      *WordList;

   extern WordList nilwords(void);
   extern WordList insert(Word, WordList);
   extern void     printwords(WordList);

#endif
```

The program unit owordlist.c is implemented in the now familiar fashion. Printing the words of the list is achieved by traversing the list and applying the print operation (printword) to each item. Individual words are correctly inserted into the ordered list using the service operation insert. This function hides a call to the ordered insert operation goinsert. The ordering of the words is determined by the library function strcmp:

```
/*
**        File:             owordlist.c
*/

#include <stdio.h>
#include <stdlib.h>
#include <string.h>
#include "golist.h"
#include "owordlist.h"

static void error(char *mess)
{
  fprintf(stderr, "%s\n", mess);
  exit(1);
}
```

```
static Word worddup(Word word)
{
  Word new = (Word) malloc(strlen(word)+1);
  if(new == NULL) error("No space (worddup)");
  return strcpy(new, word);
}

WordList nilwords(void)
{
  return gonil();
}

WordList insert(Word word, WordList list)
{
  return goinsert(worddup(word), list, (GOrder)strcmp);
}

static void printword(Word word)
{
  printf("%s\n", word);
}

void printwords(WordList list)
{
  gotraverse(list, (GOperation)printword);
}
```

Finally, the program is implemented. The program is modified from the original to read the text from a file, the name of which is given as the program command line argument. Otherwise, the logic is the same as in the original version:

```
/*
**      File:           case01.c
**
**      Read a series of words and maintain an ordered
**      list. Upon completion, print the list.
*/

#include <stdio.h>
#include <string.h>
#include "owordlist.h"

#define WORDSIZE        30
#define READONLY        "r"
#define TERMINATOR      "ZZZ"

main(int argc, char *argv[])
{
  FILE            *fp;
  char            word[WORDSIZE];
  WordList         wordlist = nilwords();
```

```
    if(argc != 2)
      fprintf(stderr, "Usage: %s filename\n", argv[0]);
    else if((fp = fopen(argv[1], READONLY)) == NULL)
      fprintf(stderr, "%s: cannot open %s\n", argv[0], argv[1]);
    else {
      fscanf(fp, "%s", word);
      while(strcmp(word, TERMINATOR) != 0){
        wordlist = insert(word, wordlist);
        fscanf(fp, "%s", word);
      }
      fclose(fp);
      printwords(wordlist);
    }
  }
```

16.9 Binary trees

In case Study 12.1 (word concordance), the sequential search algorithm was used to retrieve information from an ordered array (see function `insertword`). The difficulty with this data structure is that it is very costly to maintain if frequent insertions and deletions are required. The linked list data structure used in the revised version (Case Study 16.1) avoids these difficulties but still only supports sequential searching. The more efficient binary search is preferred if a suitable data structure can be found.

Since sequential searching is costly for long lists, it is desirable to have a data structure that implements efficient insertions and deletions, and can also be searched efficiently. The linked data structure that meets these requirements is the *binary tree*. The binary tree data structure has nodes, each having two links or pointers associated with it, one pointing to the root of its *left subtree* and the second pointing to the root of its *right subtree*. This is shown in Figure 16.17.

In particular, an *ordered binary tree* is a finite set of nodes which is either empty or consists of a root node as the *ancestor* of two disjoint binary trees called the left subtree and the right subtree. Nodes of the left subtree satisfy the ordering relation (e.g. alphabetical or numerical) when compared with nodes of the right subtree. At any level in the tree, it is permissible for either or both of the subtrees to be empty. Figure 16.17 is then an instance of an ordered binary tree.

The characteristics of the binary tree is that its definition is recursive. Each tree node has two descendants associated with it both of which are the roots of disjoint subtrees. The necessary definitions to describe a binary tree of `Datatype` values are:

```
    typedef struct node        Node;
    typedef Node               *PtrNode;
```

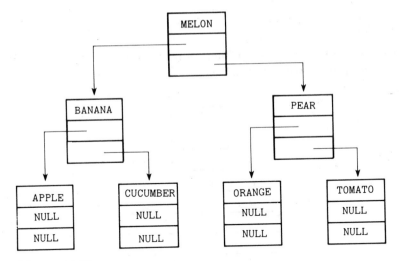

Figure 16.17

```
struct node { /* binary tree: */
    Datatype    data
    PtrNode     left;
    PtrNode     right;
};
```

The members `left` and `right` are pointer variables containing the addresses of other tree nodes. As a special case, these members may be the value NULL, denoting no further descendents.

Let us now declare some variables of type Node:

```
Node                    top,
        left,                    right,
    leftleft, leftright, rightleft, rightright;
```

and perform some assignments on these structures:

```
top.data        = 40;
left.data       = 20;
leftleft.data   = 10;
leftright.data  = 30;
right.data      = 60;
rightleft.data  = 50;
rightright.data = 70;
```

We assume in this instance that `Datatype` is defined as:

```
typedef int    Datatype;
```

A tree structure can be established by having the left member of `top` address the node `left`, and the `right` member of `top` address the node `right`. The statements are:

```
top.left        = &left;
top.right       = &right;
```

Pictorially, the effect of these pointer assignments is shown in Figure 16.18. Continuing with these pointer assignments:

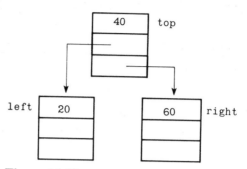

Figure 16.18

```
left.left             = &leftleft;
left.right            = &leftright;
right.left            = &rightleft;
right.right           = &rightright;
leftleft.left         = (Ptrnode)NULL;
leftleft.right        = (Ptrnode)NULL;
leftright.left        = (Ptrnode)NULL;
leftright.right       = (Ptrnode)NULL;
rightleft.left        = (Ptrnode)NULL;
rightleft.right       = (Ptrnode)NULL;
rightright.left       = (Ptrnode)NULL;
rightright.right      = (Ptrnode)NULL;
```

we ultimately construct the binary tree of Figure 16.19.

To reference the data items in this tree, there are a number of equivalent expressions. To retrieve the data item '40', we use:

```
top.data
```

The expression:

```
top.right
```

is an object of type pointer to a `struct node`. It does, of course, point to the node called `right`. From Section 15.5, a pointer to a structure permits a member of that structure to be accessed. Two expressions to reference the data value '60' are:

```
right.data
```

or:

```
top.right -> data
```

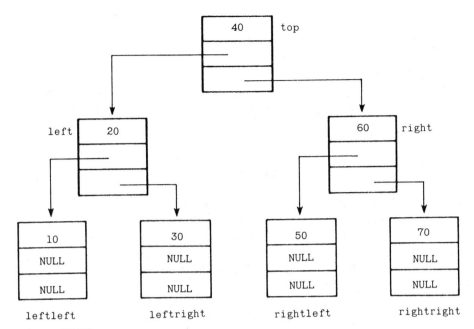

Figure 16.19

Similarly, the data item '30' can be accessed by:

```
leftright.data
```

or:

```
left.right -> data
```

or:

```
top.left -> right -> data
```

The essential feature here is that members of the objects immediately below the top node are accessible not only by their name (e.g. `leftright.data`) but also anonymously through the pointers which refer to them (e.g. `top.left -> right -> data`). If we have a variable of type `PtrNode` called `root`, declared and initialized by:

```
PtrNode root = &top;
```

then the complete tree is accessible through `root` and its pointers.

We can dispense completely with the named nodes and operate solely with anonymous nodes if each node can be created dynamically. Like linear linked lists, this is achieved with the standard library function `malloc`. If `ptrnode` is declared as:

```
    PtrNode    ptrnode;
```

then:

```
    ptrnode = (PtrNode) malloc(sizeof(Node));
```

causes space for one tree Node to be dynamically created and addressed by the variable ptrnode. The node can then be attached to the tree structure at some appropriate point.

16.10 Binary tree processing

There are numerous ways to systematically examine all the nodes of a binary tree exactly once. Several *traversal* methods are important because of the order superimposed on the data stored in the tree. A common task is to print in order the data items held in an ordered binary tree. Consider the example tree of the preceding section. The numerical ordering of this data set is:

```
    10, 20, 30, 40, 50, 60 and 70
```

When data items are stored in an ordered binary tree and printed in order, the tree traversal is called inorder.

To perform this inorder traversal of the tree, we initially start with a pointer to the root node. The data item at the node addressed by the variable root is the value '40'. Before we can print this value in its correct sequential order, we must first print all the data items in the subtree immediately to the left of the root node (data values 10, 20 and 30). All the nodes in the right subtree (data values 50, 60 and 70) are printed after the root data item. The printing order is, therefore, as follows:

1.   Print all the data items in the left subtree of root.
2.   Print the data item at the root.
3.   Print all the data items in the right subtree of root.

This sequence suggests that recursion can be used to perform the task, since as we move from the root to the left subtree, we actually apply the same process to the root of this subtree. Similarly with the right subtree. To construct a recursive function we refine steps 1 and 3 and determine the termination condition for the recursive calls. Consider that the recursive function is called inorder and has the declaration:

```
    void inorder(PtrNode r)
```

The argument r represents the root of the tree to be printed, and would be initially called by:

```
    inorder(root);
```

for the tree.

Step 1 of the process amounts to making a recursive call on `inorder` applied to the root of the subtree to the left of r:

```
inorder(r -> left);
```

Similarly, the recursive call:

```
inorder(r -> right);
```

descends to the root of the right subtree of the current node. The statements we have in our recursive implementation of `inorder` are then:

```
inorder(r -> left);
printf("%d\n", r -> data);
inorder(r -> right);
```

A series of these recursive calls follow the left subtrees until we encounter the node containing the data item '10'. When we reach this point, it is found to have a NULL left subtree. It follows that when we process a subtree whose root is NULL the recursive process terminates. The three statements are then guarded by a suitable conditional. The completed version of `inorder` is then:

```
void inorder(PtrNode r)
{
  if (r != NULL){
    inorder(r -> left);
    printf("%d\n", r -> data);
    inorder(r -> right);
  }
}
```

Traversing a binary tree using this function is illustrated in the following program. The example binary tree is first established as shown above, then the function is called to traverse the tree printing the data items in ascending order.

PROGRAM 16.5

```
/*
**      Establish an ordered binary tree of height
**      two and demonstrate an inorder traversal of the
**      structure.
*/

#include <stdio.h>

typedef int                 Datatype;
typedef struct node         Node;
typedef Node                *PtrNode;
```

```
struct node {     /* general binary tree node: */
   Datatype     data;
   PtrNode      left;
   PtrNode      right;
};

void inorder(PtrNode);

main()
{
   Node          top, left, right,
                 leftleft, leftright, rightleft, rightright;
   PtrNode       root;

   root = &top;
   top.data = 40;  top.left = &left;          top.right = &right;
   left.data = 20; left.left = &leftleft;  left.right = &leftright;
   right.data = 60;right.left = &rightleft;right.right = &rightright;
   leftleft.data = 10; leftleft.left = leftleft.right = NULL;
   leftright.data = 30;leftright.left = leftright.right = NULL;
   rightleft.data = 50;rightleft.left = rightleft.right = NULL;
   rightright.data =70;rightright.left = rightright.right = NULL;

   inorder(root);
}


void inorder(PtrNode root)
{
   if (root != NULL){               /* a further subtree? */
      inorder(root -> left);        /* traverse left side first */
      printf("%d\n", root -> data); /* print root node data item */
      inorder(root -> right);       /* then traverse right side */
   }
}
```

Two other methods for binary tree traversal are called preorder and postorder. They differ from each other and from inorder traversal in the order in which they visit the roots with respect to the left and right subtrees. We leave implementation of these two traversals as an exercise.

We define a general abstraction for a binary tree in a manner reminiscent of the general list abstraction. First, the actual implementation structure is concealed from the user of the package, removing possible direct access on the storage. Second, the explicit nature of a binary tree is supported by a suite of service operations expressing the operations on a tree. Finally, a generic version is produced from which particular versions may be instantiated.

The binary tree, like the linked list, has an associated cursor identifying the tree node in the window. The cursor positioning operators provided are: setroot, which places the cursor on the root node of the tree; parent, which moves the cursor to the parent of the current node; leftsibling (rightsibling), which moves the window to the root of the subtree to the left (right) of the current node.

Each of these treewalking operations must address special boundary conditions. They can be determined by the operation isintree which returns the logical value FALSE when the cursor does not address a tree node; otherwise it returns TRUE. If the tree is empty, then following the operation setroot, operation isintree is FALSE. If, initially, isintree is FALSE then leftsibling and rightsibling have no effect. Similarly, if isintree is FALSE, parent has no effect. If the cursor presently addresses the root node, then parent moves the cursor off the tree, and a subsequent call to isintree will yield FALSE.

From any node in the tree the cursor may move to its left or right descendant. If the left or right subtree is empty, these operators will move the cursor off the tree, leaving isintree FALSE. To avoid such outcomes it is preferable that we first determine this situation. Two predicates to detect if the subtrees of the cursor node are empty are isemptyleft and isemptyright. Similarly, the Boolean operator isroot returns TRUE if the cursor node is the root node. This condition can be detected before attempting a move with the operator parent.

An initially empty tree is produced with the operator empty. The predicate to detect an empty tree is isempty.

The data item at the cursor node can be inspected using contain. If the cursor is not addressing a tree node, then an execution error occurs. All the data items in a binary tree may be visited and operated upon with inorder. The operation to be performed upon each element is given as an argument to inorder.

The operator insertleft (insertright) inserts a new leaf node with some given data value as the left (right) subtree of the cursor node. The condition isemptyleft (isemptyright) is first tested and if FALSE the operation aborts. An additional parameter determines whether the cursor remains in its present position or inherits the position of the new node.

Similarly, the operator insertroot establishes a new root node with some data value. The existing tree hangs as either the left or right descendant according to a function parameter. Another argument determines the final position of the cursor. The cursor does not have to be on the root node to execute this operation.

The abstraction of a general binary tree which we have arrived at is given by the following header file:

```
/*
**      File:         gbtree.h
*/

#ifndef GBTREE

    #define GBTREE

    #include "boolean.h"
```

```
        typedef enum { NOMOVE, MOVE } Where;
        typedef enum { LEFT, RIGHT } Direction;

        typedef void        *GType;
        typedef void        *GBTree;
        typedef void        (*Operation)(GType);

        extern GBTree       gempty(void);
        extern Boolean      gisempty(GBTree);
        extern Boolean      gisintree(GBTree);
        extern Boolean      gisroot(GBTree);
        extern Boolean      gisemptyleft(GBTree);
        extern Boolean      gisemptyright(GBTree);
        extern GType        gcontain(GBTree);
        extern GBTree       gsetroot(GBTree);
        extern GBTree       gleftsibling(GBTree);
        extern GBTree       grightsibling(GBTree);
        extern GBTree       gparent(GBTree);
        extern GBTree       ginsertleft(GType, GBTree, Where);
        extern GBTree       ginsertright(GType, GBTree, Where);
        extern GBTree       ginsertroot(GType, GBTree, Direction, Where);
        extern void         ginorder(GBTree, Operation);

    #endif
```

The implementation of the genaral binary tree uses the same pointer technique as the list abstraction. Each tree node has pointers to its left and right descendants, and a pointer to its parent. The data item is, once again, represented by an untyped pointer. The tree has a `root` and `cursor` node pointer:

```
    /*
    **      File:       gbtree.c
    */

    #include <stdio.h>
    #include <stdlib.h>
    #include "gbtree.h"

    typedef struct tree     Tree;
    typedef struct node     Node;

    struct tree{
      Node                  *root;
      Node                  *cursor;
    };

    struct node{
      GType                 data;
      Node                  *parent;
      Node                  *left;
      Node                  *right;
    };
```

```
static void error(char *mess)
{
  fprintf(stderr, "%s\n", mess);
  exit(1);
}

GBTree gempty(void)
{
  Tree  *tree = (Tree *) malloc(sizeof(Tree));

  if(tree == NULL) error("No space (empty)");

  tree -> root = tree -> cursor = NULL;
  return tree;
}

Boolean gisempty(GBTree tree)
{
  return (((Tree *)tree) -> root == NULL);
}

Boolean gisintree(GBTree tree)
{
  return (((Tree *)tree) -> cursor == NULL);
}

Boolean gisroot(GBTree tree)
{
  return (((Tree *)tree) -> root == ((Tree*)tree) -> cursor);
}

Boolean gisemptyleft(GBTree tree)
{
  if(((Tree *)tree) -> cursor == NULL)
    error("Access violation (isemptyleft)");
  return (((Tree *)tree) -> cursor -> left == NULL);
}

Boolean gisemptyright(GBTree tree)
{
  if(((Tree *)tree) -> cursor == NULL)
    error("Access violation (isemptyright)");
  return (((Tree *)tree) -> cursor -> right == NULL);
}

GType gcontain(GBTree tree)
{
  if(((Tree *)tree) -> cursor == NULL)
    error("Access violation (contain)");
  return ((Tree *)tree) -> cursor -> data;
}
```

```
GBTree gsetroot(GBTree tree)
{
   ((Tree *)tree) -> cursor = ((Tree *)tree) -> root;
   return tree;
}

GBTree gleftsibling(GBTree tree)
{
   if(((Tree *)tree) -> cursor == NULL) return tree;
   ((Tree *)tree) -> cursor = ((Tree *)tree) -> cursor -> left;
   return tree;
}

GBTree grightsibling(GBTree tree)
{
   if(((Tree *)tree) -> cursor == NULL) return tree;
   ((Tree *)tree) -> cursor = ((Tree *)tree) -> cursor -> right;
   return tree;
}

GBTree gparent(GBTree tree)
{
   if(((Tree *)tree) -> cursor == NULL) return tree;
   ((Tree *)tree) -> cursor = ((Tree *)tree) -> cursor -> parent;
   return tree;
}

GBTree ginsertleft(GType data, GBTree tree, Where where)
{
   Node   *node;

   if(((Tree *)tree) -> cursor -> left != NULL)
     error("Existing left subtree (insertleft)");

   node = (Node *) malloc(sizeof(Node));
   if(node == NULL) error("No space (insertleft)");

   node -> data = data;
   node -> left = node -> right = NULL;
   node -> parent = ((Tree *)tree) -> cursor;
   ((Tree *)tree) -> cursor -> left = node;
   if(where == MOVE) ((Tree *)tree) -> cursor = node;
   return tree;
}

GBTree ginsertright(GType data, GBTree tree, Where where)
{
   Node   *node;

   if(((Tree *)tree) -> cursor -> right != NULL)
     error("Existing right subtree (insertright)");
```

```
   node = (Node *) malloc(sizeof(Node));
   if(node == NULL) error("No space (insertright)");

   node -> data = data;
   node -> left = node -> right = NULL;
   node -> parent = ((Tree *)tree) -> cursor;
   ((Tree *)tree) -> cursor -> right = node;
   if(where == MOVE) ((Tree *)tree) -> cursor = node;
   return tree;
}

GBTree ginsertroot(GType data, GBTree tree,
                   Direction direction, Where where)
{
  Node *node = (Node *) malloc(sizeof(Node));

  if(node == NULL) error("No space (insertroot)");
  node -> data = data;
  node -> left = (direction == LEFT ) ? ((Tree *)tree)
                                      -> root : NULL;
  node -> right = (direction == RIGHT) ? ((Tree *)tree)
                                       -> root : NULL;
  node -> parent = NULL;
  ((Tree *)tree) -> root = node;
  if(where == MOVE) ((Tree *)tree) -> cursor = node;
  return tree;
}

static void inorder(Node *root, Operation operation)
{
   if(root != NULL){
     inorder(root -> left, operation);
     operation(root -> data);
     inorder(root -> right, operation);
   }
}

void ginorder(GBTree tree, Operation operation)
{
   inorder(((Tree *)tree) -> root, operation);
}
```

CASE STUDY   16.2 Cross-referencing

Case Studies 12.1 and 16.1 produced a sorted concordance of the words in an input text. This program might be extended in a number of ways. If we associate an integer counter with each word in the list, we could maintain a count of the number of occurrences of each word in the text. Alternatively, we might produce an alphabetical list of every word, including duplicates, together with an associated line number. A second program could then read the output from the latter and display a single copy of each word with a list of the line numbers on which it appears.

We shall extend the concordance case study by a combination of the last two proposals. The specification of the concordance program is extended to produce a cross-reference list of the words used, sorted into alphabetical order, and including a list of the line numbers, in ascending order, on which each word appears.

In this new problem, there are three abstractions operating:

(a)   a stream of words and associated line numbers extracted from the input file, one word at a time;

(b)   a list of the unique words maintained in dictionary order; and

(c)   the line number list for each word.

To implement the program we must provide implementation structures and interfaces to these data types. The implementations for (b) and (c) will be derived from our generic tree and list abstractions respectively. Interfaces for the abstractions (a) and (b) are referenced directly in the program. The line number list associates with each word and interfaces with the word list abstraction.

We shall proceed by considering each abstraction in turn. A bottom-up design blends naturally with the problem, permitting the number list to be incorporated into the word list, and the word list and input stream into the program. Further, the word list and line list abstractions are derived from existing data types.

The program maintains an association between a word and a sequence of line numbers. If, for each word/line number pair received from the input stream, that word has already occurred, then the new line number is incorporated into its corresponding list of line numbers. If the word occurs for the first time, then a new line number list containing only that line number is established for this new word. If the word appears more than once on a line, then only one occurrence of the line number appears in the list.

Consider, then, the abstraction of a sequence of line numbers. The features of the abstraction required by the program (specifically the word list abstraction) are the types `LineNumber` and `LineNumberSequence`, and the operators `nilsequence`, `appendline` and `printlinenumbersequence`. An empty sequence of occurrences is established with the initializer `nilsequence`. The action of adding a line number to an existing sequence is provided by the operation `appendline`. Strictly, the line number is appended to the end of the sequence. Further, if the final entry in the sequence is the same line number as the new item, the latter is ignored. This corresponds to the situation where a word appears more than once in a line. Finally, the line number sequence is displayed with the operation `printlinenumbersequence`.

The line number sequence is derived from the general list abstraction. An empty sequence is realized by an empty list. An item is appended on to the end of the sequence by locating the cursor on the final list element and executing an `insertafter` operation. Before inserting, the check for duplicates is performed. The `insertafter` operation is called with the `MOVE` argument set, so that the cursor always associates with the final element of each sequence.

These considerations result in the following program unit and associated header file:

```
/*
**      File:           lineseq.h
*/

#ifndef LINESEQ

  #define LINESEQ

  typedef int           LineNumber;
  typedef void          *LineNumberSequence;

  extern LineNumberSequence nilsequence(void);
  extern LineNumberSequence appendline(LineNumber,
                                       LineNumberSequence);
  extern void               printlinenumbersequence
                                       (LineNumberSequence);

#endif
```

```
/*
**      File:           lineseq.c
*/

#include <stdio.h>
#include <stdlib.h>
#include "lineseq.h"
#include "glist.h"

#define PERLINE         5

static void error(char *mess)
{
  fprintf(stderr, "%s\n", mess);
  exit(1);
}

LineNumberSequence nilsequence(void)
{
  return gnil();
}

LineNumberSequence appendline(LineNumber number,
                              LineNumberSequence seq)
{
  LineNumber    *new;
```

```
    if( ! gisnil(seq) && *((LineNumber *)gcontent(seq)) == number)
      return seq;

    new = (LineNumber *) malloc(sizeof(LineNumber));
    if(new == NULL) error("No space (appendline)");
    *new = number;
    return ginsertafter(new, seq, MOVE);
}

static int perline = 0;

static void printlinenumber(LineNumber *number)
{
  if(perline == PERLINE){
    perline = 0;
    printf("\n\t");
  }
  printf("%6d", *number);
  perline++;
}

void printlinenumbersequence(LineNumberSequence seq)
{
  perline = 0;
  gtraverse(seq, (Operation) printlinenumber);
}
```

The word list abstraction must support operations to (a) record a word and line number in the list, and (b) print the entire word list content together with the line number list for every word. These services are provided by the operations insertword and printwords.

The word list abstraction is realized as an *ordered binary tree*, which is a general binary tree with the additional constraint that for a given node of the tree all values in the left subtree are less than the value at the node, and all the values in the right subtree are greater than the value at the node. Figure 16.19 is an example of an ordered binary tree.

Each tree node has a word and its associated line number sequence as its data value. The operation insertword searches the ordered tree for an occurrence of the new word. If an entry is found, the line number is appended on to the corresponding line number sequence. If no match is found, a new node is established and correctly positioned in the tree. The data for this new node is the new word and a line number sequence of unit length containing only that line number.

In the original implementation of the word concordance problem the client is unaware of the representation of the word list. This strategy is carried forward into the cross-reference variant. The implementation in program unit wordref.c contains the private data object wordxreference which represents the abstraction. The two services insertword and printwords operate on this data object. Operation insertword also performs the necessary initialization. If required, a separate service could have been provided for this task.

The outcome of this analysis is the following program unit and header file:

```
/*
**        File:              wordxref.h
*/

#ifndef WORDXREF

   #define WORDXREF

   #include "lineseq.h"

   typedef char          *Word;

   extern void insertword(Word, LineNumber);
   extern void printwords(void);

#endif



/*
**        File:              wordxref.c
*/

#include <stdio.h>
#include <stdlib.h>
#include <string.h>
#include "wordxref.h"
#include "lineseq.h"
#include "gbtree.h"
#include "boolean.h"

typedef struct{
   Word                   word;
   LineNumberSequence    linenumbers;
} WordandLineNumberSequence;

typedef void              *WordXReference;

static Boolean iswordxreferenceset = FALSE;
static WordXReference wordxreference;

static void error(char *mess)
{
   fprintf(stderr, "%s\n", mess);
   exit(1);
}

static Word worddup(Word word)
{
   Word new = (Word) malloc(strlen(word)+1);
```

```
    if(new == NULL) error("No space (worddup)");
    return strcpy(new, word);
}

static WordandLineNumberSequence
        *makewordandline(Word word, LineNumber number)
{
  WordandLineNumberSequence *new =
        (WordandLineNumberSequence *)
                malloc(sizeof(WordandLineNumberSequence));

  if(new == NULL) error("No space (makewordline)");

  new -> word = worddup(word);
  new -> linenumbers = appendline(number, nilsequence());
  return new;
}

void insertword(Word word, LineNumber number)
{
  int    comp;

  if( ! iswordxreferenceset){
    iswordxreferenceset = TRUE;
    wordxreference = gempty();
  }

  wordxreference = gsetroot(wordxreference);

  if( ! gisintree(wordxreference)){
    wordxreference =
        ginsertroot(makewordandline(word, number),
                wordxreference, LEFT, NOMOVE);
    return;
  }

  while( gisintree(wordxreference)){
    if((comp =
        strcmp(word,
                ((WordandLineNumberSequence
                *)gcontain(wordxreference))
                -> word)) == 0){
      LineNumberSequence lines =
        ((WordandLineNumberSequence *)gcontain(wordxreference)) ->
                linenumbers;
      lines = appendline(number, lines);
      ((WordandLineNumberSequence *)gcontain(wordxreference))
                -> linenumbers = lines;
      return;
    } else if(comp < 0){
      if(gisemptyleft(wordxreference)){
        wordxreference =
```

```
            ginsertleft(makewordandline(word, number),
                wordxreference, NOMOVE);
            return;
          }
          wordxreference = gleftsibling(wordxreference);
        } else {
          if(gisemptyright(wordxreference)){
            wordxreference =
              ginsertright(makewordandline(word, number),
                wordxreference, NOMOVE);
            return;
          }
          wordxreference = grightsibling(wordxreference);
        }
      }
    }

    static void printwordlines(WordandLineNumberSequence *seq)
    {
      printf("\n%s:\n", seq -> word);
      printlinenumbersequence(seq -> linenumbers);
    }

    void printwords(void)
    {
      ginorder(wordxreference, (Operation) printwordlines);
    }
```

In the original problem no account was taken of the whitespace characters between the input words other than as separators. In this new problem we must identify all occurrences of newline symbols to maintain the correct line count. A further program abstraction is thus a stream of input characters formed into words and line number pairs. The operator nextword delivers the next input word and its source text line number. If the end of file is detected, an empty word is returned. The header file and program unit is:

```
/*
**      File:           wordstrm.h
*/

#ifndef WORDSTREAM

  #define WORDSTREAM

  #include "lineseq.h"
  #include "wordxref.h"

  extern void nextword(FILE *, Word, LineNumber *);

#endif
```

```
/*
**        File:           wordstrm.c
*/

#include <stdio.h>
#include "wordstrm.h"

#define NEWLINE        '\n'
#define TAB            '\t'
#define BLANK          ' '

#define FOREVER        for(;;)

static LineNumber linenumber = 1;

static int nextcharacter(FILE *fp)
{
  int   ch;

  ch = getc(fp);
  if(ch == EOF)
    return EOF;
  else if(ch == NEWLINE){
    linenumber++;
    return BLANK;
  } else
    return ch;
}

void nextword(FILE *fp, Word word, LineNumber *number)
{
  int   ch;

  *word = NULL;
  FOREVER{                          /* skip leading whitespace */
    ch = nextcharacter(fp);
    if(ch == EOF) return;
    if(ch != BLANK && ch != TAB) break;
  }

  *number = linenumber;
  *word++ = ch;
  FOREVER{                          /* compose word */
    ch = nextcharacter(fp);
    if(ch == BLANK || ch == TAB || ch == EOF) break;
    *word++ = ch;
  }
  *word = NULL;
}
```

Finally, the program itself. The design is similar to the original. Words are read from the input stream and inserted into the word list abstraction. The process repeats until the end of file is determined. The cross-reference list is then displayed:

```
/*
**      File:          case02.c
*/

#include <stdio.h>
#include <string.h>
#include "wordstrm.h"
#include "wordxref.h"

main(int argc, char *argv[])
{
  FILE        *fp;
  char        word[20];
  LineNumber  number;

  if(argc != 2)
    fprintf(stderr, "Usage: %s filename\n", argv[0]);
  else if((fp = fopen(argv[1], "r")) == NULL)
    fprintf(stderr, "%s: cannot open %s\n", argv[0], argv[1]);
  else {
    nextword(fp, word, &number);
    while(strcmp(word, "") != 0){
      insertword(word, number);
      nextword(fp, word, &number);
    }
    fclose(fp);
    printwords();
  }
}
```

16.11 Summary

1. Static data objects are used to build dynamic data structures. These static objects, or nodes, contain pointers to other such nodes and are known as self-referential structures. The nature of the linkages reflects the underlying data structure.

2. A *singly chained linked list* is a dynamic data structure composed of one or more nodes chained together by single pointers. Variations on singly chained lists include the *circular list* and the *doubly linked list*.

3. A *tree* is a non-linear data structure with a root node that points to zero or more subtrees. In particular, in a *binary tree*, each parent may have at most two descendents.

16.12 Exercises

1.   Write a function that determines the length of a singly chained linked list of the form shown in Program 16.2. Develop two versions of the function: a non-recursive and a recursive version.

2.   Write a function reverse:

```
GList reverse(GList p)
```

which reverses the order of the items in the GList p. Use the operations defined in glist.h of Section 16.6.

3.   A stack is a last-in-first-out data type. Operation gpush places a new item on the stack top, while operation gpop removes one. If the stack is empty, gpop leaves the stack unchanged. Operation gtop delivers a copy of the top stack item. If the stack is empty, gtop reports an error and exits. Operation gnewstack creates an empty stack, and gisnewstack determines if the stack is empty. A header for a program unit to support stacks is:

```
#ifndef GSTACK
  #define GSTACK

  #include "boolean.h"

  typedef void      *GSType;
  typedef void      *GStack;
  typedef void      (*GDelete)(GSType);
  extern GStack     gnewstack(void);
  extern GStack     gpush(GSType, GStack);
  extern GStack     gpop(GStack, GDelete);
  extern GSType     gtop(GStack);
  extern Boolean    gisnewstack(GStack);
#endif
```

Implement the corresponding program unit using the generic list package of Section 16.6.

4.   Derive a program unit intqueue.c from the generic list package of Section 16.6, which implements a queue of integers. Use this package to reimplement Case Study 13.1.

5.   Provide functions preorder and postorder that are the counterparts of the function inorder given in Section 16.10. The function preorder (postorder) visits the root item before (after) visiting the items in the left and right subtrees.

6. Write a function that counts the number of leaf nodes in a binary tree.

7. Use the sorted list package developed in Section 16.8 to derive a sorted name list similar to that of Section 16.7. Develop a hash table of names, using chained hashing to resolve clashes. A possible header is:

```
#ifndef HASH
  #define HASH

  #include "boolean.h"

  typedef char     *Name;

  extern void      initialize(void);
  extern void      insert(Name);
  extern Boolean   isin(Name);
#endif
```

17

Operations on bits

IT WAS REMARKED in Chapter 1 that C was originally conceived as a systems programming language to implement the UNIX operating system. A particular feature of this activity is the processing of individual bit patterns within a computer word. These facilities are supported in C by the provision of a number of *bitwise operators*.

17.1 Bitwise operators and expressions

In addition to the bit fields associated with structured values, C also supports six operators to manipulate bit values of integral types. The six bitwise operators are shown in Table 17.1.

Table 17.1

Category	Bitwise operator	Symbol
Bitwise operators:	(unary) bitwise complement	~
	bitwise and	&
	bitwise or	|
	bitwise exclusive or	^
Shift operators:	left shift	<<
	right shift	>>

Like all C operators, the bitwise operators have rules of precedence and associativity which determine how expressions involving these and other operators are evaluated. Further, all these bitwise operators, except the *unary complement*, operate in conjunction with the assignment operator. The full table of operators is given in Appendix E.

All the bitwise operators apply to integer types only. Thus these operators may not be applied to types `float` and `double`. We will restrict our discussion to a machine with a 16-bit, 2's complement representation for a standard sized `int`. Other architectures are processed similarly.

The *bitwise complement* operator ~, also known as the 'one's complement operator', computes the bitwise negation of its single operand. The usual unary conversions apply to the operand. Every bit in the binary representation of the result is the inverse or complement of the operand. If the integer variable t has decimal value 12, the binary representation for this value is:

0000000000001100

then ~t has the binary representation:

1111111111110011

This 2's complement value equates to decimal − 13.

The bitwise operators *and* (&), *or* (|) and *exclusive or* (^) are binary operators. Each operand is treated in terms of its binary representation. Each bit of the result is computed by applying the operator and, or or exclusive or to the corresponding bits of both operands. The semantics of these three operators is given by Table 17.2.

Table 17.2

x	y	x & y	x | y	x ^ y
0	0	0	0	0
0	1	0	1	1
1	0	0	1	1
1	1	1	1	0

In the context of the following declarations and initializations:

int p = 123, q = -17;

Table 17.3 shows a series of expressions, the binary representation of the result of evaluating the expression, and the corresponding decimal value.

Table 17.3

Expression	Binary representation	Decimal value
p	0000 0000 0111 1011	123
q	1111 1111 1110 1111	−17
p & q	0000 0000 0110 1011	107
p| q	1111 1111 1111 1111	−1
p ^ q	1111 1111 1001 0100	−108

A *mask* is used to extract the desired bit pattern from an expression. For example, the int constant 3 has the binary representation:

0000 0000 0000 0011

and can be used in conjunction with the bitwise and operator to determine the low order 2 bits of an int expression value. For example, the expression:

```
y = x & 3;
```

assigns to y the rightmost (least significant) 2 bits of the integer variable x. If x has the value 17 (binary: 0000000000010001), then y has the value 1 (binary: 0000000000000001). To find the value of a particular group of bits in an expression, a mask with 1's in those bit positions and 0's elsewhere is used. Thus, the hexadecimal constant 0x30 is a mask for bits 5 and 6 from the right.

To clear the low-order byte of a 16-bit integer, the mask 0xFF00 can be used. To allow the code to work properly, independent of the size of an integer, the bitwise complement can be used to construct the necessary mask:

```
high_byte = word & (~ 0xFF)
```

Finally, there are the *shift operators*. Both are binary operators with two integral operands. The right operand is converted to an int. The type of the expression result is that of its left operand. The *left shift* operator << shifts the binary representation of its left operand the number of places to the left as specified by the right operand. The low-order bits are zero filled. The *right shift* operator >> shifts the binary representation of its left operand the number of places to the right as specified by its right operand. The bits shifted in from the left are machine-dependent. If the left operand is unsigned, then 0's are shifted in from the left. If the left operand is a signed operand, then whether 0's or 1's are shifted in is at the discretion of the implementor. On some implementations, 0's are always shifted in; on others the leftmost sign bit is regenerated as the shifted in bit. Right shifting a signed value is, therefore, highly non-portable and should be avoided. Table 17.4 shows a number of expressions, the binary representation after evaluating the result, and the corresponding decimal value. The integer variable p is assumed to have the decimal value 123.

Table 17.4

Expression	Binary representation	Decimal value
p	0000 0000 0111 1011	123
p << 4	0000 0111 1011 0000	1968
p >> 2	0000 0000 0001 1110	30
(p >> 2) & 0xF	0000 0000 0000 1110	14

Bitwise expressions can be used for data compression, making useful savings in program storage requirements. For example, on a machine with 32-bit unsigned int's, four bytes may be packed into one int. The function pack uses the bitwise operators to perform byte by byte packing:

```
unsigned int pack(char a, char b, char c, char d)
{
    unsigned int packed;
```

```
    packed = a;
    packed = (packed << 8) | b;
    packed = (packed << 8) | c;
    packed = (packed << 8) | d;

    return (packed);
}
```

The four bytes in a packed unsigned integer can be recovered with the function
unpack:

```
#define MASK          0xFF

void unpack(unsigned p, char *a, char *b, char *c, char *d)
{
  *a = p & MASK;
  *b = (p >> 8) & MASK;
  *c = (p >> 16) & MASK;
  *d = (p >> 24) & MASK;
}
```

Program 15.8 used bit fields to pack the elements of a date. We repeat the same
problem in Program 17.1 below, this time using the bitwise operators to perform the
packing and unpacking.

PROGRAM 17.1

```
/*
**        The program determines a person's age measured
**        in years given that person's date of birth and
**        today's date. The dates are packed into 16 bits
**        and stored left to right as day (5 bits), month
**        (4 bits) and year (7 bits).
*/

#include <stdio.h>

typedef unsigned int          Date;   /* packed representation */

#define DAY(D)                ((D) >> 11)
#define MONTH(D)              (((D) >> 7) & 0xF)
#define YEAR(D)               ((D) & 0x7F)

void askfordate(char *, Date *);

main()
{
  Date        dateofbirth, today;
  int         age;

  askfordate("Date of birth?: ", &dateofbirth);
  askfordate("Today\'s date?: ", &today);
```

```
      if (MONTH(today) > MONTH(dateofbirth) ||
          MONTH(today) == MONTH(dateofbirth) &&
            DAY(today) > DAY(dateofbirth))
        age = YEAR(today) - YEAR(dateofbirth);
      else
        age = YEAR(today) - YEAR(dateofbirth) - 1;

      printf("age: %d\n", age);
    }

    void askfordate(char *prompt, Date *date)
    {
      unsigned int d, m, y;

      printf("%s", prompt);
      scanf("%d/%d/%d", &d, &m, &y);

      *date = (((d << 4) | m) << 7) | y;
    }
```

CASE STUDY   17.1 Sets

A college offers ten courses in Mathematics, Physics, Chemistry, Biology, English, French, German, Italian, Accounting and Economics. Each student's enrolment is recorded in a text file, one record per line. The student's surname appears in columns 1–20 inclusive. Each course taken by a student is shown by the presence of the letter X in columns 21–30, representing, respectively, the ten courses. Design and write a program which reads the enrolment file and prints a class list for every course. It can be assumed that there are not more than eighty students.

The problem is most naturally expressed in terms of the set concept. Each student record consists of the student's name and the set of courses on which that student is enrolled. As each student record is input, each occurrence of the letter X in columns 21–30 causes the corresponding course to be included in the set of courses that the student attends. Producing a class list for a given subject is expressed by determining whether the course is a member of the set of courses attended by a student.

A *set* is fundamental to modern mathematics. A set is a collection of objects of some type. In Case Study 11.2 a set of integers was implemented. In this application, the base type for the set is the courses. We can define the enumeration type:

```
    typedef enum { MATHEMATICS, PHYSICS, CHEMISTRY, BIOLOGY,
                   ENGLISH, FRENCH, GERMAN, ITALIAN,
                   ACCOUNTING, ECONOMICS } Course;
```

Variables of type Course are declared and assigned in the usual way. For example:

```
    Course enrolled = MATHEMATICS;
```

These courses can be mixed in any combination to form the set of courses on which a particular student is matriculated. For example, a student enrolled for MATHEMATICS, ENGLISH and ACCOUNTING would be denoted by:

```
{ MATHEMATICS, ENGLISH, ACCOUNTING }
```

using { and } to denote a set (do not confuse with the C syntactic tokens { and }). If a student has enrolled on no courses, this is shown as the *empty* set:

```
{ }
```

The union of two sets is a set containing the members of both sets. The value of:

```
{ MATHEMATICS } union { ENGLISH, ACCOUNTING }
```

is the set shown above. The intersection of two sets is a set containing only the objects which are members of both sets. The value of:

```
{ MATHEMATICS, ENGLISH, ACCOUNTING }
    intersection { PHYSICS, MATHEMATICS }
```

is the set:

```
{ MATHEMATICS }
```

The difference of two sets is a set containing all the members of the first set which are not members of the second set. The value of:

```
{ MATHEMATICS, ENGLISH, ACCOUNTING }
    difference { PHYSICS, MATHEMATICS }
```

is the set:

```
{ ENGLISH, ACCOUNTING }
```

The operator ismember delivers TRUE or FALSE according to whether the left operand is a member or not a member of the second operand. The value of:

```
enrolled ismember { MATHEMATICS, ENGLISH, ACCOUNTING }
```

for the value of the Course variable as declared above, is TRUE.

Using our usual notation, we consider a package of set handling functions. The set base type is Course as defined above. The type name Setofcourses is assumed to have been defined in a typedef statement to denote an abstraction for these sets (Figure 17.1).

Function ismember has two arguments and returns a Boolean value according to whether the first argument of type Course is a member of the set obtained from the second argument. The function header is:

```
Boolean ismember(Course element, Setofcourses set)
```

The function header for join is:

```
                          Set
       ┌────────────────────────────────────────────┐
       │ Boolean ismember( ... ) { ... }            │
       │                                            │
       │ Setofcourses union( ... ) { ... }          │
       │                                            │
       │ Setofcourses intersection( ... ) { ... }   │
       │                                            │
       │ Setofcourses difference( ... ) { ... }     │
       │                                            │
       │ Setofcourses emptyset( ... ) { ... }       │
       │                                            │
       │ Setofcourses join( ... ) { ... }           │
       └────────────────────────────────────────────┘
```

Figure 17.1

```
Setofcourses join(Course element, Setofcourses set)
```

and adds the single item element to the set returning a new set as the function value.

The problem naturally divides into two parts. The first phase builds the array of student records. Each record contains the student's name and the set of courses for which that student is enrolled. The second phase produces a class list for each subject.

The internal data structure for the problem is an array of student records. Appropriate declarations are:

```
#define NAMESIZE    20
#define TEXTSIZE    (NAMESIZE+1)
#define CLASSSIZE   80

typedef struct {
  char              name[TEXTSIZE];
  Setofcourses      matriculated;
} Student;

Student      students[CLASSSIZE];
```

An external file of unknown length contains each student record, one per line. Each record is read from the file and stored in consecutive elements of the array. The reading continues until the end of file is reached. A student's record is read in two parts. First, the twenty-character name is input. Second, the ten-character course selection is read and stored in the Setofcourses member matriculated. This set variable is initialized to the empty set using the emptyset operation. For each occurrence of the letter 'X' in the input stream, the corresponding course is included in the set of courses using the join operation. The coding is accomplished by the function input:

```
/*
**      Read a series of student records from the
**      specified file. Continue until the end of
**      file is reached. Each student record is held
```

```
**         as a single line of text. The first field is 20
**         characters long and is the name of the student.
**         The next field is 10 characters long and is an
**         encoding for the 10 college courses. If a student
**         is enrolled on the course, an X appears in the
**         corresponding column. If a student is not
**         enrolled, the column remains blank.
*/

void input(FILE *fp, Student students[], int *number)
{
    Setofcourses        enrolled;
    Course              subject, successor ();
    char                ch;
    int                 k;
    *number = 0;
    while (fscanf(fp, "%20s", students[*number].name) != EOF){
        for (k = strlen(students[*number].name); k < NAMESIZE; k++)
            fscanf(fp, "%c", &ch);          /* ignore trailing blanks */
        enrolled = emptyset();
        for (subject = MATHEMATICS; subject != TRAILER;
                    subject = successor(subject)){
            fscanf(fp, "%c", &ch);
            if (ch == 'X')
                enrolled = join(subject, enrolled);
        }
        students[*number].matriculated = enrolled;
        (*number)++;
    }
}
```

The program output is a class list for each of the ten subjects. The data structure is nested. The outer loop cycles through all the subjects, while the inner loop cycles through all the students. If the named subject is a member of the set of courses on which the student is enrolled, that student's name is printed. The coding is:

```
/*
**      Produce a class list for every college course.
**      The list is presented in subject order, with
**      each enrolled student tabulated under the
**      course name.
*/

void output(Student students[], int number)
{
    Course      subject, successor();
    int         k;
    void        printcourse();

    for (subject = MATHEMATICS; subject != TRAILER;
                subject = successor(subject)){
        printcourse(subject);
```

```
      for (k = 0; k < number; k++)
        if (ismember(subject, students[k].matriculated))
          printf("\t%s\n", students[k].name);
    }
}


/*
**        Print the course title.
*/

static char *coursename[] = {
        "MATHEMATICS", "PHYSICS", "CHEMISTRY", "BIOLOGY",
        "ENGLISH", "FRENCH", "GERMAN", "ITALIAN",
        "ACCOUNTING", "ECONOMICS"
};

void printcourse(Course subject)
{
  printf("\n\n\n\n%s\n", coursename[(int) subject]);
}
```

In Case Study 11.2 the integer set was realized by an array of int's. This solution was appropriate given the number of possible values in the set and also given that an integer value may be any from the range of possible integers.

In this problem, we can take advantage of two known attributes. First, the maximum set size is 10. There can be no more than ten subjects on which a student is enrolled. Further, the values of the set elements are known; they are the values from the enumeration type Course. If, as the C compiler does, we encode each subject with MATHEMATICS = 0, ... , ECONOMICS = 9, then bit position 0 of an unsigned int can represent MATHEMATICS, bit position 1 can represent PHYSICS, and so on. The abstraction Setofcourses can be realized with an unsigned int value, such that if bit position 0 is value 1, MATHEMATICS is a member of the set, and if bit position 0 is value 0, MATHEMATICS is not a member of the set. The definition we have is then:

```
    typedef unsigned int      Setofcourses;
```

If on our particular machine the bits are numbered right to left, then the set denoted by:

```
    { MATHEMATICS, ENGLISH, ACCOUNTING }
```

is recorded in the unsigned int value shown in Figure 17.2. The empty set is readily constructed from a binary pattern of ten 0's, i.e. decimal zero. The function emptyset yields the empty set and is established by:

bit position	9	8	7	6	5	4	3	2	1	0
	0	1	0	0	0	1	0	0	0	1

Figure 17.2

```
#define emptyset()      ((Setofcourses) 0)
```

Note how this and all the other set 'functions' are written as macros. It would be possible to write them as true functions, but they are so concise that macros suffice. Further, there is no function call overhead, and the implementation is therefore efficient. Macro emptyset has no arguments and the null parameter list ( ) may be omitted. We choose to retain this redundancy to provide compatibility with the other 'functions'. Outwardly, they will all appear as C functions.

The operation join is implemented by setting the bit which corresponds to the subject encoding. To join PHYSICS to any set involves setting bit position 1. To join GERMAN, bit position 6 assumes the value 1. Consider the set denoted by:

{ MATHEMATICS, ENGLISH, ACCOUNTING }

with representation as shown above. To join GERMAN to this set, bit 6 must change to value 1, while the remaining bits are unchanged. This we achieve by creating a bit pattern containing all 0's except in bit position 6, as shown in Figure 17.3, then performing a bitwise OR operation between the two patterns. The resulting set is shown in Figure 17.4. The coding for this operation is:

bit position 9 8 7 6 5 4 3 2 1 0

| 0 | 0 | 0 | 1 | 0 | 0 | 0 | 0 | 0 | 0 |

Figure 17.3

bit position 9 8 7 6 5 4 3 2 1 0

| 0 | 1 | 0 | 1 | 0 | 1 | 0 | 0 | 0 | 1 |

Figure 17.4

```
#define join(ELEM, SET)\
    ((Setofcourses)1 << (int)(ELEM) | (SET))
```

The argument ELEM will be an enumeration value for the type Course. This value is coerced to type int by the explicit cast to produce the course encoding. A binary 1 is then left shifted that number of places to create the mask which is then OR'ed with the original set argument.

The other operators are implemented in a similar manner. As noted above, all the operators are coded as macros rather than as pure functions. The listing for this program unit and the remainder of the program appears below:

```
/*
**      File :          case01.c
**
**      A college offers a range of 10 courses. Produce
**      a class list of the student's enrolled on each
**      of the courses.
*/
```

```
#include <stdio.h>
#include "set.h"

#define READONLY        "r"

#define NAMESIZE        20
#define TEXTSIZE        (NAMESIZE+1)
#define CLASSSIZE       80

typedef struct {              /* student and enrolled courses: */
  char            name[TEXTSIZE];
  Setofcourses    matriculated;
} Student;

void    input(FILE *, Student [], int *),
        output(Student [], int),
        printcourse(Course);
Course  successor(Course);

main(int argc, char *argv[])
{
  FILE    *fp;
  Student students[CLASSSIZE];
  int     number;

  if (argc != 2)
    fprintf(stderr, "Usage: case01 filename\n");
  else if ((fp = fopen(argv[1], READONLY)) == NULL)
    fprintf(stderr, "case01: cannot open %s\n", argv[1]);
  else {
    input(fp, students, &number);
    fclose(fp);
    output(students, number);
  }
}


void input(FILE *fp, Student students[], int *number)
{
  .....
}


void output(Student students[], int number)
{
  .....
}


static char *coursename[] = .....
```

```
void printcourse(Course subject)
{
  printf("\n\n\n\n%s\n", coursename[(int) subject]);
}


Course successor(Course subject)
{
  return ((Course) ((int)subject + 1));
}




/*
**        File :            set.h
**
**        A set package, suitable for sets of small
**        integers. The integers are abstracted as course
**        names in the context of the application.
*/

typedef enum { MATHEMATICS, PHYSICS, CHEMISTRY, BIOLOGY,
               ENGLISH, FRENCH, GERMAN, ITALIAN,
               ACCOUNTING, ECONOMICS, TRAILER } Course;

typedef unsigned int          Setofcourses;
#define emptyset()\
        ((Setofcourses) 0)

#define ismember(ELEM, SET)\
        ((Setofcourses)1 << (int)(ELEM) & (SET))

#define join(ELEM, SET)\
        ((Setofcourses)1 << (int)(ELEM) | (SET))

#define union(SET1, SET2)\
        ((SET1) | (SET2))

#define intersection(SET1, SET2)\
        ((SET1) & (SET2))

#define difference(SET1, SET2)\
        ((SET1) ^ (SET2))
```

17.2 Summary

1. *Bitwise expressions* allow storage compaction and operations on the machine-dependent bit representation of integral data values. Bitwise operations are highly machine-dependent and make programs difficult to port. Where appropriate, consideration should be given to portability aspects when using

bitwise operators. In particular, code should be conditionally compiled for a number of architectures.

2.   Packing is the name given to placing bit patterns into integral data values. Unpacking is used to access these bit patterns. Masks are used to perform these operations.

17.3 Exercises

1.   Develop a C function called rotate which rotates a bit pattern a given number of places. The function header is:

```
unsigned int rotate(unsigned int value, int n)
```

The process of rotation is similar to shifting, except that when a value is rotated to the left the bits that are shifted out of the high-order bits are shifted back into the low-order bits. Similarly with a right rotation. Left and right shifts are denoted by positive and negative values for n respectively.

2.   Write a function called getbits which delivers the value of the n-bit pattern contained in the argument value starting at bit position p:

```
unsigned int getbits(unsigned int p,
     unsigned int n, unsigned int value)
```

3.   Write a function that reverses the bit representation of a byte. For example:

```
10101110 yields 01110101 when reversed.
```

4.   Develop the program unit corresponding to the BitVector header file given below. The constructor bitvector creates a vector of bits of length size intialized to the value initial. Destructor dbitvector releases any dynamic space used by the bit vector. Operation setbit assigns a particular bit in the vector. Operation getbit delivers the value of some specified bit. Operation printbitvector displays the bits in a bit vector as a bit stream:

```
#ifndef BITVECTOR
  #define BITVECTOR

  typedef enum { OFF, ON } Bit;
  typedef void          *BitVector;
```

```
extern BitVector bitvector(int size, Bit initial);
extern void      dbitvector(BitVector bv);
extern BitVector setbit(int bitno, Bit val,
                        BitVector bv);
extern Bit       getbit(int bitno, BitVector bv);
extern void      printbitvector(BitVector bv);
#endif
```

18

Miscellaneous topics

THIS IS THE FINAL CHAPTER, and one in which we introduce further features of C. Many programs can be written without the constructions presented in this Chapter. They do, however, provide more functionality.

One function may call another, and upon completion the latter returns control to the former. In a similar manner, one program may call (execute) a second program using the library function system.

Many kinds of error conditions can occur in a program. A user may enter an improper data value; a programming mistake may cause range constraints on a value to be exceeded. When errors occur a program receives a coded signal identifying the nature of the problem. Unless other arrangements have been made, the signal terminates the process. Alternatively, a sequence of statements can be identified with a particular signal to determine how the program will proceed. The section on signals is concerned with gracefully dealing with such error situations.

Perhaps, properly, we should have introduced the goto statement in Chapter 6. It is no accident that all the programs we have written have been developed without using the goto statement. Programs can be written without it. The problems associated with it and its possible limited uses are discussed below.

Similarly, the declarations in <setjmp.h> provide a way to avoid the normal function call and return sequence. This provision is, in effect, a goto from one function to another – a form of non-local goto.

18.1 Command execution

The function system provides a way to execute one program from within another C program. The function prototype is given in <stdlib.h> and appears as:

```
int system(const char *prog)
```

The effect is to suspend the current program and execute the command in the character string prog. The nature of this string is strongly dependent on the local operating system. The command prog is passed to the environment's command processor (for example, the UNIX Shell). When prog has completed, the environment returns to the current program to continue its operation.

A system-dependent integer status code is returned by the executed

444

command. Under UNIX, the status return value is that delivered by the library function exit.

If prog is NULL, system determines if a command processor is present. If a command processor does not exist, system returns zero, otherwise it returns non-zero.

Program 18.1 operates as a simple command processor, prompting, reading the user command, then executing the command. The cycle continues until the user enters the special command "exit".

PROGRAM 18.1

```
/*
**      Simple command processor. Issue a user prompt,
**      read the single user command, and execute it.
*/

#include <stdio.h>
#include <stdlib.h>
#include <string.h>

#define COMSIZE        80
#define FOREVER        for(;;)
#define EXIT           "exit"

main()
{
  char command[COMSIZE];

  FOREVER {
    printf("> ");
    if(gets(command) == NULL) continue;        /* blank line? */
    if(strcmp(command, EXIT) == 0) exit(0);     /* stop? */
    system(command);
  }
}
```

18.2 Signals

A program can be terminated by striking the interupt key, which is often DEL or CTRL-C. The program stops executing and control returns to the operating system. Normally what happens is that part of the operating system responsible for keyboard input sees the interrupt character and sends a signal called SIGINT to the program that associates with the terminal. When the program receives the signal it performs the action associated with SIGINT and terminates.

Signals do not carry information directly. This limits their usefulness as a general mechanism. However, each type of signal is given a mnemonic name, for example

SIGTERM, which indicates the purpose of the signal. Signal names are defined in the standard header file <signal.h>.

The library function signal alters the default action. It has two arguments: the first is a number that specifies the signal, usually denoted by the signal name; the second is either the address of a function, or is a code to specify that the signal is to be ignored or to be given the default action. The function argument denotes the handler for the signal. The library function signal is used in the following way:

```
#include <signal.h>
typedef void        (*Handler)(int);
Handler             oldhandler, newhandler;
int                 sig;
.....
oldhandler = signal(sig, newhandler);
.....
```

The first parameter sig identifies the signal in question. The second parameter newhandler describes the action to be associated with the signal. If, as in the example, it is the address of a function, then that function will be called when a signal of type sig is received by the program. If the signal handling function returns, control is restored to the point at which the process was interrupted. The second argument can also be one of two symbolic names defined in <signal.h>: SIG_IGN, meaning ignore this signal; and SIG_DFL, meaning restore the system's default action.

Program 18.2 shows how the interrupt signal can be caught and how the underlying mechanism operates. The program consumes some processor time repeatedly displaying a message. If the program is free to execute then it produces the output:

```
Loop value   1
Loop value   2
.....
Loop value 200
```

We can, however, interrupt the program by using the interrupt key. If this occurs before the program has executed the signal call, the program terminates since the signal has not been received. If the interrupt occurs after the signal call, control is passed to the function inthandler. The output might then appear as:

```
Loop value   1
Loop value   2
.....
Loop value   34
Interrupt handler: signo = 5
Returning from servicing interrupt
Loop value   35
.....
Loop value 200
```

PROGRAM 18.2

```
/*
**      Catch and service the interrupt signal.
**      Program a loop and interrupt its processing.
**      Service the interrupt, then allow the program
**      to continue.
*/

#include <stdio.h>
#include <signal.h>

typedef void            (*Handler)(int);
void    inthandler(int);                        /* prototype */

main()
{
  Handler       oldhandler;
  int           k;

  oldhandler = signal(SIGTERM, inthandler);

  for(k = 1; k <= 200; k++)
    printf("Loop value %3d\n", k);
}

void inthandler(int signo)
{
  printf("Interrupt handler: signo = %d\n", signo);
  printf("Returning from servicing interrupt\n");
}
```

Note how control is passed from the function `main` to `inthandler`. When `inthandler` has finished, control is passed back to the point at which the program was interrupted.

The function `signal` returns the previous value of the handler for the specific signal. If an error occurs, `signal` returns SIG_ERR. Thus we would normally perform the appropriate error checking.

Suppose a program wishes to ignore the interrupt signal SIGINT. To accomplish this we include the following logic in the program:

```
if((oldhandler = signal(SIGINT, SIG_IGN)) == SIG_ERR){
  fprintf(stderr, "Cannot ignore SIGINT\n");
  exit(1);
}
```

The interrupt may be enabled again with the call:

```
signal(SIGINT, SIG_DFL);
```

or reset to the original value with:

```
signal(SIGINT, oldhandler);
```

In the example program the interrupt handling function inthandler merely reported its existence. More realistically, the handler would take the necessary actions to allow the program to resume or to terminate gracefully. For example, suppose our program uses a temporary workfile. The following version of inthandler removes the file and terminates the program:

```
void inthandler(int signo)
{
  remove("tempfile");
  fprintf(stderr, "Program interrupted and stopped\n");
  exit(1);
}
```

The content of inthandler could be expanded depending on the number of necessary clean-up operations required.

The actions for signals are reset immediately after they are caught. This means that the program performs the default action SIG_DFL on the second and subsequent occurrence of the signal. If two or more interrupts are received by Program 18.2, only the first is caught and serviced. In Program 18.3, the last action of the interrupt handler reassociates itself with the signal.

PROGRAM 18.3

```
/*
**        Catch and service the interrupt signal.
**        Program a loop and interrupt its processing.
**        Service the interrupt, then allow the program
**        to continue. Permit catching further interrupts.
*/

#include <stdio.h>
#include <signal.h>

void    inthandler(int);        /* prototype */

main()
{
  int          k;

  if(signal(SIGTERM, inthandler) == SIG_ERR){
    fprintf(stderr, "Cannot set SIGTERM\n");
    exit(1);
  }

  for(k = 1; k <= 200; k++)
    printf("Loop value %3d\n", k);
}
```

```
void inthandler(int signo)
{
  signal(SIGTERM, SIG_IGN);
  printf("Interrupt handler: signo = %d\n", signo);
  printf("Returning from servicing interrupt\n");
  signal (SIGTERM, inthandler);
}
```

The library function `raise` sends the signal `sig` to the program itself. It returns non-zero if unsuccessful. The function prototype declaration is:

```
int raise(int sig)
```

The signal `SIGTERM` is provided for use by ordinary programs. By convention, it is used to terminate a program. Function `raise` can then be used to generate this signal when some error condition occurs, and trapped and serviced by some other part of the program. We might, for example, use this to report an error when using an abstract data type, permitting the application program to take the necessary action.

Program 18.4 deliberately raises the signal `SIGTERM` serviced by the routine `inthandler`.

PROGRAM 18.4

```
/*
**      Deliberately raise the signal SIGTERM serviced
**      by the routine inthandler.
*/

#include <stdio.h>
#include <signal.h>

void inthandler(int);              /* prototype */

main()
{
  if(signal(SIGTERM, inthandler) == SIG_ERR){
    fprintf(stderr, "Cannot catch SIGTERM\n");
    exit(1);
  }
  raise(SIGTERM);                  /* deliberately raise signal */
}

void inthandler(int signo)
{
  signal(SIGTERM, SIG_IGN);
  printf("Interrupt handler: signo = %d\n", signo);
  printf("Returning from servicing interrupt\n");
  signal(SIGTERM, inthandler);
}
```

18.3 The `goto` statement

We conclude our discussion of the C programming language by introducing the only remaining C statement. The `goto` statement permits unconditional transfers of control from one part of a function to another. The `goto` statement follows the syntax:

```
goto label;
```

where `label` is an identifier and `goto` is a reserved keyword. Labels are not declared in the sense of program variables. The label identifier in a `goto` statement must be the same as a named label associated with some statement in the current function. Labels are effectively declared on the statement with which they associate. A labelled statement is preceded by a label identifier immediately followed by a colon symbol, as in:

```
label : statement;
```

When a `goto` statement is executed, control passes immediately to the statement prefixed with the corresponding label. Examples of labelled statements include:

```
sum : a = b + c + d;
bug : printf("Execution error\n");
```

Statements may be multiply labelled, permitting one statement to be referenced by different named labels. Thus, we might have:

```
bug : recover : abort : exit(1);
```

The free-format of C would permit this last example to also appear as:

```
bug :
recover :
abort : exit(1);
```

The `null statement` may be labelled, so that we have:

```
dummy : /* null statement */ ;
```

All the programs presented in this book are solved satisfactorily using the control structures of sequence, selection and iteration. Together with the simple statement forms, they are combined into major statement groupings. Nevertheless, situations arise which make certain aspects of the program design which are awkward to solve using only these three control structures. A typical example of this problem is input data validation. Consider a function to read the elements of a three-dimensional integer array from a file. Without performing any validation, the function might appear as:

```
void input3d(fp, matrix, rows, columns, planes)
    FILE    *fp;
    int     matrix[][COLUMNS][PLANES];
    int     rows, columns, planes;
    {
```

```
        int i, j, k;
         for (i = 0; i < rows; i++)
          for (j = 0; j < columns; j++)
           for (k = 0; k < planes; k++)
             fscanf(fp, "%d", &matrix[i][j][k]);
   }
```

A robust program will check its input data and take the necessary action upon
detecting an error. In our example, one possible check we may wish to perform is to
detect the end of file condition. Function fscanf returns EOF upon encountering
the end of file. Using this value, a logical flag, and additional conditions in the for
statement, we have a revised version for this function. If the end of file is detected,
an error message is generated and the program terminates:

```
   void input3d(fp, matrix, rows, columns, planes)
      FILE     *fp;
      int      matrix[][COLUMNS][PLANES];
      int      rows, columns, planes;
   {
      int      i, j, k;
      Boolean eof_flag = FALSE;

      for (i = 0; i < rows && !eof_flag; i++)
        or (j = 0; j < columns && !eof_flag; j++)
          for (k = 0; k < planes && !eof_flag; k++)
             eof_flag = fscanf(fp, "%d", &matrix[i][j][k]) == EOF;

      if (eof_flag)
        {
          fprintf(stderr, "Unexpected eof\n");
          exit(1);
        }
   }
```

Because of the incorporation of additional conditional checks, the solution is
somewhat clumsy. A more graceful exit is achieved by simply using a goto
statement from within the nested loops to a point in the function where the error
action can take place:

```
   void input3d(fp, matrix, rows, columns, planes)
      FILE     *fp;
      int      matrix[][COLUMNS][PLANES];
      int      rows, columns, planes;
   {
      int i, j, k;

      for (i = 0; i < rows; i++)
        for (j = 0; j < columns; j++)
          for (k = 0; k < planes; k++)
             if (fscanf(fp, "%d", &matrix[i][j][k]) == EOF)
                goto abort;
      return;
```

```
abort :
    fprintf(stderr, "Unexpected eof\n");
    exit(1);
}
```

C permits a goto statement to transfer control to any other statement within the function in which it is used. Certain kinds of branching can be especially confusing and should be avoided. For example, transferring control into the middle of a compound statement from outside it bypasses any initialization of variables declared at the head of the compound statement:

```
. . . . . . . . . .
. . . . . . . . . .
goto middle;
. . . . . . . . . .
. . . . . . . . . .
{
    int sum = 0, divisor = 1;
    . . . . . . . . . .
    . . . . . . . . . .
middle :
    . . . . . . . . . .
}
```

Other restrictions that should also apply to the use of the goto statement include:

(a) branching into the 'then' or 'else' parts of an if statement from outside the if statement;
(b) branching into the body of a switch statement;
(c) branching into the body of an iteration statement.

Indiscriminate use of the goto statement must be avoided. The fact that both the selection and repetition control structures can be emulated using only if and goto statements does not mean that they should be used as substitutes. The keywords while, for and do signify repetition; if and switch denote selection. Their appearance in a program immediately indicates the desired control flow. By way of comparison, consider Program 18.5 which repeats the processing in Program 6.14. Note how the repetition is now implemented using a combined if and goto. Further, the tests are conducted with the same pairing. Overall, the program logic is much less obvious.

PROGRAM 18.5

```
/*
**      A piece of text consists of a character sequence
**      spanning a number of lines and terminated by a period
**      symbol. Count the number of "words" in the text,
**      where a word is defined as any character string
**      delimited by whitespace (blank, tab or newline)
**      symbols.
*/
```

```
#include <stdio.h>

#define PERIOD          '.'
#define BLANK           ' '
#define TAB             '\t'
#define NEWLINE         '\n'

#define FALSE           0
#define TRUE            1

main()
{
  char c;                              /* data character */
  int  words = 0;                      /* word counter */
  int  inword = FALSE;                 /* word indicator */
loop:
  c = getchar();                       /* get next character */
  if (c == PERIOD)                     /* terminator? */
    goto finish;                       /* yes - complete program */

  if (c == BLANK || c == TAB || c == NEWLINE){ /* whitespace? */
    inword = FALSE;                    /* outwith a word */
    goto loop;                         /* go fetch next character */
  }

  if (! inword){                       /* within a word? */
    inword = TRUE;                     /* now in a word */
    words++;                           /* increment counter */
  }

  goto loop;                           /* cycle for next character */

finish:
  printf("Number of words is %d\n", words);
}
```

The freedom to destroy the program structure provided by the while, if, etc., is what makes the goto statement a dangerous facility, and hence a topic for advanced study. The goto statement should only be used in exceptional circumstances, when the required control cannot be reasonably expressed by the control flow primitives introduced in Chapter 6. Most times this is so rare that the goto statement can be virtually ignored. This way, the difficulties associated with its use can be avoided.

18.4 Non-local jumps

Sometimes a program may wish to intercept an interrupt and interpret it as a request to stop its current actions and return control to its own command processing loop.

One might, for example, wish a user to return to a program's main menu when the interrupt key is pressed. This is done using the two routines called `setjmp` and `longjmp`.

A program position is saved in an object of type `jmp_buf`, which is defined in the standard header file `<setjmp.h>`. The macro `setjmp` saves the state information in `env` for use by `longjmp`:

```
int setjmp(jmp_buf env)
```

The return is zero from a direct call of `setjmp`, and non-zero from a subsequent call of `longjmp`. This bizarre behaviour means that the `setjmp` function is used to intialize the `jmp_buf` and returns zero on its initial call. Later, the function returns again with a non-zero value supplied in the call of `longjmp`.

For portability it is only safe to use `setjmp` as part of a comparison in an `if` statement or as the operand in the control expression of a `switch` statement:

```
jmp_buf    place;
.....
if(setjmp(place) == 0)
     /* here on direct call */
else
     /* here by calling longjmp */
```

Function `longjmp` passes control back to a saved position.

```
void longjmp(jmp_buf env, int val)
```

The function restores the state saved by the most recent call to `setjmp`, using the information saved in `env`, and execution resumes as if the `setjmp` function had just executed and returned the non-zero value `val`.

Program 18.6 demonstrates the use of `setjmp` and `longjmp`. The program's output is:

```
Returned via longjmp(..., 1)
```

Macro `setjmp` saves the program's state information in the `jmp_buf place` and initially returns the value 0. The program logic then results in the execution of the subordinate function `nonreturnable`. This function never returns normally but executes a `longjump` back to the saved position with return argument 1. `Setjmp` then operates with this as its return value causing the `else` clause of the `if` statement to be obeyed producing the aforementioned output.

PROGRAM 18.6

```
/*
**        Demonstration of the use of setjmp and longjmp.
*/

#include <stdio.h>
#include <setjmp.h>
```

```
void nonreturnable(void);        /* prototype */
jmp_buf           place;

main()
{
  int    jmpval;

  if((jmpval = setjmp(place)) == 0){
     nonreturnable();                    /* first return from setjmp */
     printf("Error! nonreturnable has returned\n");
     exit(1);                            /* will not occur! */
  } else {
     printf("Returned via longjmp(..., %d)\n", jmpval);
     exit(0);                            /* will occur on second return */
  }
}

void nonreturnable(void)
{
  longjmp(place, 1);
  printf("Error! longjmp has returned\n");
  exit(2);                               /* will not occur! */
}
```

18.5 Summary

1. The system library function provides a way to execute one program from within another. The behaviour is reminiscent of function calls in which the calling program is temporarily suspended whilst the called program executes.

2. The signal library function provides a programmer-defined way of handling interrupts. The library function raise generates a selected interrupt.

3. The goto statement violates the principles of structured programming. The goto statement permits unconditional transfer of control and results in unmanageable code. In the majority of cases, the structured control structures should be used. There are, however, a number of situations when the occasion demands the use of the goto statement.

4. Jumps across function boundaries is provided by the library functions setjmp and longjmp.

18.6 Exercises

1. Construct a simple command processor based around Program 18.1. The processor should support the use of variables, established with the processor command `set`:

```
set variable value
```

The value of a variable may then be used in commands with a leading dollar symbol ($).

2. Alter the command processor implemented in Question 1 to correctly handle interrupts.

3. Alter the implementation of generic lists in Section 16.6 so that an interrupt is raised when an incorrect use of the data type is made. This replaces the error reporting and program termination.

Appendix A: Hardware characteristics

Table A.1 summarizes the hardware properties of the basic data types of a C program on two typical configurations:

Table A.1

	INTEL 8088/86	DEC VAX[†]
char	8 bits	8 bits
short	16 bits	16 bits
int	16 bits	32 bits
long	32 bits	32 bits
unsigned	16 bits	32 bits
float	32 bits	32 bits
double	64 bits	64 bits

The header <limits.h> defines constants for the sizes of the integral values. The values listed below give minimum magnitudes; greater values may be employed:

CHAR_BIT	8	bits in a char
CHAR_MAX	UCHAR_MAX	maximum value of char, unsigned
	or SCHAR_MAX	or signed representation
CHAR_MIN	0	minimum value of char, unsigned
	or SCHAR_MIN	or signed representation
INT_MAX	+ 32767	maximum value of int
INT_MIN	− 32767	minimum value of int
LONG_MAX	+ 2147483647	maximum value of long
LONG_MIN	− 2147483647	minimum value of long
SCHAR_MAX	+ 127	maximum value of signed char
SCHAR_MIN	− 127	minimum value of signed char
SHRT_MAX	+ 32767	maximum value of short
SHRT_MIN	− 32767	minimum value of short

[†]VAX is a registered trademark of Digital Equipment Corporation.

457

UCHAR_MAX	255	maximum value of unsigned char
UINT_MAX	65535	maximum value of unsigned int
ULONG_MAX	4294967295	maximum value of unsigned long
USHRT_MAX	65535	maximum value of unsigned short

The names listed below are floating point constants defined in <float.h>. The given value represents the permitted minimum value. Implementations will define their own appropriate values.

DBL_DIG   10
    decimal digits of precision
DBL_EPSILON   1E-9
    smallest number x such that x + 1.0 ! = 1.0
DBL_MANT_DIG
    number of digits in the floating point mantissa for base FLT_RADIX
DBL_MAX   1E+37
    maximum double floating point number
DBL_MAX_EXP
    largest integer such that the value of FLT_RADIX raised to this integer power,
    subtract 1, does not exceed DBL_MAX
DBL_MAX_10_EXP
    largest integer such that 10 raised to this power does not exceed DBL_MAX
DBL_MIN   1E-37
    smallest normalized double floating point number
DBL_MIN_EXP
    smallest integer such that the value of FLT_RADIX raised to this integer
    power, subtract 1, is not less than DBL_MIN
DBL_MIN_10_EXP   -37
    smallest integer such that 10 raised to this power is not less than DBL_MIN

FLT_DIG   6
    decimal digits of precision
FLT_EPSILON   1E-5
    smallest number x such that x + 1.0 ! = 1.0
FLT_MANT_DIG
    number of digits in the floating point mantissa for base FLT_RADIX
FLT_MAX   1E+37
    maximum floating point number
FLT_MAX_EXP
    largest integer such that the value of FLT_RADIX raised to this integer power
    then subtract 1 does not exceed FLT_MAX
FLT_MAX_10_EXP   +37
    largest integer such that the value 10 raised to this power does not exceed
    FLT_MAX

FLT_MIN   1E−37
   smallest normalized floating point number
FLT_MIN_EXP
   smallest integer for the exponent part of a floating point number to base
   FLT_RADIX
FLT_MIN_10_EXP   −37
   smallest integer for the exponent part of a floating point number to base 10
FLT_RADIX   2
   base to which the exponent part of all floating point numbers are represented
FLT_ROUNDS
   nature of rounding used by the particular implementation:

      1: round to nearest representable value
      0: truncate toward zero
    − 1: no rule applies

LDBL_DIG   10
   decimal digits of precision in a long double
LDBL_EPSILON   1E−9
   smallest number x such that x + 1.0 ! = 1.0
LDBL_MANT_DIG
   number of digits in the floating point mantissa for base FLT_RADIX
LDBL_MAX   1E + 37
   maximum long double floating point number
LDBL_MAX_EXP
   largest integer such that the value of FLT_RADIX raised to this integer power,
   subtract 1, does not exceed LDBL_MAX
LDBL_MAX_10_EXP   + 37
   largest integer such that 10 raised to this power does not exceed LDBL_MAX
LDBL_MIN
   smallest normalized long double floating point number
LDBL_MIN_EXP
   smallest integer such that the value of FLT_RADIX raised to this integer
   power, subtract 1, is not less than LDBL_MIN
LDBL_MIN_10_EXP   − 37
   smallest integer such that 10 raised to this power is not less than LDBL_MIN

Appendix B: ASCII character set

Table B.1 lists the American Standard Code for Information Interchange (ASCII) character codes in hexadecimal, octal and decimal and the associated character symbol. The ASCII code is a 7-bit code with the range 0 to 127 inclusive. Character codes 0 through 31 inclusive, and decimal 127 are the non-printing characters or *control characters*:

Table B.1

ASCII character	Hexadecimal code	Octal code	Decimal code
NUL (CTRL SPACE)	00	000	0
SOH (CTRL A)	01	001	1
STX (CTRL B)	02	002	2
ETX (CTRL C)	03	003	3
EOT (CTRL D)	04	004	4
ENQ (CTRL E)	05	005	5
ACK (CTRL F)	06	006	6
BEL (CTRL G)	07	007	7
BS (CTRL H or BACKSPACE)	08	010	8
HT (CTRL I or TAB)	09	011	9
LF (CTRL J or LINEFEED)	0A	012	10
VT (CTRL K)	0B	013	11
FF (CTRL L)	0C	014	12
CR (CTRL M or RETURN)	0D	015	13
SO (CTRL N)	0E	016	14
SI (CTRL O)	0F	017	15
DLE (CTRL P)	10	020	16
DC1 (CTRL Q)	11	021	17
DC2 (CTRL R)	12	022	18
DC3 (CTRL S)	13	023	19
DC4 (CTRL T)	14	024	20
NAK (CTRL U)	15	025	21
SYN (CTRL V)	16	026	22
ETB (CTRL W)	17	027	23

ASCII character	Hexadecimal code	Octal code	Decimal code
CAN (CTRL X)	18	030	24
EM (CTRL Y)	19	031	25
SUB (CTRL Z)	1A	032	26
ESC (CTRL [or ESC)	1B	033	27
FS (CTRL \)	1C	034	28
GS (CTRL])	1D	035	29
RS (CTRL ^)	1E	036	30
US (CTRL ?)	1F	037	31
(space)	20	040	32
!	21	041	33
"	22	042	34
# (hash symbol	23	043	35
$	24	044	36
%	25	045	37
& (ampersand)	26	046	38
' (quote)	27	047	39
(	28	050	40
)	29	051	41
* (asterisk)	2A	052	42
+	2B	053	43
,	2C	054	44
–	2D	055	45
.	2E	056	46
/	2F	057	47
0	30	060	48
1	31	061	49
2	32	062	50
3	33	063	51
4	34	064	52
5	35	065	53
6	36	066	54
7	37	067	55
8	38	070	56
9	39	071	57
:	3A	072	58
;	3B	073	59
<	3C	074	60
=	3D	075	61
>	3E	076	62
?	3F	077	63
@ (at symbol)	40	100	64
A	41	101	65
B	42	102	66
C	43	103	67
D	44	104	68
E	45	105	69

ASCII character	Hexadecimal code	Octal code	Decimal code
F	46	106	70
G	47	107	71
H	48	110	72
I	49	111	73
J	4A	112	74
K	4B	113	75
L	4C	114	76
M	4D	115	77
N	4E	116	78
O	4F	117	79
P	50	120	80
Q	51	121	81
R	52	122	82
S	53	123	83
T	54	124	84
U	55	125	85
V	56	126	86
W	57	127	87
X	58	130	88
Y	59	131	89
Z	5A	132	90
[	5B	133	91
\ (backslash)	5C	134	92
]	5D	135	93
^ (circumflex)	5E	136	94
_ (underscore)	5F	137	95
` (grave)	60	140	96
a	61	141	97
b	62	142	98
c	63	143	99
d	64	144	100
e	65	145	101
f	66	146	102
g	67	147	103
h	68	150	104
i	69	151	105
j	6A	152	106
k	6B	153	107
l	6C	154	108
m	6D	155	109
n	6E	156	110
o	6F	157	111
p	70	160	112
q	71	161	113
r	72	162	114
s	73	163	115

ASCII character	Hexadecimal code	Octal code	Decimal code
t	74	164	116
u	75	165	117
v	76	166	118
w	77	167	119
x	78	170	120
y	79	171	121
z	7A	172	122
{	7B	173	123
| (stick symbol)	7C	174	124
}	7D	175	125
~ (tilde)	7E	176	126
delete	7F	177	127

Appendix C: Reserved keywords

The following is a list of *reserved keywords*; identifiers used by the C programming language. They may not be used as programmer-defined identifiers:

auto	double	int	struct
break	else	long	switch
case	enum	register	typedef
char	extern	return	union
const	float	short	unsigned
continue	for	signed	void
default	goto	sizeof	volatile
do	if	static	while

Appendix D: Identifiers

An *identifier* is created according to the following rule:

> An identifier is a combination of letters and digits, the first of which must be a letter. The underscore symbol (_) is permitted in an identifier and is considered to be a letter.

An identifier may be any length. However, ANSI conforming C compilers consider the first thirty-one characters as significant in an object with *internal linkage*. The thirty-second and subsequent characters in an identifier are ignored. Further, identifiers for external objects are processed by systems software other than compilers (such as linking loaders), and those may only consider the first six characters as significant. These systems may not be case sensitive and fail to distinguish between two identifiers treated as unique by the C compiler.

Appendix E: Operators

The C programming language supports an extensive list of *operators*. Table E.1 below provides the full list. The table presents the symbol(s) used to represent the operator, a description of the operator, and the operator associativity. The operators are listed in non-increasing order of precedence. Thus, the operators addition (+) and subtraction (−) have equal precedence, and both have higher precedence than the equality (==) operator. The addition and subtraction operators associate left to right. The precedence and associativity are used to determine how an expression is evaluated. The general rule is that operators with highest precedence are evaluated first. An expression involving operators of equal precedence is evaluated according to the associativity of the operators.

Table E.1

Operator	Description	Associativity
()	Function call	Left to right
[]	Array element reference	
->	Pointer to structure member reference	
.	Structure member reference	
−	Unary minus	Right to left
+	Unary addition	
++	Increment	
−−	Decrement	
!	Logical negation	
~	One's complement	
★	Pointer reference (indirection)	
&	Address	
sizeof	Size of an object	
(type)	Type cast (coercion)	
★	Mutiplication	Left to right
/	Division	
%	Modulus	
+	Addition	Left to right
−	Subtraction	
<<	Left shift	Left to right
>>	Right shift	

Operator	Description	Associativity
 <= > >=	Less than Less than or equal Greater than Greater than or equal	Left to right
== !=	Equality Inequality	Left to right
&	Bitwise AND	Left to right
^	Bitwise XOR	Left to right
|Bitwise OR	Left to right	
&&	Logical AND	Left to right
||	Logical OR	Left to right
?:	Conditional expression	Right to left
= *= /= %= += -= &= ^= |= <<= >>=	Assignment operators	Right to left
,	Comma operator	Left to right

Operands in a C expression are subject to a number of conversions. Any data item that is not one of the preferred types is automatically converted or promoted. A data item of a lower type is promoted to one of a higher type. All integer arithmetic is performed with at least the range of an `int`. As a consequence, a character or short integer appearing in an expression is first converted to `int`. This process is called *integral promotion*. The promotion results in an `int`, if an `int` can hold all of the values of the original type; otherwise the conversion will be to `unsigned int`. Thus, following these promotions, an expression can only involve data items of types `long double`, `double`, `float`, `unsigned long int`, `unsigned int`, `long int` or `int`.

In a mixed expression *arithmetic conversions* determine whether and how operands are converted before a binary operation is performed. When two values are to be operated upon in combination, they are first converted to a single common type. The result after applying the operation is also of that same common type.

The conversion is performed according to a hierarchy of types. Operands of *lower* type are converted to those of the *higher* type before executing the operator. The implicit arithmetic conversions operate much as expected. The full set of rules for arithmetic conversions is:

If either operand is `long double`, convert the other to `long double`.

If either operand is `double`, convert the other to `double`.

If either operand is `float`, convert the other to `float`.

Perform the integral promotions on both operands and if either operand is unsigned long int, convert the other to unsigned long int. Otherwise, if one operand is long int and the other is unsigned int, then if a long int can represent all values of an unsigned int then the latter is converted to a long int; if not, both are converted to an unsigned long int.

If either operand is long int, convert the other to long int.

If either operand is unsigned int, convert the other to unsigned int.

Otherwise, both operands are of type int.

When employing a function with arguments the actual and formal arguments must agree in number and type. The full set of rules on argument passing is especially complicated because of the need to support a mixture of new and old style function declarations. We can simplify matters if we insist that a function prototype be present and in scope. In that case, the arguments are converted as if by assignment to the types specified in the prototype.

Appendix F: The standard C library

Many C facilities are provided by C libraries. The facilites are categorized by their functionality and belong to a particular library. The capabilities detailed in this appendix are partitioned into the following eleven groupings:

- (F.1) operations on characters
- (F.2) operations on strings
- (F.3) general utilities
- (F.4) input/output procedures
- (F.5) mathematical functions
- (F.6) variable argument lists
- (F.7) non-local jumps
- (F.8) signals
- (F.9) diagnostics
- (F.10) date and time
- (F.11) localization

To use a function from one of these libraries, the appropriate `#include` command should be used to provide the relevant library declarations. Many functions, particularly those that provide operations on characters, are macros. All of the facilities we discuss are described as if they were functions to permit detailing the number and type of the arguments:

F.1 Character functions

The standard header file `<ctype.h>` contains a set of macros that are used to process single characters. The macros fall into two categories: test a single character, and convert a single character. The macros are made accessible by the preprocessor statement:

```
#include <ctype.h>
```

The macros which test a single character return an `int` value that is non-zero (logical TRUE) or zero (logical FALSE) according to whether the test succeeds or not. All these functions are distinguished with the prefix 'is', for example, isdigit. The functions have an argument of type int. The macros which perform character translation have the prefix 'to' (e.g. toupper) and return an int representation of some int character argument.

isalnum

```
int isalnum(c)
```

Returns non-zero if c represents an alphanumeric character; otherwise returns zero. The alphanumeric characters is any one of 0–9, a–z and A–Z inclusive.

isalpha

```
int isalpha(c)
```

Returns non-zero if c represents an alphabetic character; otherwise returns zero. The alphabetic characters are a–z and A–Z inclusive.

iscntrl

```
int iscntrl(c)
```

Returns non-zero if c represents a control character; otherwise returns zero. The control characters are the 'non-printing' characters. From the standard ASCII set, the control characters are 0x00 to 0x1F inclusive and also 0x7F.

isdigit

```
int isdigit(c)
```

Returns non-zero if c represents a decimal digit character; otherwise returns zero. The decimal digits include 0 to 9 inclusive.

isgraph

```
int isgraph(c)
```

Returns non-zero if c represents a graphics character; otherwise returns zero. From the standard ASCII character set, the graphics characters are those with codes 0x21 to 0x7E inclusive.

islower

```
int islower(c)
```

Returns non-zero if c represents a lower case alphabetic character; otherwise returns zero. The lower case alphabetics include a–z inclusive.

isprint

```
int isprint(c)
```

Returns non-zero if c represents a printable character; otherwise returns zero. From the standard ASCII character set, the printable characters are those with codes 0x20 to 0x7E inclusive.

ispunct

```
int ispunct(c)
```

Returns non-zero if c represents a punctuation symbol; otherwise returns zero. The Standard defines a punctuation character as any printable character, except the space character and any character which returns TRUE from isalnum.

isspace

```
int isspace(c)
```

Returns non-zero if c represents a whitespace character; otherwise returns zero. The whitespace characters from the standard ASCII character set are horizontal tab (0x09), newline (0x0A) and space (0x20), formfeed (0x0C), carriage return (0x0D) and vertical tab (0x0B).

isupper

```
int isupper(c)
```

Returns non-zero if c represents an upper case alphabetic character; otherwise returns zero. The upper case characters are A–Z inclusive.

isxdigit

```
int isxdigit(c)
```

Returns non-zero if c represents a hexadecimal digit character; otherwise returns zero. The hexadecimal digits are 0–9, a–f and A–F inclusive.

tolower

```
int tolower(c)
```

If c represents an upper case alphabetic character, then tolower returns the corresponding lower case character; otherwise c is returned unchanged.

toupper

```
int toupper(c)
```

If c represents a lower case alphabetic character, then toupper returns the corresponding upper case character; otherwise c is returned unchanged.

F.2 String processing

A string in C is an array of characters terminated by the ASCII NUL character ('\0'). String constants in a program are automatically constructed in this form by the C compiler.

The standard header file <string.h> contains a series of external referencing declarations to the string handling function. Generally, there are two classes of functions. The first category is concerned with varieties of string copying. The functions usually return a character pointer result. When characters are transferred to a destination string no checks are performed to ensure that the destination string is sufficiently large. Possible array overflow can then occur and corrupt other program variables. The second class of functions perform tests and return a non-zero value representing TRUE or zero for FALSE.

strcat

```
char *strcat(char *s1, const char *s2)
```

Appends the content of the string s2 to the end of the string s1. The first character of s2 overwrites the null character which terminates s1. A pointer to the first character of s1 is returned.

strchr

```
char *strchr(const char *s, int c)
```

The string s is searched for the first occurrence of the character c. If c is found, the function returns a pointer to c in s; otherwise NULL is returned.

strcmp

```
int strcmp(const char *s1, const char *s2)
```

Compares the two strings s1 and s2. If s1 is less than s2 the function returns a negative value. If s1 equals s2, zero is returned. If s1 is greater than s2, a positive value is returned. Two strings are equal if they have the same length and have identical content. String s1 is less than string s2 if (a) their content is identical to some character and then the next character from s1 is less than the next from s2 according to the character set encoding; or (b) string s2 is longer than string s1 and the contents of s1 and s2 up to the length of s1 are identical.

strcoll

```
int strcoll(const char *s1, const char *s2)
```

Compares lexicographically the strings s1 and s2. The function differs from strcmp by using information about the program's locale, as set by the function *setlocale*.

strcpy

```
char *strcpy(char *s1, const char *s2)
```

Overwrite the original content of the string s1 with the content of the string s2. A pointer to the first character of s1 is returned.

strcspn

```
size_t strcspn(const char *s1, const char *s2)
```

Compares string s1 with string s2 and returns the length in characters for which s1 consists of characters not found in s2.

strerror

```
char *strerror(int n)
```

Returns a pointer to the implementation defined string corresponding to the error number n. Useful for finding what the values in errno mean.

strlen

```
size_t strlen(const char *s)
```

Return the number of characters in the string s, not including the terminating null character. The standard header file <stddef.h> contains a typedef for the type size_t specifying some size of unsigned integer object.

strncat

```
char *strncat(char *s1, const char *s2, size_t n)
```

Append the first n characters from the string s2 to the end of the string s1. If s2 contains fewer than n characters, only these are appended. A pointer to the first character of s1 is returned.

strncmp

```
int strncmp(const char *s1, const char *s2, size_t n)
```

Compares up to n characters of the two strings s1 and s2. Returns a negative integer if s1 is less than s2; zero if s1 equals s2; and a positive integer if s1 is greater than s2 (see strcmp). If either string contains fewer than n characters, the entire string is used.

strncpy

```
char *strncpy(char *s1, const char *s2, size..t n)
```

Overwrites the original content of string s1 with the first n characters of string s2. If s2 contains fewer than n characters, the entire string is used. A pointer to the first character of s1 is returned.

strpbrk

```
char *strpbrk(const char *s1, const char *s2)
```

Returns a pointer to the first character in s1 that matches any character in s2; otherwise it returns NULL.

strrchr

```
char *strrchr(const char *s, int c)
```

The string s is searched for the last occurrence of the character c. If c is found, the function returns a pointer to c in s; otherwise NULL is returned.

strxfrm

```
size_t strxfrm(char *s1, const char *s2, size_t n)
```

Transforms string s2 using information about the program's locale, as set by the function setlocale; strxfrm then writes up to n bytes of the transformed result into the string s1, and returns the length of the transformed string. The transformation is done so that if two strings return a given result when compared by `strcoll` before transformation, then they return the same result when compared by `strcmp` following the transformation.

The `mem...` functions manipulate objects as character arrays. Unlike the string functions, these operate on a region of memory and do not stop upon encountering a null character.

memchr

```
void *memchr(const void *r, int c, size_t n)
```

Searches the first n characters in region r for character c. It returns a pointer to the character if it is found; otherwise it returns NULL.

memcmp

```
int memcmp(const void *r1, const void *r2, size_t n)
```

Compares the first n characters of the region r1 and r2 character by character. If a character in r1 is greater than the corresponding character in r2 then it returns a number greater than zero; if a character in r1 is less than the corresponding character in r2 then it returns a number less than zero; otherwise it returns zero if both regions are identical.

memcpy

```
void *memcpy(void *r1, const void *r2, size_t n)
```

Copy the first n characters from region r2 into region r1. The behaviour of memcpy is undefined if the two regions overlap. A pointer to the first character of r1 is returned.

memmove

```
void *memmove(void *r1, const void *r2, size_t n)
```

Copy the first n characters from region r2 into region r1. Unlike memcpy, function memmove operates correctly even if the two regions overlap. A pointer to the first character of r1 is returned.

memset

```
void *memset(void *r, int c, size_t n)
```

Fills the first n bytes of the region pointed to by r with copies of the character c, and returns a pointer to r.

F.3 General utilities

The header file <stdlib.h> declares a number of types and macros and several functions of general applicability. The types and macros are as follows:

MACROS

RAND_MAX   The maximum value returned by the `rand` function (see below).

EXIT_SUCCESS   Value indicating that a program executed correctly.

EXIT_FAILUR   Value indicating that a program executed incorrectly.

TYPES

div_t   The type of the structure returned by `div`.

ldiv_t   The type of the structure returned by `ldiv`.

FUNCTIONS

abort

```
void abort(void)
```

Causes abnormal program termination as if by raising the SIGABRT signal. The implementation defines whether `abort` cleans up a program by flushing buffers or closing streams.

abs

```
int abs(int n)
```

Returns the absolute value (i.e. the distance from zero) of the integer n. The behaviour is undefined if the value cannot be represented; on 2's complement machines the most negative number has no positive equivalent.

atexit

```
int atexit(void (*func)(void))
```

`atexit` registers the function func to be executed when the program exits, providing a means of performing additional clean-up operations at program termination. The functions that are registered are called upon in reverse order of their registration. At least thirty-two such functions may be registered. Zero is returned for successful registration, and non-zero for failure.

atof

```
double atof(const char *s)
```

Converts the string referred to by s into a double procession floating number. It is equivalent to the call:

```
strtod(s, (char **)NULL)
```

atoi

```
int atoi(const char *s)
```

Converts the string referred to by s into an integer. It is equivalent to the call:

```
(int) strtol(s, (char **)NULL, 10)
```

atol

```
long int atol(const char *s)
```

Converts the string referred to by s into a long. It is equivalent to the call:

```
strtol(s, (char **)NULL, 10)
```

bsearch

```
void *bsearch(const void *key, const void *base,
    size_t n, size_t size,
    int (*cmp)(const void *arg1, const void *arg2))
```

Searches the array base[0], ... , base[n−1] for an item that matches *key. The items in the array must be in ascending order. n is the number of elements in the array and size is the size in bytes of an array item. The function cmp is used to compare the search key with table entries, and returns negative (zero, positive) if the first argument is less (equal, greater) than the second. bsearch returns a pointer to the array element for which there is a match, or NULL if none is found.

calloc

```
void *calloc(size_t n, size_t size)
```

Returns a pointer to a region of memory for n objects of size size bytes. If the request cannot be satisfied NULL is returned. The space is initialized to zero in every byte.

div

```
div_t div(int num, int den)
```

Divides the numerator num by the denominator den and returns a structure of type div_t. This structure consists of two int members named quot (the quotient from num/den), and rem (the remainder from num/den).

The quotient is positive if the signs of the arguments are the same; otherwise the sign of the quotient is negative. The sign of the remainder is the same as the sign of the numerator.

exit

```
void exit(int status)
```

Gracefully terminates a program. When called, exit performs the following actions: (a) calls all the functions registered through atexit in reverse order; (b) flushes all output stream buffers, closes the streams and removes all temporary files created by tmpfile; and (c) returns control to the environment providing an implementation defined status value. Successful termination is denoted by the status value zero or EXIT_SUCCESS; failure by EXIT_FAILURE.

free

```
void free(void *ptr)
```

Deallocates a region of memory previously allocated by malloc, calloc or realloc. The argument to free points to the block of memory to be released. It is an error to attempt to free store which was never allocated or has been released.

getenv

```
char *getenv(const char *name)
```

The environment itself can make information available to a program. This information is available in an implementation-defined environment list of string pairs – a name and its defined value. Function getenv searches this list for a name corresponding to the string pointed to by name and returns a pointer to the string that defines the corresponding value; otherwise it returns NULL.

labs

```
long int labs(long int n)
```

Returns the absolute value of its long integer argument. The behaviour is undefined if the value cannot be represented – on 2's complement machines the most negative number has no positive equivalent.

ldiv

```
ldiv_t ldiv(long int num, long int den)
```

Divides the numerator num by the denominator den and returns a structure of type ldiv_t. This structure consists of two long members named quot (the quotient from num/den) and rem (the remainder).

The quotient is positive if the signs of the arguments are the same; otherwise the sign of the quotient is negative. The sign of the remainder is the same as the sign of the numerator.

malloc

```
void *malloc(size_t size)
```

Allocate a region of memory of size bytes, and return a pointer to the block of memory. The pointer is aligned for any type of object. If the request cannot be satisfied, NULL is returned. The allocated space is unitialized.

qsort

```
void qsort(void *base, size_t n, size_t size,
           int (*cmp)(const void *, const void *))
```

Sorts into ascending order an array base[0], ... , base[n-1] objects of size size bytes. The function cmp is used to compare two elements from the array and returns negative (zero, positive) if the first argument is less (equal, greater) than the second.

rand

```
int rand(void)
```

Generates and returns a pseudo random integer in the range 0 to RAND_MAX, which is at least 32767.

realloc

```
void *realloc(void *ptr, size_t size)
```

Reallocates a block of memory which has been previously allocated with the functions calloc or malloc. Hence, realloc changes the size of the object pointed to by ptr, and returns a pointer to the new space, or NULL if the request cannot be satisfied.

The content of the new region is the same as the initial part of that pointed to by ptr up to the minimum of the original size and of the argument size. If size is larger than that of the ptr region, then the additional space is unitialized.

srand

```
void srand(unsigned int seed)
```

Establish an initial seed value for the sequence of pseudo random numbers generated by rand. If no call to srand is made before using rand, it is as if the seed were initialized to 1.

strtod

```
double strtod(const char *s, char **endp)
```

Converts the string pointed to by s to a double precision floating point number. Any leading whitespace in the string s is ignored. Following the whitespace characters is the character sequence representing the floating point value as defined in Section 3.1. Any unconverted suffix in s is pointed to by *endp unless strtod is called with endp as NULL.

strtol

```
long int strtol(const char *s, char **endp, int base)
```

Converts the string pointed to by s to a long integer. Any leading whitespace in the string s is ignored. Following the whitespace characters is the character sequence representing the long value as defined in Section 3.1. Any unconverted suffix in s is pointed to by *endp unless strtol is called with endp as NULL.

Base gives the base of the number being read, from 0 to 36 inclusive. If base is zero, then strtol expects a number in the form of a C integer constant (leading 0 implies octal, and leading 0x or 0X implies hexadecimal). If base is between 2 and 36, conversion is done assuming the input is written to that base. If the base exceeds 10, then the letters a–z and A–Z are given the values $10 - 35$ respectively. An explicit base 16 also permits a leading 0x or 0X.

strtoul

```
unsigned long strtoul(const char *s,
                      char **endp, int base)
```

Operates as per strtol except that the result is unsigned, and that no leading sign is permitted in string s.

system

```
int system(const char *prog)
```

Passes the string `prog` to the environment's command processor for execution. If `prog` is NULL then `system` returns zero if a command processor exists, otherwise it returns non-zero. If `prog` is not NULL, then `system` returns an implementation-dependent value.

F.4 Standard I/O functions

The input and output functions, types and macros are defined in the standard input/output header file <stdio.h>.

All input/output functions access a file or device through a `stream`. The library supports `text` streams and `binary` streams, which are identical on some systems. A text stream is a sequence of characters composed into lines terminated by '\n'. A binary stream is a sequence of bytes used, for example, to represent a program's internal data values (for example, a structure or an array), which when read will always compare equal to data written earlier to the same stream under the same implementation.

A stream is connected to a `file` by opening it. When the stream is closed, the connection is removed. Opening a file returns a pointer to an object of type FILE, which contains all the information required to access the file. When a program begins execution, three text streams called `stdin`, `stdout` and `stderr` are open.

The macros and types defined in <stdio.h> are:

MACROS

_IOFBF	fully buffered stream
_IOLBF	line buffered stream
_IONBF	unbuffered stream
BUFSIZE	default buffer size for stream
EOF	end of file indicator
FILENAME_MAX	maximum filename length
FOPEN_MAX	maximum number of simultaneously open files
L_tmpnam	maximum temporary filename length
SEEK_CUR	seek from current position
SEEK_END	seek from the end of a file
SEEK_SET	seek from the beginning of a file
stderr	pointer to the standard error stream
stdin	pointer to the standard input stream
stdout	pointer to the standard output stream

TMP_MAX	maximum number calls to `tmpnam`

TYPES

FILE	Stream descriptor
fpos_t	Current position in a file

clearerr

```
void clearerr(FILE *fp)
```

Resets any error indication on the file identified by the file pointer fp (see also ferror).

fclose

```
int fclose(FILE *fp)
```

Closes the file identified by the file pointer fp. All internal data buffers are emptied and freed. If an error occurs, fclose returns EOF; otherwise zero is returned.

feof

```
int feof(FILE *fp)
```

Returns non-zero if the file identified by the file pointer fp is truly at the end of file; otherwise return zero.

ferror

```
int ferror(FILE *fp)
```

Return non-zero if an error condition has occurred while reading or writing the file identified by the file pointer fp; otherwise return zero. Function clearerr can be used to reset the error condition.

fflush

```
int fflush(FILE *fp)
```

Flushes any internal data buffers for the file identified by the file pointer fp. The file should have been opened for output. Function fflush returns EOF if an error is detected; otherwise zero is returned.

fgetc

```
int fgetc(FILE *fp)
```

Returns the next character from the file identified by the file pointer fp, which must be opened for input. If an error occurs or the end of file condition is determined, fgetc returns EOF.

fgetpos

```
int fgetpos(FILE *fp, fpos_t *pos)
```

Copies the current position for the file stream fp into the area referred to by pos.

This value may be subsequently used by the library function fsetpos. The function returns non-zero if an error occurs.

fgets

```
char *fgets(char *buffer, int n, FILE *fp)
```

Characters are read from the file identified by the file pointer fp which must be opened for input. The reading continues until the end of file is reached, until a newline character is read, or until n−1 characters have been input. The characters are stored in successive locations of the character array buffer, and a terminating null character is appended.

If a newline character is read, then it is stored in the array. If the end of file is encountered before any characters have been read or an error occurs, then the function returns the NULL pointer. If the input operation succeeds, then a pointer to the first character of buffer is returned.

fopen

```
FILE *fopen(const char *filename, const char *mode)
```

Function fopen opens the named file according to the indicated access mode. If the function is successful, then a FILE pointer is returned and used in subsequent I/O operations; otherwise the value NULL is returned. Both arguments to fopen are null-terminated character strings. Permissible values for the mode argument are:

"r"   open an existing file for reading;

"w"   truncate an existing file or create a new file for writing;

"a"   create a new file or append to an existing file for writing;

"r+"   open an existing file for both reading and writing, positioned at the beginning of the file;

"w+"   truncate an existing file or create a new file both for reading or writing, positioned at the beginning of this empty file;

"a+"   create a new file or append to an existing file both for reading or writing, positioned at the end of the file.

If the mode includes the suffix b, as in "rb" or "w+b", then the file is opened as a binary stream.

fprintf

```
int fprintf(FILE *fp, const char *format, ... )
```

Performs formatted output to the file identified by the file pointer fp. See printf for details.

fputc

```
int fputc(int c, FILE *fp)
```

Writes the character c to the file identified by the file pointer fp. Function fputc returns c if successful; otherwise returns EOF.

fputs

```
int fputs(char *s, FILE *fp)
```

Writes the characters in the null-terminated string s to the file identified by the file pointer fp. If any errors occur, fputs returns EOF; otherwise a non-negative value is returned.

fread

```
size_t fread(char *buffer, size_t size,
    size_t n, FILE *fp)
```

Reads a block of binary data from the file identified by the file pointer fp into buffer. The number of data items read is n, each of size bytes. The actual number of items read is returned by fread. If this value is positive and less than n, then that number of items was read before encountering the end of file. If fread returns 0, either the immediate end of file or an error has occurred.

freopen

```
FILE *freopen(const char *filename,
    const char *mode, FILE *fp)
```

Closes the file presently associated with the file pointer fp and open a new file with name filename and mode (see fopen). If the call to freopen is successful, the fp is returned; otherwise NULL is returned.

fscanf

```
int fscanf(FILE *fp, const char *format, ... )
```

Performs formatted input from the file identified by the file pointer fp. See scanf for details.

fseek

```
int fseek(FILE *fp, long offset, int origin)
```

Positions the file identified by the file pointer fp to a point that is offset bytes relative to some place dependent upon the value of origin. If origin is SEEK_SET, then the position is relative to the beginning of the file. If origin is SEEK_CUR, the position is relative to the current file position. If *origin* is SEEK_END, then the position is relative to the end of file. If the operation is successful, fseek returns zero; otherwise fseek returns non-zero.

fsetpos

```
int fsetpos(FILE *fp, const fpos t *pos)
```

Positions the stream fp at the position *pos returned by a previous call to fgetpos. The function returns non-zero if an error occurs.

ftell

```
long ftell(FILE *fp)
```

Returns the relative offset in bytes of the current position in the file identified by the file pointer fp. The value −1L is returned as an error indicator.

fwrite

```
size_t fwrite(const void *buffer, size_t size,
        size_t n, FILE *fp)
```

Writes a block of binary data from `buffer` to the file identified by the file pointer `fp`. The number of data items written is n, each of `size` bytes. The actual number of items written is returned by `fwrite`. If an error occurs, `fwrite` returns a value less than n.

getc

```
int getc(FILE *fp)
```

Reads and return the next character from the file identified by the file pointer `fp`. The value EOF is returned if the end of file is reached or if an error occurs. `getc` is usually implemented as a macro.

getchar

```
int getchar()
```

Reads and returns the next character from the standard input file `stdin`. The value EOF is returned if the end of file is reached or if an error occurs. `getchar` is normally implemented as a macro.

gets

```
char *gets(char *buffer)
```

Reads characters from the standard input file `stdin` into the buffer until a newline is read or the end of file is reached. If an error occurs, or if no characters are read because the end of file is immediate, then function `gets` returns NULL; otherwise `buffer` is returned. If the input is terminated because the newline symbol is read, the newline character is not stored in the buffer (see also `fgets`).

perror

```
void perror(const char *s)
```

Writes to `stderr` an error message asociated with the global error integer variable `errno`. The error report is formed as if by:

```
fprintf(stderr, "%s: %s\n", s, "error message")
```

printf

```
int printf(const char *format, ... )
```

Writes the arguments to the standard output stream `stdout` according to the `format` string. Function `printf` returns a negative value if an error occurs; otherwise `printf` returns the number of characters written.

The argument list is composed of comma separated expressions. The expressions are evaluated and converted according to the conversion specifications in the `format` string. The conversion specifications should agree in number and in type with the arguments. Characters in the format string which are not part of a conversion specification are copied unaltered to the output. A conversion specification is introduced by the percent symbol (%). Following the percent sign, a conversion specification is constructed from:

  flag characters

  field width

  precision

  long size specification

  conversion specifier

Only the percent sign and the *conversion specifier* are obligatory. The remaining elements are optional *modifiers* but should appear in the given order, if present. The permissible conversion operations are the single characters c, d, e, E, f, g, G, i, n, o, p, s, u, x, X or %. The conversion operation % is used as the literal representation for the percent sign, which is otherwise reserved. The effect of these conversion operations is summarized in Table F.1, then detailed later in this section.

Table F.1

Character	Data object	Action
c	int	The argument is displayed as a single character
d, i	int	Signed decimal conversion of an int or a long
e, E	double	Signed decimal floating point conversion in scientific notation
f	double	Signed decimal floating point conversion
g, G	double	Signed decimal floating point conversion using either e (or E) or f conversion whichever requires the least space
n	int *	The number of characters written thus far by this call to printf is written into the integer argument
o	int	Unsigned octal conversion
p	void *	Display a pointer value
s	char *	The argument is displayed as a string
u	int	Unsigned decimal conversion of an unsigned
x, X	int	Unsigned hexadecimal conversion using a–f or A–F as appropriate

When an argument is printed, the place where it is output is called its field. The number of characters in the field is called the *field width*. If the optional field width in the conversion specification is omitted, the minimum number of character places is used in the conversion. To demonstrate some simple uses of printf, consider the following declarations and calls. In these and further examples, the output characters are delimited by the symbols [and] to indicate the extent of the field:

```
int    j = 45, k = -123;
float x = 12.34;
char   c = 'W';
char *m = "Hello";
```

```
printf("No arguments")      No arguments
printf("Tax is 10%%")       Tax is 10%
printf("[%d]", j)           [45]
printf("[%d]", k)           [-123]
printf("[%f]", x)           [12.340000]
printf("[%c]", c)           [W]
printf("[%s]", m)           [Hello]
```

The optional modifiers in a conversion specification affect the meaning of the main conversion operation. They are summarized in Table F.2. If no modifiers are present, certain defaults occur. For example, the format %f always defaults to six decimal places of output. These defaults and the effect of the modifiers are detailed with the conversion operations.

The main conversion operations are now discussed in detail. The illustrative examples use the symbol ƀ to represent blanks (spaces) in the output.

CONVERSION OPERATION c

An int or unsigned int argument is printed as a single character which should represent a symbol from the valid character set. The minimum field width and '−' modifiers can be meaningfully employed with this conversion (see Table F.3).

```
char c = 'W';
```

CONVERSION OPERATION d

One argument of integral type (long/short if the long/short size specification is given) is consumed. A signed decimal conversion of the value is performed. A sequence of decimal digits representing the number is displayed. If no field width is given, the default is the least number of characters necessary. If the value requires fewer positions than that given by the field width, it is right justified in the field and padded on the left with spaces. If a field width is insufficient to display the converted value, then the default field width is assumed. The conversion modifier '0' uses leading zeros rather than spaces. The '−' modifier left justifies the value in the field. The '+' modifier ensures that a plus or minus symbol is output (Table F.4).

```
int      j = 45, k = -123;
long int jj = 1234567890;
```

Table F.2

Modifier	Description
−	The value to be displayed is left justified in the field
+	The value will always be displayed with a numeric sign (only for the conversion operations d, e, E, f, g, G and i)
space	Non-negative numbers are to be preceded by a blank space (only for the conversion operations d, e, E, f, g, G and i)
#	Integers displayed in octal format are preceded by a leading 0. Integers displayed in hexadecimal format are preceded by a leading 0x (or 0X). Floating point conversions always guarantee that the decimal point is displayed. For g and G, trailing zeros are removed
0 (zero)	The zero character is used as the padding to the left of the converted value, rather than with leading spaces
field width	The minimum field width, expressed as a decimal integer constant. If this minimum field width is insufficient to display the value, then that which is necessary is used. If this field width is specified by an asterisk symbol (*), the field width is given by the next argument to printf, which should be an integer
precision	The precision is expressed as a decimal integer constant and is used to indicate the maximum number of digits to the right of the decimal point in an e, E, f, g or G conversion. When used with a d, i, o, u, x, or X conversion, it specifies the minimum number of digits. When used with an s conversion, the precision determines the maximum number of characters to be displayed. If the precision is specified by an asterisk symbol, then the precision is provided by the next argument to printf which should be an integer
h	The short size specification is used in conjunction with the conversion operations d, i, o, u, x and X and indicates that the argument is a short int or an unsigned short int
l	The long size specification is used in conjunction with the conversion operations d, i, o, u, x and X and indicates that the argument is a long int or an unsigned long int
L	When used before an e, E, f, g or G conversion, it indicates that the corresponding argument is a long double

Table F.3

Function call	Output
printf("[%c]", c)	[W]
printf("[%3c]", c)	[ØØW]
printf("[%-4c]", c)	[WØØØ]

Table F.4

Function call	Output
printf("[%d]", k)	[-123]
printf("[%4d]", j)	[45]
printf("[%-5d]", j)	[45]
printf("[%05d]", j)	[00045]
printf("[%2d]", k)	[-123]
printf("[%+4d]", j)	[+45]
printf("[%ld]", jj)	[1234567890]
printf("[%+05d]", j)	[+0045]

CONVERSION OPERATIONS e AND E

Signed decimal floating point conversion is performed on an argument of type double. An argument of type float is automatically converted to type double in the usual way. Thus these conversion operations are equally applicable to variables of type float and double. The conversion produces a value in scientific notation form − d.dddddde + dd (for e conversion) or − d.ddddddE + dd (for E conversion). The leading minus sign is optional. The precision specifies the number of decimal digits following the decimal point. If no precision is given, a default value of 6 is assumed. If the precision is given as 0, no fractional value is present nor is the decimal point (unless the '#' modifier is used). The exponent is always signed and consists of at least two decimal digits (Table F.5).

```
float  x = 12.345;
double y = -678.9;
```

Table F.5

Function call	Output
printf("[%e]", x)	[1.234500e+01]
printf("[%E]", x)	[1.234500E+01]
printf("[%14.4e]", x)	[1.2345e+01]
printf("[%-12.1E]", y)	[-6.8E+02]
printf("[%+12.2E]", x)	[+1.24E+01]
printf("[%.2e]", y)	[-6.79e+02]
printf("[%10.0e]", x)	[1e+01]
printf("[%#10.0e]", x)	[1.e+01]

CONVERSION OPERATION f

A signed decimal floating point conversion is performed on a value of type double (or float). The output value consists of a sequence of decimal digits with an imbedded decimal point. At least one digit appears before the decimal point. The number of digits in the fractional part is determined by the precision. If no precision is given, the default is six decimal places. If the precision is given as 0, no fractional value is present in the output, nor is the decimal point (unless the '#' modifier is used) (see Table F.6).

```
float   x = 12.345;
double  y = -678.9;
```

Table F.6

Function call	Output
printf("[%f]", y)	[-678.900000]
printf("[%-10.2f]", x)	[12.35ƀƀƀƀƀ]
printf("[%+8.1f]", x)	[ƀƀƀ+12.4]
printf("[%.2f]", y)	[-678.90]
printf("[%08.2f]", x)	[00012.35]
printf("[%+06.1f]", x)	[+012.4]
printf("[%#4.0f]", x)	[ƀ12.]

CONVERSION OPERATIONS g AND G

A signed decimal floating point conversion is performed on a value of type double (or float). The conversion is as for either the f or e (or E when G is used) conversions whichever is the shortest (see Table F.7).

```
float   x = 12.345;
double  y = -234567.89;
```

Table F.7

Function call	Output
printf("[%g]", x)	[12.345000]
printf("[%G]", x)	[12.345000]
printf("[%.1g]", y)	[-2.4e+05]
printf("[%.1G]", y)	[-2.4E+05]

CONVERSION OPERATION i

Same as conversion operation d.

CONVERSION OPERATION n

This conversion specification takes a pointer to an integer argument into which it writes the number of characters printed thus far by the present printf call. It does not affect the string generated by printf (see Table F.8).

```
int k = 45;
int nchar;
```

Table F.8

Function call	Output
printf("[%d]%n", k, &nchar)	[45]
printf("[%d]", nchar)	[4]

CONVERSION OPERATION o

The argument, which should be of integral type, is output as an unsigned octal value. The value is displayed as a sequence of octal digits in a minimum field unless the field width specification is given. No leading 0 prefixes the octal value unless the '#' modifier is used (see Table F.9).

```
int          k = 45;
unsigned int j = 0123;
```

Table F.9

Function call	Output
printf("[%o]", j)	[123]
printf("[%5o]", k)	[ＢＢＢ55]
printf("[%#6o]", j)	[ＢＢ0123]
printf("[%-4o]", k)	[55ＢＢ]

CONVERSION OPERATION p

This conversion sequence prints, in a system-dependent manner, a void * pointer object. For example, in a machine with segmented architecture this value may be displayed in the form segment:offset (see Table F.10).

```
int k = 45;
int *ptr = &k;
```

Table F.10

Function call	Output
printf("[%p]", ptr)	[115E:1FFE]

CONVERSION OPERATION s

The argument is printed as a string of symbols. The argument is expected to be of type pointer to char. If no field width is specified, the string is displayed without change, otherwise the string is displayed right justified in the field. If a precision specification p is given, then the first p characters of the string or the string itself, whichever is the shorter is displayed. The only appropriate modifier is '−' which left justifies the string in the field (see Table F.11).

```
char *mess = "Hello";
```

Table F.11

Function call	Output
printf("[%s]", mess)	[Hello]
printf("[%8s]", mess)	[␣␣␣Hello]
printf("[%-8s]", mess)	[Hello␣␣␣]
printf("[%6.2s]", mess)	[␣␣␣␣He]
printf("[%-10.6s]", mess)	[Hello␣␣␣␣␣]

CONVERSION OPERATION u

The u operation performs unsigned decimal conversion of an unsigned int. A sequence of decimal digits representing the value of the argument is displayed. The field is as short as possible unless a field width modifier is present (see Table F.12).

```
unsigned int t = 123;
```

Table F.12

Function call	Output
printf("[%u]", t)	[123]
printf("[%6u]", t)	[␣␣␣123]
printf("[%-4u]", t)	[123␣]

CONVERSION OPERATIONS x AND X

An argument of integral type is printed as an unsigned hexadecimal value. The conversion operation x uses the hexadecimal digits 0–9a–f, while the X operation uses the hexadecimal digits 0–9A–F. If the '#' modifier is used, then the prefix 0x for the x operation (or 0X for the X operation) is prepended (see Table F.13).

```
int k = 0xf4;
```

putc

```
int putc(int c, FILE *fp)
```

Writes the single character c to the file identified by the file pointer fp. If an error occurs, putc returns EOF; otherwise the value of the written character is returned.

Table F.13

Function call	Output
printf("[%x]", k)	[f4]
printf("[%X]", k)	[F4]
printf("[%6x]", k)	[ﬀﬀﬀf4]
printf("[%#6X]", k)	[ﬀﬀ0XF4]

putchar

        int putchar(int c)

Writes the single character c to the standard output. If an error occurs, putchar returns EOF; otherwise the value of the written character is returned. Normally, putchar is implemented as a macro.

puts

        int puts(const char *buffer)

Writes the null-terminated character string in buffer to the standard output. A newline symbol is automatically written following the last character in the buffer (see also fputs). If an error occurs, puts returns EOF; otherwise a non-negative value is returned.

remove

        int remove(const char *filename)

Removes the named file. Subsequent attempts to open the file will fail. This function returns non-zero if the operation is unsuccessful.

rename

        int rename(const char *oldname, const char *newname)

Changes the name of a file from the string pointed to by oldname to the string pointed to by newname. The function returns non-zero if the operation is unsuccessful. If rename fails then the original file is unaffected. If newname refers to an existing file, then the behaviour is implementation-dependent.

rewind

        void rewind(FILE *fp)

Resets the file indicated by the file pointer fp back to the beginning of the file. It is equivalent to:

```
(void) fseek(fp, 0L, SEEK_SET);
clearerr(fp);
```

scanf

        int scanf(const char *format, ...)

Function scanf reads items from the standard input according to the format string. The arguments after the format string must all be pointers. Converted values read from the standard input are stored in the locations referenced by the pointers. Function scanf returns the number of successful assignments. If this number is less than the number of arguments given to scanf, the input operation has prematurely terminated either because end of file has been reached or because an error has occurred. If end of file occurs before any assignments have been performed, scanf returns EOF.

The *format* string is a picture of the expected input, and may contain:

1. Whitespace characters, which match optional whitespace characters in the input stream. One or more whitespace characters in the format string are considered as one. This equivalent single whitespace character matches any number of whitespace characters in the input. The first non-whitespace character remains in the input as the next character to be read.

2. Non-whitespace characters, other than the percent symbol (%), which must match exactly the next input character. If there is no match, the operation is terminated and the failed input character remains in the input stream as the next available character.

3. A conversion specification which is introduced by a percent symbol (%). A conversion specification is constructed from:

        percent symbol
        assignment suppression symbol
        field width
        short or long size specification
        conversion operation

    Only the percent symbol and the conversion operation are obligatory. The remaining modifiers are optional but should appear in the given order, if present. The conversion operations are, with one exception, a single character from: c, d, e, E, f, g, G, o, s, u, x, X, % or [. The exception is the operation [, which is followed by a series of characters ending in]. The effect of all these conversion operations is summarized in Table F.14.

Except for character input and the [conversion operation, an input field consists of a sequence of non-whitespace characters, appropriate to the conversion operation. The first inappropriate character terminates the field or the field width is exhausted (if specified), whichever comes first. Except for the same two exceptions, a field may be preceded by a sequence of whitespace characters.

The optional modifiers in a conversion specification alter the meaning of the main conversion operation. The effect of these modifiers is summarized in Table F.15.

The main conversion operations are now discussed in detail. Each subsection discusses the operation and the effect of any modifier. The symbol ƀ is used in the examples to denote a blank or space symbol.

Table F.14

Character	Action
c	Read and assign one or more characters
d, i	Signed decimal conversion and assignment to a short, int or a long
e, f, g	Signed decimal floating point conversion and assignment to a float, double or long double
n	Returns as an integer the number of characters read by this call thus far
o	Unsigned octal conversion and assignment to a short, int or a long
p	Read a void * pointer previously written using the %p conversion by the printf family
s	Read and assign a string
u	Unsigned decimal conversion and assignment to an unsigned int, unsigned short int or an unsigned long int
x, X	Unsigned hexadecimal conversion and assignment to a short, int or a long
%	A percent symbol is expected in the input
[	A string of characters from the input stream is read and assigned. The permissible set of scanned characters are enclosed between the [and a matching] symbols. If the first character in the list is a circumflex (^), the scanning characters are any not drawn from the list

Table F.15

Modifier	Description
*	The assignment suppression flag. Characters are read from the input and processed in the normal way for the conversion operation, but no assignment is performed. No argument to scanf is used
field width	The maximum field width, expressed as an unsigned decimal integer constant which is not zero
size specification	The size specification is either the character 'h' (meaning short), or the character 'l' (meaning long). Both may be used in conjunction with the d, i, n, o, u and x conversions, and specifies that the argument is a pointer to a short or a pointer to a long (respectively). When used with the e, f or g conversions, the character 'l' specifies that the argument is a pointer to a double rather than a pointer to a float. The character 'L' in conjunction with the conversions e, f or g specifies a long double pointer argument

CONVERSION OPERATION c

One or more characters are read and stored at the location(s) addressed by the pointer to char argument. Note that the c conversion does not skip over any initial whitespace characters. If a field width is given, then that number of characters is read and stored. The pointer argument is considered to be the address of an array of characters in which the input is stored. Note that no null terminator is appended to the stored input characters (see Table F.16).

```
char ch1, ch2, text[6];
```

Table F.16

Function call	Input	Effect
scanf("%c", &ch1)	ABC123	ch1 = 'A'
scanf("%c%c", &ch1, &ch2)	AØBC	ch1 = 'A', ch2 = ' '
scanf("%*4c")	ABC123	skip ABC1
scanf("%2c", text)	ABC123	text[0] = 'A',
Note no address operator with text.		text[1] = 'B'

CONVERSION OPERATION d

Signed decimal conversion and assignment to an int or to a short (if h size specification given) or to a long (if l size specification given) (see Table F.17).

```
short sx;
int   xx;
long  lx;
```

Table F.17

Function call	Input	Effect
scanf("%d", &xx)	ØØØ123Ø	xx = 123
scanf("%2d", &xx)	1234	xx = 12
scanf("%*2d%d", &xx)	1234ØØ	xx = 34
scanf("%hd", &sx)	ØØ-12A	sx = -12
scanf("%ld", &lx)	Ø+123Ø	lx = 123
scanf("%d/%ld", &xx, &lx)	12/34ØØ	xx = 12, lx = 34

CONVERSION OPERATIONS e, f, g

Signed decimal floating point conversion. The conversion e, f and g expect an argument which is a pointer to a float. The same conversions preceded with the long size modifier 'l' expect a pointer to a double argument. A preceding long size modifier 'L' specifies a long double. All these operations accept a floating point value. The form of a floating point value is an optional sign, zero or more decimal digits, an optional decimal point, and zero or more decimal digits. These formats may then be followed by the letter 'e' or 'E', an optional sign and zero or more decimal digits (see Table F.18).

```
float  x;
double y;
```

Table F.18

Function call	Input	Effect
scanf("%f", &x)	ƀƀ12.34ƀ	x = 12.34
scanf("%lf", &y)	+1.23AB	y = 1.23
scanf("%*f%e", &x)	ƀƀ−6.2ƀƀ1e+1	x = 10.0
scanf("%f", &x)	ƀƀ2ƀ	x = 2.0
scanf("%2f%e", &x, &y)	1234A	x = 12.0, y = 34.0
scanf("%le", &y)	1.ƀ	y = 1.0
scanf("%2f%lg", &x, &y)	1.79ƀ	x = 1.0, y = 79.0

CONVERSION OPERATION i

Decimal conversion and assignment to an int or to a short (h) or to a long (l); leading 0 implies an octal and leading 0x or 0X implies hexadecimal (see conversion operation d).

CONVERSION OPERATION n

Write into the corresponding argument the number of characters that scanf has read up to this point. No data is input with this conversion.

CONVERSION OPERATION o

Unsigned octal conversion and assignment to an int or to a short (if h size specification given) or to a long (if l size specification given). A leading zero in the input stream is not necessary (see Table F.19).

```
short sx;
int   xx;
long  lx;
```

Table F.19

Function call	Input	Effect
scanf("%o", &xx)	ƀƀƀ17ƀ	xx = 15
scanf("%2o%h2o", &xx, &sx)	1234ƀ	xx = 10, sx = 28
scanf("%*3o%lo", &lx)	74117A	lx = 15

CONVERSION OPERATION p

Read a pointer value as produced by the %p conversion of the printf family. Details are system-dependent.

CONVERSION OPERATION s

Read a string of characters and assign to the argument which must be of type pointer to char. Any leading whitespace characters in the input are ignored. Non-whitespace characters are input until the first occurrence of a whitespace character, or until the maximum number of characters have been read if a field width is specified. The characters are stored in the array and terminated with the null character (see Table F.20).

```
char tl[10], t2[12];
```

Table F.20

Function call	Input	Effect
scanf("%s", tl)	␣␣ABC␣	tl = "ABC"
scanf("%s %s", tl, t2)	␣AB␣␣CDE␣	tl = "AB", t2 = "CDE"
scanf("%4s", tl)	␣␣ABCDEF	tl = "ABCD"
scanf("%*4s%s", t2)	␣␣ABCDEF␣	t2 = "EF"
scanf("%1s", tl)	␣␣XYZ␣	tl = "X"

CONVERSION OPERATION u

Perform unsigned decimal conversion and assign to an argument which must be of type pointer to unsigned (or pointers to unsigned short or unsigned long for size specifications 'h' and 'l'). Leading whitespace symbols are ignored. Characters are read until the first occurrence of a non-digit or until the maximum field width has been read (see Table F.21).

```
unsigned int ux;
```

Table F.21

Function call	Input	Effect
scanf("%u", &ux)	␣␣123␣␣	ux = 123
scanf("%2u", &ux)	␣␣23␣␣	ux = 12
scanf("%*2u%u", &ux)	␣␣123␣␣	ux = 3

CONVERSION OPERATION x

Unsigned hexadecimal conversion and assignment to an int or to a short (if h size specification given) or to a long (if l size specification given). The conversion accepts 0—9a—fA—F as valid hexadecimal digits. Leading whitespace is ignored. Hexadecimal digits are read until a non-hexadecimal digit appears in the input, or until the maximum field width has been used. Leading 0x or 0X is not necessary, but if present are counted toward the field width (see Table F.22).

```
int xx;
```

Table F.22

Function call	Input	Effect
scanf("%x", &xx)	◖◖◖1F◖	xx = 31
scanf("%2X", &xx)	◖FFF◖	xx = 255
scanf("%*2x%x", &xx)	◖FFF◖	xx = 15

CONVERSION OPERATION [

Read a string of characters and assign to the argument which must be of type pointer to char. The input characters are stored in the array and null-terminated. The set of characters between [and the matching] denote those that may be read as part of the input. The first input character not a member of the set terminates the input operation. Leading whitespace characters are not skipped by this operation. If the first character following the [is the circumflex symbol ˆ, then the input is any character other than those in the set (see Table F.23).

```
char t1[10], t2[12];
```

Table F.23

Function call	Input	Effect
scanf("%[ABC]", t1)	ABAB◖	t1 = "ABAB"
scanf("%[ABC]", t1)	◖◖ABAB◖	t1 = ""
scanf("%[ABC]", t2)	ABACD	t2 = "ABAC"
scanf("%[ˆABC]", t1)	ABAB◖	t1 = ""
scanf("%[ˆABC]", t1)	◖◖ABAB◖	t1 = "◖◖"

setbuf

```
void setbuf(FILE *fp, char *buffer)
```

When function fopen and freopen open a stream they automatically establish a buffer for it. This buffer is BUFSIZE bytes long, as defined in <stdio.h>. Function setbuf changes the buffer for the stream referenced by fp from its default to the argument buffer. This function can only be used after fp has been opened and before any data has been read or written.

If buffer is set to NULL, then fp is unbuffered.

setvbuf

```
int setvbuf(FILE *fp, char *buffer,
        int mode, size_t size)
```

When functions fopen and freopen open a stream they automatically establish a buffer for it. This buffer is BUFSIZE bytes long, as defined in <stdio.h>. Function setvbuf changes the buffer for the stream referenced by fp from its default to the argument `buffer` and sets its length to `size`. Argument `mode` defines the manner of the stream buffering using the macros _IOFBF, _IOLBF and _IONBF. This function can only be used after `fp` has been opened and before any data has been read or written.

`setvbuf` returns non-zero for any error occurring.

sprintf

```
int sprintf(char *buffer, const char *format, ... )
```

The values of the arguments are converted according to the `format` string (see `printf`) and are placed in the character array pointed to by `buffer`. The character string in `buffer` is null-terminated. Otherwise, the function operates in a manner similar to `printf` (see Table F.24).

```
int   jj = 45;
char *m = "Hello";
char text[80];
```

Table F.24

Function call	Effect
sprintf(text, "[%d]", jj)	text = "[45]"
sprintf(text, "[%-8s]", m)	text = "[Helloɓɓɓ]"

sscanf

```
int sscanf(const char *buffer, const char *format, ... )
```

Values as specified by the `format` string are input from the character array `buffer` and stored in the arguments. Otherwise, function `sscanf` operates in a manner similar to `scanf`.

```
int   jj;
char *m = "Hello";
char tl[10];
```

Table F.25

Function call	Effect
sscanf("45", "%d", &jj)	jj = 45
sscanf("first second", "%s", tl)	tl = "first"
sscanf(m, "%2s", tl)	tl = "He"

tmpfile

```
FILE *tmpfile(void)
```

Creates a temporary binary file, opened for update, and returns a pointer to the stream for that file. The file is removed automatically when it is closed or when the program ends. The function returns NULL if it could not create the file.

tmpnam

```
char *tmpnam(char *name)
```

Constructs a unique file name and stores the string in name and returns the address of name as the function value. The string name must have space for at least L_tmpnam characters. A different name is produced each time tmpnam is called; at most TMP_MAX different names are guaranteed during program execution.

If the actual argument is NULL, then tmpnam stores the file name in an internal static array and returns a pointer to that array.

ungetc

```
int ungetc(int c, FILE *fp)
```

The character c is pushed back on to the file identified by the file pointer fp. The next call to an input function will then read this same character. Only one character may be put back into a file. Between two calls to ungetc, there must be at least one read operation on that file. Function ungetc returns the character c if successful; otherwise ungetc returns EOF.

vfprintf

```
int vfprintf(FILE *fp, const char *format,
    va_list args)
```

Performs formatted output to the file identified by the file pointer fp. See vprintf for details.

vprintf

```
int vprintf(const char *format, va_list args)
```

Function vprintf is equivalent to the function printf except that the variable list of arguments associated with the latter is replaced by args which will have been initialized by va_start and perhaps calls to va_arg. See Appendix F.6 for <stdarg.h>, and Section 10.4.

The following example prepares and delivers a multi-argument error message.

```
void fatal(char *format, ...)
{
  va_list args;

  va_start(args, format);
  vprintf(format, args);
  va_end(args);
}
```

vsprintf

```
int vsprintf(char *buffer, const char *format,
    va_list args)
```

The values of the arguments are converted according to the format string and placed in the character array buffer. See sprintf and vprintf for details.

F.5 Mathematical functions

The mathematical functions are declared by the library header file <math.h>. For all the functions a domain error occurs if an input argument is outwith the domain over which the function is defined (for example, taking the square root of a negative value). If this occurs, errno (defined in <errno.h>) is set to the constant EDOM (defined in <math.h>), and the function returns a result that is implementation-dependent.

For all functions a range error occurs if the result of the function cannot be represented by a double. In this case errno is set to the constant ERANGE (defined in <math.h>), and the function returns the value ±HUGE VAL (defined in <math.h>) with correct sign.

In the following, arguments x and y are of type double, n is of type int, and all the functions return a double. Trigonometric functions operate with radian values.

acos(x)	trigonometric arc cosine of x, the result expressed in radians between 0 and Π.
asin(x)	trigonometric arc sine of x, the result expressed in radians between − Π/2 and Π/2.
atan(x)	trigonometric arc tangent of x, the result expressed in radians between − Π/2 and Π/2.
atan2(x, y)	trigonometric arc tangent of x/y, the result expressed in radians between − Π and Π.
ceil(x)	returns the floating point equivalent of the integer value not less than x.
cos(x)	trigonometric cosine of x, where x is expressed in radians.
cosh(x)	hyperbolic cosine of x.
exp(x)	exponential of x.
fabs(x)	absolute value of x.
floor(x)	returns the floating point equivalent of the largest integer not greater than x.
fmod(x, y)	floating point remainder of x/y with the same sign as x. If y is zero the result is implementation-defined.
frexp(x, int *exp)	partitions the double vale x into its *mantissa* and *exponent* parts. It returns the mantissa m such that $0.5 <= m < 1$ or m = 0. The exponent is placed in the area pointed to by exp.

`ldexp(x, n)`	computes x multiplied by 2 raised to the power n.
`log(x)`	natural logarithm.
`log10(x)`	logarithm of x to the base 10.
`modf(x, double *ip)`	splits the argument x into its integral and fractional parts (each having the same sign as x). It stores the integral part in `*ip` and returns the fractional part.
`pow(x, y)`	computes x to the power y.
`sin(x)`	trigonometric sine of x, where x is expressed in radians.
`sinh(x)`	hyperbolic sine of x.
`sqrt(x)`	square root of x.
`tan(x)`	trigonometric tangent of x, where x is expressed in radians.
`tanh(x)`	hyperbolic tangent of x.

F.6 Variable argument lists

The header file `<stdarg.h>` declares and defines routines that are used to traverse a variable length function argument list. It declares the type `va_list`, and the functions `va_start`, `va_arg` and `va_end`. Generally these operations are implemented by macros.

Before any attempt is made to access a variable argument list, `va_start` must be called. It is defined as:

```
void va_start(va_list ap, lastarg)
```

The macro initializes ap for subsequent use by `va_arg` and `va_end`. The second argument is the identifier naming the rightmost parameter of the calling function.

Following initialization, macro `va_arg` can be used to sequentially access the anonymous arguments of the calling function. It is effectively defined as:

```
type va_arg(va_list ap, type)
```

Each call to this macro returns the value of the subsequent argument. The second argument to this macro is the name of the type of the required argument and is the type of the value returned. The macro modifies ap for further calls.

The macro:

```
void va_end(va_list ap)
```

must be called once following processing of the variable argument list. This must be done before the calling function returns to ensure proper cleanup of the environment.

F.7 Non-local jumps

The declarations in `<setjmp.h>` provide the elements that perform non-local jumps. The header file contains the type `jmp_buf`, the macro `setjmp` and the function `longjmp`:

```
int setjmp(jmp_buf env)
```

The macro `setjmp` copies the current environment into `env` for use with `longjmp`. `Setjmp` returns zero when called directly and non-zero for a subsequent call of `longjmp`. The actual value returned by `setjmp` is established by the `longjmp` call. The proper use of `setjmp` is in the conditional expressions associated with `switch`, `if` and loop statements:

```
if(setjmp(environment) == 0)
    /* direct call */
else
    /* call from longjmp */
```

Function `longjmp` restores the state saved by the most recent call to `setjmp`. It is defined as:

```
void longjmp(jmp_buf env, int val)
```

Execution resumes as if the `setjmp` function had just executed and returned the non-zero value `val` using the information in the environment `env`.

F.8 Signals

The header `<signal.h>` provides facilities for handling exceptional conditions arising during program execution. These conditions arise from program errors or from interrupt signals from external sources. The header contains the macros:

SIG_DFL	default signal handling indicator
SIG_ERR	error when setting a signal
SIG_IGN	ignore a signal
SIGABRT	abort signal
SIGFPE	arithmetic signal
SIGILL	illegal instruction
SIGINT	interrupt signal
SIGSEGV	segmentation violation signal

SIGTERM   program termination signal

and declarations for the functions signal and raise.

```
void (*signal(int sig, void (*handler)(int)))(int)
```

Function signal determines how signals are to be handled. If handler is SIG_DFL, the implementation-defined default behaviour is followed; if it is SIG_IGN, the signal is ignored; otherwise, the function referred to by handler is called with the signal value as its argument.

If signal is successful it returns a pointer to the previous handler for that signal. If an error occurs, signal returns SIG_ERR. If the handler returns, execution resumes where signal had occurred.

The function:

```
int raise(int sig)
```

sends the signal sig to the currently executing program. It returns non-zero if unsuccessful.

F.9 Diagnostics

The header file <assert.h> defines the macro assert effectively declared by:

```
void assert(int expression)
```

providing a simple diagnostic aid. The macro checks the value of the expression and if zero (logical FALSE) prints a message on the standard error stream then calls abort to terminate the program. The message takes the form:

```
Assertion failed : expression, file filename, line nnn
```

where expression is that given to assert, and filename and nnn are given by the preprocessor macros __FILE__ and __LINE__.

To disable assert, define the macro NDEBUG prior to including the header <assert.h>:

```
#define NDEBUG
#include <assert.h>
```

F.10 Date and time

The header file <time.h> declares types and functions for manipulating date and time values. The header file contains declarations for the following data types:

clock_t   implementation-defined arithmetic type used to represent system time;

time_t   arithmetic type used to represent the calendar time;

tm   a structure with the components of a calendar time:

```
struct tm {
        int tm_sec;       /* seconds 0..59 */
        int tm_min;       /* minutes 0..59 */
        int tm_hour;      /* hour of day 0..23 */
        int tm_mday;      /* day of month 1..31 */
        int tm_mon;       /* month since January 0..11 */
        int tm_year;      /* year since 1900 */
        int tm_wday;      /* day of week 0..6 (Sun..Sat) */
        int tm_yday;      /* days since Jan 1, 0..365 */
        int tm_isdst;     /* daylight saving time flag ... */
                          /* > 0 if dst operational */
                          /* == 0 if not dst */
                          /* < 0 if information unavailable */
};
```

and prototype declarations for the following functions.

asctime

```
char *asctime(const struct tm *tp)
```

Converts the calendar time structure *tp into an ASCII string of twenty-six characters (including the null terminator) having the form:

```
DDD MMM dd hh:mm:ss YYYY\n\0
```

where

DDD	day of week
MMM	month
dd	day of the month
hh:mm:ss	hours:minutes:seconds
YYYY	year

For example:

```
Wed Aug 23 09:45:20 1989\n\0
```

The calendar time *tp can be obtained by a call to localtime.

clock

```
clock_t clock(void)
```

Returns an approximation of the amount of processor time used by the calling program. The return value is converted into a number of seconds by division by the value of the macro CLK_TCK (defined in <time.h>).

ctime

```
char *ctime(const time_t *tp)
```

THE STANDARD C LIBRARY

Converts the calendar time `*tp` to local time in the form of an ASCII string (see `asctime`). It is equivalent to:

```
asctime(localtime(tp))
```

difftime

```
double difftime(time_t t1, time_t t2)
```

Returns the difference, in seconds, between the times `t1` and `t2`.

gmtime

```
struct tm *gmtime(const time_t *tp)
```

Converts the calendar time `*tp` into Greenwich Mean Time. If the time is unavailable, `gmtime` returns NULL.

localtime

```
struct tm *localtime(const time_t *tp)
```

Converts the calendar time `*tp` into local time, putting the result into a struct `tm`, and returning a pointer to that structure.

mktime

```
time_t mktime(struct tm *tp)
```

Function `mktime` converts the local time in the structure `*tp` into a calendar time, effectively the complement of the functions `localtime` and `gmtime`. If the value cannot be represented, then the function returns the value − 1 coerced to the required type.

Note that the original values of the fields in the `tm` structure need not be restricted to the values described at the beginning of this section. For example, we might increment the member `tm_hour` to determine the calendar time one hour hence, even if that causes `tm_hour` to exceed 23. When the function `mktime` has completed, the values of the fields in the `tm` structure are adjusted to their normal limits to conform to the newly calculated calendar time.

strftime

```
size_t strftime(char *s, size_t smax,
        const char *format, const struct tm *tp)
```

Formats date and time information from `*tp` into the character array `s` according to the format string `format`. At most `smax` characters are placed in `s`. The `format` string behaves analogously to a `printf` formatter. Ordinary characters appearing in `format` are copied unchanged into `s`. Each `%c` combination is replaced as described below:

%a	abbreviated weekday name (e.g. Sun)
%A	full weekday name (e.g. Sunday)
%b	abbreviated month name (e.g. Dec)

%B	full month name (e.g. December)
%c	local date and time representation
%d	day of the month (01–31)
%H	hour (00–23)
%I	hour (01–12)
%j	day of the year (001–366)
%m	month (01–12)
%M	minute (00–59)
%p	local equivalent of AM or PM
%S	second (00–59)
%U	week number of the year (00–53); regarding Sunday as the first day of the week
%w	weekday (0–6, Sunday is 0)
%W	week number of the year (00–53); regarding Monday as the first day of the week
%x	local date representation
%X	local time representation
%y	year without century(00–99)
%Y	year with century prefix (e.g. 1989)
%Z	timezone name, if any
%%	the % character

time

```
time_t time(time_t *tp)
```

Returns the current calendar time, or − 1 (suitably coerced) if the time is unavailable. If tp is not NULL, then the return value is also assigned to *tp.

F.11 Localization

C was originally designed as the implementation language for the UNIX operating system. Since its introduction C has evolved beyond its original setting and its country of origin. It now has international status. Localization is concerned with the character set, formatting information and language features of a given country.

The header file <locale.h> declares the function setlocale and a number of macros with the prefix LC_X where X is an upper case word. The function prototype is:

```
char *setlocale(int part, const char *locale)
```

and is used to set all or part of the locale information, or to query information about the current locale.

The portion of the locale to be set or queried is identified by the part argument. The Standard defines a number of macros for this purpose:

LC_ALL	Set or query *all* locale specific information. The following locale categories are affected.
LC_COLLATE	Set or query information concerning the collating functions strcoll and strxfrm (see Appendix F.2).
LC_CTYPE	Set or query information about character handling functions.
LC_MONETARY	Set or query monetary specific information.
LC_NUMERIC	Set or query information concerning the formatting of numeric strings, e.g. this may change the decimal point character for formatting input/outout and string conversion routines.
LC_TIME	Set or query information concerning the formatting of time strings by the strftime function.

Setting the argument locale to the null string "" directs setlocale to perform a query operation. The enquiry identifies that portion of the locale specific information required by one of the above macros. A pointer to a string containing the required information is returned by the function, or NULL if the enquiry fails.

If a non-null string is given for the argument locale, the string associated with the nominated part for the new locale is returned. If the setting cannot be performed, a null pointer is returned and the original locale is unchanged.

When a C program begins, it operates as if the call:

```
setlocale(LC_ALL, "C")
```

has been executed. This is the minimal set of locale specific information required to translate C source code.

The Standard does not describe the mechanism by which setlocale makes locale information available. It is implementation-dependent.

Appendix G: Compiling under UNIX

A C program is composed of one or more program text files. The files can be either header files or program unit files. Normally, header files have the suffix '.h' in the filename and program units have the suffix '.c'. Under UNIX, program files are compiled with the cc command. Strictly, cc is not the C compiler proper, but a driver program that initiates the phases associated with macro preprocessing, compiling, linking and loading. The general form of the cc command is:

```
cc option file1 file2 ....
```

The options are distinguished by a leading hyphen symbol (−). They alter the effect of the cc command.

A program that is created as one source file, say 'prog.c', is compiled with the command:

```
cc prog.c
```

Any errors that appear in the program are reported on the standard error output stream. A program with no errors produces no report. The command translates the C source code into an executable object program in the file 'a.out'. This executable program image can be run by entering the command:

```
a.out
```

Normally, compiled programs are retained in files with the same name as the program source filename but with the '.c' suffix removed. The object filename is given to the compiler command with the option '−o':

```
cc −o prog prog.c
```

The '−o' option is followed by the filename of the destination file, as opposed to 'a.out' which is the default. These arguments may be given in any order to the cc command. It is perfectly valid to enter:

```
cc prog.c −o prog
```

The executable program image in file 'prog' is now executed by entering the command:

```
prog
```

Consider now a program split over two files (say, 'prog1.c' and 'prog2.c'). the two files can be compiled and combined to produce an executable program file called 'prog' with the command:

```
cc -o prog prog1.c prog2.c
```

The cc command actually does its work in a number of stages. The source program file 'prog1.c' is processed up to and including the compilation phase. An object file called 'prog1.o' is created. Similarly, an object file 'prog2.o' is created for the second file. The two object files are then linked together to produce the executable program file 'prog'. The two '.o' files are automatically deleted after the linking phase.

In a typical edit/compile/run cycle, we can retain the '.o' object files by using the '-c' option. If a program resides in two '.c' files, say 'main.c' and 'file.c', then each may be separately compiled to produce the object files 'main.o' and 'file.o'. The commands are:

```
cc -c main.c
cc -c file.c
```

The two object files are linked to produce the executable program file 'prog' with the command:

```
cc -o prog main.o file.o
```

Note that both the named files have '.o' suffices. The cc command recognizes these as object file names and does not attempt to recompile them. This last example simply executes the linking phase of the cc command.

If a later change is made to, say, the source file 'file.c', then it alone may be recompiled by:

```
cc -c file.c
```

then relinked with the unchanged 'main.o' using the previous command. Alternatively, the source file 'file.c' may be compiled then linked with the original 'main.o' file with a mix of file types in the command:

```
cc -o prog main.o file.c
```

The '-D' option provides a compile time macro definition. This option has two forms:

```
-Dname
```

or

```
-Dname=def
```

The first form has the effect of including the preprocessor statement:

```
#define name
```

in the source program file. In the second form, the statement effectively incorporates into the program text:

```
#define name      def
```

The first example might be used to define a macro name which is the subject of a `#ifdef` or `#ifndef` preprocessor statement. The second example establishes a definition for a macro name. Two practical examples are:

```
cc -c -DVAX code.c
cc -c -DBITS=16 interp.c
```

The `cc` command automatically searches the standard C library during the linking phase. The library functions referenced in the program file (for example, `printf`) are copied from the library and linked with the program to produce the object code. The '−l' option permits other libraries to be specified. The command:

```
cc -o prog statistics.c -lm
```

compiles the program 'statistics.c' and links it with functions from the mathematical library. The program would be expected to reference one or more math library functions (e.g. `sqrt`) and incorporate a `#include <math.h>` preprocessor statement. It is important that the '−lm' option is placed after the program filename. This is because the linker searches only for those functions referenced by program source files named preceding the '−l' option in the `cc` command. The general form for the '−l' option is:

```
-lname
```

where 'name' is the name of the library to be searched. No intervening space appears between '−l' and the library name.

G.1 `Make`: **Maintaining computer programs**

It is common practice to divide large programs into smaller, more manageable pieces (see Chapter 7). The pieces may require different treatments: some may be run through a macro processor, and others may be processed by a sophisticated program generator. The outputs from these utilities may have to be compiled with special options and with certain definitions and declarations. The code may then need to be loaded with certain libraries under the control of particular options. Unfortunately, it is very easy for the programmer to forget which files depend upon which others, which files have been modified recently, and the exact sequence of operations needed to make a new version of the program. One may easily lose track of which files have been changed and which object modules are still valid. Forgetting to compile a routine that has been changed or that uses changed declarations usually results in a program that will not work, and a bug that is very difficult to identify. On the other hand, recompiling everything just to be safe is very wasteful.

Make mechanizes many of the activities of program development and maintenance. Make provides a simple mechanism for maintaining up-to-date versions of programs. This is achieved by telling make the sequence of commands that create certain files, and the list of files that require other files to be current before the operations can be performed. Whenever a change is made in any part of the program, make will create the files simply, correctly and with the minimum of effort.

The basic operation of make is to update a target file by ensuring that all of the files on which it depends exist and are up to date. To illustrate, consider a simple example: a program named prog is made by compiling and loading three C-language files x.c, y.c and z.c with the lm library. By convention, output of the C compilations is found in the files named x.o, y.o and z.o. Assume that the files x.c and y.c share some common declarations in a file named defs.h, but that z.c does not. That is, x.c and y.c have the line:

```
#include "defs.h"
```

The following text describes the relationships and operations:

```
prog:     x.o y.o z.o
        cc -o prog x.o y.o z.o -lm

x.o y.o:  defs.h
```

If this information is stored in a file named makefile, the command:

```
make
```

will perform the operations needed to recreate prog after any changes have been made to any of the source files x.c, y.c, z.c or defs.

Make operates using three sources of information: the user supplied description file (as above), file names and time stamps from the file system, and built in rules. In the example, the first line states that prog depends on three '.o' files. Once these object files are current, the second line describes how to create prog. The final line says that x.o and y.o depend on the file defs.h. From the file system, make discovers that there are three '.c' files corresponding to the required '.o' files, and uses built in knowledge to generate the object files from the source files (that is, it issues a cc -c file command).

If none of the source or object files had changed since the last time prog was created, all of the files would be current, and the make command would announce this fact and stop. If, however, the defs.h file had been changed, x.c and y.c (but not z.c) would be recompiled and then prog created from the new '.o' files.

G.2 SCCS: Source code control system

A large software system may involve hundreds of program units and thousands of lines of code produced by many programmers. A number of different versions of the system, tailored to different environments, may have to be produced. Major problems of large software systems include keeping track of the development and maintenance of program units, determining the interdependence of components, and ensuring the consistency of code common to different versions of the system.

SCCS is a system for recording changes to a system module. Each time a program unit is changed, that change is recorded and stored in a delta. Subsequent changes to a unit are also recorded as deltas. The latest version of a system is then created by SCCS by applying all the deltas in turn to the original code. A series of deltas D1, D2, . . . is shown in Figure G.1. SCCS permits generation of any version in the chain. Systems at different stages of the development can thus be produced. For example, a customer using version 1.2 may report a bug. In the meantime, development is presently working on version 1.3. To identify the source of the user bug, version 1.2 may be recreated and the fault diagnosed.

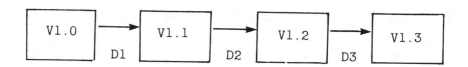

An extension of this feature is the ability to freeze development of a system at any point in the chain. For example, the customer released version may be to V1.3. Further system development may continue in parallel, with new deltas constituting a new release of the system, for example, delta D2.1 may apply to V1.3 producing V2.1. To produce release 1 of the system, the SCCS user requests that those deltas pertaining to release 1 are applied. Further, additional deltas can be introduced to version 1 while development to release 2 is in progress.

Index of symbols

+ addition operator 5, 21, 466
& address operator 41, 71, 466
\a alarm escape sequence 14
= assignment operator 5, 26, 467

\ backslash 14
\\ backslash escape sequence 15
\b backspace escape sequence 14
& bitwise and operator 430, 431, 467
^ bitwise exclusive or operator 430, 431, 467
| bitwise or operator 430, 431, 467
~ bitwise unary complement operator 430
{ brace 4, 6, 48
} brace 4, 6, 48

, comma operator 32, 101, 467
/* comment delimiter 6
*/ comment delimiter 6
−c compiler option 509
−D compiler option 186, 509
−l compiler option 510
−o compiler option 508
2's complement 12
` complement operator 430, 466
+ = compound assignment operator 28, 467
− = compound assignment operator 28, 467
% = compound assignment operator 28, 467
?: conditional operator 94, 467
% conversion specification 38, 488, 492
%% conversion 38, 488, 492
%[conversion 42, 492, 497
%c conversion 38, 42, 484, 485, 493
%d conversion 38, 42, 484, 493
%e conversion 38, 42, 484, 487, 493, 494
%E conversion 38, 484, 487
%f conversion 38, 42, 484, 487, 493, 494
%g conversion 38, 42, 484, 488, 493, 494
%G conversion 38, 484, 488
%i conversion 38, 42, 484, 494
%n conversion 38, 42, 484, 494
%o conversion 38, 42, 484, 489, 493, 495
%p conversion 38, 42, 484, 494

%s conversion 38, 42, 484, 489, 493, 496
%u conversion 38, 42, 484, 490, 493, 496
%x conversion 38, 42, 484, 490, 493, 496
%X conversion 38, 42, 484, 490, 493, 496

/ division operator 21, 466
" double quote 4, 15
\" double quote escape sequence 15

e power 13
E power 13
... ellipsis 218
= = equality operator 91, 467

\f formfeed escape sequence 14

> greater than operator 89, 466
> = greater than or equal operator 89, 466

* indirection operator 73
! = inequality operator 91, 467

<< left shift operator 430, 432, 466
< less than operator 91, 466
<= less than or equal operator 91, 466
&& logical and operator 93, 466
! logical negative operator 93, 466
|| logical or operator 93, 466
l long integer suffix 12
L long integer suffix 12

__DATE__ macro, predefined 177
__FILE__ macro, predefined 177
__LINE__ macro, predefined 177
__STDC__ macro, predefined 177
__TIME__ macro, predefined 177
% modulus operator 21, 466
* multiplication operator 21, 466

\n newline escape sequence 4, 14
\0 null character 15